Therapeutic Cultural Routines to Build Family Relationships

Crowning Glory. Malian girl wearing traditional hair style. Artist: © Jean Lewis

Marva L. Lewis • Deborah J. Weatherston
Editors

Therapeutic Cultural Routines to Build Family Relationships

Talk, Touch & Listen While Combing Hair©

Springer

Editors
Marva L. Lewis
School of Social Work
Tulane University
New Orleans, LA, USA

Deborah J. Weatherston
Alliance for the Advancement of Infant Mental Health
Southgate, MI, USA

ISBN 978-3-030-83725-9 ISBN 978-3-030-83726-6 (eBook)
https://doi.org/10.1007/978-3-030-83726-6

This Springer imprint is published by the registered company Springer Nature Switzerland AG
The registered company address is: Gewerbestrasse 11, 6330 Cham, Switzerland

Foreword

As a very young child, I was subjected to a daily ritual of hair combing. I would sit on a stool between the strong legs of my great-grandmother who would carefully part my tresses, inserting the hair grease she had generously placed on the back of her hand onto my scalp. She would brush each section and finish with a set of neat and intricate braids. At the end, she would announce "don't you look pretty"! Running to finally release myself from the position on the stool where I had been for a half hour (two hours on hair-washing days), I would take a glance in her mirror and feel as pretty as she said I was.

As Lewis and Weatherston profess in this pioneering book, such hair combing interactions go beyond simple custodial care. They represent an opportunity for a stronger emotional bond between parent and child, but also can be an adverse experience for some children. Fortunately for me, through these hair combing and myriad other interactions, my great-grandmother provided the sensitive, responsive care that contributed mightily to my sense of myself as being worthy and capable, and my sense of her as a sensitive and responsive caregiver—an angel in my nursery.

Lewis, Weatherston, and their colleagues intensively explore the process of hair combing, in a manner that has not been achieved in the early childhood mental health arena. Situating hair combing in the context of the adverse racialized experiences of African Americans, they suggest that colorism and other structural, interpersonal, and intrapersonal factors affect how caregivers perceive and behave during the hair combing process. As the authors postulate, children with short and kinky hair are often exposed to a negative hair combing experience that makes them feel less attractive externally, which impacts their internal well-being. One of the principles of early childhood mental health is to consider how the adults' own caregiving experiences affect their approach to caring for their own children. As Lewis argues, an assessment of parents' own ghosts in the nursery around hair combing can contribute to an intervention experience that may enhance their own approach to interacting with their children.

The authors devote considerable attention to using this cultural routine as an antidote to the legacy of historical trauma with which African American children must contend. They encourage therapists and other mental health personnel to use hair combing in their work with African American families, as a mechanism for enhancing parents' responsiveness and attunement to their children. They are careful to emphasize that understanding and utilizing such cultural routines should be done in the context of high-quality reflective supervision, for both African American and non-African American practitioners, so they can reflect upon any culture-specific responses to families that may negatively affect their practice.

This is a seminal book for those in the early childhood mental health field who are serious about building on families' cultural practices to promote child and family well-being. Using rich case studies and capitalizing on extant clinical and empirical literature, Lewis, Weatherston, and their colleagues explore a critical facet of African American child-rearing. Like most cultural routines, hair combing in the African American community has positive and negative characteristics, and the authors courageously examine both aspects of this process. They encourage practitioners to use hair combing as a mechanism to enhance parental responsiveness to young children, to validate the child's sense of internal and external beauty. Through this groundbreaking work, these authors have given practitioners a vital tool to enhance the relationships between parents and young children—the overarching goal of all early childhood mental health interventions.

Brenda Jones Harden
Professor Emerita
University of Maryland School of Social Work
College Park, MD, USA
June 7, 2021

About the Book

The book is composed of four parts. In Part I, *Talk, Touch & Listen While Combing Hair*, we begin with the research and the story of the case that led Dr. Marva L. Lewis to return to graduate school and focus on hair combing as a context for research. The findings from this research established hair combing interaction as a routine and ritual that includes the parenting behaviors that strengthen attachment. We present a structured assessment procedure to understand the childhood racial and ethnic experiences of parents and caregivers.

The chapters in Part II, *Reflective Supervision and Practice*, highlight the clinical dynamics of same race, different race client-therapist-family triads. Dr. Deborah J. Weatherston created the reflective questions that appear at the end of the chapters to provide opportunities to further explore these clinical dynamics. In Chap. 6, Wilson, Weatherston, and Hill define the reflective supervision experience, integrating traditional thoughts about reflective processes with rapidly emerging understanding of racial trauma as experienced by Black and Brown families, professionals, and those who supervise them. In Chaps. 7 and 8, Norwood and Wright, respectively, each illustrate the power of attention to hair combing interactions as an opportunity to understand the childhood experiences of racial acceptance and rejection. Both Norwood and Wright bring a clinical lens to assess the trauma of colorism. Both share case histories of their work with small children and their responses to the topic of skin color and hair type. Their case studies illustrate the use of hair combing time to observe and assess strengths and risks, as well as intervention when working with infants, young children, and parents or primary caregivers.

In Chaps. 9 and 10, Wilson and Hill, African American professionals working in a northern community mental health agency, conclude with personal reflections about culture and race as experienced through their work with White and Black, Indigenous, and People of Color (BIPOC) families and in supervision with White supervisors and consultants. Both offer windows into the possibility of healing and hope when working across differences within the mental health and early childhood communities.

In Part III, *Reflections on Community-Based Interventions*, the manualized, *Talk, Touch & Listen While Combing Hair©* curriculum, based on the research about hair combing tasks, has been used with groups of parents in community agencies, homeless shelters, and with a college summer camp in several cities around the country. Each of the contributors offers personal and professional stories about their experiences around the culture of hair combing and interlace theory with promising practices that can lead to healing and change.

In Part IV, *Tools for Observation, Assessment and Intervention*, authors Lewis and White introduce a projective tool, *The Neck-up* drawing, for the assessment of caregivers' childhood memories and perceptions of their racial features. Several drawings and stories illustrate the vivid memories and powerful emotional responses this simple procedure may elicit from a caregiver as part of an assessment protocol. *The Neck-up* drawing provides a standardized method to understand a caregiver's unconscious memories of their racialized features and emotions associated with their hair type and getting their hair combed. Caregivers are then given the opportunity to "tell their story" about the emotions selected at the completion of the drawing.

The *Childhood Experiences of Racial Acceptance and Rejection* (CERAR) is a semi-structured interview that provides a more detailed story of the person's relationship with their caregiver, hair, and racial features. A tender-headed rating scale is also part of the tools that might be used to assess the experiences of a caregiver during hair combing time. These tools will provide the clinician with relationship-based content to further explore with a caregiver.

Chapter 17, *Guidelines to Identify Child-Endangering Hair Styling Practices: Medical, Legal, and Psychosocial Perspectives*, by Lewis, Dunjwa, and Cohen (a psychologist, chemist, and juvenile court judge), introduces information regarding hair styling practices and processes that endanger children. The authors identify several resources available for caregivers with information on styling and appropriate hair products for young children.

Part IV concludes with a summary and next steps for research specific to Talk, Touch, & Listen While Combing Hair.

Preface

Hair Combing Routines with Children Matter

The Critical Role of Culture and Relationships in the Reconstruction of a Post-pandemic America

The year 2020 will be recorded as one of the most important eras in the history of the United States and the world. In the span of one year, beginning in February 2020, two worldwide events occurred, a deadly pandemic and protests for racial justice. These two events, the COVID-19 pandemic spreading death through an unseen virus to people in countries around the world and the global protests for racial justice in response to the police killing of George Floyd, at first glance appear unrelated. Yet, both were fueled by legacies of our shared racist past: the high number of Blacks dying from COVID-19 due to race-related comorbidity factors and the disproportionate number of Black males targeted for violence and killed by police.

Shortly after the death of George Floyd and worldwide protests began, a local New Orleans judge and professor sent the following statement to students and alumni of the course she taught on the constitution: "It is fundamentally true that we are in the second reconstruction of our nation. We are all a part of it ..." (personal communication, Palmer, 2020).

Writing a book about the simple task of combing children's hair during the pandemic of the COVID-19 virus and nationwide protests for racial justice is hard. The contributors to this book sit alone in makeshift home offices, quarantined from friends, family, and workmates. My brain throbs from cognitive dissonance as I stare transfixed by the daily, frightening news feed of the death tolls and violence from these twin pandemics. How can I write a book when people I know and love are hospitalized and dying? To write a book about hair combing interaction with infants and young children seems frivolous and almost sacrilegious. During the early days of the outbreak in March 2020, feelings of fear and depression, with underlying complicated responses of grief and loss, took place as I opened email with news that another African American choir member, student's relative, a colleague's client, and a local celebrity had died from the COVID-19 virus.

As I watched the extraordinary explosion of nationwide protests and police brutality after the death of George Floyd, a kernel of ambivalence took its place among my list of emotions. Writing a book about the developmental value of the cultural practice of combing a young child's hair seemed out of sync with these passionate protests for social justice for Black lives. The constant news feed of increasing numbers of people around the world marching for social justice triggered exhilarating memories of fighting for Civil Rights as a teenager in the turbulent 1960s. We proudly wore our uniforms of colorful Dashikis that identified our African heritage as we righteously proclaimed, "I'm Black and I'm Proud."

The shocking television images of the city of Portland, Oregon, burning after protests of police brutality, triggered traumatic memories of my beloved city, Detroit, Michigan, burning during the city riots protesting police brutality of 1967. Over 50 years later in 2020, seeing identical images on the six o'clock news of an American city in flames created a sense of Déjà vu and cognitive disorientation. The daily rollercoaster of emotions I experienced, ranging from rage and anger to feelings of fear and hopelessness, distracted me from the discipline needed to write a book for social workers about building family relationships using cultural routines.

I shared these feelings with my co-editor, practitioner, and long-time friend, Deborah Weatherston. I said with intense emotion, "People are dying, cities are burning, and I'm writing a book about combing children's hair?" I confessed how hard it was to put pen to paper amid emotional turmoil triggered by experiences of historical trauma, modern realities of structural racism, and inequities associated with COVID-19. I acknowledged the reluctance I felt to ask authors, many of whom are women of color, White friends, and allies facing similar emotional challenges in their various cities around the country, to work quickly to finish their revisions to meet a looming deadline.

I also admitted my ambivalence about the worth of the project. Over decades of doing research on the topic of hair combing interaction, submitting multiple applications for grants that were subsequently denied, arguing with publishers, journal editors, and peer reviewers to keep words like "nappy-haired ghosts" in the title, my uncertainty was all too familiar. Since completing my dissertation in 1993, I had worked hard to translate this seemingly frivolous topic, hair combing, into hard science. Using rigorous, culturally informed research methods, I explored the psychological and sociocultural factors that lead to variability in the quality of combing hair and its impact on mother-child relationships (Lewis, 1999). My commitment to the publication of this book is to increase cultural awareness and to provide psychosocial tools based on hair combing interactions for social workers, mental health practitioners, and others working with children and families of color. My vision is for parents to connect emotionally with their children, culture, and communities. I turned to my co-editor for a little help. With clinical understanding and decades of experience as an infant mental health practitioner, supervisor, and advocate, she urged me to write about these feelings and share them with my co-authors. Breathing a sigh of relief, I felt motivated to return to the tasks of writing, reaching out, and editing.

A nation torn apart by race. That same day, I opened an email from Constitutional Law Professor, Martha Palmer of nearby Loyola University Law School. In the Spring of the previous year, I had the honor of participating in an enriching course on civic engagement and the United States Constitution. The email included the quote at the beginning of this preface. You might ask, "What does the Constitution of the United States have to do with mothers combing their children's hair or how social workers and others provide services to families of color?" The phrase, *the second reconstruction of America*, helped me contextualize the wide range of emotions I experienced from a broader human rights perspective. My beloved country, the United States, was again in emotional turmoil, caused by the twin pandemics of an unrelenting virus and unresolved structural and individual racism. I asked, "What could I do at this advanced stage of my professional life? Cover myself in protective gear to volunteer at the hospitals to provide food and relief for the overwhelmed first responders? Join the protesters in the street?" Neither idea was feasible.

The Colors of Racism and Politics of the Pandemic. Both the pandemic and protests for social justice were framed in chronic and emotionally charged histories of racial trauma. Racial disparities in the social determinants of health drive the comorbidity factors, for example, asthma, diabetes, and obesity, that place African Americans at the highest risk for death after exposure to the virus. The traumatic images of George Floyd dying under the knee of a White police officer matched hundreds of years of violence at the hands of authority figures targeting African American communities (Ashing, Lewis, & Stevens, 2017). The Civil War fought to end slavery in the United States and led to the social divisiveness that tore White families with sons passionately fighting in blue uniforms for the Union or gray uniforms of the Confederate army. In 2020 the toxic climate of red and blue political parties emboldened demonstrators in multiple cities, declaring their constitutional rights to not wear face masks. In Lansing, Michigan, the city of my undergraduate education at Michigan State University, I watched the nightly news in disbelief as gun toting White males marched on the capital, challenging the female democratic governor's authority to order that businesses remain closed to stop the spread of the virus. The social media was filled with videos of emotionally charged fights between store clerks and people refusing to wear masks, fights between neighbors, and estrangement within families over the politics of the day. The historic bloody civil war and bloodshed today reflect a continuing and significant racial divide.

Why Hair? The power of routine and rituals to shape relationships of shared identity.

The interventions created from the findings in my research center on strengthening mother-child (parent-child) relationships through *talking*, *touching*, and *listening*. The parent education curricula developed from that research highlight relationship-based dynamics that attachment researchers have identified as critical to the healthy development of infants and young children (Bowlby, 1969). The systematic analysis of hours of videotaped interaction of African American mothers combing their infant child's hair revealed core relationship-based activities that occur during this daily routine—verbal interaction, physical touch, and the need for the mother or caregiving parent to listen and respond to the child's cues, for example, the smiles or the cries or the tears, during hair combing. Our research team observed differences in hair combing interactions: the quality of verbal interactions, the warmth and nurturance of physical touch, and the promptness of the mother's or primary caregiver's response based on the accuracy of understanding the infant or young child's cues. This daily, warm, and dynamic interaction provides a firm foundation for the mother or father or caregiving parent and child to form a relationship. The quality of this relationship allows the child to feel secure, to safely explore the world of people and things, and to reach developmental milestones in a timely way, including social, emotional, and cognitive skills needed for multicultural citizens to live in harmony with one another. These skills can be learned and practiced during what appears to be the simple task of combing hair, making a child presentable to the world. The everyday task of a mother lovingly combing her young daughter's hair may be the unrecognized cultural pearl to cultivate loving, respectful, and kind relationships in families and communities in a reconstructed post-racial pandemic America.

This tiny task of combing a child's natural hair embodies the core elements needed to reconstruct racially wounded relationships, which brings me full circle to the importance of the simple, everyday routine and ritual of combing infants' and toddlers' hair. To create authentic partnerships to work for social justice, citizens need three primary relationship-based skills: Talk, touch, and listen.

1. Black and White citizens will need communication skills, to authentically and respectively *talk* with each other to form working partnerships.
2. Partners working for social justice must be open to accepting and giving warm physical *touch*, in the form of a firm handshake or a hug as anti-racist allies.
3. Healthy partners recognize the need to *listen* deeply to each other. Just as we have learned to adjust to the new "norms" of social distance and the wearing of masks needed to mitigate the spread of the COVID-19 virus, we must courageously break the silence of racial divides. We must learn to be comfortable in the discomfort as we acknowledge the human realities of living in a society structured for centuries by the virus and violence of racism. These same interpersonal social skills are key components of the everyday task of hair combing interactions—talking, touching, and listening—that will be taught to a new generation of children in a post-pandemic world.

I can now emerge from my emotional fog that had me stuck in the past and afraid of the future. I accept "why" writing this book is important. The parallel skills needed for relationships between parents and infants to create a close attachment and bond, or among people of different racial or diverse identity groups working for social justice, are the same—*talking*, *touching*, and *listening*. These are the fundamental reasons why writing this book is important. This purpose—strengthening parent-child relationships during hair combing time—will prepare these young children with the skills needed for healthy development as well as to be engaged and effective citizens living and working for social justice for all.

A Post-Pandemic World. The era following the end of the Civil War and a divided United States was labeled as a time for the reconstruction of America. A time of healing the North/South, Red/Blue, Black/White divides of our relationships. The phrase the "second reconstruction of America" used by Martha Palmer sparked a ray of hope and psychological energy for me. I fervently believe that by leveraging our individual privileges, building on our strengths, and working together as equal citizens of the United States, we will heal and move us forward.

Finding ways to talk about this shared history as well as being heard and emotionally understood by an empathetic listener will bring healing to individuals as well as future generations. I offer you a metaphor of the pearl, a jewel, created in the unlikely environment of the belly of a clam. Tiny changes serve as catalysts for revolutionary changes to take place. A tiny parasite invades the inner lining of a healthy clam. It becomes a tiny irritant to the clam, though not fatal. The natural biological system responses of the clam fights back by releasing a thick fluid to cover the invader and stop the irritation to its insides. The clam continues releasing the soothing fluid, and it builds up around the invader until a beautiful pearl is formed. This pearl, born out of the pain of the foreign invader, now becomes a valuable jewel, admired for its luster and flawless iridescent color. The irritant, now buried beneath layers of protective covering called "nacre," remains a part of the pearl. The protective covering prevents the pain. The protective covering is what is admired and recognized for its distinct beauty.

Parent-infant relationships are the pearls of a just community. The body of the mother's natural biological system releases the protective hormones of nurturance that covers the pain of childbirth. Over time, through daily interactions, emotional warmth, nurturing physical touch, and affirming verbal responses, the vulnerable newborn develops a protective attachment relationship. This secure relationship ensures the growth and development of the dependent infant. The memories of the protective and nurturing warmth of these early interactions provide support for the child as an adult to function in relationships with other adults, with their children, and with members of their cultural and social groups. The "pearl" of secure parent-child relationships are families and communities of positive adults. These adults will become engaged citizens of communities that develop cultural norms of social justice. The tiny task of hair combing interaction will contribute to building these positive relationships.

The skills learned in early childhood during hair combing time when children learn to talk, touch, and listen in nurturing family relationships create new, healthy citizens for society and communities. We may then build the beloved community that reflects Martin Luther King's dream of a civil and just society for all.

I have hope.

New Orleans, LA, USA
July 4, 2020

Marva L. Lewis

Acknowledgments

A Personal Note from Marva L. Lewis

I begin my acknowledgments with appreciation for the wonderful journey of motherhood given to me by my daughter, Mahalah Renée. Thank you for being you, with your wonderful easy temperament, artistic eye, baking skills for those Keto bagels, and steadfast commitment to social justice. Combing your thick, beautiful 4c hair led to a research question and maternal worry, "Will I get the parts straight when combing your hair?" I love you and appreciate you. Thank you, Dollwyn Pierre and Mrs. Ruby Taylor, for your love, practical parenting guidance, and wisdom for raising Mahalah.

There are many, many shoulders on which I stand who must be acknowledged in my academic journey. I thank you and appreciate you. The thoughtful, loving people who stepped up put me back on my path, as I faltered under the weight of earning tenure as a single mom with a three-year-old daughter. These folks have been my educators, dearest friends, colleagues, and comrades in the battle for prevention of child abuse and work for social justice. I am Blessed with a long list of people to say … thank you.

I want to also acknowledge the organizations that played a central role in my intellectual journey resulting in this book.

The transformative experience, often buried in the many credentials and degrees that populate my curriculum vitae, was with my participation in the Upward Bound Program at Oakland University, during my teenage years. I participated in the Upward Bound Program from 1967 to 1969. Created in 1964 as part of the Federal Economic Opportunity Act, it began as an experimental program to encourage access to higher education for low-income students. So, I was part of an experiment, profiting from superb leadership, intellectual stimulation, and guidance offered by the kind, wise faculty of this program. Thank you to those dedicated staff who guided us, the politicians who fought for funding of this nationwide program, and the dear peers who populated the program and remain lifetime friends. The high school I attended in Ferndale, Michigan, was predominantly White; there were 65

Black students in a class of 400 students, with a total school enrollment of 2000. Being 16 in the 1960s was one of the most exciting, exhilarating, and transformative times of my development. Upward Bound provided the safety and structure needed by exuberant adolescents, keeping us focused on our education as we marched for Civil Rights in our local communities. I went from being a Negro to "I'm Black and I'm Proud." This experience set the stage for my research agenda to end colorism, and the work to end racial disparities in the foster care system.

I thank all the everyday parents who voluntarily participated in the research and shared the time, expertise, and stories of hair combing memories. Finally, I acknowledge the love and support of my family. My seven brothers and sisters who patiently supported me in my numerous "projects." My parents, Ward Lewis, Jr., and Martha Williams Lewis, who celebrated 72 years of marriage. They were part of the urban migration of that Isabella Wilkerson (2011) wrote about with millions of other African American families journeying from the Jim Crow south to all points north, west, and east in the United States. My family arrived in Detroit in the late 1940s with dreams of getting "a good job in the car factory." Though they did not complete high school their charge to all of us was to "get an education," work hard, pray, and play. My childhood memories include my mother reading to us as we sat on the floor transfixed. She first read to us from the King James Bible and the book *Paradise Lost, Paradise Regained* from the Jehovah's Witnesses, a religion she had recently joined. She read these passages in standard English. She would then pick up the book *Uncle Remus Tales* about Brer' rabbit escaping the traps of his arch nemesis Brer' Fox. She read these hilarious tales' lively Ebonics, spoken in the rich oral tradition of African American culture. These tales of the trickster, Brer Rabbit, taught me to fight using my wit rather than my fists. The bilingual story time taught me the beauty of language, creativity, and commitment. These stories led to my understanding of how parents can persevere and joyfully rear children in oppressive contexts.

My parents raised eight children with an ACE score of zero (0), no adverse childhood experiences. All eight of their children completed high school; seven completed college obtaining master's degrees and doctorates, including Michigan State University, Harvard University, and University of Michigan.

Thank you, Mom, thank you, Dad. Your love of family, reading, and books lives on.

Marva Leatrice Lewis

From the Two of Us

We are filled with gratitude for the authors who contributed to this book during a particularly painful period of sociocultural upheaval, racial oppression, a global pandemic, and economic distress. Some worked in isolation, confined to their homes, without the usual comradery of colleagues or friends. Others worked from home, balancing work and family 24-7, their children needing supervision throughout the school year. All shared a commitment to telling the story of hair combing and colorism, through the lens of cultural, ethnic, and racial experience, past and present, that shape a child's internal model for relationship and evolving sense of self.

Thank you to individuals who took time from their work lives, professional lives, in the middle of this pandemic, to edit early drafts of chapters. Thank you to Natasha Eberly, Zelda Lewis, and Michelle Simpson. Your careful editing, suggestions, and support have been invaluable to the completion of this work. We extend a special thank you to Hiram E Fitzgerald, who agreed to review early versions of the chapters. Thank you, we appreciate your expertise and wisdom.

Central to our work is the belief that relationships impact relationships, offering the possibility for continued growth and change, beginning with the parent-infant relationship, and throughout the lifespan. We give special thanks for the relationships that have strengthened and sustained us over many years, and to those with whom we have worked so closely these past few years while collaborating on the completion of *Therapeutic Cultural Routines to Build Family Relationships: Talk, Touch & Listen While Combing Hair.*

We have been on a reflective journey together, strengthening our relationship with each other and our relationship to the work. We have worked by my side, at a distance, supporting the creation of this book, deftly holding each other's worries when often overwhelmed by daily life, frantic texts, emails, and phone calls. For this we are both incredibly grateful.

With genuine thanks, admiration, and affection,

Deborah J. Weatherston and Marva L. Lewis

References

Chase, R. (2002). *The complete tales of Uncle Remus by Joel Chandler Harris.* Houghton Mifflin Company.

Watch Tower Bible and Tract Society. (1958). *From paradise lost to paradise regained.*

Wilkerson, I. (2011). *The warmth of other suns: the epic story of America's great migration.* Penguin Books.

Endorsements

"This timely gift to the field of infant and early childhood mental health urges practitioners to question and transform dominant paradigms of practice and knowledge offering tools to effectively recognize, elevate and prioritize non-dominant ways of knowing, sources of strength, and pathways to healing in Black, Indigenous and Other People of Color (BIPOC) families and communities. Through intimate stories of caregivers and their young children, practitioners and families, supervisors and supervisees, and their relationships, the authors vividly illustrate the power of a relational-dyadic intervention with Black families (Hair Combing Interactions) that centers on cultural traditions, acceptance of racialized physical features and differences and improvement in racial identity for the restoration attachment relationships. The reflective questions woven throughout the book challenge practitioners to engage in critical self-reflection about race, racism and the formation of internal working models of relationships, the origin of personal values and beliefs, their impact on who we are and what we do and on our responsibility in changing practice to promote liberation."

Carmen Rosa Noroña, Child Trauma Clinical Services and Training Lead, The Child Witness to Violence Project – Division of Developmental and Behavioral Pediatrics, Boston Medical Center

"It is a pleasure to write an endorsement for this important book, Therapeutic Cultural Routines to Build Family Relationships: Talk, Touch & Listen While Combing Hair, edited by Dr. Marva Lewis and Dr. Deborah Weatherston. This book introduces many new and important perspectives related to racism, colorism, and ways to understand the impact of historical trauma on early parent-child relationships. Dr. Lewis, over many years of work, has developed an evidence-based intervention to address racial disparities and support the relationship within African American families through the important cultural routine of combing hair. When we worked together earlier in her career, she shared her interest in the area and the development of this culturally sensitive way to support the early relationship. It is very exciting to see how these ideas have come to fruition and the broad influence

of this work across different perspectives, addressing the important concerns at this time. In collaboration with co-editor, Dr. Weatherston, additional perspectives are incorporated on reflective supervision and practice encouraging the reader to thoughtfully consider issues of culture, ethnicity, and racial equity. I highly recommend this book to social workers and to infant and early childhood mental health providers as they will gain important perspectives about culturally sensitive ways to support early relationships."

Joy D. Osofsky, Paul J. Ramsay Endowed Chair of Psychiatry and Barbara Lemann Professor of Child Welfare, Louisiana State University Health Sciences Center

"Contributors to this volume present case studies and ethnographic approaches confirming the power of Talk, Touch & Listen hair combing interactions for reducing mother-child stress and enhancing interpersonal resilience in families affected by historic trauma and continued contemporary racism and discrimination. Talk, Touch & Listen, a culturally and historically anchored process, is a valuable relationship-based clinical intervention for enhancing mother-child mental health and well-being and should be read by everyone who works with marginalized families."

Hiram E. Fitzgerald, University Distinguished Professor Emeritus, Michigan State University

"What a wonderful account of the 'magic of everyday moments.' This book, filled with reflections derived from close attention to the care of children's hair, is sure to stimulate creative thinking about the ways we can improve our loving attention to each other in our daily lives. Thank you all for sharing this work with us."

Paul Spicer, President of the Board of Zero To Three and Professor of Anthropology, University of Oklahoma

Contents

About the Editors and Contributors

Editors

Marva L. Lewis, PhD, IMH-E® earned a PhD in Sociocultural Psychology and is Associate Professor at Tulane University School of Social Work in New Orleans, Louisiana. She is endorsed by the Alliance for the Advancement of Infant Mental Health as Mentor-Research/Faculty IMH-E®. She is a former child protection worker and children's counselor at a domestic violence shelter. While completing her graduate degree in Boulder, Colorado, she worked with Janet Dean and Rae Sullivan as a psychotherapist on a nurse/therapist outreach team for the Community Infant Project and helped develop the *Circulo Infant Outreach* program for Latina mothers. She completed a postdoctoral fellowship at Louisiana State University Department of Psychiatry with Dr. Charles Zeanah and Dr. Joy Osofsky, where she was part of the original Infant Team. She conducts research on cultural rituals and routines of hair combing interaction and parent-infant attachment. She developed strengths-based community interventions. Her research focuses on the development of strengths-based, culturally valid, community-based interventions to support African American families to address intergenerational messages of acceptance or rejection of children based on colorism. Dr. Lewis serves on as a Consulting Editor for the Infant Mental Health Journals and co-authored (in press) the article, Call to Action: Centering Blackness and Disrupting Systemic Racism in Infant Mental Health Research and Academic Publishing. Since 2020 she served as chair of the work group, *Engage Diversity and Difference in Practice*, for the steering committee of the Erikson Institute and Council on Social Work Education (CSWE), *Curricular Guide for Infant and Early Childhood Mental Health and Developmental Neuroscience.* In 2011 she was commissioned by the National Zero to Three Safe Baby Court Teams to provide consultation, coaching, and training on issues of bias, historical trauma of slavery, and workforce contributions to racial disparities in the child welfare system. She worked with the national Center for Social Science Policy (CSSP) to develop the *Race Equity Assessment Tool* for Safe Babies Court Teams. In 2021 she chaired the development of an online introductory resource module and toolkit for leadership training on *Racism, Prejudice, Implicit Bias and the Psychological Maltreatment of Children.*

Deborah J. Weatherston, PhD, IMH-E® began her career as a developmental and clinical specialist in an infant mental health home visiting program through Michigan's Community Mental Health system. Her commitment to this two-generational, preventive intervention approach to service, working with the parent and infant or young child together, in the intimacy of their own home, led to the co-development of the Graduate Certificate in Infant Mental Health in 1988 at the Merrill-Palmer Institute of Wayne State University in Detroit, Michigan. She was the Director of that program until 2002 when she became the Executive Director of the Michigan Association for Infant Mental Health (2002–2016), an organization promoting infant mental health training, education, and reflective practice experiences for professionals across disciplines and in multiple service settings. She co-developed and served as the first Executive Director of the Alliance for the Advancement of Infant Mental Health, Inc.®., a nationally and internationally recognized organization whose mission is to promote workforce development through the competency-based *Endorsement for Culturally Sensitive, Relationship-Focused Practice Promoting Infant Mental Health* (2016–2018). She is currently an infant mental health supervisor and consultant in private practice in Michigan.Dr. Weatherston's interest in promoting infant mental health is reflected in her service on the Board of Directors for the World Association for Infant Mental Health (WAIMH), where she was the Editor of WAIMH *Perspectives in Infant Mental Health* from 2009 to 2019, as a Consulting Editor for the *Infant Mental Health Journal*, and as a ZERO TO THREE graduate fellow. In addition, she has written extensively about infant mental health principles and practices and, most recently, about reflective supervision as a cornerstone for effective work with infants, very young children, and families.

Contributors

Samuel L. Bradley Jr., DSW earned a doctorate in Social Work from Tulane University in New Orleans, Louisiana, and is currently appointed as faculty at the Boston College School of Social Work in Massachusetts. His research focus is on innovation and equity in academic innovation. Dr. Bradley is an accomplished musician, community activist, and administrator with extensive experience in fundraising and communications. He is particularly passionate about utilizing design thinking as a strategy for developing innovation in higher education as well as leveraging higher education programs to support community outcomes in marginalized communities.

Ojore Lateef Bushfan, MA, MS, LMFT earned an MS in Counseling and a License in Marriage and Family Therapy. He currently works as a licensed therapist in Counseling and Psychological Services at San Diego State University and the Health and Wellness Center at Grossmont College in California, providing therapeutic interventions to college students with social emotional challenges that impede their academic success. He was a research assistant and facilitator for the *San Diego Caregiver-Child Connection Project Hair Combing Interactions Study.* He is passionate about working within school systems, providing mental health services to college students with behavioral and social-emotional challenges, and developing creative and culturally responsive ways of working with this population. His interests include attachment theory, adolescents, African American males, body-centered/somatic work, challenging dominant male discourses/male socialization, grief and loss, and sound healing.

Nola M. Butler Byrd, PhD, LPCC is a multicultural counselor educator, social justice activist and Licensed Professional Clinical Counselor, and Certified Radix Body-Centered Personal Growth Work Practitioner. She holds a doctorate in Education-Multicultural from the San Diego State University (SDSU)/Claremont Graduate University Joint Doctoral Program in Education, an MA in Education-Counseling from SDSU, and a BA in Theater-English from Wesleyan University. Affiliated with San Diego State University for over 20 years, she is currently Associate Professor and Director of the Community-Based Block (CBB)

Multicultural Counseling and Social Justice Education Program. The 47-year-old CBB Program prepares counselor/change agents who serve diverse, marginalized communities. Additionally, she is a doctoral faculty member in the College of Education. Dr. Butler Byrd has served for many years on the SDSU University Senate and the Academic Senate of the California State University System. Dr. Butler Byrd is immediate Past President of the California Association for Licensed Professional Clinical Counselors and a Past President of San Diego Chapter of the Association for Black Psychologists. Her teaching, research, and service are in the areas of community-based multicultural counseling and social justice education, culturally responsive teaching and supervision, and deliberative democratic processes.

Natasha Byars, MS, MSW, LICSW earned an MS in Child Development from Erikson Institute and an MSW from Loyola University Chicago, Illinois. She currently serves as Assistant Director at Southwest Human Development, overseeing the Professional Development Institute at Educare Arizona. She serves as faculty for the Harris Infant and Early Childhood Mental Health Training Institute, has consulted on international SEL curriculum development, and worked in an indigenous village preschool in Chiapas, Mexico.She volunteers on the Arizona Early Childhood Professional Development Project ECHO Action Team. She was a Project LAUNCH clinician and Department of Psychiatry Social Work Fellow at Boston Children's Hospital, and a ZERO TO THREE Academy Fellow (class of 2018–2020), Ms. Byars led the Massachusetts Young Children's System of Care Project at Boston Public Health Commission, collaborating across the state to integrate IECMH teams into primary care and support IECMH professional development and capacity building in communities and systems. She holds the principles of inclusion, representation, and honoring families as central to her work.

Barbara Cheatham, MA is a retired Public Health Program Manager, and a certified life coach. She received a BA degree from National University, San Jose, California, and her Master of Arts degree from City University, Seattle, Washington (Bay Area side). She has over 30 years of experience in the areas of Behavioral Science and Social Sciences and has done additional work through her project, *Team Two Resumes & Such*, on life skills, careers, and life enrichment for youth. She formerly served as the Staff and Healthcare Education Coordinator for Healthy Start New Orleans (Louisiana). Other experiences include management, outreach, education, and training for the Alameda County Public Health Department in EMS, Safe Kids, childhood injury prevention, and the Prevention Health Department Division of AIDS and Communicable Disease Immunization Project. Her publications include poetry analogies presented in the Bay Area Black United Fund African American Health Summit 2003–2007.

Constance Cohen, JD, MSE served as an Associate Juvenile Judge in Des Moines, Iowa, from June 1994 until July 2014.She presided over one of the original Safe Babies Court Teams beginning in 2005. Following her retirement from the bench, she served as the judicial consultant for the Quality Improvement Center for Research-Based Infant and Toddler Court Teams from 2014 to 2018.She earned her law degree from Drake University Law School in 1986.She also holds BA and MSE degrees from Drake University.Her legal career included positions as Prosecuting Attorneys Training Coordinator for the Iowa Attorney General's Office, Executive Director of the Iowa County Attorneys Association, Assistant Dallas County Attorney, and sole practitioner of law. She also served as an adjunct professor at DMACC and Drake University Law School.She is a frequent lecturer at local, state, and national trainings. She is currently enjoying teaching, consulting, volunteering, traveling, and unhurried time with family, which happily includes five grandchildren.

Mumbi Dunjwa, MISM, CNMT is the Founder and CEO of Naturaz (www.naturaz.com), a family-centered, 100% vegan hair care product line that is scientifically formulated for textured hair. She is an award-winning chemist from the American Chemical Society, and she has utilized her background and experience to create Naturaz. Ms. Dunjwa has 11 years of experience in one of the world's largest pharmaceutical companies. She has also practiced as a Certified Nuclear Medicine Technologist in large Trauma 1 teaching hospitals in Massachusetts, Kansas, Georgia, and Pennsylvania.She has a deep-rooted passion for education and is committed to empowering women and youth. Ms. Dunjwa holds a Masters of Information Systems Management degree from Carnegie Mellon University and a Bachelor of Science degree in Chemistry and Nuclear Medicine Technology from Worcester State University and the University of Massachusetts.

Ava L. Gill, MA is an EOPS (Extended Opportunities Programs and Services) Counselor and NextUP (a program for current and former foster youth) Foster Youth Counselor Liaison at Grossmont College in California. She is also an EOPS Counselor at San Diego Mesa College, where she not only works with EOPS students but also Project Restart students, a program for men and women who have been formally incarcerated and are choosing to attend college. Ava received her Master's degree in Educational Counseling from San Diego State University's Community-Based Block (CBB) Program. She served as a research assistant and facilitator for the *San Diego Caregivers Child Connection Project Hair Combing Interaction Study*. Ava has a love and passion for the population that she serves. She feels that it is a privilege and an honor to help her students become the best they can be and reach their desired educational goals and beyond.

Stefanie Hill, LMSW, IMH-E® (IV) is a Social Worker at Starfish Family Services in Livonia, Michigan, where she currently supervises staff of the Home Base Program, including infant and early childhood mental health staff. Prior to that position she has worked for over 25 years in the field of Infant Mental Health (IMH). She has worked as an IMH Home Visitor, Supervisor, and Reflective Consultant, training many professionals, as well as parents, in the power of relationships to effect change. She has presented several times at the Michigan Association of Infant Mental Health (MI-AIMH) conference, for the Wayne County Fatherhood Initiative, and Head Start, as well as other conferences across the state. Ms. Hill was very instrumental in developing Detroit-Wayne County's Baby Court Model on behalf of children under 5 years and their families who come to the attention of the Child Welfare system. She is the fourth Black Infant Mental Health Specialist who has earned endorsement as an Infant Mental Health Mentor in Michigan. Stefanie is married, has four children and five grandchildren, reflecting her commitment to relationships in life, as well as in her work.

Kathleen Baca Leanos, MA, MSW, LCSW is a bilingual and bicultural social worker who earned a Master's in Social Welfare at UCLA Luskin School of Public Affairs in California, with an emphasis on Public Child Welfare, and an MA in Education with a Concentration in Counseling from San Diego State University's Community-Based Block (CBB) Program. She served as a research assistant and facilitator for the *San Diego Caregiver-Child Connection Project Hair Combing Interactions Study.* Mrs. Baca Leanos's focus has been emergency response social work with families and communities of color. She worked as a Childrens' Social Worker at Los Angeles County Department of Children and family services and now serves Ventura County Behavioral Health as a Senior Crisis Team Clinician.

Afiya M. Mbilishaka, PhD being in love with hair her whole life, grew up as her family's hairstylist, graduating from lawn chairs at cookouts to eventually holding space in her college dorm room for a mini-salon. She earned her degrees from the University of Pennsylvania and Howard University. At the age of 26, Dr. Afiya earned a PhD in Clinical Psychology and was a full-time therapist at Columbia University. She is now Professor and Head of the Psychology Program at the University of the District of Columbia. Dr. Afiya is a natural hairstylist at N Natural Hair Studio in Silver Spring, Maryland, where she loves creating art with locs, twists, and afros. Dr. Afiya innovated the practice and research of "PsychoHairapy©," where she uses hair as an entry point for mental health services in beauty salons and barbershops, as well as through social media. Dr. Afiya has provided engaging multimedia talks at universities throughout the country, and in the intimate setting of hair care spaces.

Rhonda Norwood, PhD, LCSW-BACS is Assistant Professor of Professional Practice at the Louisiana State University School of Social Work in Baton Rouge. She earned her doctorate in social work at Louisiana State University. Dr. Norwood has 20 years of clinical and supervisory experience in a variety of agency settings and private practice. Her area of expertise is infant mental health, which includes working with young children and their families and perinatal mood disorders. Dr. Norwood's area of research interest includes integrating effective interventions with child welfare services, parental representations of their children, and children's narratives as representations of their relationships and worlds.

Michelle J. Rowe-Odom, MA is a professional counselor and counseling educator with over seven years of teaching experience at the graduate level, training students in a community-based social justice multicultural counseling education program in San Diego, California. She is also an academic counselor for the California Community Colleges, serving student-parents, asylee, and refuge-seeking populations. Michelle has over ten years of experience serving in the areas of early-childhood and K-12 education, parent-education, and social services, combined. Michelle has earned her Master's in Education with a concentration in Multicultural Counseling from the Community-Based Block (CBB) Program at San Diego State University, California, and served as a research assistant and co-facilitator for the *San Diego Caregiver Child Connections Project (SDC3)*. She is a mother and community activist organizing for anticolonial program development in the areas of mental health, child care, education, and economic development for African (Black) and oppressed communities.

Olivia Saito, MPH graduated from Tulane University School of Public Health and Tropical Medicine in New Orleans, Louisiana, where she did her practicum with Dr. Marva Lewis and the *Talk, Touch & Listen* Program. Upon graduating, she worked for the Healthy Start Program in New Orleans. When she moved to California, she took on a supervisory role in a child abuse prevention program that supported mothers and children in the Long Beach area. She currently works for Soka Gakkai International-USA, an organization that serves to empower people to transform their life circumstances through Buddhist practice and faith.

Aditi Subramaniam, LMHC, R-DMT, IECMH-E® (IV-C), is a licensed mental health clinician and registered movement psychotherapist. She earned her MA in Mental Health Counseling and Expressive Arts Therapy from Lesley University in Cambridge, Massachusetts, and MA in Clinical Psychology from the University of Delhi, India. She is a Massachusetts Association for Infant Mental Health (MassAIMH) Endorsed® practitioner as an Infant and Early Childhood Mental Health Mentor–Clinical. She currently works at the Massachusetts Society for the Prevention of Cruelty to Children (MSPCC) as the Infant and Early Childhood Mental Health Partnership Manager, leading a statewide partnership between MSPCC and MassAIMH. She serves as faculty at Jewish Family and Child Services in the Infant Parent Training Institute. She is a national trainer at the Brazelton Institute at Boston Children's Hospital, a Brazelton Touchpoints center. She lives in Boston, Massachusetts, with her husband and five-year-old daughter and enjoys dancing, making art, and is humbled in parenting and learning from the tiny wonders of childhood from her daughter.

Mary G. Warren, PhD, IMH-E® (IV-P) (Infant Mental Health Mentor for Policy), teaches Cross-Cultural Understanding, Law, Policy and Advocacy, and Reflective Practice in the online Infant and Early Childhood Development PhD Program of Fielding Graduate University (2013 to present) in Santa Barbara, California.She co-developed the Best for Babies Court Team in Maricopa County, Arizona, and has been an active Baby CASA. She co-developed Arizona's Statewide Early Childhood System, was an ACE trainer, and member of the Executive Committee of the Arizona ACE Consortium.As the founding Secretary for the international Alliance for the Advancement of Infant Mental Health, she represented the Infant Toddler Mental Health Coalition of Arizona where she was the Endorsement Coordinator. She was both founding faculty for the Master of Applied Studies in Infant Family Practice at Arizona State University (ASU) (2008–2011) and founding director for the Family Impact Seminars at ASU (2007–2008). The US Department of Health and Human Services Administration on Children, Youth, and Families named her the 2012 Commissioner's Award recipient in Arizona for her work in prevention and intervention in child maltreatment.

Virginia White, MSW DSW, received a Doctorate of Social Work from Tulane University School of Social Work in New Orleans, Louisiana. She received a bachelor's degree in Psychology from Dillard University and a Master of Social Work degree from Southern University at New Orleans. Dr. White is passionate about advocacy, social justice, and eliminating health disparities. She co-authored publications on the prevalence of health disparities among African American males with renal cell carcinoma. She also presented at the 2012 Summit on the Science of Eliminating Health Disparities in Washington, DC. She was recently selected as a fellow in the 2021 Interdisciplinary Minority Fellowship Program funded by the Substance Abuse and Mental Health Services Administration (SAMHSA). Dr. White has additional experience in trauma-informed care, school social work, restorative practices, juvenile justice, and facilitating focus groups.

Karol A. Wilson, LMSW, IMH-E® (IV) is a Social Worker and one of the Program Supervisors at Starfish Family Services in Dearborn, Michigan. She has been a member of the Infant Mental Health Community for over 25 years as an infant mental health home visitor, reflective supervisor, and consultant. She has trained nationally and internationally on reflective supervision, attachment, and diversity. She was one of the first Michigan Association of Infant Mental Health Diversity Fellows and the first Black Infant Mental Health Specialist to be Endorsed as an Infant Mental Health Mentor. She is an elected Board Member of the Alliance for the Advancement of Infant Mental Health. She is a published author, specializing in infant and early childhood mental health. Married with two adult children, she plans to continue in private practice after her retirement from her administrative duties in June 2021.

Danielle K. Wright, DSW, LCSW, MPH earned a Master's of Social Work and Public Health and Doctorate of Social Work from Tulane University in New Orleans, Louisiana. She has been a licensed clinical social worker with over 10 years of experience in the areas of trauma, toxic stress, infant mental health, social and emotional learning, and certification in Disaster Mental Health. Dr. Wright was trained in Infant Mental Health through the LSUHSC Department of Psychiatry's Harris Infant Mental Health Fellowship. She is the founding Director of Navigate Nola, the child well-being division of the Deep South Center for Environmental Justice. Dr. Wright is also the founder and CEO of the New Orleans Wellness Institute and works as a therapist, in private practice, at Atlas Psychiatry. She also served as an adjunct clinical field faculty member at Tulane University School of Social Work. She is a member of several volunteer service organizations including the Links Inc., Crescent City Chapter.

'Sankofa with the Comb'©[1]

A word in the Akan language of Ghana that translates as "reach back and get it" also refers to the Asante Adinkra symbol represented by a bird with its head turned backward taking an egg off its back. The feet are turned forward to the future. The artistic insertion of a wooden African hair pick into the belly of the bird symbolizes the opportunity that hair combing interaction provides for caregivers to talk, touch, and listen to children connecting their family and cultural past to the future generations of children's lives.

A Place for Natural Connections

[1] Sankofa with the Comb created by Marva L. Lewis.

Part I
Talk, Touch & Listen While Combing Hair

Chapter 1
Childhood Experiences of Racial Acceptance and Rejection

Marva L. Lewis

A Snapshot of the Morning Routines in Two Families

One morning, as Terri[1] hurriedly combed through her daughter's soft mass of curly, kinky, coarse hair, the plastic comb hit a tangle. Recoiling from the harsh punishment combing, three-year-old Tonisha reflexively pulled away. Glancing at the stark red numbers displayed on the microwave, Terri whispers through clenched teeth, "Damn it! I told you to keep still. I'm trying to comb your nappy hair!" With narrowed eyes and tightly pressed lips she angrily hits her daughter's legs and arms with the back of the hairbrush.

The only time Tonisha is alone with her mother – who works the night shift, in addition to a daytime job as a hotel maid – is during the time she gets her hair combed. Silently, carefully using the same curse words to chastise her small body for flinching from the searing pain of the fine-tooth comb in her thick, curly hair, Tonisha commands her body, "Damn it, I say stay still!" She busies her mind with the well-worn question that no one seems to know the answer: "Why my mama hate me so much? Why my hair so bad?" The next day the Day Care Center teacher makes a mandated call to Child Protective Services to report the bruising on the visible part of Tonisha's arms and legs.

That same morning, in the apartment across the hall from Terri, another mother, Regina also combs her daughter's hair. Known to her many family and friends as Gina, she gently brushes her daughter Ashley's soft mass of curly, kinky, coarse hair. She smiles at Ashley's antics, marveling at how adept her twenty-four-month-old daughter was at imitating family members' voices in a pretend conversation on her play phone as she lovingly completes her daily routine of combing Ashley's hair. As Gina carefully parts Ashley's hair, the mother and daughter spontaneously sing the popular song,

"I love you. You love me" Later, Gina tenderly kisses and hugs her daughter as she drops her off at the same day care center that Terri's daughter attends.

[1] All names and other personal identifiers included in clinical stories/vignettes in this chapter have been changed to protect privacy and confidentiality.

M. L. Lewis (✉)
School of Social Work, Tulane University, New Orleans, LA, USA
e-mail: mlewis@tulane.edu

M. L. Lewis, D. J. Weatherston (eds.), *Therapeutic Cultural Routines to Build Family Relationships*, https://doi.org/10.1007/978-3-030-83726-6_1

Both single mothers live with their children in the same crowded low-income apartment complex. Both experience the same environmental toxic stressors of poverty, their urban neighborhood under siege with high rates of violence, and general neglect. To pay the subsidized rent and her portion of childcare, 25-year-old Terri works two minimum-wage jobs.

Both of their children attend the same Head Start Child Care Center. Both complete the same daily hair-combing task. Each of these mother's responses to the stress of their environments has important outcomes for their emotional relationship with their child. Each child will have memories of having their hair combed. Yet, each child will have qualitatively different memories of relationship with their mothers (Emde, 1989; Stern, 1985).

Keeping Children Safe from the Harm of Child Abuse

Imagine you are the child protection social worker who takes the call from the daycare center. Where do you start your investigation? You hear from other social workers that the public housing area is dangerous. There was a police shooting that just happened in the past week. And you are White. You will stand out in all-Black neighborhood. Everyone will recognize that you are the social worker coming to remove the child from parents. Should you take the police with you for protection? If I ask the juvenile court to remove the children from their parents, will the parent think I am prejudiced against Black people?

Imagine you are the African-American daycare owner that Terri and Gina's children attend. The law mandates that you report this incidence of suspected child abuse. As you reluctantly search for the number, you notice Tonisha's hair is neatly combed and her clothes clean and neat. You think back to your own hair combing time with a smile. Memories also pop up of the few times you got spanked as a child and think, "I was spanked and I'm okay." You ask yourself, "How can I turn in another mother to Child Services who looks like me? How can I convince a White judge that this mother will keep her children safe and that there will not be any more child maltreatment?"

Both providers are dedicated professionals. They both believe passionately about need for the protection of infants and young children from the harms of child abuse or neglect. The daycare owner loves and believes that her mission in life is to provide the highest-quality childcare and early education for Black and Brown children. She knows how vital childcare is to working single mothers and for two parent households struggling at minimum wage jobs. She knows there are few options for childcare when the entire family must work. They don't have the privilege of having only one parent to work as a stay-at-home parent.

A 10:29 Second Intervention to Build Attachment. As mandated reporters of child abuse and neglect, infant and early childhood educators are under enormous pressure to make life-and-death decisions for children. Would you like to learn how to use an evidence-based, ten minute and twenty-nine second (10:29) home-based intervention that builds parent attachment with infants and toddlers? Are you interested in learning about the science behind the development of a manualized intervention that can prevent intergenerational child maltreatment? Do you need more culturally valid tools that can help families of color heal from racial wounds as they learn about the evidence-based parenting strategies with infants and toddlers? Finally, are you interested in more effective ways to do your job that will help prevent burnout in hard-working social workers and early childhood educators?

Helping Black and Brown Parents Build Attachment Relationships with Infants and Healing Racial Wounds

Infants are at the highest risk for child maltreatment. Young children of color and their families experience additional stress associated with their racial group. In 2021, the American Professional Society on the Abuse of Children has proclaimed that racism experienced by youth is a form of psychological maltreatment or child abuse. The American Psychological Association (2016) and Academy of Pediatrics have declared the psychosocial harm of racism-based stress on young children of color (National Academies of Sciences, Engineering, and Medicine, 2019; Trent et al., 2019). Structural inequalities based on race lead to childhood adversities that shake the foundations of children's health and well-being (Shonkoff et al., 2021). The traditional indexes of childhood adversity now include developments in epidemiology, neurobiology, and describe the biomedical and epigenetic consequences of toxic stress of urban experiences of racism and discrimination for children of color and their families (Pachter et al., 2017). Consistent findings from research on early childhood environments, adversity, and resilience report the role of physiological disruptions of race-related toxic stress and disparities, health outcomes, and chronic stress responses in children and caregivers (Shonkoff et al., 2021; Slaughter-Acey et al., 2020). The unique effect of structural racism calls for a compelling public health approach (Sotero, 2006), to "… to protect the developing brain and other biological systems from the physiological disruption of [race-based] toxic stress" (Shonkoff, et al., 2021, p. 115).

Prevention is one of the most important strategies to prevent child abuse. The research on the causes of child maltreatment is clearly identified risks. The children at highest risk live in poverty with parents who are isolated, stressed, and lack the simple knowledge of child development or are repeating childrearing practices that have been passed down in families for generations. "This is the way children should be disciplined," she thinks. Making the decision to call Child Protection to remove an infant or child from the family is one of the most painful points in the life of dedicated professionals who love children. People who go into infant or early childcare do not do it for the money, but for their love of children. To make those hard decisions to report and recommend removal, most providers need the effective tools to see the glimmers of strength in the family. Building on a parent's existing strengths and increasing the provider's confidence that infants and toddlers are safe in their homes is a dedicated professional's dream. We invite you to add one more tool to your first aid kit.

Fighting child abuse and structural racism at the same time is daunting and overwhelming. Trying to maintain an authentic antiracist posture in the face of deadlines, paperwork, old policies, sometimes uninformed supervisors, and undereducated staff contributes to feelings of helplessness and hopelessness. Yet, the passion to do the best work with infants and young children keeps professionals in their jobs. They need new tools that are both culturally valid and effective for best observation, assessment, and decision making. Professionals need tools that can sustain the small gains in treatment plans for families that can last through the predictable developmental challenges that will be faced by parents as their child grows and blossoms. The use of the hair combing task provides a simple complement to the existing, evidence-based attachment interventions such as Healthy Families Home visiting, Circle of Security, Attachment Bites (National Academies of Sciences, Engineering, and Medicine, 2019).

We invite you to read further about the use of the at-home routine of combing hair that can be added to your first aid kit for children and families of color. As you read the stories contributed by the authors in this book, you will have the opportunity to learn how these simple everyday tasks provide you with a window into the quality of the relationship between a parent or primary caregiver and young child. Does this relationship appear to be strong and secure or in trouble? Does this parent need developmental guidance or on-going support? Is there evidence of a developmental delay?

Finding Strengths Through Assessment and Intervention Using Rich Cultural Routines

'How can I do anti-racist work with infants and young children? Both the social workers and the childcare providers described at the beginning of this introduction have attended mandatory training on implicit bias and structural racism leading to racial disparities in the child welfare system. As early childhood providers they are endorsed and embrace the Diversity Tenets designed to help eliminate bias in infant and early childhood practice (Ghosh-Ippen et al., 2012). Yet, the issues of client engagement with different race and same race providers continues. Much of the existing infant and early childhood interventions that are committed to antiracist practice have few tools that directly address the racial wounding to Black and Indigenous People of Color (BIPOC) children and families. We argue that the use of the tools presented in this book with consistent racially informed reflective practice as described in Part II of this book will help you achieve goals for equity and social justice.

Colorism and Nappy-Haired Ghosts in the Nursery

The phenotype of racial features readily distinguishes Black Indigenous People of color from other racial groups as well as within their same racial group. The caste-like characteristics of skin color and hair remain a source of conflict and rejection within families and communities of color (Arnold et al., 2004; Branch & Newcombe, 1986; Wilkerson, 2020). Racial features include skin color, ranging from very light to very dark; hair texture, ranging from very straight and wavy to very tightly curled, coarse, and kinky; nose and lip size, ranging from broad to narrow and thick to thin; and, buttocks, ranging from flat to protruding and round. These racial features vary among individuals identified as Black, as well as among children within the same family. In addition, many Black infants' hair texture may change during these early years from straight or wavy and easy to manage to a coarse and tightly curled texture that requires more attention, time, and patience to style.

These features are all associated with the complex, multilayered legacy of racism and stereotypes about Black people (Bogel, 1989; Russell et al., 1992; Okazaw-Rey et al., 1987; Rooks, 2001). From birth, young children may be either highly prized or summarily rejected simply based on the lightness of their skin tone or straightness and length of their hair. Comments and messages based on these stereotypes of African racial features may have been a source of ongoing ridicule or shame within the child's network of relationships with family, extended family or school, and community. Conversely, Blacks born with more European racial features such as light skin color and long straight hair may have experienced rejection by other Blacks or been reinforced with socially sanctioned vanity and "specialness" (Porter, 1991). Stigmatized racial characteristics then become a salient part of the daily life of young Black children (Fegley et al., 2008).

In the case of three-year-old Black boys, there is an increased risk factor for expulsion from preschool, and for Black girls, school expulsion and criminal charges (Crenshaw, 2015; Gilliam & Shahar, 2006). A parent's childhood experiences of colorism and emotional acceptance or rejection of infants and children by parents, extended family, and the community may become the unrecognized factor in caregiver sensitivity, the "ghost" in the nursery (Rohner, 1975, 1986).

African-American hair texture and skin color have been the symbol of centuries of painful stereotypes, the basis for economic and social discrimination and emotional trauma of racial and gender prejudice, (Bogel, 1989; Fannon, 1968; Davis et al., 1998; Rooks, 2001). These legacies also may be manifested in biased attitudes of internalized oppression related to "light skin" and "dark skin" and known as "colorism" – valuing lighter skin tones and straight or wavy hair over dark skin and "nappy" hair (Russell et al., 1992). Over the past century, the emotional baggage associated with hair and skin color has been a recurrent theme in popular movies, books, articles, and topics in church and professional seminars in Black communities around the United States (e.g., Byrd & Tharps, 2001; Golden, 2004; Harris & Johnson, 2001; Russell et al., 1992; Straight, 2000).

Racial features of hair and skin color can be trauma triggers in the formation of African-American mother–infant attachment relationships. Behavioral evidence is available from the everyday task of combing hair, a focus of stereotypes, racial pride, and shame (Lewis, 1993). For example, the mother may perform this task in a perfunctory manner or simply assign the task to someone else if she has negative associations with kinky hair and has a young daughter with kinky hair. A colorist-historical trauma framework provides a conceptual means to understand the continued socioemotional impact on the psychological well-being of caregivers and parents of color (Ortega-Williams et al., 2019). In addition, research findings from observations of behavioral interactions during hair combing time suggest that a parent's or caregiver's unresolved childhood experiences of colorism impacts how the caregivers – a mother, grandmother, or early childhood teacher – may interact with Black and Brown children (Gilliam & Shahar, 2006; Lewis, 2015).

A Colorist-Historical Framework

A colorist-historical trauma framework identifies colorism as a key dimension of structural racism that negatively impacts the psychological and physical well-being of Black, Indigenous caregivers of color. (Ortega-Williams et al., 2019). This framework provides an intersectional lens of colorism and historical trauma to unpack the gendered stereotypes of hair and skin tone during the developmental experiences of young children. The intersection of children's developmental experiences tied to their immutable racial features creates a type of social paradox leading to a child's perception that their fate is linked to their hair texture and skin color (Hochschild et al., 2007). In this book, we argue that childhood experiences of the historical trauma of colorism influence parent–infant interactions during hair combing and subsequently the quality of the formation of parent–child attachment (Lewis et al., 2013).

The Intergenerational, Biopsychosocial Impact of Colorism – Evidence from Research

Throughout the chapters in this book, we discuss racial trauma and the concept of colorism – valuing lighter skin tone or straight hair textures – that shape the attachment relationship between parents or primary attachment figures and their infants and young children through *childhood experiences of racial acceptance and rejection* (CERAR). The compelling evidence from research of the intergenerational impact of historical trauma and structural racism on physical health and well-being of Black Indigenous families of color calls for the need for parents and infant and early childhood educators to recognize the impact of colorism on children. Racial disparities are triggered by implicit bias and stereotypes associated with racial phenotype, specifically skin color, or hair type. These responses to skin tone and hair are barriers to health-promoting resources for children in the social determinants of health, employment, education, and housing (National Academies of Sciences, Engineering, and Medicine, 2019).

Large racial disparities exist in preterm delivery and other birth outcomes with African-American women experiencing more negative outcomes as reported in a longitudinal study of health disparities in adverse birth outcomes in two generations of a sample of 1350 Black/African-American women (Slaughter-Acey et al., 2019, 2020). The researchers studied the role of skin tone and the relationship between experiences of racial microaggressions – chronic or episodic, daily, race-related hassles; negative social experiences; and prenatal health care. They found differences in the rates of preterm care based on the skin tone and generation. In other words, the access to prenatal care for women with light brown skin tones differed from women with medium and dark brown skin tones.

We invite you to read the stories of professional providers representing a wide array of social backgrounds, races, and experiences using the everyday routine of hair combing interaction (HCI) as a tool for observation, assessment, and intervention. As you read the short biographies of each author, you will see the depth of skills, training, education, and commitment to infants and the early childhood field. Many of the authors tell their story of using the *Talk, Touch, and Listen While Combing Hair* curriculum or simple observational task to inform their work with children and families of color. The authors each use a racial trauma-informed reflective practice lens to describe their work, insight, and implementation of the tools based on hair combing interaction.

What You Will Learn from Reading This Book?

The developmental framework in which infants and young children grow and change is made up of several interdependent ecological dimensions (Lewis, 2000): a nurturing environment, a sustaining environment, and the collective experience of trauma and resilience. Norton (1993) describes the nurturing environment as composed of family and socioemotional processes and the sustaining environment, composed of resources such as housing, employment, and education. More specifically, the sustaining environment includes the family's cultural, ethnic, and racial prescriptions for behavior, values, and beliefs about infants and young children, as well as the role and expectations of parents for their children. The third context, affecting the social and emotional development of infants and young children, includes the collective experiences of historical trauma and resilience (Lewis, 2019; Brave Heart, 2000; van der Kolk, 2014), their cultural or ethnic group's history, the larger social setting in which the family resides, including the policies, access to resources and health care, and the dynamics of the social networks of family and friends.

We offer a colorist-historical trauma framework to both address issues of internalized stereotypes of colorism – the acceptance or rejection of children that may place young children at risk for child maltreatment during the critical developmental stages of birth through toddler.

Decades of mixed methods research on parent–child interactions during hair combing led to the selection of this conceptual framework. Laboratory studies of the interactions between African-American parents and their infants and young daughters were conducted using traditional developmental assessment methods such as observation of free play and reading. The dyads were also videotaped combing their child's hair as they do at home. Hours of systematic analysis of videotaped caregiver child interaction during hair combing time revealed individual differences of mothers, fathers, and caregivers combing children's hair. This analysis found that on average, caregivers spend 10:29 seconds from start to finish combing their young child's hair. Individual differences included the position they held the child (proximity) and opportunity for physical touch during hair combing time; the amount of verbal interaction and topics of talk, as well as how well the caregiver responds to the infant's cues.

Combing the hair of an infant or child with a difficult temperament requires a different skill set to accomplish the task than a child born with an easy temperament. Similarly, the degree that a young child is "tender headed" – that is, extremely sensitive to physical touch to the scalp – will dictate the experience of both the caregiver and child during the battle to get the child's hair in a semblance of order.

The other individual factors include the general parenting style of the caregiver. A parent or primary caregiver combing hair who generally uses an authoritarian parenting style with their children is likely to use a firmer, no-nonsense parenting style while combing children's hair.

These findings have been translated into a manualized curriculum, *Talk, Touch, and Listen While Combing Hair*© (Lewis et al., 2009). This research will be discussed throughout the book as well as in chapters where authors share experiences implementing the curriculum in diverse cities in the United States. Authors will also share stories about the use of some tools such as the projective tool of the *"Neck up" drawing"* presented in Chap. 16.

Hair combing interaction (HCI) and the observations of the amount of physical touch, the verbal interactions, and response by caregivers provide a window into the quality of parenting styles and child compliance. Providers may use HCI as both a context for observation and assessment and/or intervention with relationships that need support or to serve as a simple primary prevention tool (Miller & Goodnow, 1995). Figure 1.1 presents interdependent, interactive, and dynamic developmental, individual, and sociocultural factors to help providers understand the outcome of the interactions – the quality of parent–child attachment. Providers may use this graphic depiction of the relationship to select choice points for interventions with infants from birth to assess individual needs.

The "call and response" of emotional synchrony between a caregiver and child begins from birth. The developmental importance of these interactions and routines are described in several chapters in the book. The individual factors that shape HCI interactions located in the young child and the parent or primary

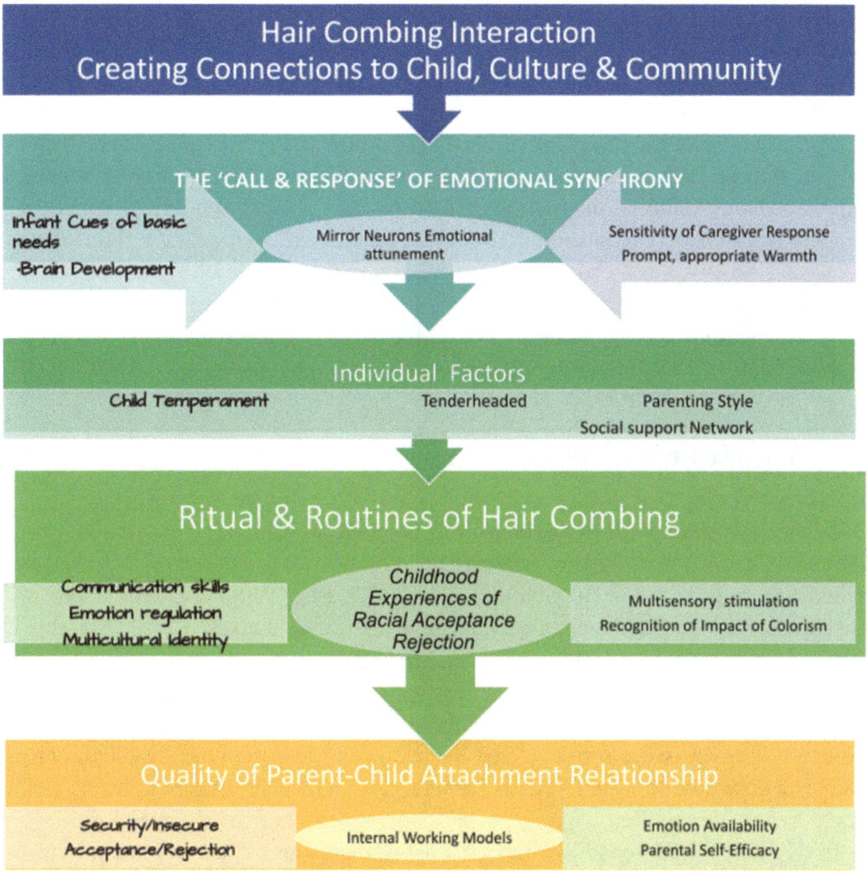

Fig. 1.1 Building attachment and intergenerational memories through hair combing interaction

caregiver constitute the challenges and strengths that contribute to the building blocks for the quality of relationships.

One of the most unique sets of factors you will read about in this book and learn to assess are the psychological legacies of historical trauma that led to the parents' childhood experiences of racial acceptance or rejection based on colorism (Lewis et al, 2013). Internal Working Models (Bowlby, 1969) of relationships that include racial wounding are unrecognized factors that may lead to the continued intergenerational practices of race-based psychological maltreatment of children.

The third level of the ecological niche is the rituals and routine of combing hair. Chapter 3 will expand on this multidimensional experience of hair combing time as an event that connects parents and primary caregivers to their child, culture, and community. This level also includes the racial context of parent–child interaction. Chapter 4 details the influence of a parent's childhood experiences of acceptance and rejection based on their racial features. We argue that the individual differences in the parenting styles Keisha and Regina introduced during the hair combing task at the beginning of the chapter, may be due, in part, to unrecognized trauma memories associated with hair or skin color. The act of combing a child's hair may be a trauma triggered by the mother's race-based stress experiences in her workplace and community. These trauma memories may also be triggered by childhood experiences of messages of racial acceptance or rejection within the mother's family and social network of friends and strangers.

The outcome of the interplay of these individual and relationship-based factors evident during HCI will help build secure bonds of attachment. Jointly viewing videotaped hair combing interactions, social workers and other helping professionals may work with a parent to identify their strengths, recognize their child's emotions, and set goals for change. Most importantly, the continued practice of hair combing interactive behaviors – talking, touching, and listening – will continue to sustain the gains made by one-hour weekly therapy sessions mandated by the courts or prevention and early intervention programs to enhance parenting capacities.

Why We Wrote This Book?

Over the past two decades of providing workshops, training, and serving as a University faculty member in graduate-level social work education, I was compelled to write this book. In Chap. 2, A Social Worker's Story, I write about my twelve years of experience as a new, bright-eyed social worker in child protective services equipped with few tools to make life and death decisions for children. The repeated requests from social workers for better assessment and intervention tools with African-American families led to my return to graduate school. What you will read in this book is the result of that decision. The research and development of everyday, low-cost tools for social workers grew out of my worries, fears, and a desire to help all children, with a special focus on African-American children.

In addition to relationship-based HCI assessments and interventions, providers need one more tool in their first-aid kits – racially informed reflective practice. Throughout the book, you will read stories of the reflections of experienced and seasoned social workers and therapists who come from a variety of cultural backgrounds, education, and experiences who work with children and families identified to be at risk for relationship failure or whose young children are in foster care for substantiated abuse and neglect.

You will hear their process of reflecting on the role of racism and legacies of oppression as the authors, one of Indian heritage, and one of mixed African-American heritage in Boston, Massachusetts, implements the hair combing task with a variety of families. You will read chapters by a cadre of authors that includes students led by their experienced community counseling professor, using the *Talk, Touch, and Listen* Curriculum with families who are homeless in San Francisco, California. You will read stories by therapists' reflective work with families reported for child maltreatment in Baton Rouge Louisiana and with children in foster care. You will read of the thoughtful reflections of a team of social work students in New Orleans, Louisiana, and the creativity they called on to present *Miranda's Green Hair* puppet show about a little girl of color who doesn't want to get her hair combed.

Each chapter ends with reflective practice questions that invite you to think about what you have read, to consider thoughts and feelings awakened by the material, and to encourage continued exploration about culture, ethnicity, and race, leading to greater self-awareness. Of interest, Chap. 6 introduces the reader to reflective supervision with a particular focus on diversity, ethnicity, race, and inclusion. In Chaps. 8 and 9, you will read the experiences of two seasoned social workers who are women of color as they offer personal and professional reflections about emotionally charged, cross-race experiences that center on hair and colorism with families and reflective supervisors.

Recognition of the Impact of Colorism: A Form of Psychological Maltreatment

The racial disparities that exist in child welfare and educational systems contribute to the racial psychological maltreatment of infants, children, and families of color (American Professional Society of Child Abuse, 2020). These disparities often lead to difficulties in engaging clients to participate in services offered through community agencies. The often daugnting, and overwhelming work for diversity, equity, and inclusion work must be addressed at the individual, family, and systems level. We offer a cultural practices approach through hair combing routines as a method to address these disparities and mitigate their impact, using conceptually complimentary tools to assess family strengths, to continue the fight for equity and justice at the systems level.

Messages based on skin tone and hair type, the immutable characteristics that children cannot change, is a form of trauma and race-based psychological maltreatment of young children. A central goal of our interventions that centers on the application of the research on hair combing interactions and colorism is enhancing parental reflective functioning, the ability to sort through early experiences of racial wounding and prevent passing on these internalized hurts to their children (Ordway et al., 2015). Throughout the chapters in this book, we highlight the unrecognized form of raced-based child psychological maltreatment, colorism, the valuing of light skin and straight hair by family and community, that is a legacy of the historical trauma of slavery for families of color. This historical practice had been used as a form of psychological terrorism to maintain power and subjection of millions of enslaved Africans over hundreds of years (Wilkerson, 2020; Hochschild, 2007).

Using HCI Tools to Build Strong Bonds with Children

It is of critical importance for infant and early childhood mental health therapists, educators, social workers, and policy makers to understand the depth of this invisible, insidious practice of colorism. Each caregiver's distinct *ethnobiography* may include an unconscious and long buried history of acceptance or rejection in response to their skin color and hair textures by a network of family and community people. These memories may currently shape their approach to the everyday task of combing an infant or young child's hair. This acceptance or rejection may be tacitly communicated during the routine of combing hair.

The goal of hair combing interventions is three-fold: Through the daily interactions of combing hair, caregivers of infants and young children may strengthen their emotional bond with their child, process their early childhood experiences of acceptance and rejection based on their racial features, and reach an understanding of the past as it impacts the present. The central goal of all HCIs is to recognize that messages based on colorism about light skin and straight hair as pretty, or dark skin as ugly and curly "nappy hair" bad, are internalized and remembered from generation to generation.

In this book, we will share tools, strategies, and experiences to provide support for families of color with infants and young children. We introduce a *Colorist-Historical Trauma Framework for Reflective Practice* as a conceptual foundation for practice that incorporates the wounds of racism to families and client [therapist relationships. This framework ties together the psychosocial tools introduced throughout the book. Each chapter ends with reflective questions tied to the sociocultural and emotional content described regarding colorism and hair type. We invite the reader to think reflectively about the information shared and, at the same time, to consider personal thoughts and feelings about culture, ethnicity, and race that may have been evoked by the experiences and materials described.

We hope the stories shared in this book will help practitioners use the simple routine of combing children's hair to provide support for parents and primary caregivers to lovingly connect with their children, build on their rich cultural strengths, and gain support from strong, vibrant communities.

Reflective Questions

1. Hair combing interaction (HCI), as described in this chapter, can awaken memories about your own early care experiences. Take this opportunity to reflect on who combed your hair and the thoughts and feelings surrounding those hair combing experiences. It is part of your long journey to self-reflection, essential to your work with children and families of color.
2. How does the concept of colorism as a legacy of historical trauma invite you to think about deeply embedded racial disparities and colorism in our culture?
3. How might you incorporate the observation of hair combing interaction to help you learn about the quality of relationship between a parent and child referred to you for services?
4. Can you use hair combing time to support and strengthen parent–child relationships in clients referred to you for service?

Resource:
Video and Discussion of Colorism with Dark Skinned Girls, https://www.youtube.com/watch?v=UW31Te1awVw

References

Arnold, M. S., Janson, C., Natt, T., & Parmer, T. (2004). Physical attractiveness as a process of internalized oppression and multigenerational transmission in African American families. *The Family Journal: Counseling and Therapy for Couples and Families, 12*(3).

Bogel, D. (1989). *Toms, Coons, Mulattoes, Mammies, and Bucks: An interpretive history of Blacks in American films*. Continuum.

Bowlby, J. (1969). *Attachment and loss: (Vol. 1). Attachment.* New York: Basic Books.

Branch, C., & Newcombe, N. (1986). Racial attitude development among young black children as a function of parental attitudes: A longitudinal and cross-sectional study. *Child Development, 57*, 712–721.

Brave Heart, M. Y. T. (2000, Winter/Spring). Wakiksuyapi: Carrying the historical trauma of the Lakota. Disaster and traumatic stress research and intervention. In M. Zakour (Ed.), *Tulane studies in social welfare* (Vols. XXI–XXII, pp. 245–266). Tulane University.

Byrd, A. D., & Tharps, L. L. (2001). *Untangling the roots of Black hair in America*. St. Martin's press.

Crenshaw, K. W. (2015). *Black girls matter: Pushed out, overpoliced and under protected*. African American Policy Forum, Center for Intersectionality and Social Policy Studies.

Davis, K. B., Daniels, M., & See, L. A. (1998). The psychological effects of skin color on African Americans' self-esteem. *Journal of Human Behavior in the Social Environment, 1*(2/3), 63–90.

Emde, R. N. (1989). The infant's relationship experience: Developmental and affective aspects. In A. Sameroff & R. N. Emde (Eds.), *Relationship disturbances in early childhood: A developmental approach* (pp. 33–51). Basic Books.

Fannon, F. (1968). *The wretched of the earth*. Grove Weidenfeld.

Fegley, S. G., Spencer, M. B., Goss, T. N., Harpalani, V., & Charles, N. (2008). Colorism embodied: Skin tone and psychosocial well-being in adolescence. In W. Overton, U. Mueller, & J. Newman (Eds.), *Developmental perspectives on embodiment and consciousness* (pp. 281–311). Mahwah, NJ: LEA.

Ghosh-Ippen, C., Noroña, C. R., & Thomas, K. (2012). From tenet to practice: Putting diversity-informed services into action. *Zero to Three Journal, 33*(2), 23–28.

Gilliam, W. S., & Shahar, G. (2006). Preschool and childcare expulsion and suspension: Rates and predictors in one state. *Infants & Young Children., 19*(3), 228–245.

Golden, M. (2004). *Don't play in the sun: One woman's journey through the color complex*. Doubleday.

Harris, J., & Johnson, P. (Eds.). (2001). *Tenderheaded: A comb-bending collection of hair stories*. Pocket Books.

Hochschild, J. L. Weaver, V. (2007). The skin color paradox and the American racial order. *Social Forces* 86 (2) 643–670.

Lewis, M. L. (2015). Getting the parts straight: The psychology of hair combing interaction between African American mothers and daughters. In K. T. Craddock, (Ed.), *Black Motherhoods(s): Contours, contexts, and considerations*. pp 204–220, Bradford, ON: Demeter Press.

Lewis, M. L. (2019). The intergenerational transmission of protective parenting responses to historical trauma. In H. E. Fitzgerald, D. Johnson, D. Qin, F. Villarruel, & J. Norder (Eds.), *The handbook of children and prejudice: Integrating research practice and policy* (pp. 43–61). Springer. https://doi.org/10.1007/978-3-030-12228-7

Lewis, M. L., (2000). The cultural context of infant mental health: the developmental niche of infant-caregiver relationships. In (Ed.) C. H. Zeanah, *Infant Mental Health*, 2nd ed., (pp. 91-107). New York: Guilford.

Lewis, M. L., (1993). *Factors influencing the interpretation of emotions in infants by African American mothers.* Unpublished dissertation, University of Colorado, Boulder.

Lewis, M. L., Foppa, L., Dardar, S., & Porré, R. (2009). *Talk, touch & listen while combing Hair©: A culturally, centered, visualization approach to parent education: A manual*. Tulane University School of Social Work.

Lewis, M. L., Noroña, C. R., McConnico, N., & Thomas, K. (2013). Colorism, A Legacy of Historical Trauma in Parent-Child Relationships: Clinical, Research, & Personal Perspectives. *Zero to Three Journal, 34*(2), 11–23.

Miller, P. J., & Goodnow, J. J. (1995). *Cultural practices as contexts for development* (New directions for child development, No. 67) (pp. 5–16). Jossey-Bass, Inc.

National Academies of Sciences, Engineering, and Medicine. (2019). *Vibrant and healthy kids: Aligning science, practice, and policy to advance health equity*. The National Academies Press. https://doi.org/10.17226/25466

Norton, D. (1993). Diversity, early socialization, and temporal development: The dual perspective revisited. *Social Work, 38*, 82–90.

Okazaw-Rey, M., Robinson, T., & Ward, J. V. (1987). Black women and the politics of skin color and hair. *Women and Therapy, 6*(1–2), 89–102.

Ordway, M. R., Webb, D., Sadler, L. S., & Slade, A. (2015). Parental reflective functioning: An approach to enhancing parent-child relationships in pediatric primary care. *Journal of Pediatric Health Care, Vol, 29*(4), 325–334.

Ortega-Williams, A., Crutchfield, J., & Hall, J. C. (2019). The colorist-historical trauma framework: Implications for culturally responsive practice with African Americans. *Journal of Social Work., 0*(0), 1–16. https://doi.org/10.1177/1468017319890083

Pachter, L. M., Lieberman, L., Bloom, S. L., & Fein, J. A. (2017). *Developing a community-wide initiative to address childhood adversity and toxic stress: A case study of The Philadelphia ACE Task Force* https://www.academicpedsjnl.net.https://www.academicpedsjnl.net/article/S1876-2859(17)30168-7/fulltext

Porter, C. P. (1991). Social reasons for skin tone preferences of Black school-age children. *American Journal of Orthopsychiatry, 61*(1), 149–154.

Rohner, R. (1975). *They love me, love me not*. HRAF Press.

Rohner, R. P. (1986). *The warmth dimension: Foundations of parental acceptance-rejection theory*. Sage.

Rooks, N. (2001). Wearing your race wrong: hair, drama, and politics of representation for African American women at play on a battlefield. In M. Bennet & V. D. Dickerson (Eds.), *Recovering the Black female body: Self-representations by African American women* (pp. 279–283). Rutgers University Press.

Russell, K., Wilson, M., & Hall, R. (1992). *Color complex: The politics of skin color among African Americans*. Anchor Books/Doubleday.

Shonkoff, J. P., Slopen, N., & Williams, D. R. (2021). Early childhood adversity, toxic stress, and the impacts of racism on the foundations of health. *Annual Review of Public Health, 42*, 115–1334.

Slaughter-Acey, J. C., Sneed, D., Parker, L., Keith, V. M., Lee, N. L., & Misra, D. P. (2019). Skin tone matters: Racial microaggressions and delayed prenatal care. *American Journal of Preventive Medicine., 57*(3), 321–329.

Slaughter-Acey, J. C., Brown, T. N., Keith, V. M., Dailey, R., & Misra, D. P. (2020). A tale of two generations: Maternal skin color and adverse birth outcomes in Black/African women. *Social Science & Medicine*. https://doi.org/10.1016/j.socscimed.2020.113552

Sotero, M. M. (2006). A conceptual model of historical trauma: Implications for public health practice and research. *Journal of Health Disparities Research and Practice., 1*(1), 93–108.

Stern, D. N. (1985). The representation of relational patterns: Developmental considerations. In A. Sameroff & R. N. Emde (Eds.), *Relationship disturbances in early childhood* (pp. 52–69). Basic Books.

Straight, S. (2000, December). Talking heads: With this simple ritual we braid our lives together. *Reader's Digest*, 59–64.

Trent, M., Dooley, D. G., & Dougé, J. (2019). The impact of racism on child and Adolescent Health. American Academy of Pediatrics. *Pediatrics, 144*(2), e20191765. https://doi.org/10.1542/peds.2019-1765

van der Kolk, B. (2014). *The body keeps the score: Brain, mind, and body in the healing of trauma.* Penguin.

Wilkerson, I. (2020). *Caste: the origins of our discontents.* Random House.

Chapter 2
A Social Worker's Story: How Can I Help This Young Mother and Her Little Children?

Marva L. Lewis

Introduction

I was a social worker, new to the field. A young mother had been referred to my agency for neglectful care of her children and was assigned to me. When I knocked on the door, Lisa,[1] a very young African-American mother cautiously opened the door. I introduced myself as a case worker from Child Protective Services and asked permission to enter her home to ask her a few questions about the referral. Rolling her eyes with disgust, Lisa reluctantly waved me into the house. I stepped slowly into the small living room and saw her four small children peeking around the corner from the kitchen. According to the referral sheet, they were all under the age of five.

The youngest child, barely a year, held onto her older sister's hand, curious about who was talking to her mother. She sucked contentedly on a bottle of what looked like grape Kool-Aid. Lisa bent down and protectively scooped up the toddler to her bosom. With carefully measured words and a trace of impatience, she asked me, "*What is it now*?" I moved further into her immaculately clean, sparsely furnished, government-subsidized, townhome. "*May I sit down*?" She motioned me to a plastic molded chair in a corner of the living room. Taking out my green referral sheet, I told her that the agency had received a call reporting that her young children had been left alone last night without supervision. "*Is that true?*" I asked. Breathing deeply and closing her eyes Lisa softly stated, "*I had to leave them alone. I knocked*

[1] All names and other personal identifiers included in clinical stories/vignettes in this chapter have been changed to protect privacy and confidentiality.

M. L. Lewis (✉)
School of Social Work, Tulane University, New Orleans, LA, USA
e-mail: mlewis@tulane.edu

M. L. Lewis, D. J. Weatherston (eds.), *Therapeutic Cultural Routines to Build Family Relationships*, https://doi.org/10.1007/978-3-030-83726-6_2

on the neighbor's door, but they wasn't home. Please don't take my kids. There was no one I could turn to for help. I had to get a restraining order to protect us from my baby's daddy, Jason. He will hurt them." She softly repeated, "*Please don't take my kids. I love them.*"

Lisa told me her story as I listened carefully. She described her past year of living with domestic violence. Last week her twenty-year old boyfriend, Jason, got upset, because he couldn't find his solid gold neck chain. He repeatedly punched her as she held the baby, Tina. The baby slipped out of her arms and landed on the floor. Her infant daughter screamed in terror as she lay flat on the floor. At that moment, Lisa resolved to protect her children from Jason's temper and violence. She called the police and they asked if the baby had been bruised or injured. She replied, "*Not this time, but he left bruises on her in the past.*" The police officer stated that without a restraining order, they could not order her child's father to remain off the premises. She had to go to the court to obtain the necessary order but could not take all four children on city buses to get to the courthouse. She continued tearfully, "*There was no one to look after them. I am all on my own.*"

Lisa's Story

With substantiated neglect, I opened a noncourt case on 19-year-old Lisa and her four stair-step children, five-year-old Natasha, four-year-old Thomas, three-year-old Carlos, and 14-month-old Tina. After reviewing her thick, fifteen-year case file, I was saddened by the experiences of abuse and neglect Lisa had experienced throughout her childhood. Her mother had abandoned her and her two siblings shortly after Lisa's birth. They were moved about among the few family relations of her mother's already overwhelmed extended family. She recalls resentful remarks by their family caretakers. She and her siblings were viewed as burdens, "*...extra mouths to feed and more nappy-heads to comb, and no help from the government.*" During this era in the child welfare system, relatives were not eligible for foster care subsidies.

Lisa continued her report of a childhood of trauma at the hands of relatives. Lisa described physical neglect and abandonment until she was finally removed from her relatives' home at about age six years due to sexual abuse by a male cousin. She lost contact with her birth family after her mother had been jailed and her parental rights terminated. As an older child and then a teenage mom, Lisa had been placed in a series of foster homes but never adopted. She finally aged out of the foster care system and was now in her own home with four young children. She had spent the majority sixteen of her nineteen years on earth, living in relatives or foster homes. She experienced many childhood traumas, including sexual abuse, foster care, incarcerated parent. What I didn't know how to assess as a new social worker, were her positive and protective experiences that led to her resilience (Briggs et al., 2021). Over the next several months, we developed a treatment plan to get her childcare services and domestic violence counseling. My worry at the conclusion of each home visit was the same, *"With my limited skills, how can I help this young mother?"*

Noticing Lisa's Mood Barometer – What Was the State of the Children's Hair?

During my visits to Lisa's home to check on the status of the children, I noticed two things about her parenting skills. First, I noticed that her home, though sparsely furnished, was always neat as a pin. She took good physical care of the children. They appeared well-fed, with clean clothes, happy, and smiling. The second thing I noticed was that even though the children were neatly dressed, and the house was in pristine order, the children's hair was often sometimes uncombed. Unconsciously, I began to use the state of the children's hair as a symbolic gauge of Lisa's emotional state. When Lisa was having a good day, the home was clean, and her children's hair was neatly combed. When Lisa was in a depressed mood, although the home was clean, the shades were drawn, and the children's hair was matted and uncombed. It was if she didn't have the emotional energy to take the last step to complete the children's hair combing routine: that is, to put her children's hair in order.

Lisa had survived childhood trauma, abandonment, and multiple placements with strangers in the foster care system. She had no secure-base primary attachment figures to call for help. When we met, she was trying to protect her children. As a domestic violence survivor with few supportive resources, she had called the police to help keep her children from harm. Without an order for protection, the police could not help her. She made the desperate decision to leave the children alone to obtain this critical document to protect her children. Lisa's current turmoil and her story of surviving childhood trauma and domestic violence led me to consciously recognize the state of her children's hair as a metaphor for her emotional state.

Searching for Strengths: A Question for Research

Lisa's strengths propelled me to wonder as a novice social worker, how to separate an individual's strengths from alarming risk factors. This became the basis for the scientific study and my research on the everyday routine of combing children's hair. From the start, I was curious as to how this young mother who had experienced so many childhood harms, whose internal working model of attachment figures was barren and brutal, could have the emotional energy to form attachments with not one but four young, needy infants and toddlers? How could she manage to keep her home clean and in order, despite the memories of loss and disorder because of being moved from home to home? How could she build a protective attachment relationship with each of her children when she had so few memories of being protected and loved herself? How could she build trust with me, a stranger, a social worker, another one in the nameless parade of social workers in her childhood? I stood there with the power to deem her an "unfit mother." A stranger with the power to petition the juvenile court to remove her children from her custody and place them into the same foster care system she had spent her childhood in. How could this young mother build trust with people after her experiences of betrayal and violence from the father of her youngest child?

What was the significance of Lisa's ability to keep her children dressed and in order during their daily routine, except for their hair? As I investigated hundreds of other referrals I received as a child protection worker, a foster care worker, and later as a prevention services worker, the image of Lisa's daughter's neatly combed hair stood out in my mental image of Lisa. This young lady had some psychological strengths that translated into protective parenting practices and loving order. It is important to understand, from birth to age three years – the same ages as Lisa's youngest two children – children with disconnected and stressed parents are at highest risk for child abuse, neglect, removal from the home, and death (Hayes-Grudo & Morris, 2020).

During one of our home calls, Lisa shared her worry about her three-year-old child. She said that it was very hard to understand his words, as if his tongue was too thick in his mouth to form words. She asked the nurse at the free clinic, but the nurse had dismissed her concerns and simply said, "*Don't worry, he will grow out of it.*"

During my conversations with Lisa and her children in her home, she would offhandedly refer to one of her children as having some "*tough, nappy hair to comb.*" My social work risk alert system went off in my head! These were the same dismissive words her family had used to describe her and her sister's hair. I understood that the unconscious, unexamined, and negative stereotypes associated with African origin hair and dark or light skin may intensify the messages of acceptance or rejection for some children of color.

What was it about Lisa's ability to keep her children's hair in order? As an African-American woman, my memories of getting my hair combed unconsciously provided an answer, but I did not yet have scientific evidence to support my thinking. Lisa's story awakened memories of a special time alone with my mother, of sitting on the floor between her legs, with my arms easily draped across her legs, and feeling the brush gently pulled through my mass of unruly, curly/kinky hair. My mother who started out her parenting role as a 17-year-old teen mother lovingly established order in my hair. My mother was far away in the northern environs of Michigan, far away from her extended family in the southern state of Alabama, where she and my father had left in the early forties with the great urban migration from the south to the north. My internal working model (Bowlby, 1969) based on loving interactions with my primary attachment figure, my mother, included our daily routine of hair combing time. Sitting in the warm embrace of her legs as she combed my hair, I gulped in my daily dose of warmth and connection, with all the attention focused on me and not my other seven brothers and sisters. Seeing 19-year-old Lisa, who looked like mothers in my community and network of friends and family, I was motivated to find answers. What were her strengths? How could I as a novice social worker support Lisa's goal of lovingly protecting her children and interrupting the World of Abnormal Rearing (WAR) (Dettlaff & Boyd, 2021), cycle of generational child abuse?

I wanted to find a way to understand the significance of hair combing in the context of family trauma and the worry of risk in intergenerational practices of child abuse or neglect. Many children experience the trauma of child abuse and the disruption of growing up in multiple foster homes. Unlike the outcome predicted by the WAR cycle, Lisa worked hard to protect her children from abuse and harm. Her children were thriving. Lisa's deep love for her children was reflected in their everyday routines of making sure they were fed, had clean clothes, and their hair neatly combed; this was a testament to her resilience in the face of a complex trauma history. On the days when she was emotionally exhausted, the children's uncombed hair became a barometer of her mood and the emotional energy needed to handle the memories of childhood trauma, or what pioneering psychoanalyst Selma Fraiberg termed "ghosts in the nursery" (Fraiberg et al., 1975). It was in these times that Lisa's children's hair reflected her own childhood experiences of neglect, disorder, and disarray.

Hair Combing Time as a Psychosocial Tool for Assessment and Intervention. I began to understand that hair combing time offers an unrecognized opportunity for sensitive, responsive caregiving that leads to the formation of healthy parent–child attachment relationships. It was Lisa's story that propelled me back to graduate school to find answers to the question about what was cultural, what was abusive, and the power of the parent–child attachment relationship. Lisa's story also led to my curiosity and commitment to understand unconscious parenting practices based on an indelible characteristic of skin color and hair type that led to acceptance or painful rejection of their children

Lisa's demographic profile checked all the boxes of risk: her adolescent age, a history of child abuse, her placement in foster care, her status as a single parent household, and poverty. She had several other risk factors, including the number and developmental status of dependent children, the absence of a support network of extended family or friends, and the latest, domestic violence. Lisa was valiantly fighting a lonely parenting battle to simply keep her children safe.

But at that time as a young social worker with a mission to help children and families, I had no training to recognize Lisa's strengths – only the risk factors (Brooks, 2016; Martin & Martin, 1995; Narayan, Rivera, Bernstein, Harris, & Lieberman, 2018). I had no method to assess the protective factors that could support healthy attachment relationships or the loving memories that her children Carlos, Tina, Natasha, and Thomas would carry into the future. I wondered, "*What were her strengths? How could I sort out cultural practices, vulnerabilities, and risk factors for child abuse?*"

My observations of her pristine housekeeping and the general good care of her children left me wondering, "*How does she fit the traditional profile of a neglectful mother*?" There was no evidence of physical abuse, yet she had referred to spanking her young children. An alarm went off in my head. I wondered if she was simply parroting a widely held, cultural norm of "*spare the rod and spoil the child*"?

Understanding the strengths of cultural practices and the assessment of risk for child abuse and neglect in African-American families had been given little attention by social science researchers (Bass et al., 1982; Hale-Benson, 1982; Hill, 1972). As a new social worker, I had participated in a one-day training, then charged to make daily decisions on the welfare and safety of children in their homes. It was the mid-1970s, and we had few theoretical tools in our social work toolbox beyond Ray Helfer's and Ruth Kempe's work on the *World of Abnormal Rearing* (Dettlaff & Boyd, 2021). This research documented that parents who had a history of being abused or neglected as a child were at higher risk for committing child abuse as a parent. This factor alone placed Lisa's children at high risk.

At the time, it was not well understood that the racial group of which Lisa was a member was disproportionately reported for child maltreatment and subsequently placed in the child welfare system (Dettlaff & Boyd, 2021). In a predominantly White urban community where African Americans composed only 11% of the population, her referral added to the pile of disproportionately high numbers of Black families on my caseload of 32 families to investigate. Lisa's 1978 social profile easily reflects the 2021 recognition of the racial adversities that impact families of color, (Shonkoff et al., 2021), and the racial disparities that may have contributed to Lisa entering and aging out of the foster care system.

How to help a young African-American single mother. I had enthusiastically entered the social work profession with the starry-eyed goal to "help people." Though only armed with a bachelor's degree in psychology, and with limited life-experiences of a 23-year-old, I was confident I could help families. Having grown up in a supportive all-Black community, and in a loving and supportive Black, two-parent, Christian family of eight children, and having come of age in the heady era of Civil Rights activism of the 1960s, I was especially committed to helping Black families. The thought of asking a juvenile court judge, at the time all White males, to remove these beautiful young children from this young mother who looked like the family I grew up with motivated me to find answers. To do the job that I loved, I needed more effective tools to help parents, such as Lisa.

Conclusions

In the mid-1970s, as a new social worker, I wanted to help Lisa, a young, struggling mother. As a member of the African-American community, having come of age during the Civil Rights era and the Black Pride movement, my heart was divided into two directions. One side of my heart filled with an urgent passion to help right the wrongs, the neglect, abuse, and trauma that this young Black woman had experienced in the hands of other African Americans. With the rallying cries of Martin Luther King's protests for social justice, I wanted to fight the racial disparities of the child welfare system that had harmed Lisa.

Lisa had survived childhood trauma, abandonment, rape, and repeated placements with strangers in the foster care system. When I met her, she was doing the number one duty expected of parents, trying to protect the children she fervently loved from harm with few resources or social support. It was her story that propelled me to enroll into graduate school to find scientific answers to the questions and observations of what abusive parenting was, and what was cultural.

The first question that I asked led to this line of research, "How can secure attachment relationships develop while parenting in a social environment of stress?" Other questions relating to this followed. "Were spanking and corporal punishment necessary to rear children in challenging urban environments? What types of support and interventions could help parents find the joy and pleasure in carrying out their duties as parents?" The second set of research questions that came to mind included: "What was the role of culture in the childrearing practices of parents, and their beliefs about children? Were my observations of Lisa's care of her children's hair coupled with my personal memories of getting my hair combed a reflection of culture? Was studying hair combing an acceptable cultural practice for scientific study?"

The observation of Lisa's ability and capacity to maintain the simple everyday routine of combing hair as she struggled with daily stressors planted the seeds of what developed into a program for research. To understand the cultural significance of hair for African Americans, specifically to understand the meaning of Lisa's ability and inability to comb her children's hair, led to a series of research studies. The findings from this research served as the basis for the development of the tools presented in this book.

Lisa's story embodies the answer to "why" hair combing interaction provides an unrecognized opportunity to strengthen parent–child attachment relationships. Her story led to my commitment to understand the sociocultural meaning of hair and the psychological trauma of colorism (Lewis, 2015; Lewis et al., 2013), in families, as well as bias and discrimination within the child welfare system (Lewis & Swift, 2014; Lewis, 2017). Why might unconscious parenting practices, that had origins in the larger sociocultural environment, those "nappy-haired ghosts in the nursery," lead to the acceptance or rejection of children based on their skin color or hair type?

The evidence of the impact of toxic stress on the mental health and well-being of parents and children and the additional unrecognized historical and modern racial stressors facing African-American parents is growing (Ashing et al., 2017; Lewis, 2019). With these culturally valid tools, we hope you will be able to use the hair combing task to identify risk factors and yet find the parent's strengths and rich cultural protective factors (Lewis, 1999; Miller & Goodnow, 1995), to better support families of color with young children.

"The rest of the story." My story as a psychologist and researcher began with a worry about how I could best support a young African-American mother to care for her children appropriately and sensitively, breaking the predictable intergenerational cycle of child abuse and neglect. I wondered how I could build on her cultural strengths and prevent her children from entering the child welfare system. My motive stemmed from the universal wish of many helping professionals, social workers, and counselors, to "help children and families who are struggling." This might be part of your motivation to read this book.

Divided into four parts, the book tells the story of hair combing from a culturally grounded, relationship-based, reflective practice framework. Part I provides an overview of the research and cultural foundations of the hair combing task as a ritual and routine. The research conducted on the hair combing task provides support for understanding the behavioral structure of hair combing time that strengthens parent–child attachment relationships.

Part II focuses on the practitioner's use of hair combing time as a context for observation, assessment, and intervention. We call attention to the "nappy-haired ghosts in the nursery," of colorism – the practice of valuing lighter skin colors and straight hair – a legacy of the historical trauma of slavery as it impacts a parent's perception of the child. Several chapters discuss reflective practice and supervision within a lens of culture, diversity, equity, and inclusion. Included are personal reflections about social work practice with very young children and families, as well as supervisory relationships, where race is at the heart of deeply felt discussions.

Part III presents the experiences of practitioners who implemented community-based interventions using the *Talk, Touch, and Listen While Combing Hair* curriculum. The authors reflect on their experiences as cofacilitators, students, and people of diverse identities and cultural backgrounds while implementing this curriculum.

Part IV introduces psychosocial tools for the practitioner for assessment and intervention using hair combing time. Case studies are presented based on the use of the "Neck-up" projective tool and the semistructured interview of Childhood Experiences of Racial Acceptance and Rejection (CERAR). Both tools may be used to simply begin a conversation with a client or parent group or used by a practitioner to assess a participant's internal working model of their early relationship experiences in response to their racial features and developing sense of self.

The authors invite you, the reader, to create your own story of incorporating hair combing time as part of your practice or educational setting. Each chapter provides reflective questions to guide you in thinking more personally about issues of racial disparity, equity, and inclusion, and the psychological impact of racial trauma and colorism, during the hair combing experience.

Reflective Questions

1. After reading the story of the young social worker's eagerness to help and lack of training and experience, what were your first thoughts about the first time you worked with a family of color?
2. Thinking back to your early years working with families from a different cultural background, do you recall your understanding of cultural practices and childcare routines?
3. What were some of your most challenging moments in work with families from a different cultural background?
4. How might knowledge of cultural practices help engage families in social work practice?

References

Ashing, K. T., Lewis, M. L., & Walker, V. (2017). Attending to children's wellbeing after witnessing race-based violence. *Journal of the American Medical Association*. https://doi.org/10.1001/jamapediatrics2017.0137

Bass, B. A., Wyatt, G. E., & Powell, G. J. (Eds.). (1982). *The Afro-American family: Assessment, treatment & research issues*. Grune & Stratton.

Brooks, B. (2016). *Black single mothers and the child welfare system. A guide for social workers on addressing oppression*. Routledge.

Briggs, E. C., Amaya-Jackson, L., Putnam, K. T., & Putnam, F. W. (2021). All adverse childhood experiences are not equal: The contribution of synergy to adverse childhood experiences scores. *American Psychologist, 76*, 243–252.

Bowlby, J. (1969). *Attachment and loss: (Vol. 1). Attachment*. Basic Books.

Dettlaff A.J., Boyd R. (2021) Towards an Anti-Racist Child Welfare Future. In: Dettlaff A.J. (eds) Racial Disproportionality and Disparities in the Child Welfare System. Child Maltreatment (Contemporary Issues in Research and Policy), vol 11. Springer, Cham. https://doi.org/10.1007/978-3-030-54314-3_22

Fraiberg, S., Adelson, E., & Shapiro, V. (1975). Ghosts in the nursery. *Journal of the American Academy of Child Psychiatry, 14*(3), 387–421.

Hale-Benson, J. E. (1982). *Black children: Their roots, culture, and learning styles*. The Johns Hopkins University Press.

Hayes-Grudo, J., & Morris, A. S. (2020). *Adverse and protective childhood experiences: A developmental perspective*. American Psychological Association.

Hill, R. (1972, 2003). *The strengths of black families*. University Press of America, Inc.

Lewis, M. L. (2017). Ten guideposts to abolish bias in child welfare. In *Advancing equitable outcomes for infants and toddlers involved in child welfare*. Quality improvement center for research-based infant-toddler court teams. www.qicct.org

Lewis, M. L. (2015). 'Getting the Parts Straight': The Psychology of hair combing interaction and African American mother-daughter relationships. In K. Craddock (Ed.), *Black motherhoods*. Demeter Press.

Lewis, M. L. (2019). The Intergenerational Transmission of Protective Parenting Responses to Historical Trauma. In (Editors) H. E. Fitzgerald, D. Johnson, D. Qin, F. Villarruel, and J. Norder. The Handbook of Children and Prejudice: Integrating research practice and policy, pp. 43-61. Springer Publishers. https://doi.org/10.1007/978-3-030-12228-7

Lewis, M. L. (1999). The hair-combing task: A new paradigm for research with African American mothers and daughters. *American Journal of Orthopsychiatry, 69*, 1–11.

Lewis, M. L., & Swift, A. (2014). Promoting social justice in families. In series Editors: C. Johnson & H. Friedman; Volume Editors: C. Johnson, H. Friedman, J. Diaz, B. Nastasi, & Z. Franco, *Praeger handbook of social justice and psychology* (Vol. II, pp. 39–58). Praeger.

Lewis, M. L., Noroña, C. R., McConnico, N., & Thomas, K. (2013). Colorism, a legacy of historical trauma in parent-child relationships: clinical, research, & personal perspectives. *Zero to Three Journal, 34*(2), 11–23.

Miller, P. J., & Goodnow, J. J. (1995). *Cultural practices as contexts for development* (New directions for child development, No. 67, pp. 5–16). Jossey-Bass, Inc.

Narayan, A. J., Rivera, L. M., Bernstein, R. E., Harris, W. W., & Lieberman, A. F. (2018). Positive childhood experiences predict less psychopathology and stress in pregnant women with childhood adversity: A pilot study of the benevolent childhood experiences (BCEs) scale. *Child Abuse and Neglect, 78*, 19–30.

Shonkoff, J. P., Slopen, N., & Williams, D. R. (2021). Early childhood adversity, toxic stress, and the impacts of racism on the foundations of health. *Annual Review of Public Health, 42*, 115–1334.

Chapter 3
The Interactive Stages of Hair Combing: Routines and Rituals

Marva L. Lewis

> *Let's see. First, I have to find something to sit her still with, be it a toy, or the television, or a book. And once we do that and get that established, she's fine to sit there for about 20 minutes and get her hair comb. And if I'm going to do something other than one ponytail, two ponytails, three ponytails I have to find a lot of things to keep her content. She is very, very busy. She just likes different things, different activities and stuff.* (Keisha[1], mother of Rae Donna)

The above quote is from the mother of a 24-month-old toddler, Rae Donna, who participated in the African-American mother–daughter interaction research study at Tulane University (Lewis, 2000a). Her words illustrate how she perceives hair combing time as part of her daily caregiving routine with her young child. Hair combing time is conceptualized as a relationship-based ritual and a consistent, interactive routine. Observing hair combing interaction (HCI) offers social workers and early childhood practitioners an opportunity to observe and assess the socio-emotional quality of the parent–child relationship to support families of color.[2] The daily routine of HCI provides the parent or caregiver an opportunity to practice nurturing behaviors learned during the intervention. In addition, the positive behavioral changes made by the parent meet the professional's and parent's shared goal to sustain positive changes in the parent–child relationship.

Families from diverse socioeconomic, ethnic, racial, and cultural groups benefit from the psychological rewards of positive routines and rituals for mental health

[1] All names and other personal identifiers included in clinical stories/vignettes in this chapter have been changed to protect privacy and confidentiality.

[2] Throughout the chapter, there will be references to families of color as a general category of families. The terms African American or Black will be used for specific references to this group.

M. L. Lewis (✉)
School of Social Work, Tulane University, New Orleans, LA, USA
e-mail: mlewis@tulane.edu

M. L. Lewis, D. J. Weatherston (eds.), *Therapeutic Cultural Routines to Build Family Relationships*, https://doi.org/10.1007/978-3-030-83726-6_3

(Butterfield, 2002; Fiese et al., 2006; Kubicek, 2002; see M. Warren's Chap. 5). For infant and early childhood clinicians and researchers, the routine of a mother, father, or primary caregiver combing a child's hair may serve as a clinical window into a family's intimate shared identity, providing an opportunity for a deeper understanding of behavioral and emotional characteristics of their relationship. Similarly, values associated with colorism, off-hand messages to children as "pretty and light-skinned" or with "good-hair" based on the straight or wavy texture of the child's hair, are reinforced during the routine of combing hair. As the child grows into adulthood, these values become part of the emotional quality of internal working models of attachment or relationship-based behaviors and the parenting role (Bowlby, 1979). This unconscious lens shapes the parent's perception of the task of hair combing and unwittingly transmits acceptance or rejection of the child.

Talk, Touch, and Listen While Combing Hair! Hair combing time offers parents a relaxed context in which to practice language and listening skills, along with the interpretation and expression of emotions. Daily hair combing routines and rituals teach parents their child's emotional communication and teach children the expression of emotions (Ekman, 1999). Language socialization is accomplished through two primary means: the mechanism of ordinary, everyday talk, and the culturally organized features of social life of the family and cultural group (Miller & Goodnow, 1995). Everyday talk includes storytelling about incidents that occurred in the family's life or may be a response to the latest event in the media or environment. This storytelling reinforces cultural values held by the parent and family. For example, during a loud thunderclap of a sudden summer rainstorm, a caregiver may relate a childhood story of getting caught in a rainstorm on the way to school and describe with laughter the strong emotions of startle and fear as they saw a bolt of lightning strike a tree in the distance. These verbal interactions offer an example of what occurs during hair combing time that enriches the parent–child relationship.

Hair combing routines offer developing toddlers opportunities to learn from birth how to be a "standard normal person" (Ossorio, 2005) in their family and cultural group. The repetition of loving touch reinforces what is acceptable behavior in this family. Yet, the experience of harsh touch through hits to the legs with a hairbrush or minimal amount of touch during hair combing routines reinforces negative messages and emotions expressed by caregiving parents toward infants and young children (Duhn, 2010).

Hair salons and Barbershops for Black Male Toddlers Participating in the rich and positive interactive rituals of hair combing time, young boys and girls learn ancient cultural standards of beauty represented in the amount of care and adornments given to this part of their body (Battle-Waters, 2004; Cowen et al., 1979; Mbilishaka et al., 2020). In the qualitative, semistructured interviews, African-American mothers in the AMDIS-1 study were asked, "*At what age should an infant boy have his hair cut?*" The responses ranged from 9 to 24 months with an average age of 12 months for infant boys' first haircut. In African-American communities, the ritual of the first trip to the local barbershop for a toddler boy's first haircut is considered a ritual and rite of passage. The community acknowledges that the first haircut for a "baby boy" recognizes that he has become a "little man." For example, clinical psychologist, Dr. Afiya Mbilishaka, (Chap. 13) obtained an additional cosmetology license to train beauticians in microcounseling skills to support their customers during their regular visits to the beauty salon. Another national initiative focuses on preparing professional barbers to creatively use their customers' weekly trip to the barbershop as an opportunity to promote health and wellness, mental health, and general life skills for Black men and boys (The Confess Project, 2021). The vision of the Barber's Coalition states, *"I am more than a pair of clippers; I am improving my community through the barber chair. one client at a time."*

Stages of HCI as an Observational Tool for Assessment of the Quality of Relationship

This chapter discusses how the routine of hair combing offers an opportunity for mother–daughter, father–daughter, or caregiver–child interaction. Based on research about the hair combing task, five observable stages of HCI were identified, including relationship-based interactions distinct to each stage (Lewis, 2015). These interactions included verbal interactions (e.g., family storytelling), nuanced communication and emotional attunement through physical touch, and caregiver listening with sensitivity. Each step that characterizes rituals and routines, as defined by anthropologists, was used to describe hair combing interaction. We then examined the potential psychological benefits of this daily interaction as a ritual and routine between a parent or primary caregiver and child during the critical developmental phase of cognitive, social, and emotional development. The intimate interactions during the stages of hair combing may contribute to a very young child's developing self-concept, ethnic awareness, and gender identity formation.

The Power of Routines, Rituals, and Celebrations to Build Relationships in Families and Communities

The celebrations, traditions, and patterned family interactions compose the powerful rituals that create a family's identity, values, and traditions in cultural groups around the world (Bossard & Boll, 1950; Fiese et al., 2006). The repetitive nature of these routines establishes and preserves a family's collective sense of identity or who we are in the world (Wolin & Bennett, 1984). The rituals of a cultural group serve as powerful organizers of family life (Fiese et al., 2006; Wolin & Bennett, 1984). Rituals are defined as "a symbolic form of communication that, owing to the satisfaction that family members experience through its repetition, is acted out in a systematic fashion over time" (Wolin & Bennett, 1984, p. 402). Though they may vary in significant ways across cultures, rituals serve several functions and provide meaning to our collective family life. Across the life course, beginning prenatally with baby showers and more recently, gender-reveal parties to celebrate the pending birth of a child, rituals provide a structure for emotionally satisfying connections among a network of family and friends. In times of collective trauma and stress, such as the events of the COVID-19 of the 2020 pandemic described in the preface of the book, familiar and predictable routines provide stability to young children.

Rituals Connect Families, Culture, and Identity

Rituals are composed of a sequence of activities involving gestures, words, actions, or objects performed in a sequestered place and according to a set series of stages (Wikipedia, 2021). Every member of the cultural group knows their role in the ritual, the behavioral rules, and precisely when and where they are supposed to carry out the ritual. The performance of what may be centuries old rituals emotionally satisfies all the participants. People who participate in cultural rituals follow a prescribed set of steps identified as *separation, transitional,* and *reintegration* (Fiese et al., 2002). The enactment of the cultural ritual begins *a separation* of the individual or family for special preparations for the event. Next people who participate in the ritual experience *transition* themselves in new, transformative ways and take on new roles. The symbolic hairstyle or freshly cut hair of a young child may symbolize the child as a "big girl" or a "big boy" who is now ready for school. The cultural ritual ends with the *reintegration* of the members with newly transformed identities to assume their new roles into the family, community, and society.

Hair as a Symbol of Social Identity, Acceptance, and Belonging

Each step in the process of hair combing routine represents a psychological process of identity consolidation, commitment to a moral standard, and ceremonial acknowledgement by the broader social groups. The structure of the stages of hair combing time provides guidelines for the developing toddler, family, and community with a prescribed set of expectations and cultural rules for behavior ('*I said, sit still while I comb your hair*!'). By successfully accomplishing the task, the parent or caregiver reinforces the child's identity, new status, and connection to their cultural group. Participation by the child in these ritual ends with an emotional experience of satisfaction, strengthened identity, and acceptance by their family and community (Lewis, 2013).

The Socioemotional Benefits of Routines and Children's Development

Routines differ from rituals in that they are practiced everyday by families or groups. Defined as observable practices, daily and weekly routines include bedtime stories, mealtime, bathing routines, chores, or simply watching favorite television shows together (Wolin & Bennett, 1984). Families' unique routines teach children behaviors based on each family's values. The way the family meal is prepared, who sits next to whom at the dining room table, reflects a unique practice of the family.

These everyday routines provide the opportunity for young children to experience parent–child or caregiver–child interactions that provide meaning to their collective identity as a member of a family group (Fiese et al., 2002). For example, the narrative talk during mealtime routines helps children with literacy skills needed to complete school tasks (Snow & Beals, 2006). There are other cognitive benefits to some routines carried out by families. For example, research demonstrates the benefits of a bedtime routine that includes reading to young children can improve their cognitive skills, along with an increase in their emotional vocabulary to label their feelings. Children with regular bedtime routines show more adaptability and resilience (Fiese et al., 2002). These same benefits may be experienced by children during the hair combing routine.

Hair Combing Interaction and the Development of the Child's Sense of Self

Developmental theorists offer additional complexity to our understanding of the relationship evolving between mother and child or caregiving parent and child during hair combing interaction (HCI) with the concept of "sensitive" periods (Stern, 1985). Stern (1985) proposes that there are "epochs of change" that define different domains of self-experience and social relatedness. They are the sense of an "emergent self," which forms from birth to age 2 months, the sense of a "core self," which forms between 7 and 15 months, and finally, the formation of a "verbal self" (Stern, 1985, p. 8). The sense of self that emerges at about 15–18 months can now create shared meaning about the self and the world with the new capacity for symbolization as evidenced by language.

African-American mothers begin combing the infant's hair from birth due to the rich texture of the infants' hair, ranging from bald, or wavy or very tightly curled. This process may be a few gentle strokes with the hand or a soft baby brush, or in the case of bald infants, an adornment with a festive headband. Thus, hair combing interaction with an infant may contribute to the significant cognitive and emotional dynamics of Stern's epochs of change. Stern (1985) notes that during this period, there is now the possibility for shared meaning and the capacity to engage in symbolic action such as play.

During this period, there is now a shift in the dominant type of interaction between parent and child, that is, from concrete physical interaction to abstract mental events and the meaning of the events (Garner, 2006; Garner & Spears, 2000). For developmental researchers or clinical practitioners, analyzing videotaped hair combing interactions may offer an ideal opportunity to empirically evaluate this shift. This theory suggests that during hair combing time, there may be higher levels of physical directing, prompting, and less verbal exchange at earlier periods (12–13 months), as well as an increase in verbal exchanges at the 15- to 18-month shift. The young child will have an increased ability to verbally make wishes known and better respond to the caregiver's directions. For example, during earlier preverbal stages, the infant and toddler may simply scrunch up their face to show hurt or pull away to express their opposition as the mother attempts to brush or comb their hair.

The various physical positions of proximity may provide the opportunity for affect sharing between caregiver and infant. Stern's theory suggests there should be greater affect attunement and increased capacity for shared meaning between synchronous dyads during HCI. These growing socioemotional skills during the 15- to 18-month shift may be observed during each of the discrete stages of hair combing interaction. For example, in the final stage of HCT, "the closing ritual," a three-year-old's growing cognitive capacity of "mentalizing" (Stern, 1985), may be evidenced by behavior in front of the mirror and the expression of clear preferences for hairstyles. Developmental milestones that might be evident during HCI may be the use of verbal labels, names, and pronouns to designate self. For example, 18-month-old Rae donna might declare, '*Ow! comb hurts Rae-Rae.*'

Multiple social identities that are objective categorizations of the self, with the establishment of core gender, ethnic, and racial identities, may emerge during this sensitive period (Spencer & Markstrom-Adams, 1990; Spencer et al. 2019) Experiences of healthy caregiver–child interaction may help consolidate these developing socioemotional skills during each interactive stage during the routine of hair combing.

The Routine and Rituals of the Five Stages of Hair Combing Interaction

The findings from the analyses of videotapes of African-American mothers[3] combing their daughter's hair provides support for Stern's description of the epochs of change over the early months of infant and toddler development (Stern, 1985). The study used qualitative methods to provide mothers with the opportunity to describe their daily routine of combing their child's hair. For example:

> Interviewer: *Describe a typical hair combing session, at home, with you and your daughter. Is there a routine that you go through?*

[3] See the African American Interaction Study (Lewis, 2000b) for description of the research study.

> Keisha: *Like, I get up in the morning, wash her face, brush her teeth, she eat her breakfast, then I do her hair... Every day she has to get her hair combed. Sometimes I comb her hair two times a day, sometimes once.*

The analyses of the videotaped interaction revealed five stages of interaction that occur during the hair combing task. The average amount of time spent combing hair was approximately 10 minutes 29 seconds. In this period, there were distinct observable stages in the type of mother–daughter interaction. These stages, *preparation, negotiation, combing hair, play,* and *closing rituals*, reflect a synchrony of interactive relationship dynamics distinct to each stage (Lewis, 2015). The interaction may be directed primarily by the mother or the daughter. Fathers also participate in caregiving routines developing their specific father–daughter dynamics (Bocknek, 2018). Infants and toddlers may practice and strengthen socioemotional skills during each of these stages.

Social and psychological factors stemming from the parent's or primary caregiver's individual *ethnobiography* discussed earlier (Lewis, Chap. 4) may shape their behaviors during the interactive stages of hair combing. At the same time, these daily interactions may reinforce powerful messages of respect, love, acceptance or rejection, shared affect, and socialization into family values.

A researcher might study the interactive stages of HCI asking questions such as *What are the normative developmental processes that occur between a caregiver and child during hair combing time*? *Do these processes change over time as a child reaches cognitive, social, emotional, or physical developmental milestones?* A service provider, therapist, or clinician might observe or wonder, *"Does the parent or primary caregiver use active listening skills during hair combing time?"* Both the researcher and helper might keep these questions in mind or ask the caregiver directly and sensitively about the developing attachment relationship during the interactive stages of hair combing time:

1. How much talk (verbal exchanges) occurs during the HCI?
2. What are the topics of talk during the HCI?
3. How does the caregiver interpret and respond to the cues of the child?
4. Who initiates the conversation during HCI?
5. How much time is spent in each of the stages?

Stage 1 of Hair Combing Interactions – *Preparation*

In the first stage of HCI, the parent caregiver prepares to comb the child's hair. During this stage, the parent caregiver will likely be dominant in the observable interactive dynamics. The clinician or therapist might observe and empathize that it takes a lot of time to stop whatever they are doing or other distractions in order to fully focus attention on the child.

The parent then selects the hair combing tools, the combs, brushes, hair picks, sprays, ointments, or hair pomades, for example, she may use to comb through the child's hair. In some cases, there may be several versions of the same tool: for example, a wide-tooth comb for initial combing through tight curls, and a fine-tooth comb to make precise parts at the scalp to separate the hair for styling. She may carefully organize the tools in the sequence that she will use the tools. With the tools now ready and close by, she positions the chair that the child will sit in to have her hair combed.

Some parents may prepare children verbally and/or physically to engage in the task. They may begin by calling the child's name or use a favorite nickname. The pattern or style of the parent's or primary caregiver's invitation to have the child sit in the designated place where she combs hair – her lap, in a chair, or on the floor sitting between her legs – may become the coordinated interaction that forms the relationship.

The parent verbally announces the task of combing hair is about to begin. For example, she may ask the child, "*Do you want to get your hair combed*?" Or she may look directly at the child and state in a no nonsense voice, "*Come here right now to get your hair combed.*" Her voice may be loud, soft, or firm to make the announcement. She may give a warning, threat, or other form of enticement during this first stage of preparation.

Some parents or primary caregivers may skip this stage of preparation and dive right into the task, ignoring their child's emotional readiness. The mother's steps in preparation may model how the daughter, as an adult, prepares for work or to study.

An example of the steps taken to prepare for the task is illustrated in one mother's response to the research interviewer's question, "*Describe a typical hair combing session at home with you and your daughter.*"

> Mother*: Let's see. First, I have to find something to sit her still with; be it a toy, or the television or a book. And once we do that and get that established, she's fine to sit there for about 20 minutes and get her hair combed. And if I am going to do something other than one ponytail, two ponytails, three ponytails, I have to find a lot of things to keep her content. She is very, very busy. She just likes different things, different activities, and stuff like that.*
> Interviewer: *Is there a routine you go through?*
> Mother: *I'm . . . like I get up in the morning, wash her face, brush her teeth, she eats her breakfast, then I do her hair. After she eats, she might be a little more content 'cuz she is full, so she might sit still for a little while.*
> Interviewer: *How long does it usually take?*
> Mother: *Well, it depends on how she feels, so if this is an everyday day, she has to get her hair combed. Sometimes I comb her hair two times a day, sometimes once.*

A Case Example of Preparation to Comb Hair

The parent or caregiver begins to mentally plan the type of hairstyle she will create for the child in preparation for the hair combing time. Particular hairstyles will require more or less time and may be influenced by where the child may be going, for example, outside to play versus to church. The parent or primary caregiver may ask, "*Will I create a regular everyday hair style, or a special occasion hair style, such as one for the first day of school or for a family photo?*"

The community recognizes the mother or primary caregiver as meeting the community's standards of a "good mother" based on the demonstrated care given in combing the child's hair. In the AMDIS-1 interviews, an African-American mother[4] was asked about the meaning of combing her daughter's hair:

> Interviewer: *What would it mean if you did not comb your children's hair?*
> Mother: *It would mean that I didn't have time to comb their hair or sometimes on the weekends or Saturdays if we don't comb their hair for that day, I may let it go unless we go somewhere I may not comb their hair that day. But . . .ummm it doesn't mean anything to me."*

Another mother's response to the same question in the study reflects a community standard:

> Interviewer: *What does combing her hair mean to you?*
> Mother: *Neatness. Like, if I let her hair go, and I don't clean her, then, I mean, I feel like I am not doing my job as a parent because she can't keep up with herself. So, I have to do that for her until she is old enough to do it for herself. . .. but now I have to do it because if I don't, it make me, you know, it reflects badness on me in a way and I don't care, so I have to make sure everybody, you know, everybody know I care enough about her to comb her hair and to go the extra length to keep her clean and neat."*

At the societal level, a parent's attention or lack of attention given to groom a child's hair may lead to legal action. Matted, dirty, and unkempt hair may call attention to the physical neglect of a child resulting in a parent being reported to Child Protective Services. Once the first step is completed, the individual is ready to move through the final two steps of the cultural ritual.

Stage II of Hair Combing Interactions – *Negotiation*

Now that the parent or primary caregiver has prepared the utensils and tools needed to accomplish the task of combing hair, engaging the child becomes the next task. The second interactive stage identified in the research is labeled *Negotiation,* to describe the type of caregiver–child interaction that may be observed.

Typically, the most emotionally challenging times of parent–child relationships are the onset of walking at about age 9 months–12 months (Emde, 1989). Selma Fraiberg (1959) used the term "infant scientist" to describe the 12- to 24-month-old infant's increased cognitive and verbal skills (p. 23). The toddler's increasing demands for autonomy and independence at 24–36 months also present challenges to parents (Bowlby, 1973; Mahler, 1975). Attachment theory suggests that the caregiver's recognition of the infant's growing social and esteem needs for autonomy and exploration may influence how she responds to the infant during the hair combing task.

During this stage of *Negotiation*, caregivers may use voice commands, verbal repetition, promises, play, or physical touch to engage reluctant young children in

[4] All names and other personal identifiers included in clinical stories/vignettes in this chapter have been changed to protect privacy and confidentiality.

the task of hair combing. A caregiver might use a variety of approaches to entice a rambunctious 15-month-old child into the task. As a well-practiced routine, the caregiver may have established physical cues, such as pulling out the hair combing paraphernalia in full view of the child. An active twenty-month-old "scientist," with well-consolidated walking skills, may be interested in everything but sitting still for hair combing. This stage may require the skills of a wartime Ambassador negotiating peace in the Middle East.

The interaction during this second stage presents the caregiver with the rich opportunity to build verbal skills in the developing child. The simplified speech used by the caregiver to refer to various characteristics of the child's hair, appearance, personality, or behaviors during this interactive stage of hair combing time supports the child's social construction of the self and autonomy (Mahler et al, 1964; Miller & Goodnow, 1995).

The life lessons learned with this type of interaction between the mother and daughter might teach the child tactics for future life skills of negotiation on the playground or the bedroom with their romantic partner (Barbarin, 1993; Coard, 2004). During HCI Stage II, some parents or caregivers may state family rules and expectations of behavior. By incorporating cultural or gendered themed storytelling and vocabulary words during this phase of negotiation, the caregiver enhances the social group connection of family and ethnicity.

Negotiating the Hair Combing ask with a Tender-Headed Child

Crystal, an older mother who participated in the AMDIS study, used a carefully worded series of questions to engage her 36-month-old daughter, Adrian who was extremely tender headed with medium curly hair, into the process of having her hair combed. In preparation, Crystal positioned Adrian gently across her lap and in a very soft and soothing voice announced:

> Crystal: *'Ok, I'm going to comb your hair now. I know that it hurts, but I've got to comb your hair. Be sure to tell me if it hurts, OK?*

Crystal very slowly and gently touches the wide-tooth comb to Adrian's scalp carefully and watches her reaction. With her eyes closed, Adrian, with a pacifier in her mouth, lets out a scream of anticipation of a familiar searing pain to the scalp, she reaches her small hand up and pulls the comb away from her head.

> Crystal: *Ok, I know it hurts. How about I just part your hair with my hands. OK? I'm putting the comb down and I will just use my hands. OK?*

Crystal then takes a few strands of hair, separates it from the other hairs, and slowly plaits the strands together, winding one strand over the other. She went through this process for the next fifteen minutes as Adrian drifted off to sleep in or on her lap. Yet, Adrian visibly reacted to touch, even in her sleep as Crystal began to brush through the curls with a baby brush.

The developmental lesson learned by Adrian during this interaction included the communication skill of nonverbal interaction. Though equipped by an outstanding vocabulary of words evidenced at the outset of the interaction, when Adrian defiantly answered "No, I don't want to get my hair combed!" she understood that if she communicates nonverbally, with a pained look on her face, her mom will respond sensitively with understanding, "*I know it hurts*."

During this second interactive stage, in varying degrees, children very clearly participate in a negotiation process with their parent or primary caregiver. Based on the analysis of the videotaped interactions from the AMDIS-1 study, the following sequence of interactions occurred during this stage of negotiation that describe the relationship dynamics:

a. *The parent or caregiver's statement of intent.* The parent verbally announces to the child a sequence of events and what is about to happen. They may describe what is they will do, what they may do together, or use neutral terms that describe what the activity will be. For example, the they may say, *"I'm about to comb your hair now*." Or "*You're going to get your hair combed now*." Or "*We've got to comb your hair now*." Or "*Combing your hair is next on the agenda*."
b. *The parent or caregiver extends the invitation.* The parent may sit or stand in a place where hair combing will take place and then invite the child to participate. The parent or caregiver may look at the child with a comb or brush in hand and smile invitingly, saying calmly, "*Come on and get your hair combed*." Or using a more authoritarian parenting style, the caregiver may not smile but look grim and issue a command or directive to the child, "*Get over here and get your hair combed*!"
c. *The child responds.* The child shows a response to the parent's words. This response may be verbal or nonverbal. A smile, grimace, tears, fear or anger, or a playful challenge may be part of the child's response.
d. *The parent or caregiver approaches.* The parent may physically approach the child, stoop down, and talk to the child with a hand touching part of the child's body. They may also join in or acknowledge the child's activity before directing the child to the hair combing task. They either allow time for the child to respond or physically takes the child to the chair or place to get her hair combed.
e. *The child responds.* This primary action during his stage ends when the parent and child are in the position to complete the task of combing hair. This stage ends as the caregiver begins to comb the child's hair.

Stage III of Hair Combing Interactions – *Combing Hair*

The actual task of combing hair occurs during this stage. The child is placed in a primary position of proximity to the caregiver. The parent may first offer soothing words of praise or comfort to the child for complying. She may offer the child a toy or bottle as they settle into the task. The caregiver chooses an implement, ointments, or spray bottle. She then positions the child and proceeds to comb the child's hair.

The parent or caregiver brushes, combs, parts, plaits, braids, and generally manipulates the child's hair. She may use her hands or fingers to smooth the hair in addition to using the comb and brush. The child's position may change periodically, but the parent or caregiver returns a child to the primary position throughout the task. The caregiver or child may dominate in directing or using physical behavior during this stage.

The Synchrony of Hair Combing Interaction

Emotional attunement or synchrony between an infant and parent or primary caregiver begins at about age two to three months. Synchrony is the coordinated interaction between a growing infant and parent in which each responds to and influences the other. This coordinated relationship-based experience helps the infant learn to express and read emotions (Stern, 1985). There may be reciprocal interactions where the child directs the caregiver's attention to something that is going on in the environment. The caregiver continues combing hair but responds to the child.

Stage IV of Hair Combing Interactions – *Play*

The relationship dynamics during this stage are very interactive; either the child or parent caregiver may initiate the type of actual or symbolic play during this stage. During this stage, both the parent and child are relaxed, fully committed, and engaged in accomplishing the task of combing hair. The strong message of relationship and attachment is communicated to the child during this relaxed exchange Stifter et al. 2020). Together, they are empowered, sharing in an activity, and emotionally attuned to each other. This stage is characterized by playful talk and chatter between the parent and child. There may be a pleasurable give and take, verbal exchange, singing, humming together, or storytelling. There may be joint laughter and joking, and shared facial expressions by parent or caregiver and child during this fourth interactive stage of the hair combing.

Symbolic play (Orr & Geva, 2015) may be acted out by the child when she picks up a doll and begins to brush the doll's hair in the same manner her hair is being combed. There is shared affect, loving touch directed by the mother toward the child or by the child toward the mother. The mother may include instructive play during this time using a counting game by clapping hands with her 11-month-old son as she gently brushes his hair.

Stage V of Hair Combing Interactions – *Closing Rituals*

A ritual, defined as a sequence of activities involving gestures, words, actions, or objects, is performed according to a set sequence (Wolin & Bennett, 1984). The parent or caregiver signals to the child that the task is now completed and ends. The parent or caregiver may express praise, reinforcing specific behaviors about gender, ethnicity, racial identity, or sexual training. In a balanced routine or ritual, both the parent and child participate (Lewis, 2013). The parent may gently pat the child's hair and ceremoniously pronounce, "*There, now we are all finished*." The child may respond by looking in a mirror or affirming the parent's work. Perhaps, the child quietly says, "*Thank you*." The quality of the ending of the session may be abrupt, happy, relieved, or angry. It may be a helpless giving up on the part of the caregiver. The caregiver may make a comment such as "*good girl*," which may reflect gender socialization, obedience, or respect. Moreover, there may be a comment such as, "*You are such a pretty Black girl!*" providing racial socialization. The caregiver may praise, hug, or kiss the child and express a warm or nurturing touch at the end.

The Cultural Significance of the Stages of Hair Combing Interaction
Anthropologists have determined the universal symbolism of hair (Firth, 1973). Yet, there are individual differences in how caregivers carry out the everyday routine of combing a child's hair that reflect their cultural values and goals for socialization. In homes around the world, cultural rituals and familiar routines define family identity and serve as a core determinant of their everyday behaviors (Minturn & Lambert, 1964, p. 2; Spencer et al. 2019).

The following dialog captures one mother's response to the research interviewer's questions about what goes on during the hair combing routine at home and what she does to prepare to comb her daughter's hair.

Interviewer: *What normally goes on at home when your daughter – when your children get their hair combed?*

Mom: *Meaning . . .*

Interviewer: *What other activities are you doing. . . what else is going on at your house?*

Mom: *Sometimes the television is on and they are looking at TV while I'm combing their hair. She's oh, I don't know. I guess she and her sister are playing with or trying to comb their baby doll hair or something or they want to read a book or something like that, that's what usually goes on.*

Interviewer: *Okay, what do you do next, what is your routine when you are doing their hair?*

Mom: *First, I did all the . . .. I have a little box with all their barrettes, and comb and brush. I go get that. Then I umm, tell them to go get their chair. When they get their hair combed, they will go get their chair, a little red chair, then they'll go sit in it and I'll . . . you know take their hair off loose, take the plait a' loose, and then I'll put grease on it... and you want everything?*

Interviewer: *Yes, yes, yes!*

Mom: *I'll grease it and then I'll you know, part, and brush it and then plait*[5] *put the barrettes on it and sometimes I play with the braid, they want to pick out the barrettes and*

[5] *Plait*, means to braid.

> *I let them know to choose their barrette even though it doesn't match, I'll let them choose it sometimes. Then after that I'll put the barrettes up and just tell them how pretty they look and they'll model turn around and "go show your daddy how pretty you look" and they'll do that and that's it interviewer: okay [why do you why do you do it that way] you said that you have them model and go see their daddy why do you do that* Mom: *because I'm just to let them know they are pretty you know that when they get their hair done you know they should want their hair to be neat that their hair being combed and neat is nice and they're pretty it makes them pretty when they get their hair combed.*

This mother describes each of the stages of combing hair with her two daughters aged 18 months and 48 months. She creates a routine with preparing her combing utensils, having a special place to store the adornments for the hair. She involves the children by issuing directions to them to "go get their little red chair" that they learn is the designated place for the hair combing to take place. This mother spends little time in the *negotiation stage* with her daughters. Although she does indicate some flexibility and allows them the option of "looking at TV," or playing with their doll and trying to comb their doll's hair or reading a book. She moves through the hair combing process to Stage five, the "closing ritual" phase with the adornments of ribbons, and barrettes. She engages the father in the hair combing time by instructing the children to "go show your daddy" and he verbally acknowledges them at the conclusion by saying, "How pretty you look!"

Jaia and Jalisha: Mother–Child Interaction During the Stages of Hair Combing Time

The following interaction was recorded in the university laboratory through a one-way mirror as part of the *African-American Mother–Daughter Interaction* study described earlier. The mother, Jalisha, and daughter, Jaia were in a playroom setting. The researcher instructed the mother to *"Comb your child's hair as you do at home."* The researcher then left the room and remained behind the one-way mirror until the mother signaled, she had completed the task.

1. *Preparation.* The mother brings a colorful cloth bag of hair combing tools over to where she will sit. She carefully holds on to a nearby chair as she kneels onto the floor. She methodically organizes the combs and brushes and makes sure they are within her reach. She happily announces to Jaia, *"Mommy's going to comb my girl's hair."*
2. *Negotiation.* Jaia whimpers and reaches her arms out toward the bottle of milk that sits on the table across the room. Jalisha firmly states, *"After we finish your hair."* There is no negotiation with this 11-month-old toddler. There is no transition. The mother commences to comb her hair.
3. *Combing hair & Stage 4 Play.* A few minutes into the combing, Jalisha hands Jaia a bottle of bubbles to distract her while she does her hair. A couple of times,

Jaia moves from left to right and wiggles. The Mother follows her physically and keeps brushing her hair. Jaia flips over her mother's leg as Jalisha steadily holds Jaia's hand, and quietly laughs. She playfully acts as if she was going to "get" Jaia and then pulls her to her lap to finish combing her hair.

4. *5. Closing ritual* When the task is complete, Jalisha puts down the brush, and claps her hands. In a high, singsong voice, she expresses praise for Jaia for sitting still throughout the session. She pronounces with much flair, *"Look how pretty you are."*

Conclusions

Throughout each of these stages, the task of hair combing offers the clinician, counselor, or social worker an opportunity to understand the quality of the developing parent–child or caregiver–child relationship through a a strengths-based lens of attachment (Anderson, 2019). Analyzing videotapes of hair combing interaction with either the hair comber or alone, the practitioner can assess the parent's reflective capacity to nurture the child through gentle touch, to soothe the preverbal toddler's distress, and to engage the child (Butler Byrd et al. 2019). The practitioner may observe the parent respond sensitively to the child's smile as they gently smooth the child's fine hairs – known as "baby hair" – around the hairline that surrounds their chubby-cheeked face during the closing ritual stage.

The practitioner may also observe the growing child's ability for self-regulation during HCI. As the caregiver pulls the comb through a curly tangle that may hurt, the infant may reach for a bottle or pacifier to withstand the discomfort. During the preparation stage, the caregiver may position the bottle or pacifier in anticipation of the needs of the infant during the time that the hair is brushed and combed.

During the time spent in any of the five stages, the quality of verbal interaction, responsiveness, listening, and physical touch varies from dyad to dyad. Further, who dominates or leads the interaction varies from dyad to dyad. The quality of interaction during the HCT may parallel the consolidation of the attachment relationship during these socioemotional shifts in the toddler. Thus, the observed individual differences may be an important area for further assessment and basis for further research.

The social worker or infant and early childhood provider, in partnership with the parent or researcher in the laboratory, may view videotaped hair combing interaction to assess what goes on between a parent or primary caregiver and young child. The time spent, the type of interaction, and the quality of the interaction between a caregiver combing a young child's hair and the child's response may reveal both the areas that may need further assessment and understanding, as well as the strengths on which to build and support.

Reflective Questions

1. Think about a child and parent or primary caregiver you have observed while they were carrying out the ritual of hair combing. What did their interactions with each other during hair combing tell you about their relationship? What did the impact of the parent's touch, conversation, and ability to listen have on the young child's experience of loving acceptance or rejection?
2. More personally, how have hair combing routines or rituals contributed to who you are, affected significant relationships with those who cared for you, and influenced core values and beliefs that you carry with you.
3. As you review this chapter about the rituals and routines of daily hair combing interaction (HCI), reflect on how you can use these observations as a tool to provide support for parents and primary caregivers to understand the significance of these cultural practices as they interact and connect with their young children.
4. How might HCI inform your own understanding of culture, ethnicity, racial trauma, and injustice?

References

Anderson, L. A. (2019). Rethinking resilience theory in African American families: Fostering positive adaptations and transformative social justice. *Journal of Family Theory & Review, 11(3), 385–397.* https://doi.org/10.1111/jftr.12343

Barbarin, O. A. (1993). Coping and resilience: Exploring the inner lives of African American children. *Journal of Black Psychology, 19*(4), 478–492. https://doi.org/10.1177/00957984930194007

Battle-Walters, K. (2004). *Sheila's shop: Working-class African American women talk about life, love, race, and hair. Rowman & Littlefield.*

Bocknek, E. L. (2018). Family rituals in low-income African American families at risk for trauma exposure and associations with toddlers' regulation of distress. *Journal of Marital and Family Therapy, 44*(4), 702–715. https://doi.org/10.1111/jmft.12293

Bossard, J., & Boll, E. (1950). *Ritual in family living*. University of Pennsylvania Press.

Bowlby, J. (1973). *Attachment and loss: (Vol. 2.) Separation, , anxiety and anger*. Basic Books.

Bowlby, J. (1979). The Bowlby-Ainsworth attachment theory. *Behavioral and Brain Sciences, 1(3), 436–438.* https://doi.org/10.1017/S0140525X00064955.

Butler Byrd, N. M., Rowe-Odom, M. J., Bushfan, O. L., Gill, A., Baca, K., & Lewis, M. L. (2019). Using hair-combing interactions to enhance relationships between Black women and girls impacted by homelessness. *Women and therapy.* https://doi.org/10.1080/02703149.2019.1622912

Butterfield, P. M. (2002). Childcare is rich in routines. *Zero to Three, 22*(4), 29–32.

Coard, S. J., Wallace, S. A., Stevenson, H. C., & Brotman, L. M. (2004). Towards culturally relevant preventive interventions: The consideration of racial socialization in parent training with African American Families. *Journal of Child and Family Studies, 13*(3), 277–293.

Cowen, E. L., Gestin, E. L., Boike, M., Norton, P., Wilson, A. B., & DeStefano, M. A. (1979). Hairdressers as caregivers. A descriptive profile of interpersonal help-giving involvement. *The American Journal of Community Psychology, 7*(6), 633–647.
Duhn, L. (2010). The importance of touch in the development of attachment. *Advances in Neonatal Care, 10(6), 294–300.*
Ekman, P. (1999). Basic emotions. In T. Dalgleish & M. J. Power (Eds.), *Handbook of cognition and emotion* (98(45–60), 16). Wiley https://doi.org/10.1002/0470013494.ch3
Emde, R. N. (1989). The infant's relationship experience: Developmental and affective aspects. In A. Sameroff & R. N. Emde (Eds.), *Relationship disturbances in early childhood: A developmental approach* (pp. 33–51). Basic Books.
Fiese, B. H., Tomcho, T. J., Douglas, M., Josephs, K., Poltrock, S., & Baker, T. (2002). A review of 50 years of research on naturally occurring family routines and rituals: Cause for celebration? *Journal of Family Psychology, 16*(4), 381–390.
Fiese, B. H., Tomcho, T. J., Douglas, M., Josephs, K., Poltrock, S., & Baker, T. (2006). A review of 50 years of research on naturally occurring family routines and rituals: Cause for celebration? *Journal of Family Psychology, 16*(4), 381–390. https://doi.org/10.1037//0893-3200
Firth, R. (1973). Hair as private asset and public symbol. In *Symbols* (pp. 262–298). Cornell University Press.
Fraiberg, S. H. (1959). *The magic years: Understanding and handling the problems of early childhood.* Scribner's Sons.
Garner, P. W. (2006). Prediction of prosocial and emotional competence from maternal behavior in African American preschoolers. *Cultural Diversity and Ethnic Minority Psychology, 12(2), 179.* https://doi.org/10.1037/1099-9809.12.2.179
Garner, P. W., & Spears, F. M. (2000). Emotion regulation in low- income preschoolers. *Social Development, 9(2), 246–264.* https://doi.org/10.1111/1467-9507.00122
Kubicek, L. F. (2002). Fresh perspectives on young children and family routines. *Zero to Three, 22*(4), 4–9.
Lewis, M. L. (2000a). African American parents and their interpretations of emotions of infants. In J. D. Osofsky & H. E. Fitzgerald (Eds.), *WAIMH Handbook of infant mental health* (Vol. 1, pp. 59–63). Wiley.
Lewis, M. L. (2000b). The cultural context of infant mental health: The developmental niche of infant-caregiver relationships. In C. H. Zeanah (Ed.), *Handbook of infant mental health* (2nd ed., pp. 91–107). Guilford Press.
Lewis, M. L. (2013). Black mother-daughter interactions & hair combing rituals. In H. Jackson-Lowman (Ed.), *Afrikan American women: Living at the CROSSROADS of race, gender, class, and culture* (pp. 345–368). Cognella Press.
Lewis, M. L. (2015). Getting the parts straight: The psychology of hair combing interaction between African-American mothers and daughter relationships. In K. Craddock (Ed.), *Black motherhood(s): Contours, contexts and considerations.* Demeter Press.
Lewis, M. L., Noroña, C. R., McConnico, N., & Thomas, K. (2013). Colorism, a legacy of historical trauma in parent-child relationships: Clinical, research, & personal perspectives. *Zero to Three Journal, 34*(2), 11–23.
Mahler, M. (1975). *The psychological birth of the human infant.* Basic Books.
Mahler, M. S., Pine, F., & Bergman, A. (1964). *The psychological birth of the human infant: Symbiosis and individuation.* Basic Books.
Mbilishaka, A. M., Mbande, A., Gulley, C., & Mbande, T. (2020). Faded fresh tapers and line-ups: Centering barbershop hair stories in understanding gendered racial socialization for black men. *Psychology of Men & Masculinities.* Advance online publication. https://doi.org/10.1037/men0000317.
Miller, P. J., & Goodnow, J. J. (1995). Cultural practices: Toward an integration of culture and development. In J. J. Goodnow, P. J. Miller, & Kessel (Eds.), *New directions for child development* (Vol. 67, pp. 5–104). Jossey-Bass Publishers.
Minturn, L., & Lambert, W. W. (1964). *Mothers of six cultures: Antecedents of child rearing.* Wiley.

Orr, E., & Geva, R. (2015). Symbolic play and language development. *Infant Behavior and Development, 38*, 147–161. https://doi.org/10.1016/j.infbeh.2015.01.002
Ossorio, P. G. (2005). "What actually happens": The representation of real-world phenomena. In *The collected works of Peter G. Ossorio* (Vol. IV). Descriptive Psychology Press.
Snow, C. E., & Beals, D. E. (2006). Mealtime talk that supports literacy development. *New Directions in Child and Adolescent Development, 111*, 51–66.
Spencer, M. B., & Markstrom-Adams, C. (1990). Identity processes among racial and ethnic minority children in America. *Child Development, 61*(2), 290–310.
Spencer, M. B., Lodato, B. N., Spencer, C., Rich, L., Graziul, C., & English-Clarke, T. (2019). Innovating resilience promotion: Integrating cultural practices, social ecologies, and development of sensitive conceptual strategies for advancing child well-being. *Advances in Child Development and Behavior, 57*, 101–148. https://doi.org/10.1016/bs.acdb.2019.05.005
Stern, D. N. (1985). *The interpersonal world of the infant*. Basic Books.
Stifter, C., Augustine, M., & Dollar, J. (2020). The role of positive emotions in child development: A developmental treatment of the broaden and build theory. *Journal of Positive Psychology, 15*(1), 89–94. https://doi.org/10.1080/17439760.2019.1695877
The Confess Project. (2021). https://www.theconfessproject.com/
Wikipedia. (2021). *Ritual*. https://en.wikipedia.org/wiki/Ritual
Wolin, S. J., & Bennett, L. A. (1984). Family rituals. *Family Process, 23*(3), 401–420.

Chapter 4
The Observing Professional and the Parent's Ethnobiography

Marva L. Lewis and Deborah J. Weatherston

Black and Indigenous families of color have experienced much racial wounding. The words of popular children's tunes about a wonderful day in the neighborhood may not describe the physical environment of some parents[1] or primary caregivers. Frequently, the childhood communities of Black Indigenous parents of color are segregated, underresourced, urban, and rural neighborhoods (Fitzgerald et al., 2019; Murry & Brody, 2002; Shonkoff et al., 2021). Parents may silently and emotionally bury experiences of racial wounding to protect and ensure the survival of their children (Lewis, 2019), rightly understanding – as the American Psychiatric Association and recently stated (2019) – that young children are impacted by racism. Overwhelming evidence from research documents the effects of racism on children (Fitzgerald et al., 2019; Shonkoff et al., 2021).

As discussed in the preface of the book, the current social context includes urban violence, the stress and isolation of the COVID-19 pandemic, and repeated police shootings (Ashing et al., 2017). Additionally, racial stressors can directly impact the mental health and well-being of parents of color and their children (National Academies of Sciences, Engineering, & Medicine, 2019; Shonkoff et al., 2021). The socioemotional impact of these chronic and familiar stressors can shape the quality of the growing parent–child attachment relationship. A therapist or other helping professional must include in their formulation how race-based oppression may be at play within family dynamics and relationships, potentially increasing risk, coping, and unhealthy parenting styles. Understanding a family's traumatic or

[1] Parent or primary caregiver references the child's primary attachment figure.

M. L. Lewis (✉)
School of Social Work, Tulane University, New Orleans, LA, USA
e-mail: mlewis@tulane.edu

D. J. Weatherston
Alliance for the Advancement of Infant Mental Health, Southgate, MI, USA

M. L. Lewis, D. J. Weatherston (eds.), *Therapeutic Cultural Routines to Build Family Relationships*, https://doi.org/10.1007/978-3-030-83726-6_4

affirming race-based experiences, defined as the family's *ethnobiography*[2], broadens the therapist's understanding of factors that may shape routine parent–child interactions. The *ethnobiography* captures the story of a parent's cultural, ethnic, and racial experiences that shape their beliefs and attitudes about racial features of skin tone and hair type, including both risk, resiliency, and positive protective factors (Narayan, Rivera, Bernstein, Harris, Lieberman, in press). By assessing the family's ethnobiography through a cultural and racially informed lens, the observing helper may gain a deeper understanding of the care a parent gives a young child through interactions during hair combing routines.

Both the parent and young child experience responses from others triggered by their skin tone or hair type (Fitzgerald et al., 2019). For example, Regina[3], the mother described in Chap. 1, may face veiled microaggressions from coworkers at her workplace associated with her natural hair style of dreadlocks. Aware that she is the only employee in the office wearing her hair in this manner, she is hypervigilant for remarks about her "ghetto fabulous" hair style. She sometimes finds herself working extra hard to dispel any myths that she is taking advantage of government assistance. As with any chronic stressor, the sight of her daughter's bushy hair, stereotyped in the media for centuries as "ugly" and "bad," may trigger a harsh response as she combs her daughter's hair. Thus, a parent of color's *ethnobiography* may influence interactions with the developing infant or toddler during the task of combing hair (Lewis, 2013, 2016; Lewis & Swift, 2014).

Traditional assessment tools of childhood trauma now include urban experiences related to an urban context, such as witnessing community violence, being bullied, felt discrimination, or living in foster care. More recent attention has been given to the positive benevolent experiences in childhood leading to resilience and positive developmental outcomes (Briggs et al., 2021). These benevolent experiences included having at least one adult caregiver with whom they felt safe. Having adults in their family or community who provided them with support or advice to make sense of racial events such as the police murder of George Floyd in 2020 and frankly answer their questions are included in positive childhood experiences.

The therapist may offer a nonthreatening way to begin a conversation with the parent or caregiver about the community they live in and the community the parent grew up in as a child. The ethnobiography provides a conversational, semistructured "storytelling" tool the clinician may use to understand the sociocultural context of the developing parent–child relationships. The therapist should be mindful that talking through these experiences with a parent may raise awareness of long buried traumas related to racial characteristics (See Lewis & White, Chapter 16, on broaching the topic of race). This assessment may give insight into a parent's behaviors, attitudes, and beliefs that may be triggered during hair combing interactions with their child. This tool provides a window into how a parent was socialized into the

[2]Copyright pending for the term "Ethnobiography" to M. L. Lewis & D. Weatherston 2021.

[3]All names and other personal identifiers included in clinical stories/vignettes in this chapter have been changed to protect privacy and confidentiality.

culture of their ethnic group. For Black, Indigenous, and people of color (BIPOC), this tool provides information on their racial socialization (Congress & Kung, 2013), their current racial and ethnic identity, and several internalized stereotypes they hold about their racial group included in the assessment. A parent's ethnobiography includes childhood experiences of racial protection and acceptance as well as fragments of memories of rejection by their primary attachment figures including extended family, teachers, peers, and strangers in the grocery store.

Table 4.1 presents various sources of childhood race-based trauma memories and experiences that compose their unique ethnobiography. Column 1 of Table 4.1 lists the sociocultural factors that shape the group's experience. From the family, the individual's quality of attachment or physical resemblance to specific family members or absent caregiver may serve as a trigger during the hair combing task. Their family's access to resources to meet their basic survival needs may also form an important part of the assessment. Column 2 of Table 4.1 describes the individual factors unique to the parent's ethnobiography.

Table 4.1 Sociocultural factors of the developmental niche and the family ethnobiography

Sociocultural factors of the caregiving environment	Family ethnobiography
Phenotype of biological racial group	Individual phenotypic: skin color, hair texture, nose & lip size
Status of racial, ethnic, religious, or immigrant group as minority/dominant within the host society: ♦ Group experiences of historical trauma, targeted for oppression and violence ♦ Social and economic power of group	Quality of family resources available to meet basic developmental needs: ♦ Housing ♦ Employment/welfare support ♦ Medical care ♦ Education
♦ Socialization into traditions, values of cultural group ♦ Racial socialization ♦ Emotional display rules ♦ Customs of childcare within family and community ♦ Communication styles	♦ Degree of acculturation to their childhood cultural group ♦ Ethnic Identity: subjective identification with the group What stage of racial identity development is your client?
Family Ethnobiographies: ♦ Family secrets ♦ Physical characteristics of family heroes/scapegoats/spouse ♦ Family stress (financial, social, marital/partner violence, mental health: Adverse Childhood Experiences (ACEs)	♦ Quality of attachment to primary caregivers ♦ Birth order, temperament, and personality ♦ Toxic physical resemblance to specific family members or absent parents ♦ Social support resources
♦ Stereotypes or privileges associated with status of group	♦ Degree of internalization of stereotypes about groups
♦ Childrearing practices of racial acceptance and rejection associated with racial features	♦ Experiences of positive, negative, or ambivalent messages from family, friends, or strangers

Sociocultural Factors of the Caregiving Environment

A family's ethnobiography stems from sociocultural factors that define the racial or cultural group experience. These group factors include the racialized phenotypic characteristics including skin color, hair type, nose, or lip size. The historical social status, including experiences of historical trauma and general stress experienced by BIPOC families in the form of poverty, employment, housing discrimination, education, etc., may be shaped by racial disparities in the social determinants of health (Brave Horse, 2000; National Academies of Sciences, Engineering, and Medicine, 2019; Tribal Behavioral Health, 2018). Ethnic or racial group factors can include the general stereotypes about the group. Over time, these group stereotypes may be diminishing, such as "all Native Americans are alcoholics" or reflect a stereotype of a "model minority," such as "all Asians are good at math."

The culture of the group provides another level of factors contributing to the broad category of the ethnobiography of the group. The cultural niche includes socialization into the traditions, values, and rules for displaying emotions (Rogoff, 2003). The cultural background of the group may also influence communication styles between and among family members.

The Parent's Ethnobiography

The Parent's Childhood Neighborhood

A parent's unique individual ethnobiography includes an additional set of ecological factors. These factors include the neighborhood and community that the parent or primary caregiver grew up in as a child, racial disparities in the parent's quality of housing during childhood, access to medical care, and the quality of segregated or underresourced education. Another potential factor is if the parent spent their childhood in a community with historical practices with origins in racism: for example, the practice of "red-lining" city blocks or neighborhoods with a high percentage of people of color and denying mortgages to these families or historical practices that kept out African Americans (or sometimes Chinese Americans, Jewish Americans, etc.) by force, law, or custom. These communities were known as "sundown towns," because there were posted signs at their city limits reading, "N-word, don't let the sun go down on you in [name of town]."

Childhood Experiences of Racial Acceptance and Rejection (CERAR).

Included are the parent's childhood experiences of racial acceptance and rejection by their primary attachment figures (Wilson et al., 2018). The ethnobiography provides the therapist with ideas about how the parent was socialized into their culture of origin, their current racial and ethnic identity, and the ethnic pride and racial stereotypes they may have internalized about their ethnic groups (Lewis, 2001). These childhood experiences include positive and affirming, as well as negative messages, from any member of their developmental niche, including extended family, teachers, and peers (Narayan et al., in press). Hurtful messages include off-hand remarks about their hair texture as "bad," from strangers in the grocery store as they stand in a check-out line.

The caregiver's CERAR may also include intergenerational legacies of historical trauma and messages about racial features, which could come from loved ones as well as the impersonal media images. Off-hand remarks and comments from grandma about the value of one skin color over another or the beauty of one hair type over another may evolve into a racial trauma that stems from internalized stereotypes and implicit racial bias. There may be patterns of practices of favoritism to lighter- or darker-skinned children by specific relatives within the extended family network. Intergenerational messages related to family secrets may be associated with racial features of children (Neal-Barnett et al., 1996). For example, a lighter-skinned child in a family of dark-skinned members may be a reminder of a past indiscretion of the parent. There may be entire sets of cousins who are of a lighter-skinned tone than their darker-skinned cousins, an unspoken reminder of traumatic legacies of rape throughout slavery. Finally, specific family members across generations may be held as family heroes or family failures and a source of pride or shame within the family systems.

> A 'colored Creole' writes: *"My mother says I am Creole. My teacher says I am Negro. Some Europeans say I am Colored, and others call me 'N----.' Who am I?"*
> Aline St. Julien (Penner & Ferdinand, 2009)

These early messages of acceptance or rejection based on skin color and hair type become part of the parent's internal working model of relationships. These mental models of racial hurts and remembered wounds may subtly guide the parent's behaviors during the hair combing task. The positive, protective, and affirming messages may be the foundation for resilience and thriving recalled by the parent about their childhood racial experiences (Gonzales et al., 1995; Hill, 1972; Norton, 1993).

Positive and Affirming CERAR Messages

The broad scope of the individual ethnobiography must provide an opportunity for the description of the positive and affirming experiences. The ethnobiography includes the experiences of racial acceptance, protective parenting (Lewis, 2019), and positive benevolent adults such as coaches, teachers, or an understanding extended family member such as an uncle or aunt. These childhood experiences lead to resilience and positive developmental outcomes (Briggs et al., 2021). In addition, racial socialization by the parent that prepares the child for coping with racial prejudice and discrimination becomes part of the adult's internal working models of relationships and concept of self (Collins, 1990; Lewis & Craddock, 2019; Lewis et al., 2018).

Racial Identity, Personality, and Temperament

A child's unique temperament may impact his or her response to the hair combing experience, impacting the formation of their racial identity, and have implications for their process of racial identity formation (McAdoo, 1985; Peters, 2002). From birth, a child may be described as having an *easy*, *slow to warm up* or *difficult* temperament (Chess & Thomas, 1989). How a child responds to external stimuli will be influenced by natural personality factors. At the level of personality, the individual's ethnobiography also includes their level of ethnic identification with their group. In the theory of racial identity formation, William Cross (2002) describes the African American's process of assimilation into the enormous standards of the dominant group. He identified five stages of an individual's process in embracing identification as a member of the Black racial group. At each of these stages, the individual shows a growing awareness of psychological issues significant for Black people. (See Box 4.1)

Box 4.1

Five stages of (Cross et al., 2002)

1. **Pre-encounter**: Seeks to assimilate into the dominant culture. 2. **Encounter**: Individual is forced to acknowledge his/her differences through a single or series of events. 3. **Immersion/Emersion:** Strong desire to surround oneself with visible symbols of one's racial/cultural identity. 4. **Internalization:** Individual is secure in their racial/cultural identity and seeks to establish meaningful relationships of one's racial/cultural identity. 5. **Internalization-commitment**: The individual discovers ways to communicate their commitment to the concerns/needs of their own racial/cultural group.

Two of specific stages in the parent's ethnobiography are important to understand. In the first stage, the *pre-encounter* stage, a person seeks to assimilate into the dominant culture by denying the importance of race or remaining oblivious to interactions with different racial group members. A person of color may emulate and endorse stereotypes of other Black people or even family members. They are referred to by friends or same race acquaintances, as an "Oreo" – "black on the outside and white on the inside" – at times in their life. The second stage, the *encounter* stage, is where a person is forced to acknowledge the felt experience of racial difference through an event. For example, a person may experience a microaggression, when a waiter at a restaurant jokingly remarks, "*And what will you have, sir? I know we don't have any chitlins or soul food on the menu, but the ham sandwiches are pretty good.*" These types of encounters with the reality of racial group membership triggered by their skin color or hair type can remain buried by parents dealing with the daily stress of their lives.

As a therapist, you might explore whether a parent had ever experienced microaggressions where they felt that the person responded to their skin color in a stereotypic way or treated them as if they were invisible.

Skin Color and Parent's Ethnobiography

Physical features that infants are born with categorize them into a racial group. Skin color and hair type are the most visible of these characteristics. Skin color may range from very light to very dark brown skin tones. As discussed in the introduction, the experiences of colorism, where lighter skin tones are valued over darker skin tones, may lead to experiences of racial acceptance or rejection for children, parents, other caregiving adults, and other family members. Figure 4.1 presents the standardized skin tone color bar (Spencer, 2005), used in the research on colorism (Lewis et al., 2021). The participants in this online inquiry used the color bar in Fig. 4.1 to select their skin tone.

The skin color of a newborn child is of great concern in some families of color. Informal reports from audience members at presentations on colorism and from parents during parenting group sessions share stories of being asked at birth about their child's skin color or hair type. The question begins with, 'What color is the baby's ears or the skin around their fingernails?' Many African-American babies are born with lighter skin tones and straight hair. As they develop, their skin tone darkens to the color of their ears and fingers. Likewise, during the first few months of life, the newborn's straight or wavy hair curls up to the texture it will remain for their life.

Thus, each family's attitudes toward colorism may create negative experiences as part of a parent's ethnobiography of skin tone. In the Colorism study, participants used the a chart of different types of hair to select their hair type (https://www.medicinenet.com/what_are_the_four_types_of_hair/article.htm). Their hair textures may range from very straight to wavy to very curly.

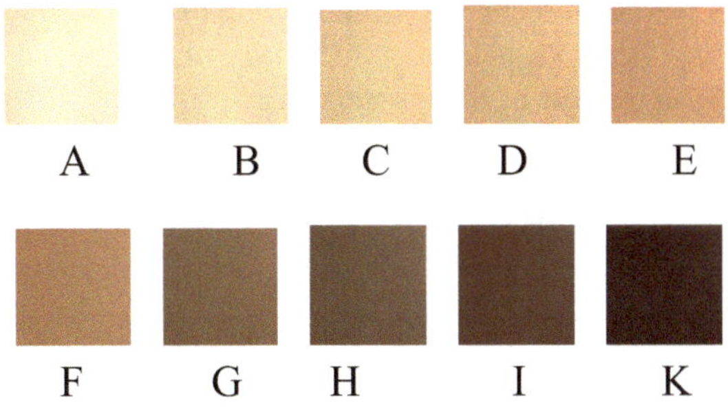

Fig. 4.1 The visual inventory for skin tone assessment (VISTA) (ColorBar) (Spencer, 2005). (Place your finger beside the color bar and then select the box that best matches your skin tone. [Letter _____])

Hair Type and Parent's Ethnobiography

The everyday task of combing hair has long been the focus of toxic negative stereotypes, and even shame. Conversely, feelings of racial pride emerged during the Civil Rights era, with big Afros and cornrows symbolizing political stances as well as connection with African culture (Mbilishaka, Chap. 13). Anthropologists and journalists, Harris & Johnson (2001), compiled an entire book of essays by diverse African-American women recalling their early experiences of getting their hair combed. The emotions they recalled spanned the continuum from anxiety to anger, contented to excited. The emotions associated with these experiences may be important indicators of the general quality of the evolving parent–child relationship. As part of an assessment, the therapist may explore the emotions the parent shared in the "neck-up drawing" (Lewis & White, Chap. 16).

Tender-Headed Scalp

According to research by dermatologists and nursing (Aronow et al., 2003; Tiwary, 1997), tender-headed condition is the degree of sensitivity to the scalp. There is little research on this condition familiar to many women of all racial groups. There is a medical condition in a review of the literature on the medical condition of *trichodynia* (hair pain), a condition where a person experiences a painful sensation of their scalp (Rebora, 2016). The pain is sometimes described as burning. In a meta review of the literature, Rebora (2016) reported that there is an underlying psychosomatic cause, such as stress, depression, or anxiety. Only a few studies have been conducted on this condition. A theory behind the condition is that nerves innervating scalp hair follicles send pain messages back to the brain when the follicle no longer has a hair in it, in a similar way to "phantom limb" pain. Another theory is that people who have this condition (sometimes called "ponytail syndrome") have supersensitive nerves in their scalp.

A young child who is tender headed may not be believed by their caregiver as there is no other visible physical indicator to account for the child's physical state. A parent with a tender-headed scalp or with a child with a tender-headed scalp may have negative memories of getting their hair combed. This childhood condition becomes part of the parent's individual ethnobiography and an area that the counselor or therapist may inquire to understand the origins of the emotional response of combing hair. A new screening tool, *'The Tender Headed Rating Scale'* (Lewis, 2020), is included in the Appendix. This ten-item tool provides questions on the degree of physical pain the person experienced as a child while having their hair combed and the response by the adult hair comber. These areas may be explored by the therapist in conjunction with the emotions used to describe the person's feelings about hair combing.

In the following example from the AMDIS-1[4] study, the researcher asks the mother about any differences in her two daughters' responses to getting their hair combed. She first has the mother rate the level of tender headedness of each on a scale of 1 to 5 with one being not tender headed at all and five being very or extremely tender headed. The mother rates her youngest daughter as a "1" and the oldest daughter as a "5" on the tender-headed rating scale. The mother describes the response of the tender-headed daughter:

> *My oldest daughter is very, very tender headed. So I mean, the hair combing process is totally different. With my oldest daughter, I would comb her hair like every three days, trying to wrap it up, you know, trying not to get into it all really, but you know you can't avoid it. With A'lia, we do it every day, sometimes twice a day, you know, depending on what we are doing, where we're going. It's just totally, it's like day and night really.*

These factors, related to the client's ethnobiography, provide several windows for exploring the internal working models of a parent's early relationships (Bowlby, 1969). The childhood experiences of racial acceptance or rejection may be carried forward as an unconscious basis for their caregiving behaviors with a young or growing child during hair combing time.

The Observing Professional

We invite the reader to explore race through the lens of ethnobiography, awakening thoughts about experiences, subtle or intentional, of racial trauma, discrimination, and prejudice. The awareness of the evocative nature of these memories we carry introduces the reader to consider the power of the racial past. Together the parent and helper may explore how these racial memories shape parental caregiving and the interpersonal relationships in the present. Extending an invitation to parents for a psychological safe space to explore their lived history of racial trauma, including the everyday microaggressions from family, friends, and coworkers to, the racial inequities of neighborhood, offers an extraordinary pathway to growth. Unearthing memories of healthy racial coping strategies in response to childhood experiences of racial trauma, as well as identifying those positive and protective adults who served as role models for coping will support this growth trajectory.

The ethnography offers a profound examination of family and parent or primary caregiver experiences, which may influence nurturing and hair combing routines. The assessment, using the ethnobiography, can help parents and professionals alike understand the ghosts and angels in a nursery, offering new strategies for intervention, hope, and repair.

[4]AMDIS-1 refers to the African-American Mother–Daughter Interaction Study-1 described in Chapter 3 of this book. The name of the child is a pseudonym.

Reflections

Assessing a family's race-based experiences broadens the understanding of risk and resiliency and offers a pathway to greater understanding and more effective clinical work. The family's ethnobiography captures the cultural, ethnic, and racial experiences that shape caregiver beliefs and attitudes about racial features of skin tone and hair type. Further, these cognitive beliefs impact their behaviors including their parenting styles and interactions with their infants and young children. With the family ethnobiography in mind, the observing professional can witness a parent's exchange with a child through the intimate hair combing experience, to ask questions, and engage in personal conversation. The observation experience becomes a rich platform for remembering and storytelling, evocative for both the parent and professional (See Wright, Chap. 8; Wilson, Chap. 9; and Hill, Chap. 10).

Key Questions for Racially Informed ReflectionKey questions to encourage professional and personal growth through reflective practice for readers from diverse ethnic and cultural backgrounds.

1. As an observing professional, what did you find yourself thinking about as you read this chapter about race and the use of *Ethnobiography* as an assessment tool with families?
2. What cultural, ethnic, and racial experiences have shaped your beliefs and attitudes about race, especially skin tones and hair types of Black, Indigenous People of Color (BIPOC)?
3. Did memories about your early life, the neighborhood you lived in, the social class and status of your family, the schools you went to, and the friends you had, come alive for you as you read this chapter?
4. Did memories about your hair type or skin color come to mind as you read this chapter?
5. How might your personal, cultural, and racial experiences shape your work with *children and families* who are from the same or different cultural group?
6. How might your personal cultural and racial experiences shape your work *as a member of a team* or with other students, faculty, professional colleagues who are from the same or different cultural group?
7. How do your cultural and racial experiences impact your ethnic identity?
8. Growing up, did you have at least one parent or primary caregiver with whom you felt safe?
9. Did you have good neighbors?
10. Was there an adult (not a parent/caregiver or the person from #9) who could provide you with support or advice about racial events or questions?
11. How might you manage the thoughts and feelings aroused in you after reading about racial hurts, trauma, microaggressions, or inequities?
12. Did anything in this chapter surprise you?

Clinicians and other helping professionals are encouraged to enter into a formal relationship with a racially informed and culturally aware supervisor who can listen to the thoughts and feelings awakened as they carry out emotionally charged work with children and families. Consistent and reliable relationship-based supervision will support personal and professional growth of helpers leading to best practice with families and self-awareness (Garcia et al., 1999; Heffron et al., 2007; Stroud, 2010; Van Horn, 2019). (See Chap. 6 for more discussion about culturally informed Reflective Supervision).

Reflective Questions

1. Do the neck-up exercise in the Appendix. What was your hair and skin tone growing up? What emotion words did you select? What stories come to mind about your hair or skin tone and what feelings are evoked as you recall them?
2. Complete the tender-headed rating scale. Were you tender headed as a child? What did this mean to you long ago and what does this mean to you now?
3. Go to the website and search the "sundown" states database to determine if the town you grew up or currently reside was a sundown town. As you reflect on this term, what thoughts and feelings are aroused? https://sundown.tougaloo.edu/sundowntowns.php
4. Is the term "sundown town" new to you? What thoughts and feelings does the term evoke? Are you from or currently live in a former "sundown town"?

References

Aronow, S. P., Aronow, H. D., Blanchard, T., Czinn, S., & Chelimsky, G. (2003). Hair relaxers: A benign caustic ingestion? *Journal of Pediatric Gastroenterology and Nutrition, 36*(1), 120–125.

Ashing, K. T., Lewis, M. L., & Walker, V. P. (2017). Thoughts and response to authority-perpetrated discriminatory, and race-based violence. *Journal of American Medical Association Pediatrics, 171*(6), 511–519. https://doi.org/10.1001/jamapediatrics2017.0137.

Bowlby, J. (1969). *Attachment and Loss: Vol 1.* Basic Books

Brave Heart, M. Y. H.. (Winter/Spring 2000). Wakiksuyapi: Carrying the Historical Trauma of the Lakota. *Disaster and Traumatic Stress Research and Intervention (Ed.)* M. Zakour, Volumes XXI–XXII pages 245–266. Tulane studies in social welfare: Tulane University, New Orleans, LA.

Briggs, E. C., Amaya-Jackson, L., Putnam, K. T., & Putnam, F. W. (2021). All adverse childhood experiences are not equal: The contribution of synergy to adverse childhood experiences scores. *American Psychologist, 76*, 243–252.

Chess, S., & Thomas, A. (1989). Issues in the clinical application of temperament. In G. A. Kohnstamm, J. E. Bates, & K. Rothbart (Eds.), *Temperament in childhood* (pp. 377–386). New York: Wiley.

Collins, P. H. (1990). Black women and motherhood. In *Black feminist thought.* Boston: Hyman.

Congress, E. P. & Kung, W. W. (2013). Using the Culturagram to assess and empower culturally diverse families. pp. 1–20. *Multicultural Perspectives in Social Work Practice with Families.* Springer Publishing Company.

Cross, W. E., Vadiver, B., Worrell, F., & Fhagen-Smith, P. (2002). Validating the cross racial identity scale. *Journal of Counseling Psychology, 49*(1), 71–85. https://doi.org/10.1037/0022-0167.9.1.7.1.

Fitzgerald, H. E., Johnson, D., Qin, D., Villarruel, F., & Norder, J. (Eds.). (2019). *The Handbook of children and prejudice: Integrating research practice and policy*. Springer Publishers. https://doi.org/10.1007/978-3-030-12228-7.

Garcia Coll, C. T., & Meyer, E. C. (1999). The sociocultural context of infant development. In C. H. Zeanah (Ed.), *Handbook of infant mental health* (pp. 56–70). New York: The Guilford Press.

Gonzales, N. A., Hiraga, Y., & Cauce, A. M. (1995). Observing mother-daughter interaction in African American and Asian American families. In H. I. McCubbin, E. A. Thompson, A. I. Thompson, & J. A. Futrell (Eds.), *Resiliency in ethnic minority families* (pp. 135–142). Madison: University of Wisconsin, Center for Excellence in Family Studies.

Harris, J., & Johnson, P. (Eds.). (2001). *Tenderheaded: A comb-bending collection of hair stories*. New York: Pocket Books.

Heffron, M. C., Grunstein, S., & Tilmon, S. (2007). Exploring diversity in supervision and practice. *Zero to Three Journal, 28*(2), 34–38.

Hill, R. (1972). *The strengths of Black families*. New York: Emerson Hall.

Lewis, M. L., (April 2001). The childhood experiences of racial acceptance and rejection scale: Development, reliability, and validity. Poster symposium presented at the Biennial Meeting of the Society for Research in Child Development, Minneapolis, Minnesota.

Lewis, M. L. (2013). Black mother-daughter interactions & hair combing rituals. In H. Jackson-Lowman, Editor, Afrikan American Women: Living at the Crossroads of Race, Gender, Class, and Culture, pp. 345-368. San Diego, CA: Cognella Press.

Lewis, M. L. (2016). African-American families a daily task to combat negative stereotypes about hair. Published in "The Conversation." https://theconversation.com/for-african-american-families-a-daily-task-to-combat-negative-stereotypes-about-hair-60154

Lewis, M. L. (2019). The intergenerational transmission of protective parenting responses to historical trauma. In H. E. Fitzgerald, D. Johnson, D. Qin, F. Villarruel, & J. Norder (Eds.), *The Handbook of children and prejudice: Integrating research practice and policy* (pp. 43–61). Springer Publishers. https://doi.org/10.1007/978-3-030-12228-7.

Lewis, M. L. (2020). *The Tender Headed Rating Scale. Unpublished measure*. New Orleans, Louisiana: Tulane University.

Lewis, M. L., & Craddock, K. T. (2019). Mothering while Black: Strengths and vulnerabilities in a sociopolitical racial context of structural inequality. In L. O'Brien Hallstein, A. O'Reilly, & M. V. Giles (Eds.), *The Routledge Companion to Motherhood* (1st ed.). Routledge.

Lewis, M. L., & Swift, A. (2014). Promoting social justice in families. In series Editors: C. Johnson & H. Friedman. Volume Editors: C. Johnson, H. Friedman, J. Diaz, B. Nastasi, & Z. Franco, *Praeger Handbook of Social Justice and Psychology – II*, 39-58. Santa Barbara, CA: Praeger.

Lewis, M. L., McConnico, N., & Anderson, R. (2018). Making meaning from trauma and violence: The influence of culture and traditional beliefs and historical trauma. In J. D. Osofsky & B. M. Groves (Eds.), *Violence, and trauma in the lives of children: Vol. 2 Prevention and intervention* (pp. 7–24). Santa Barbara, CA: Praeger Publishers.

Lewis, M. L., Nastasi, B., Parrott, L. (2021, in process). A Pilot Study of Childhood Experiences of Race-based Trauma from Colorism: Messages of Skin Color and Hair Type. Tulane University, New Orleans, Louisiana, USA.

McAdoo, H. P. (1985). Racial attitude and self-concept of young Black children over time. In H. P. McAdoo & J. McAdoo (Eds.), *Black children* (pp. 213–242). Beverly Hills, CA: Sage.

Murry, V. M., & Brody, G. (2002). Racial socialization processes in single-mother families: Linking maternal racial identity, parenting, and racial socialization in rural, single-mother families with child self-worth and self-regulation. In H. P. McAdoo (Ed.), *Black children: Social, educational, and parental environments* (2nd ed., pp. 97–118). Thousand Oaks, CA: Sage.

Narayan, A. J., Rivera, L. M., Bernstein, R. E., Harris, W. W., & Lieberman, A. F. (in press). Positive childhood experiences predict less psychopathology and stress in pregnant women with childhood adversity: A pilot study of the benevolent childhood experiences (BCEs) scale. *Child Abuse and Neglect.*

National Academies of Sciences, Engineering, & Medicine. (2019). *Vibrant and healthy kids: Aligning science practice, and policy to advance health equity*. Washington, DC: The National Academies Press. https://doi.org/10.17226/25466.

Neal-Barnett, A. López, I. & Owens, D. (1996, August). Neither Black nor White. The Impact of Skin Color in the Puerto Rican Community. In A. Neal Barnett (Chair), Women of Color on Color: Healing wounds, and building legacies. Round table discussion conducted at 104th annual meeting of the American Psychological Association, Toronto, Canada.

Norton, D. (1993). Diversity, early socialization, and temporal development: The dual perspective revisited. *Social Work, 38*, 82–90.

Penner, D.R., & Ferdinand, K.C. (2009) Aline St. Julien. In: Overcoming Katrina. *Palgrave studies in oral history*. Palgrave Macmillan, New York. https://doi.org/10.1057/9780230619616_1

Peters, M. (2002). Racial socialization of young Black children. In H. P. McAdoo (Ed.), *Black children* (2nd ed.). Thousand Oaks: Sage.

Rebora, A. (2016). Trichodynia: A review of the literature. *International Journal of Dermatology, 55*(4), 382–384. https://doi.org/10.1111/ijd.13204.

Rogoff, B. (2003). *The cultural nature of human development*. New York: Oxford University Press.

Shonkoff, J. P., Slopen, N., & Williams, D. R. (2021). Early childhood adversity, toxic stress, and the impacts of racism on the foundations of health. *Annual Review of Public Health, 42*, 115–1334.

Spencer, M.B. (2005). Skin Color Opinions and Perceptions Evaluation (SCOPE). Unpublished manuscript, University of Chicago.

Stroud, B. (2010). Honoring diversity through a deeper reflection: Increasing cultural understanding within the reflective supervision process. Special Issue, Putting reflective supervision into practice. *Zero to Three, 31*(2).

Tiwary, C. M. (1997). A survey of use of hormone/placenta-containing hair preparations by parents and/or children attending pediatric clinics. *Military Medicine, 162*(4), 252–256.

Tribal Behavioral Health Agenda. (2018). SAMHSA, Tribal Behavioral Health Agenda https://store.samhsa.gov/product/The-National-Tribal-Behavioral-Health-Agenda/PEP16-NTBH-AGENDA

Van Horn, J. (2019). Exploring professional ethics through diversity-informed reflective supervision. *Zero to Three Journal, 40*(1).

Wilson, I., Mbilishaka, A. M., & Lewis, M. L. (2018). "White folks ain't got hair like us": African American Mother-Daughter Hair Stories and Racial Socialization. *Women, Gender, and Families of Color, 6*(2), 226–248.

Chapter 5
Cultural Routines and Reflections: Building Parent–Child Connections—Hair Combing Interaction as a Cultural Intervention

Mary G. Warren

The hair combing experience provides a culturally based intervention to support parent–child relationships that need therapeutic support. Hair combing interaction (HCI) offers a time for parent and child to be present with one another, to talk, to laugh, and to engage positively. It is also an opportunity to build the young child's feeling that they are cared about, lovable, beautiful, all leading to positive self-esteem.

HCI can involve talking with a trained therapist using hair as a focus to help a parent or primary caregiver sort out relational difficulties with children or personal conflicts. HCI can also explore how family and societal culture influences what we think about ourselves and others; what we think about hair in general; and what cultural values can be passed on while engaging in the everyday routine of combing children's hair.

What Is Family and Societal Culture?

Most definitions suggest culture includes "the beliefs, language(s), and behaviors valued in a community" (Barrera & Corso, 2002, p. 104). Barbara Rogoff (2003) states culture is dynamic, not static. Culture changes as we participate in it. Cultural communities evolve through processes by which "[i]ndividuals and generations shape practices, traditions, and institutions at the same time that they build on what they inherit in their moment in history" (Rogoff, 2003, p. 62). Culture is a powerful source of belonging—belonging to a family, a group of people, and/or to a place.

M. G. Warren (✉)
Fielding Graduate University, Infant and Early Childhood Development (IECD), Santa Barbara, CA, USA
e-mail: mgwarren@fielding.edu

M. L. Lewis, D. J. Weatherston (eds.), *Therapeutic Cultural Routines to Build Family Relationships*, https://doi.org/10.1007/978-3-030-83726-6_5

Place can be a specific geographic location or more broadly encoded in memories. For example, for the Potawatomi Indian nation, "place" is where sweetgrass grows and can form part of the smells and tribal traditions to represent the hair of Mother Earth (Kimmerer, 2013).

There are many aspects to this belonging or culture—not only race/ethnicity, but also gender/sexual orientation, age, refugee or immigrant status, socioeconomic status, education level, religion. Many of these factors exist in the same person. We call these "intersectionality." A single, White, lesbian woman with a high school diploma and an income from multiple sources inhabits a different cultural niche from a college educated male living in a refugee camp with his whole extended Muslim family. Intersectionality blends together to influence how we live our lives and what cultural norms influence our actions, values, and beliefs.

When families are formed by the joining of two people in marriage (of whatever form) and children are born/adopted/reared, how parents care for the children transmits culture—those values, beliefs, and everyday routines that pass on belongingness. How parents care for children—and their hair—can become a battle to belong or an easy opportunity to learn family cultural norms. This chapter discusses how the act of hair combing can be a dominant cultural function in the development of children and their relationships with caregivers.

Hair Is Personal. Hair Is Social

Hair reflects both an individual and the norms of the collective society. Hair—how it is styled, combed, covered, or not—influences and is influenced by cultural norms. Cultural norms are dynamic, evolving as humans interact with each other and their environments (Rogoff, 2003). Envision this as a mobile, hanging from the child with all other elements moving around the child on the same level. The parts can bump into and bounce off each other, including the elements in the outer ring (see Fig. 5.1). How hair is combed, protected, and styled, particularly in early childhood, reflects this cultural evolution and the subject of this chapter.

Our lives are steeped in culture. Hair care is part of how we learn about, are influenced by, and revise our inner self and our own culture. Mothers and other primary caregivers are the first architects of how our hair reflects us. Through hair combing interactions, parents have many opportunities to express pride in their child, to celebrate—or denigrate—the child's developing self, and even reinforce cultural messages about the importance and appearance of one's hair.

Growing up, who first took care of your hair? Probably this person was your Mother or another primary caregiver. She washed it, dried it, combed it, and when there was enough to tie up some way, you may have sprouted a palm tree or two little tuffs out of the top of your head, or a ponytail in the back. Or, may be your hair was cut short to make caring for it easy. Where you lived as a baby, who composed your close family, and what the cultural norms said about children's hair all influenced how your Mother or other caregiver cared for your hair. These same elements still influence your hair care—either due to your continued conformance, or your rebellion.

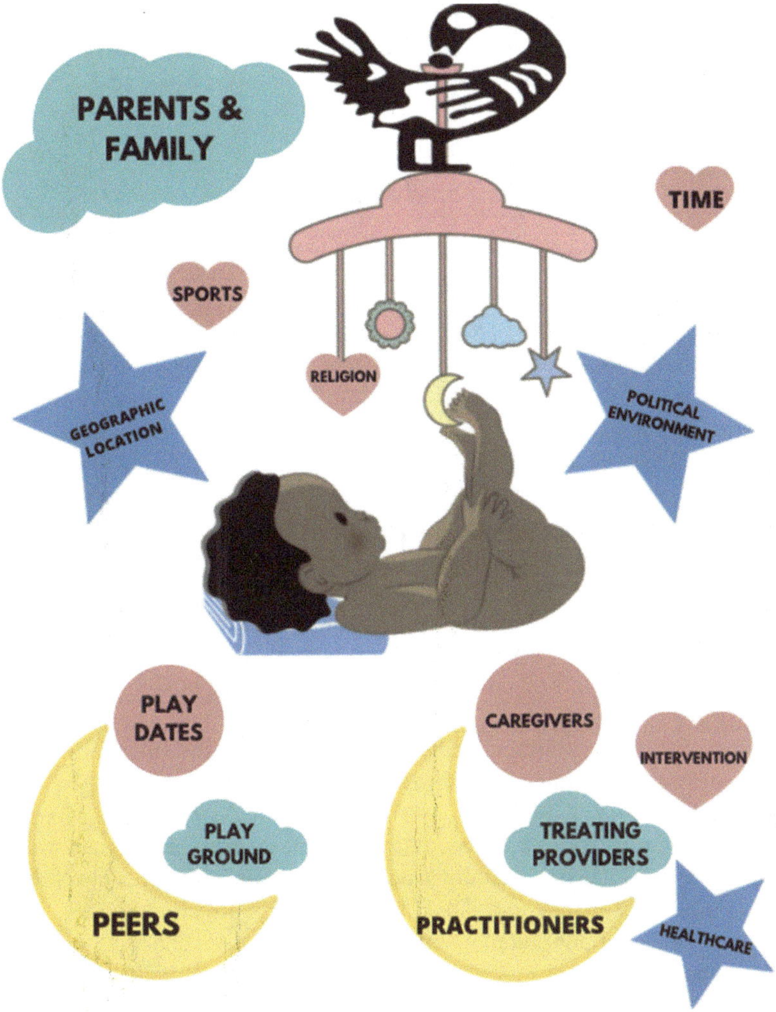

Fig. 5.1 The sociocultural influences on parent–infant interactions during hair combing time

How Is Family Culture Instilled?

The daily routines of living together, keeping house, feeding, and clothing family members all establish the family's culture (Wolin & Bennett, 1984). Often, these routines are passed down intergenerationally. They may change over time with the addition of children, moves to different geographic locations, deaths of grandparents. How parents think of their roles, sometimes based on typically gendered roles, sometimes fixed due to employment schedules, perhaps changing with social norms, all influence who typically cares for the children's hair. Religion, school, and the celebrations that these institutions may generate—like baptism, graduation, prom—affect a family's culture, and certainly how hair is combed and styled.

Why Is the Culture of the Family Important?

Family connotes cohesion, a sense of belonging, a safe place. We know the importance of secure attachment between child and caregiver as the inception of learning, exploring, and building trust. Trust in the comfort and safety of the mother or primary caregiver's continuous care sets the stage for the child's ability to grow and build relationships with others throughout life. Beginning in the first days of early caregiving, the child's attachment to his/her parent comes from daily interactions; routines that are predictable and that involve "serve and return" conversations or dialog where caregiver responds to child's bids for attention and interaction and the caregiver is sensitive in response (Center on the Developing Child at Harvard, 2013). When a caregiver is contingently responsive to a young child and responds in timely, positive, nurturing ways, the attachment relationship begins to unfold, over the first years of life, to be a secure one for the child. The young child learns to trust that the caregiver is a loving person, available for affection, comfort, and ongoing response. Hair combing interactions can reinforce the attachment relationship for the child—or not.

As part of a family, children learn to rely on predictability (first we get dressed, then comb hair), the fun of anticipation (hurray! next week we get to go to Disneyland!), how to negotiate the hierarchies of power (should I ask Mom or Dad about this?). Family stories are passed on during meals, bedtime routines—and during hair combing. How one's family handles disruptions like moves, divorce, death, job loss may be explained and talked about during hair care activities. Learning about expressing emotions, coping with uncertainty, and the changing strategies for managing people and actions are valuable lessons that can be picked up during hair combing. Parenting and culture are intertwined with the primary goals of successfully transmitting the culture across generations and embedding the next generation into the existing culture (Bornstein et al., 2011; Rogoff, 2003).

Hair care is influenced by family, of course, but today's child grows up in multiple environments (childcare, church, playground) that can influence how the child and caregiver perceive norms around hair. Research findings suggest that cultural practices are "not stable within racial or ethnic contexts, or even within country of origin, language/dialect, social class, gender, religion, immigration history, experience with racism and segregation, and neighborhood" (Reid et al., 2019, p. 979).

How might young children be exposed to cultural norms? What parents and caregivers believe about children, about their own role as parents and caregivers and about hair demonstrate cultural norms. Have you heard early childhood professionals or parents suggest any of these practices?

1. Children learn by observation. "Do as I do, vs. do as I say." (Rogoff, 2003)

2. "Use your words!" to encourage children to label emotions and feelings as communication to others as well as self-learning about the impact of actions.
3. "Let's get something to get that hair out of your face."

Hair combing can incorporate lessons on vocabulary (barrettes, ribbons, scrunchies), math ("Let's measure the length of your hair." "How many rows can we braid on the side of your head?"), colors ("Mom's hair is brown, and your hair is blonde."), and shapes ("We can make a round bun with your hair.").

Lessons from current events might influence how hair is cared for and styled. Episodes like the COVID-19 virus pandemic of 2020 dramatically affected how hair was styled. When salons were closed, people had to cut their own hair. As months passed during the pandemic, women adopted extreme hair styles, for example, pink or green highlights (Bosworth, 2020).

How males versus females wear their hair demonstrates many variations between the sexes, and similarities. These gender norms begin in early childhood. Usually, males wear their hair cut short, while females may grow their hair longer. Hair length and styles vary significantly among the sexes depending on immediate social, ethnic, religious, and generational norms. For those identifying as nonbinary, not fixing one's hair consistent with prevailing hair care norms can be a statement of independence from adherence to norms. How celebrities and sports figures wear their hair can form models for children to emulate—or entreat parents to allow them to emulate. Celebrations like dances and other social get-togethers can provide opportunities for extra care and consultation around hair care products, fancy designs, and creative accessories. Or both males and females may prefer to wear their hair long.

Rituals and Routines and Therapeutic Intervention

Therapists may use observations of hair combing interactions (HCIs) as opportunities to understand the cultural influences being passed on in the family through daily caregiving routines, including hair combing. Eliciting the responses to the methods suggested in the questions below can be ports of entry through observation into understanding the parent–child relationship and identifying opportunities for helpful interventions when needed.

1. Who combs the young child's hair? Grandma? Mama? Daddy?
2. Is the child invited to bring barrettes, comb/brush, ribbons to the parent to comb or style the hair? Is this part of the daily routine or does the parent ask the child every time?
3. Is the young child expected to sit still and not fuss as the parent combs and styles his/her hair? How does the parent/caregiver let the child know this? What is the facial expression and/or tone of voice of the parent/caregiver? Is the child physically and/or verbally reminded to sit still? What is the experience like for the young child? The parent?
4. Is the child entertained by an electronic device while sitting to have her hair fixed? What are the parameters around device use? Which device/s is the child

allowed to use? Which software programs or internet links are allowed? Can the sound be heard?

5. Do the child and parent engage in conversation while sitting to fix hair? Are both the child and parent sitting? Do they seem comfortable with one another? Is the child standing in front of the parent?
6. Is the child allowed to comb his/her own hair, using barrettes/ribbons at will?
7. How does the parent talk about the child's hair? Is it beautiful just the way it is? Does the caregiver refer to the child having "good" hair or "bad" hair? Does it need to be "tamed"? (See personal recollections.)

Conversations and Personal Recollections for Exploring Therapeutic Assessments and Interventions

Our childhood experiences influence how we feel about ourselves and how we will care for or nurture our child/children. When working with parents, social workers or other practitioners may have opportunities to engage in conversations about a parent's memories of early care, relationships with those who took care of them, and, of special interest to this book, hair combing interactions. This section discusses multiple childhood memories that may be fruitful for parents and practitioners to explore to strengthen the therapeutic relationship and lead to greater understanding of the past as it enters or influences the present.

Scandinavian Roots?

A grandmother remembers, "My daughters' Scandinavian hair, fine and very straight, was hard for me to braid. To this day my girls are upset with me for not teaching them to braid their hair." (Personal Communication, B.W., 2019).

A social worker or professional might ask how Grandmother views her Scandinavian cultural roots. Are these terms ("fine and very straight") applicable to her Scandinavian cultural norms? In what ways? Does this mother continue to worry or wonder about her daughters' upset? Does the upset affect how her daughters now parent their own children? As grandparent and professional reflect together, does grandmother express feeling sad or incompetent as a mother to her girls?

Multicultural Hair

A mother of 2 biracial (Canadian and Caymanian) boys in the Cayman Islands says:

> In our culture people talk about 'good hair'...which is hair that is more like white people... straighter, easier to comb. Our boys have very different hair and people will comment...'oh, this one got the good hair' (Personal Communication, S.S., 2019).

A social worker or practitioner might ask the mother if she can say a little more about "good hair" or "bad hair" and what it means to her. She may ask if there are other stories about hair in her family and empathize about either the "good" or "bad" hair or how it relates to feelings of self-worth or self-esteem carried today.

Sibling Relationships/Jealousy

A Chinese-American adult female says, "My sisters and I all have different textured hair. Chinese 'good' hair is straight and silky. Mine is coarse and curly. I wish I had my sister's good hair." (Personal Communication, J.M., 2019)

Canadian/Caymanian mom says "My friend has two daughters both with *very different hair texture and curls*. There were a lot of tears growing up around the issue of hair" (Personal Communication, S.S., 2019).

A social worker or practitioner might ask about the mom's daughters' rivalries/jealousies due to their different hair textures. Why was this important to them and how was it played out in their developing sibling relationship? What was the mom's experience around these struggles about hair?

Ribbons Today

An adult female from Panama City, Panama says,

> My mom used to say, "We are poor, but they don't have to see that we are pigs." We were not poor, but how your child looks, that idea of having clean clothes, pressed uniforms for school, this was all part of how others could judge and perceive you and your family, and infer how good a mother you are.
>
> I absolutely hated everything about hair care growing up. My mother used to buy expensive ribbons to match my uniform color, and I would always lose them because my hair is so straight and fine. My mother would be enraged and pulled on my hair "to teach" me not to lose my hair ties; I still got home without them. The first time I had a haircut my mother cried, because my long hair was cut to shoulder length. (Personal Communication, R.L., 2019).

A social worker or practitioner might help the adult caregiver reflect on how she felt as a child and today about ribbons and rules, or how solidly cultural norms influence parent emotions about being a "good" parent.

Questions Social Workers or Practitioners can use to tease out issues affecting society and/or family culture to work towards resolution.

1. Ask how Mother or Grandmother views her country's cultural roots. Are her terms to describe her daughters' hair ("fine and very straight") applicable to her country's cultural norms? Might these words reflect a political or societal view in general?
2. Ask Mother/Father to say a little more about "good hair" or "bad hair" and what it means to her/him. Empathize about either the "good" or "bad" hair, or how it relates to feelings of self-worth or self-esteem carried today.

3. Are there other stories about hair in the family?
   1. Ask about sibling rivalries/jealousies due to their different hair textures or abilities to work with or style their hair. Why was this important to them and how has it played out in their developing sibling relationship?
   2. Help the adult caregiver reflect on how she felt as a child, as well as today, about ribbons and rules around hair, hair coverings, hair colors. Might these feelings be coloring her interactions with her child?
   3. Can the adult recognize that a child is upset with how her/his hair is combed or styled?
   4. What is the mom's felt experience around struggles about hair? Does she express feeling sad or incompetent as a mother to her children?
   5. Reflect with adults how solidly cultural norms influence parent emotions about being a "good" parent.

Cultural Socialization: How Children Learn Cultural Norms

Behaviors arise out of beliefs. Parent behaviors are the foundation of daily routines that pass on cultural beliefs to the child. Children are active participants in the cultural processes that constitute interactions between child and adult. As Rogoff (2003) suggests, culture is dynamic, the result of people interacting with other people, technology, objects, and thoughts. The child's agency (Reid et al., 2019, p. 979) in these interactions can be observed in the daily activities around caring for hair, bedtime routines, and feeding.

Is Hair Combing part of the bedtime routine? *Does the family demonstrate:*

a. Affectionate bedtime routines—Child bathes as play, brushes teeth, combs hair, reads, cuddles, enjoys hugs. Child sleeps in own bed.
b. Instrumental bedtime routines—Child bathes to get clean, says prayers, and sleeps in own bed.
c. Permissive bedtime routines—Child takes bath, roughhouses, has a snack and water to drink. Child sleeps where he or she wants.
d. Bedtime as an extension of waking time—Child is expected to finish meals and chores, and wash hands and face. Child sleeps with parent.

Is Hair Combing Part of the Feeding Routine? *Does the family demonstrate differences in the way children are treated:*

e. Special Needs—Child has special food, special feeding chair, spoon/cup. Hair is combed away from the face. Food is part of conversation time, can be played with, and textures explored.
f. Part of family—Child's food is made from the family meal. Child is expected to wash hands and comb hair prior to coming to the table. Child is a silent observer, food can be explored to an extent, but not wasted.

g. Begged to eat—Child's appearance is chubby, desirable; so, food holds critical daily importance. Child is begged to eat.
h. Fed—Food cannot be wasted. Children are not allowed to touch food until physical dexterity can be tested and food not dropped.

Social workers and other practitioners can talk about routines such as these to assess family cultural beliefs, interactions, and relationships. Sometimes beliefs that the therapist or professional and parent have may clash. Acknowledging this clash as part of a Reflective Supervision session can be helpful. (see Wilson, Weatherston & Hill, Chap. 6, Reflective Supervision).

Therapists Exploring Personal Connections with Hair

Behavioral Health practitioners, social workers, and other child and family practitioners, first of all, must be self-aware. They must learn to know their own culture and biases (St. John et al., 2012; Diversity-Informed Tenets, 2018). Discussing personal beliefs about ethnicity and race, as well as cultural values, with a reflective supervisor may strengthen understanding of one's own biases that could interrupt the work with a child and family. These biases, as well as differences in cultural practices that are unseen and unacknowledged by the professional, may create barriers between family and professional and lead to a disruption in the professional–family relationships (See Wilson, Chap. 9).

Social workers, therapists, and mental health practitioners will find themselves interacting with others not of their same culture. *What do you do when you don't feel like you belong 'in the room', like you can't 'speak the language'*? A good place to start is to be curious about the cultural meanings of children's and families' own feelings, thoughts, and actions, and their feelings and thoughts about your culture. Curiosity may lead to greater self-awareness and understanding about how others ascribe meaning to their own (the practitioner's) feelings, thoughts, and actions (Bowman & Stott, 1994). As suggested earlier, talking with a reflective supervisor about your own feelings and biases or perceived conundrums working with this child/family can be helpful.

Using what the therapist learns about the child/family culture and "taking into consideration the family goals for children's development and learning, leads to positive family engagement and relationships between practitioner and family." (Reid et al., 2019, p. 985). HCI offers a template for the child to develop positive relationships with peers and other adults, even when the parent may not incorporate the gentle, nurturing efforts suggested. Continued modeling and talking about HCI can be a powerful force to change current patterns of interaction between parent and child, and therefore for the child to learn to do with others.

Social workers and other professionals may also benefit from dialog with each other about the varied family cultural patterns they find, the approaches, values, and strategies families use when interacting with children, and the effects thereof on the children and on themselves (See Byars & Subramaniam, Chap. 12). Using humor and patience with themselves, the parents, and the children will further embody the HCI program.

Conclusions

Children develop in all domains as they interact with their parents and other primary caregivers. Hair combing interactions offer opportunities to maximize children's development in language, cognition, social-emotional development, interoception, proprioception, and fine motor control. When parent or primary caregiver interactions are positive, nurturing, and contingent, the child learns to trust that mother, father, or caregiver—and by extension the world—is positive, affirming, and responsible to care for the child's well-being. When a child experiences such a safe haven, his environment is a place worth exploring and learning about. HCI offers practices for children and parents or caregivers to interact positively and build a safe haven, a secure and trusting relationship, a strong foundation for a child's social and emotional development across the lifespan.

It is vital for researchers, interventionists, and other outside observers to understand how a family's culture contributes to a child's resiliency. The family history and connections to people and places, and the child's current participation in a safe and secure home environment, set the stage for our children to be coconstructors of cultures around the world that promote peace, equity, and inclusion. Caregivers and their attitudes are key. HCI provides a culturally enriched and informed way to create and reinforce this trusting environment.

Reflective Questions

1. *Culture is a powerful source of belonging—belonging to a family, a group of people, and/or to a place.* Take a few minutes to think about how you have developed a sense of belonging to your family. What cultural beliefs, practices, and traditions have helped to shape who you are and how you perceive the world.
2. The consideration of personal beliefs about ethnicity and race, as well as cultural values, is an important part of professional growth and development. What are some of those beliefs or values and how do they influence your practice with children and families if you are from another culture?
3. Do you have a personal story about hair combing or cultural rituals as they relate to your current professional identity or self-esteem?
4. Consider how you might informally invite parents to share stories about their hair combing experiences as a child or with their current children. Explore with them any differences in their child's individual response to

having their hair combed. For example, one child was tender headed and another was not. Was their response to getting their hair combed consistent with the child's personality?

5. Thinking about the ways that culture was defined in this chapter, try to identify a core value or belief you currently hold about parent's responsibilities. How similar or different are these beliefs from your family of origin? Reflect on what occurred that led to you continuing to practice or led to your ending a cultural practice from your family of origin.

References

Barrera, I., & Corso, R. M. (2002). Cultural competency as skilled dialogue. *Topics in Early Childhood Special Education, 22*(2), 103–113.

Bornstein, M. H., Putnick, D. L., & Lansford, J. E. (2011). Parenting attributions and attitudes from a cross-cultural perspective. *Parenting, 11*(2-3), 214–237. https://doi.org/10.1080/15295192.2011.585568

Bosworth, S. (2020). Wanted: Unboring hair. *Wall Street Journal.*

Bowman, B., & Stott, F. (1994). Understanding development in a cultural context: The challenge for teachers. In B. Mallory & R. New (Eds.), *Diversity and developmentally appropriate practice(s): Challenge for early childhood education.* Teachers College Press.

Center on the Developing Child at Harvard Resources Archive. (2013). https://developingchild.harvard.edu/resources; https://devhcdc.wpengine.com/science/key-concepts/serve-and-return/social-media/

Diversity- Informed Tenets. (2018). https://diversityinformedtenets.org/

Kimmerer, R. W. (2013). *Braiding sweetgrass.* Milkweed Editions.

Reid, J. L., Kagan, S. L., & Scott-Little, C. (2019). New understandings of cultural diversity and the implications for early childhood policy, pedagogy, and practice. *Early Child Development and Care, 189*(6), 976–989. https://doi.org/10.1080/03004430.2017.1359582

Rogoff, B. (2003). *The cultural nature of human development.* Oxford University Press.

St. John, M. S., Thomas, K., & Noroña, C. R. (2012). Infant mental health professional development (Infant Mental Health Tenets). *Zero to Three Journal, 33*(2), 13–22.

Wolin, S., & Bennett, L. (1984). Family rituals. *Family Process, 23*(3), 401–420.

Part II
Reflective Supervision and Practice: Experiences Shared by Infant and Early Childhood Mental Health Practitioners

Chapter 6
Introduction to Reflective Supervision: Through the Lens of Culture, Diversity, Equity, and Inclusion

Karol A. Wilson, Deborah J. Weatherston, and Stefanie Hill

Reflective Supervision Defined

Grounded in Infant and Early Childhood Mental Health (IECMH) theory and practice, reflective supervision (RS) is a supportive relationship that develops over time between a supervisor and supervisee, highlighting strengths and vulnerabilities, and inviting attention to the awakening of thoughts and feelings that occur in the presence of vulnerable children and their families.

Reflective supervision invites introspection and deep exploration of cultural beliefs, traditions, and values that in turn can lead to greater self-awareness through reflective process. Of additional importance, the supervisor and supervisee look closely at the impact of relationships on other relationships – the infant's or child's relationship as it impacts the parent, the parent's relationship as it impacts the practitioner or supervisee, and the practitioner or supervisee as it impacts the supervisor, and the reverse (Emde, 1991). This allows the supervisee to unearth new understanding, new strategies, and new interventions, encouraging continuing reflection and curiosity about child and family dynamics and personal growth.

According to Shahmoon-Shanock (2009), a prominent leader in the field of IECMH, RS is vital for those working in mental health and other clinical fields to enhance their professional development and competency. However, as the IECMH field has grown and gained recognition for its careful attention to relationships and the critical role that parents play in supporting the social and emotional well-being

K. A. Wilson (✉)
Starfish Family Services, Dearborn, MI, USA
e-mail: wilsonkarol726@gmail.com

D. J. Weatherston
Alliance for the Advancement of Infant Mental Health, Southgate, MI, USA

S. Hill
Starfish Family Services, Livonia, MI, USA

M. L. Lewis, D. J. Weatherston (eds.), *Therapeutic Cultural Routines to Build Family Relationships*, https://doi.org/10.1007/978-3-030-83726-6_6

of infants and young children, RS is recognized as an all-important tool to help service providers in a variety of settings and across disciplines to address multifaceted issues faced when engaging in IECMH work (Watson et al., 2016; Weatherston et al., 2010). Experienced clinicians define RS as collaborative, consistent, and reflective (Eggbeer et al., 2010; Schafer, 2007). The supervisory relationship deepens as each experiences trust in the other, honesty, authenticity, and acceptance.

The supervisor and supervisee together create a relational space that offers an invitation for the participants to be curious and vulnerable about their work with infants, young children, and families (Weatherston & Barron, 2009). This relationship between family and practitioners is one that develops over time, through many deeply felt interactions and shared stories about work with children and families (Weatherston & Ribaudo, 2020). IECMH work with children and families is intimate, intricate, and at times very painful. The supervisee carries the smell, tears, fears, and joys of what was witnessed during home or clinical visits into the supervisory space. Pawl and St. John (1998) propose that RS serves as the anchor for the supervisee to get support, processing the emotions that may be overwhelming, leading to shared understanding of the infant and family referred, as well as greater understanding of oneself. The supervisory relationship, often intense, may withstand disruptions and misunderstandings, leading to the need for repairs and ultimately new understanding and growth.

The Importance of Reflection

Research has shown that RS supports the supervisee in building clinical and reflective strategies to better serve infants and families. Regular engagement in RS reduces burnout (Heller & Ash, 2016; Shea, 2019) and compassion fatigue while awarding the opportunity to paint a picture of their work with words, examining multiple perspectives, and reflecting on the infant, the parent, and the caregiving environment. During RS, the supervisor strives to utilize skills and share knowledge about IECMH work to create a felt experience for the supervisee that in turn is offered to the parent and ultimately to the infant or child. The supervisor is also working to regulate and manage his or her own emotional response to remain present, curious, and nonjudgmental. This example of Jeree Pawl's mantra, "Do unto others as you would have others do unto others" is the foundation of RS and the parallel process (Pawl & St. John, 1998, p. 7). The supervisee and the reflective supervisor partner together to build emotional safety, which allows them to wonder about the work and engage in thoughtful interactions with each other (Schafer, 2007; Weatherston & Barron, 2009).

Many of the families served have not experienced safety that offers coregulation to assist them in organizing their strong feelings. Their experiences of relationship with a helping professional may be threatened by trauma, loss, violence, and insecure attachments (Osofsky, 2011; Osofsky & Lieberman, 2011). RS fuels the supervisee to attend to the dysregulation that families may convey and helps create an environment where parents of infants and young children can delight in and respond to a range of emotions and developmental milestones. The supervisee may be the first to offer the family a supportive and consistent relationship where each member is held in positive regard (Weatherston & Tableman, 2015).

RS is consistent in that sacred time is set aside to meet for a minimum of one hour weekly, where possible. The supervisee is also given space to reflect on thoughts and feelings carried in the body, heart, and mind in response to their work (Schafer, 2007). These feelings provide valuable information about the infants, young children, and families with whom they work and often lead to greater self-awareness within the RS relationship. It is essential to be able to sit with someone who understands one's work. It can be difficult, however, to share negative feelings and what's not going well. There may be fear of judgement, rejection, and shame for having negative thoughts. Yet, those times of discomfort may offer the most insight and greatest moments of clarity. At the same time, the risk of reprisal can feel too great to enter that space of vulnerability.

Supervisory Relationship

Conversations regarding racial and cultural differences may unintentionally create relationship disruptions in RS if the supervisee is a person of color. The supervisee may feel pressured to educate or take care of the White supervisor's feelings of discomfort, which can dismiss the experience of the supervisee. So how does this crucial conversation begin and who initiates it? The answer varies, but it is important to remember that differences are recognized early in infancy as the infant perceives the world constructed through relationships with primary caregivers. Over time and through multiple interactions, the child develops a working model for relationship that becomes more complex as past experiences form a framework for how the developing child views himself/herself (Bowlby, 1969). This model is internalized and influenced through the infant's or child's biology, environment, and culture. In this way, the child gains an understanding of his or her own value and worth (Zeanah, 2019).

Of importance, even though race does not have an integral physical or biological meaning, we cannot ignore the power behind it (Gannon, 2016). Race is said to be a political construct based on societal rules and phenotypic characteristics. Babies as young as six months of age notice photos of people whose skin color differs from their own (Kelly et al., 2005). By age two or three, children are also aware of gender differences, physical features and may notice people who are differently abled. It is within the caregiving relationship that the baby learns to delight, fear, or avoid those who are different. Core beliefs about race and culture are grounded in histories that can trigger painful memories that are not easily shared (Kelly et al., 2007; Lee et al., 2013).

Attention to race in the IECMH field has increased as families enrolled in services have continued to be disproportionately affected by social injustice. Advances in technology have brought racism and social injustices to the forefront. There is more awareness of the atrocities that are the result of systemic racism. It is recommended that being intentional in addressing issues of diversity, inequity, and exclusion that families face is essential (Thomas et al., 2019).

Internal Working Model: Journey to Becoming Who We Are

According to John Bowlby (1969, 1988), the internal working model serves as a coherent characterization of how the child develops a sense of the world and others. These experiences help the child to determine if he or she is worthy, valuable, and able to successfully engage in relationships. It is imperative to think about how the internal working model is impacted by racism. The internal working model is constructed as the attachment between the young child and primary caregiver is developed. Through the caregiving relationship, the baby develops strategies to keep the caregiver close and navigate the balance between proximity and exploration. To do this, the child must experience coregulation before they can regulate on their own and begin to explore (Bretherton et al., 1990). Attachment theory concludes that a pattern is set during infancy, which becomes the basis for predictable interactions and expectations for relationships across the life span during infancy (Brown et al., 2008). The caregiver who has been plagued by systemic racism may unintentionally create experiences of fear of exploration in the presence of people from varying races to keep the child safe and protected from racism and violence. (Note: when these children are with family and people who look like them, they may exhibit more secure attachment behaviors.) The perceived fear of being misunderstood or potentially harmed by those who are White can serve as a template for what the child expects from relationships within dominant cultures. As the child reaches school age and continues through to adulthood, the child, now a professional, has learned to be more cautious and eventually, the Black supervisor or supervisee may enter an RS relationship with initial feelings of mistrust. These feelings may be unconscious, making the relationship between the supervisor and supervisee tenuous and uncomfortable. To combat these barriers, the supervisor and supervisee need to talk about race sensitively and bravely and how those early experiences have not only impacted who they are but how those experiences can also serve as a vehicle to inform their work in the IECMH field.

The supervisor is not only a teacher and guide but is usually seen as a cherished mentor who is admired and well respected in the IECMH community. In IECMH work, supervisees of color often have supervisors who are White. This can make conversations about race and culture more difficult to engage in. The supervisor may feel apprehensive about how to invite these important conversations, because they don't want to say the wrong thing, offend the supervisee, or be misunderstood. The supervisee may feel vulnerable and even angry, having assumed that the supervisor will not and cannot understand their personal experiences. The stress of racism is not only magnified by a specific occurrence but in the dismissing of others to believing and acknowledging the person's experience. The weight of this dismissal creates ongoing stress within the Black supervisor or supervisee. Opportunities to engage in conversations to examine the stressors can offer relief and regulation to the supervisor and supervisee and strengthen the space between (Watson, 2016). In this instance, space is created to encourage conversations regarding the fear, anxiety, anger, and hurt one has felt regarding racial injustice while maintaining a reflective stance of compassion, empathy, and positive regard (Harrell, 2000, 2014).

The supervisor and supervisee can reflect on the following, with an understanding that trust develops over time. Tackling the injustices of racism is not easy but is necessary to examine as part of the reflective process. If this continuous examination is done in RS, it will support the supervisee in being able to invite discussions about race and differences with families. Together the supervisee supervisor and supervisee can reflect on the following:

1. *What is it like to be with families who have different racial and ethnic backgrounds from you?*
2. *We both have different experiences that may make it difficult to talk about the discomfort we may be feeling. I would like to invite you to talk about any feelings you have that make you feel unsafe in our RS relationship.*
3. *Uncomfortable feelings may continue to enter our RS space as we are reminded of race. We may be triggered by the experiences of the families we are talking about. Hopefully, we can talk about how to address these feelings.*

Examining Race in RS

The Irving Harris Foundation first published the Diversity-Informed Tenets for Work with Infants, Children and Families in 2012 and revised them in 2018. These principles are foundational to the infant and early childhood mental health (IECMH) community and include purposeful attention to diversity informed practices, equity, intersectionality, privilege, and reflection (Ghosh-Ippen et al., 2012; Noroña et al., 2012; St. John et al., 2012). The first and central principle of diversity-informed practice is self-reflection, coming to know oneself, especially one's culture, beliefs, and values as they shape understanding and response to systemic racism, oppression, disparity, and trauma. Other tenets clearly direct practitioners and advocates in the IECMH field to protect the rights of all children, to fight discriminatory practices, to honor diverse family structures, and to uphold justice in all aspects of our work. The Diversity-Informed Tenets support and strengthen reflective supervision as a context for personal and professional examination of one's own thoughts, feelings, and experiences while working closely with others whose culture, ethnicity, or race differ from their own.

Embedded in these tenets is the overarching theme of cultural humility. Experienced practitioners suggest that cultural humility is a lifelong process of honoring the uniqueness of individuals and engaging in opportunities to support varying perspectives (Lekas et al., 2020; Morris et al., 2005). To practice cultural humility, there needs to be an appreciation and understanding that there is always more to learn about ourselves and others. Barrera et al. (2012) emphasize careful inquiry about differences that are offered with respect to each other's history. The interactions are reciprocal in that the supervisor and supervisee will share in the vulnerability and transparency of sitting with the discomfort of their own cultural and racial journey and how those journeys may have contributed to barriers.

Conversations about power and privilege (Mcintosh, 2015) can also be hard to tackle, but are not exclusive to those who are White. Privilege can present itself in many ways in IECMH work. Privilege becomes a barrier when those who benefit from social, economic, and racial advantages don't recognize, validate, or attempt to understand those who don't have the luxury of not thinking about race. One example might be the professional/supervisee who decides who the family is based on the referral information. The supervisee makes assumptions, before meeting the family first to note the observable strengths and risks, and to share their story. Another example might be the professional/supervisee who tries to be the expert about what the infant or young child needs, and how to begin services rather than respecting the parent's voice and strategies. Wearing privilege as a coat of armor and ignoring its impact could be a contributing factor in creating disruptions in the relationship with families as well as in the RS relationship. When it is not examined, the person who holds the privilege may be dismissive and defensive, making it difficult to engage in conversation.

Although arduous, careful attention and commitment are needed to address and combat privilege, it is important to be mindful that in most instances, these disruptions are not intentional and can be repaired. Problems arise when the supervisee and supervisor remain silent. The supervisor and supervisee need to be responsive in that both are inviting conversation to talk about how relationships have been harmed by inequity and social injustice. These crucial conversations in this reflective space are not entered into to blame or ridicule but to deepen and strengthen the RS relationship and IECMH work. When ignored, the persistent ghost will continue to invade the protected space. (Patterson, 2012; Wilson et al., 2018).

Greater Understanding and Connection

The first of ten Irving Harris Diversity Informed Tenets is self-awareness, leading to better services for infants, young children, and families (Ghosh-Ippen et al., 2012). This tenet is fundamental when offering IECMH services. To assure quality, the family's concerns need to be individualized. This requires the family and provider to partner together, to develop a plan that includes considerations of race and culture. The IECMH provider needs to be intentional in thinking about core beliefs carried within as these affect developing relationships with families. Heller and Ash (2016) emphasize self-knowledge and awareness as an essential component in IECMH work and that it is enhanced through the RS relationship. Self-knowledge encourages the supervisee to examine his or her own internal working model and the importance of acknowledging mental states, which impact the capacity for reflection. Intentional exploration includes the supervisee's consideration of the impact of race, culture, and ethnicity in IECMH work. RS is enriched when the supervisee and supervisor bravely and authentically engage in dialogue that supports self-reflection, professional development, and understanding. The RS relationship deepens as trust develops. The journey to establishing trust can be both joyous and painful as stories about oneself and one's work are shared, heard, responded to, and honored. When the reflective partners are truly invested in their quest to understand the meaning of behaviors, their own and those they are working with, their work deepens and leads to new understanding and change.

Reflective Questions

1. What is required of a reflective supervisor and supervisee to enter honest conversations about race, power, equity, and belonging?
2. Why is it important for supervisors and supervisees to share their thoughts and feelings about race, ethnicity, privilege, and culture within their supervisory relationship?
3. What impact could a courageous conversation with a supervisor, in which you share personal reflections, perceptions, or misperceptions about power, privilege, social injustice, or race about race, ethnicity, and culture, have on your own development, the supervisory relationship, and on your work with children and families?
4. How might your own cultural and racial experiences shape your engagement in a reflective supervisory relationship with a person who is from a different cultural or racial group?

References

Barrera, I., Kramer, L., & MacPherson, D. (2012). *Skilled dialogue for responding to cultural diversity in early childhood* (2nd ed.). Paul H. Brookes Publishing Co..

Bowlby, J. (1969). *Attachment and loss*, 1(3). Basic Books.

Bowlby, J. (1988). Attachment, communication, and the therapeutic process. In *A secure base: Parent-child attachment and healthy human development* (pp. 137–157). Routledge.

Bretherton, I., Ridgeway, D., & Cassidy, J. (1990). Assessing internal working models of the attachment relationship: An attachment story completion task for 3-year-olds. In M. T. Greenberg, D. Cicchetti, & E. M. Cummings (Eds.), *Attachment in the preschool years: Theory, research, and intervention* (The John D. and Catherine T. MacArthur Foundation series on mental health and development) (pp. 273–308). University of Chicago Press.

Brown, D., Hawkins Rodgers, Y., & Kapadia, K. (2008). Multicultural considerations for the application of attachment theory. *American Journal of Psychotherapy, 62*(4), 353–363.

Diversity-Informed Tenets for Work with Infants, Children & Families. (2018). https://diversity-informedtenets.org/

Eggbeer, L., Shamoon Shanock, R., & Clark, R. (2010). Reaching toward an evidence base for reflective supervision. *Zero to Three Journal, 31*(2), 39–45.

Emde, R. N. (1991). The wonder of our complex enterprise: Steps enabled by attachment and the effects of relationships on relationships. *Infant Mental Health Journal, 12*(3), 164–173.

Gannon, M. (2016). *Race is a social construct, scientists argue. Scientific American.*

Ghosh-Ippen, C., Noroña, C. R., & Thomas, K. (2012). From tenet to practice: Putting diversity-informed services into action. *Zero to Three Journal, 33*(2), 23–28.

Harrell, S. P. (2000). A Multidimensional conceptualization of racism-related stress: Implications for the well-being of people of color. *American Journal of Orthopsychiatry, 70*(1), 42–47.

Harrell, S. P. (2014). Compassionate confrontation and empathic exploration: The integration of race related narratives in clinical supervision. In C. A. Falender, E. P. Shafranske, & C. J. Falicov (Eds.), *Multiculturalism and diversity in clinical supervision. A competency-based approach* (pp. 83–110). American Psychological Association.

Heller, S. S., & Ash, J. (2016). The provider reflective process assessment scales (PRAS): Taking a deep look into growing reflective capacity in early childhood providers. *Zero to Three Journal, 37*(2), 22–28.

Kelly, D. J., Liu, S., Ge, L., Quinn, P. C., Slater, A. M., Lee, K., Liu, Q., & Pascalis, O. (2007). Cross-race preferences for same-race faces extend beyond the African versus Caucasian contrast in 3-month-old. *Infants, 11*(1), 87–95. https://doi.org/10.1080/15250000709336871

Kelly, D. J., Quinn, P. C., Slater, A. M., Lee, K., Gibson, A., Smith, M., Ge, L., & Pascalis, O. (2005). Three-month-olds, but not newborns, prefer own-race faces. *Developmental Science, 8*(6), F31–F36. https://doi.org/10.1111/j.1467-7687.2005.0434a.x

Lee, K., Quinn, P. C., Pascalis, O., & Slater, A. (2013). Development of face processing abilities. In P. D. Zelazo (Ed.), *Oxford handbook of developmental psychology* (Vol. 2, pp. 338–370). Oxford University Press.

Lekas, H.M., Pahl K., & Fuller Lewis, C. (2020, December 20). Rethinking cultural competence: Shifting to cultural humility. *Health Serv Insights, 13*, 1178632920970580. https://doi.org/10.1177/1178632920970580. PMID: 33424230; PMCID: PMC7756036.

McIntosh, P. (2015). Extending the knapsack: Using the white privilege analysis to examine conferred advantage and disadvantage. *Women & Therapy, 38*(3–4), 232–245.

Morris, J. A., Brotheridge, C. M., & Urbanski, J. C. (2005). Bringing humility to leadership: Antecedents and consequences of humility. *Human Relations, 58*(10), 1323–1350.

Noroña, C. R., Heffron, M. C., Grunstein, S., & Nalo, A. (2012). Broadening the scope: Next steps in reflective supervision training. *Zero to Three Journal, 33*(2), 29–34.

Osofsky, J. (2011). *Clinical work with traumatized young children.* Guilford Publications.

Osofsky, J. D., & Lieberman, A. F. (2011). A call for integrating a mental health perspective into systems for care for abused and neglected infants and young children. *American Psychologist, 66*(2), 120–128.

Patterson, K. (2012). *Crucial conversations: Tools for talking when stakes are high.* McGraw-Hill.

Pawl, J. H., & St. John, M. (1998). *How you are is as important as what you do in making a positive difference for infants, children, and families.* National Center for Infants, Toddlers and Families.

Schafer, W. (2007). Models and domain of supervision and their relationship to professional development. *Zero to Three Journal, 28*(2), 9–16.

Shahmoon-Shanok, R. (2009). What is reflective supervision? In S. S. Heller & L. Gilkerson (Eds.), *A practical guide to reflective supervision* (pp. 7–24). Zero to Three.

Shea, S. E. (2019). Reflective supervision for social work field instructors: Lessons learned from infant mental health. *Clinical Social Work Journal, 47*, 61–71.

St. John, M. S., Thomas, K., & Noroña, C. R. (2012). Infant mental health professional development. *Zero to Three Journal, 33*(2), 13–22.

Thomas, K., Noroña, C. R., & St. John, M. S. (2019). Cross-sector allies together in the struggle for social justice: Diversity-informed tenets for work with infants, children, and families. *Zero to Three Journal, 33*(2), 23–28.

Watson, C. (2016). Using the reflective interaction observation scale as a framework for defining infant mental health reflective supervision. Alliance for the Advancement of Infant Mental Health Annual Retreat. Phoenix, AZ.

Watson, C., Harrison, M., Hennes, J., & Harris, M. (2016). Revealing the space between: Creating an observation scale to understand infant mental health reflective supervision. *Zero to Three Journal, 37*, 12–19.

Weatherston, D. J., & Barron, C. (2009). What does a reflective supervisory relationship look like? In S. S. Heller & L. Gilkerson (Eds.), *A practical guide to reflective supervision* (pp. 61–80). Zero to Three.

Weatherston, D. J., & Ribaudo, J. (2020). The Michigan infant mental health home visiting model. *Infant Mental Health Journal, 41*(2), 166–177.

Weatherston, D. J., & Tableman, B. (2015). *Supporting competencies/reducing risks* (3rd ed.). Michigan Association for Infant Mental Health.

Weatherston, D. J., Weigand, R., & Weigand, B. (2010). Reflective supervision: Supporting reflection as a cornerstone for competency. *Zero to Three Journal, 31*(2), 22–30.

Wilson, K., Barron, C., Wheeler, R., & Estele-Avelini Jedrzejek, P. (2018). The importance of examining diversity in reflective supervision when working with young children and their families. *Reflective Practice, 19*(5), 653–665. https://doi.org/10.1080/14623943.2018.1538956

Zeanah, C. H., Jr. (Ed.). (2019). *Handbook of infant mental health* (4th ed.). The Guilford Press.

Chapter 7
Summoning Angels in the Nursery with Hair Combing Interactions

Rhonda Norwood

Introduction

Although it is widely known that attachment quality is dependent on the parent or primary caregiver's responses to the infant's needs and cues (Ainsworth et al., 1978), it is often very challenging to assist some parents in becoming more sensitive and responsive to their young children. This can be particularly true with dyads involved with the child welfare system who have experienced maltreatment within the context of their caregiving relationships. Complex trauma has been defined as adverse experiences that occur during childhood that are usually ongoing (e.g., persistent maltreatment or neglect), have potential to negatively affect the child's developmental processes, beginning in infancy, and occur within the caregiving context (Ford & Courtois, 2009). Attachment theory provides a salient framework for understanding why complex trauma so profoundly and pervasively affects most children who experience it. In addition to the pervasive nature of complex trauma, which can impact every developmental domain of the growing child, the parent or primary caregiver as the very source of the distress is a fundamental violation of the infant or child's expectation of protection and comfort (Bowlby, 1979).

As a result, maltreated children are more likely to have a *disorganized attachment* (see Cyr, Euser, Bakermans-Kranenburg, & van IJzendoorn for a meta-analysis), which is used to describe the attachment behaviors of young children who exhibit contradictory, undirected, or otherwise odd behaviors (Main & Solomon, 1986) during assessment reunions with the caregiver (Main & Cassidy, 1988). This disorganized classification is associated with having a frightening or frightened parent or primary caregiver, as is often seen in situations involving maltreatment, other violence, or parental unresolved loss (Main & Hesse, 1990; Schuengel et al., 1999).

R. Norwood (✉)
School of Social Work, Louisiana State University, Baton Rouge, LA, USA
e-mail: rhondan@lsu.edu

M. L. Lewis, D. J. Weatherston (eds.), *Therapeutic Cultural Routines to Build Family Relationships*, https://doi.org/10.1007/978-3-030-83726-6_7

The incoherence of the behaviors during the reunion episodes is attributed to the conflict between competing behavioral systems in the young child. Specifically, the child instinctually needs to seek comfort from the parent or caregiver due to the distress of the separation, but the parent or caregiver is also a source of distress or fear. This results in an unsolvable conundrum for the child who needs to simultaneously be near and at a safe distance to the primary caregiving figure (Main & Hesse, 1990). To further complicate the clinical picture of these dyads, infants or very young children with a disorganized attachment are more likely to later develop externalizing behavioral issues than children with secure attachments (Fearon et al., 2010), and their primary caregiving figures are more likely to feel a sense of helplessness as caregivers (Lecompte & Moss, 2014).

In this chapter, I will describe three dyads who were referred for therapy to a forensic infant mental health clinic that provides intervention to very young children and their families who were involved with the child welfare system. These case studies highlight the difficulty of working with dyads with a disorganized attachment. Hair combing interactions (HCIs) were used with each of these dyads to address different issues within these mother–child relationships. All dyads were assessed using several of the relationship-based assessments common in infant mental health (see Larrieu et al., 2019 for a review) with a focus on both mother and child behaviors, their reciprocal interactions, and representations of one another (Stern-Bruschweiler & Stern, 1989).

Case 1: D'Atria[1]

D'Atria was the 18-year-old Black mother of 40-month-old Jakayla, who had been in foster care for approximately 13 months when they were first referred for treatment. Jakayla entered foster care after a neighbor reported that they could hear the young child, 27 months old at the time, crying in the neighboring apartment for hours. When the Police and Department of Children and Family Services (DCFS) responded, they found Jakayla alone, and placed her into foster care. She was taken for a medical evaluation after the foster mother expressed concerns that she cried when she was touched; examination revealed that she had multiple fractures in various stages of healing. D'Atria was found several days later, and she admitted to leaving Jakayla alone, because she was using drugs. She was angry that Jakayla was taken into care and stated, "I left her there because it wasn't safe where I was!" She denied that she had ever physically hurt Jakayla, and she often expressed that, "The doctors got it wrong, ain't nothing wrong with my baby." Although she initially participated minimally in recommended addictive disorders and parenting services, D'Atria began to engage with services and consistently attended her supervised

[1] All names and other personal identifiers included in clinical stories/vignettes in this chapter have been changed to protect privacy and confidentiality.

visitation with Jakayla approximately 9 months into the case. DCFS referred them to the clinic for therapeutic services approximately 2 months later. Their visits were described as "chaotic," and Jakayla was reported to "actively avoid her mother, who then responds to the child in anger." Jakayla was also having significant difficulty with emotional and behavioral regulation in the foster home and at her preschool for several days following each visit with her mother.

In terms of their interactions, Jakayla did indeed avoid her mother physically. She often stood in the corner of the room farthest from her mother's chair, walked around the perimeter of the room to retrieve a toy to maintain maximum physical distance from her, and froze or actively pulled away when her mother tried to engage her.

When Jakayla completed a narrative story stem task (NSST) to assess her representations of relationships, particularly within attachment contexts (Bretherton et al., 1990), her NSST revealed great inconsistencies in her representations and expectations of caregiving behaviors. For example, she enacted scenes with the mother doll driving the car (with the child doll in it) off a cliff, the mother doll stomping on the child doll during a scene that described the family losing the keys, and the mother doll transforming into the "something scary" in a bedtime story. On the other hand, she also enacted scenes when the mother figure was a nurturing, authoritative figure who soothed and bandaged the child doll after hurting her knee, cleaned spilled juice, gently reminded the child doll to be careful, and helped the child doll to search for a lost pet. It was unclear if the 11 months that Jakayla had spent in a sensitive, responsive foster home had been helping her to reconstruct her representations of caregivers or if D'Atria had also provided sufficient moments of sensitive caregiving prior to Jakayla entering care.

D'Atria's assessments likewise revealed several struggles that she had in interacting with Jakayla. She was very abrupt and harsh in her tone and words, often yelling at Jakayla and calling her names at times (e.g., "Girl, you so stupid!"), and she had great difficulty recognizing Jakayla's cues and responding to them. For example, one of the assessment tasks (Crowell and Feldman, 1988) tasks required Jakayla to build a small structure using a model made out of Legos, and Jakayla struggled greatly with this (as would be expected for her age). D'Atria was unable to recognize that she needed help with this, chided her for not being able to get it right, and then took what she had managed to put together and pulled it all apart and laughed at her. Jakayla began to cry and moved away from her mother. At this point, D'Atria seemed genuinely surprised and said, "Oh come on, I was just kidding. Don't be a baby!" D'Atria's parental representations, assessed with the Working Model of the Child Interview (WMCI; Zeanah et al., 1994), also revealed several concerns, and her representations of her child were coded as being *distorted,* with a tendency to be "self-involved." This is a classification given when the majority of responses are more about the caregiver than the child. For example, when D'Atria was asked to describe Jakayla's personality, she responded,

> I don't know. She's cute. You know I was 15 when I had her, and I was just so worried that she'd be ugly. And she was at first. I didn't want to show her to my friends. But I ain't had to worry about that long, 'cause my friends didn't stick around after I had her. My mama

> didn't want us with her either. That bad little thing cried too much, drove me crazy. Everyone was so worried about what I done to her, what about what she done to me? And what about what happened to me when I was little? You wanna talk about abuse, I got it all, but no one worried about me or took me away.

Although the question was about Jakayla's personality, D'Atria briefly referenced Jakayla's physical appearance before pursuing tangents about the problems that Jakayla's birth and crying caused for her. She then seemed to become competitive with Jakayla, comparing her own childhood experiences with Jakayla's and expressing resentment that she was not helped as Jakayla was being helped now. This theme repeated itself throughout the interview and often resurfaced in dyadic and individual sessions that followed.

Therapeutic Visitation

During the first few visits at the clinic, D'Atria often complained about Jakayla not playing with her. She seemed to "tattle" on Jakayla to the clinician. When Jakayla physically avoided her mother, D'Atria sometimes responded with anger, yelling at Jakayla to "Stop being mean!" At other times, she physically grabbed and jerked Jakayla around, forcing her to sit next to her and play with toys. Sometimes she ignored Jakayla completely and focused on her conversation with the clinician, while at other times she tried, unsuccessfully, to make Jakayla laugh by intrusively tickling her or tossing toys at her.

Because of Jakayla's distress during and after the visits, D'Atria's clinician worked with D'Atria individually to try to quickly improve her capacity to be sensitive to Jakayla's needs during the visits. D'Atria agreed to a treatment plan that consisted of elements of a few different interventions. Prior to the visits, Visit Coaching (Beyer, 2008) techniques were used to assist D'Atria in using her strengths to have effective visits. During the visits, which were video-recorded, the clinician primarily used Child Parent Psychotherapy (CPP; Lieberman et al., 2015). D'Atria then remained for an individual session following the visit, and occasionally came in between the weekly visits, to watch the videos and discuss their interactions. During these individual sessions, I provided information about attachment, young children's cues, and assisted D'Atria in identifying Jakayla's needs and developing a repertoire of sensitive responses to those needs. We also spent time discussing D'Atria's own childhood attachment experiences and processing how those experiences were affecting her interactions with Jakayla. With this combination of efforts, I observed some small changes in D'Atria's interactions with Jakayla, but Jakayla continued to avoid interacting with her mother the majority of the visits, often overwhelming D'Atria's developing capacities to regulate her own emotions and behaviors when with Jakayla.

Another barrier to progress was that D'Atria also spent a great deal of time complaining about Jakayla's foster mother, often deflecting conversations about herself to criticize the foster mother. One issue that D'Atria consistently complained about was how the foster mother was styling Jakayla's hair. D'Atria repeatedly made statements like, "I never let her go around looking like that, and y'all think she's a better mom than me?" She sometimes criticized Jakayla's hair during the visits, and she once told Jakayla, "You tell that lady to stop making you so ugly."

D'Atria's *Ghosts*

Fraiberg et al. (1975) used the now well-known metaphor "ghosts in the nursery" to describe the intergenerational effects of psychopathology in caregiving contexts. Specifically, unresolved conflicts from a parent's own childhood can be re-enacted with that caregiver's new baby, causing a self-perpetuating cycle of dysfunction from generation to generation.

D'Atria's struggles to be sensitive with her daughter seemed to be the result of several issues. She reported that she had entered foster care several times as a young child because her mother was "a crack head," and D'Atria did not remember her mother providing much care for her at all. D'Atria was also sexually abused by several different men who her mother allowed in the house. She became pregnant right before her fifteenth birthday, and her mother then surrendered her parental rights so that D'Atria could live in a group home for pregnant teens. D'Atria was typically dismissive of this neglect, abuse, and abandonment, but, at other times, she was very angry that "the system" did not help her like they were now helping Jakayla. This anger was sometimes directed at "the system," but it was also often directed at Jakayla, as if she had somehow prevented her mother's rescue from her abusers.

D'Atria's *Angels*

In contrast to the *ghosts,* "angels in the nursery" are those memories and current experiences that are positive influences for a caregiver and are elicited as an agent of change, providing the parent with hope of a better future with their child (Lieberman et al., 2005). D'Atria did not have many good memories of her mother, nor did she have many memories of her foster homes as her stays with them were typically brief. However, once, during another discussion about Jakayla's hair, she showed me a picture of herself in the 6th grade, and she pointed out how nice her hair looked in that picture:

> D'Atria: That was when I was living with Miss Nellie. Miss Nellie was the nicest foster mom; she was the only one who made sure my hair looked good.
>
> Clinician: Sounds like you have some good memories of living there?
>
> D'Atria: I used to get teased at school, because my hair was never combed. But Miss Nellie did my hair every Saturday morning so that we could go to church the next day. And all those church people would tell me how pretty I was. When I went back home after Miss Nellie, I tried to do my hair like she did.

Further discussions about Miss Nellie revealed that she was the only caregiver that D'Atria believed valued her. She described Miss Nellie as making her favorite foods for dinner, and, when she (often) got into trouble at school, Miss Nellie would tell her, "Now, where's my smart girl? You know better than that, I want you to go back and show everyone how good you can be." But many of her stories about Miss Nellie were about times when she would comb D'Atria's hair, like this one:

D'Atria: We always sat in the living room. She had everything laid out on the footstool next to her, and I sat between her feet. Sometimes we watched tv; she liked all these old, crazy shows, but she would laugh so much, and that would make me laugh. Sometimes she would sing church music to me, and then I heard them in church. That was the only time I've ever been to church. I liked it. But I liked it best when we just talked. I didn't tell her much, but I told her more than anyone I ever did.

Clinician: How do you remember feeling during those times?

D'Atria: Loved.

Clinician: I've noticed that you often comment on Jakayla's hair style. What do you think when you see her hair?

D'Atria: I think she ain't got no style! It's all straggly. Make her look ugly, and my baby ain't ugly.

Clinician: Tell me about when you did Jakayla's hair when she lived with her.

D'Atria: I did it every week. She looking like they do it once a month now. She looked good with me.

Clinician: So, you kept up with it and made sure that she looked good. That's pretty important to you.

D'Atria: Yeah, she must be feeling like they don't like her.

Clinician: So, Miss Nellie always combed your hair, and you enjoyed that time with her. You also said that you felt loved by Miss Nellie. When you see Jakayla's hair not combed, you worry that she is not feeling loved. That she's not feeling like you felt when you were with Miss Nellie?

D'Atria: If they loved her, they wouldn't let her go around looking like that. I know it. I love her, and I always had her looking good.

Clinician: When you talked about Miss Nellie loving you, you gave me a lot of details about the time she spent with you combing your hair, and the things you enjoyed doing together during the combing. You also told me how good you thought your hair looked, but it seems to me that your face just lights up when you talk about laughing, talking, and singing together. So, I'm wondering, do you think your best memories are about how good you looked, or how you felt spending that time with her?

D'Atria: (Long pause) She just made me feel loved. That's the only time I've ever felt that way.

Clinician: Tell me about the time that you spent with Jakayla doing her hair. What was that time like for you?

D'Atria: I don't know. I got excited to do it all the time. I would think about how I was going to fix it, and then I'd buy barrettes and sometimes I'd get ribbons, and I'd get so excited to show her. Sometimes she act like she don't care. And that piss me off. I done spent all this money, and she don't want to do it.

Clinician: How do [you] imagine Jakayla felt during those times you were combing her hair?

D'Atria: Just like she do here- she pulled away from me, fought me.

Clinician: And why do you think she reacted that way?

D'Atria: I keep telling you, she mean.

Clinician: Ok, I hear you. She didn't like it, and she didn't want to do it. But how do you think she *felt* when spending that time with you having her hair combed?

D'Atria: (shrugs her shoulders and looks away)

Clinician: (after a long moment of silence) Do you think she felt the way you felt with Miss Nellie?

D'Atria: No. Jakayla don't love me.

Reflective functioning (Fonagy et al., 2002) is the capacity for a parent or caregiver to understand the infant or child's mental states and recognize that those mental states are different from the caregivers' mental states. Children's well-being is inherently dependent on caregiver reflective functioning as it guides the caregiver's interaction and attunement with the child. Reflective functioning, therefore, is important as it influences the positivity of caregivers' behaviors, particularly in terms of sensitivity to the child, and it affects the child's development in all domains, ability to regulate emotions, attachment security, and development of psychopathology (see Camoriano, 2017 for a review). This excerpt illustrates how D'Atria's unresolved trauma was interfering with her ability to see Jakayla as a separate person with her own needs and feelings. She perceived Miss Nellie to be warm, sensitive, and responsive, and she, therefore, felt loved and valued, worthy of those responses. She, in turn, valued and loved Miss Nellie, and she had great experiences during their HCIs. D'Atria clearly loved and valued Jakayla, and she attempted to recreate her treasured combing experiences with her own daughter, but, given the harsh interactions observed in the visits, it is likely that she was not delivering the same sensitive, nurturing combing experience that she received from Miss Nellie. Although her intentions were good, her capacity for recognizing, understanding, and responding to Jakayla's cues was so impaired that she remained absolutely bewildered by Jakayla's rejection of her and the hair combing.

Clinician: You said that you often felt excited to comb Jakayla's hair. Can you tell me what you imagined that it would be like to comb her hair?

D'Atria: I thought she would love it like I did. I could have sat there for hours. She don't sit at all.

Clinician: What do you think is different?

D'Atria: I liked Miss Nellie, she (Jakayla) don't like me.

Clinician: You said you were in 6th grade when you lived with Miss Nellie. Jakayla was much younger when she lived with you. Do you think that may make a difference?

D'Atria: (Paused) Maybe, I don't know. I would have wanted my mama to comb my hair when I was little though. I would have wanted to look good. But my mama was too mean. If she was even awake long enough to do it, she would've been too mean.

D'Atria was convinced that the problems in her relationship with Jakayla were the result of Jakayla not liking her, for some reason unknown to her. In asking the guided question about developmentally appropriate expectations regarding a toddler's ability to sit still compared with that of a 12-year-old, I wanted to test her openness to considering alternatives to explain Jakayla's behaviors, particularly those alternatives that would help D'Atria to recognize and join with Jakayla's subjective experiences. D'Atria's response was encouraging in that she did consider the effects of Jakayla's age. Although she quickly continued to compare herself with Jakayla, she also added a memory of negative interactions with her biological mother. While this may have been a logical entry point to discuss how her mother's harsh behavior made her feel and attempt to then connect that to her own harsh interactions with Jakayla, I doubted that D'Atria could handle that discussion at this early point in her therapy.

I felt hopeful that we could continue to work on her representations of Jakayla and of herself as a parent, as we were trying to do with the dyadic CPP sessions, but I now wondered if incorporating HCIs into sessions, specifically eliciting the *Angel*-effects of Miss Nellie, would help D'Atria to develop sensitivity to Jakayla's needs and boost her confidence as she became more competent in responding to Jakayla appropriately.

Clinician: You felt very loved and cared for with Miss Nellie combing your hair, and you want Jakayla to have those same experiences with you, right? (Note: So far, D'Atria was primarily focused on her own needs and experiences when interacting with Jakayla. I used statements like these to try to reframe and refocus D'Atria on Jakayla's experiences and needs.)

D'Atria: Right, but it ain't going to happen.

Clinician: Well, I can't say for sure if it will definitely happen, but it seems like it may be worth a try. What do you think about us spending some time in your visits with you combing her hair? What would that be like for you?

D'Atria: Frustrating! She ain't going to sit there.

Clinician: Well, I agree that she probably wouldn't sit there if we just brought her in here right now and asked her to have her hair combed, but I'm wondering if you and I can't come up with a gradual plan to have her feel more comfortable with you combing her hair?

D'Atria: I don't know how to do that, but I'll try.

With this agreement, we planned to focus on increasing Jakayla's comfort with physical proximity. Although video review of dyadic interventions is very often used in infant mental health, D'Atria had refused to watch any of the videos of her visits with Jakayla up until this point. With hair combing as the new goal, though, D'Atria agreed to watch some of the videos as an investigative mission of discovering what Jakayla liked and did not like. In these first review sessions, I heavily edited several videos so that we could initially focus only on moments that were less negative (at this point, there were very few positive interactions). D'Atria seemed to enjoy these sessions, and she soon began to start the individual sessions with comments like, "Did you see when Jakayla grabbed those blocks and moved away from me, and I just sat there and still talked to her? She kept getting closer to me, and then she handed me a block. I couldn't believe it."

With each visit, D'Atria became a bit less intrusive and harsh, and Jakayla cautiously began to engage with her mother a bit more often. When D'Atria began to react negatively to Jakayla, she was able to "hear" the clinician speaking for Jakayla and adjust her behavior better and better over time. As she was making improvements in her interactions, we were able to begin to watch the good, the bad, and the ugly in the video reviews. Our conversations connected the present interactions with D'Atria's experiences with her own childhood ghosts; as D'Atria began to understand herself more within the context of being an abandoned, maltreated child who now had an abandoned, maltreated child, we were able to elicit those angels to look to the future.

Jakayla was now better tolerating physical proximity to her mother. We started to gradually get Jakayla closer to her by reading books or playing with toys that required closeness, and then D'Atria began to slowly touch Jakayla more often. At this point, D'Atria relied heavily on me for encouragement with these touches. She had begun to think about how her actions affected Jakayla, but she still did not trust herself to know how to interact with her. She became fairly adept at reading my subtle signals to her during the sessions, and we would use this new skill to become better at reading Jakayla's cues as we started the hair combing. D'Atria did have many moments of frustration with this slow process, but I allowed her plenty of time to vent in her individual session to prevent angry outbursts in front of Jakayla. We also continued to use video reviews to highlight the positive ways that Jakayla was responding to her mother's interactions to encourage and motivate D'Atria to continue to work toward the goal.

Hair Combing

Like D'Atria had been doing in the visit coaching, we planned every detail of the first HCI prior to that session. Because we could not predict Jakayla's responses, and D'Atria still struggled with her own emotional regulation and outbursts, we spent quite a bit of time on "worst-case" scenarios and contingency plans. Similarly, I repeatedly reminded her of the goals of this first session, which was to focus on Jakayla's cues and to respond to them, rather than to complete a style or add predetermined accessories. Finally, we focused on keeping this interaction into perspective; should the worst-case scenario occur, both D'Atria and Jakayla would be safe, and there would be more opportunities to improve.

When Jakayla entered the visit this session, we spent a few minutes interacting and following Jakayla's lead as usual. Once Jakayla settled to play near her mother, D'Atria then began to touch Jakayla's hair, eventually stroking it. She then asked Jakayla if she could comb it "just a little bit," and Jakayla immediately froze and looked at this clinician. D'Atria noticed this, and she told Jakayla, "Mama used to be mean when combing your hair, but I'm different now. It's gonna be soft, and you can tell me to stop and I will." I reflected on both D'Atria's words and Jakayla's posture; Jakayla did continue to sit next to her mother, so D'Atria took the comb and slowly approached Jakayla. We had set up a mirror in front of them so that D'Atria could closely watch Jakayla's responses, but D'Atria seemed to avoid looking at her. She was also very tense. She gingerly touched her hair with the comb a few times, and Jakayla sat there and stared ahead. D'atria barely combed a few strands, and then she said, "That's good, let's play." Both were fairly quiet as they set up a doll house, but they slowly resumed their normal level of play within approximately 15 minutes.

In the individual session following, D'Atria avoided eye contact and was quiet. When asked how she felt about the HCI, she shrugged her shoulders.

Clinician: You seemed fairly tense. How were you feeling?
D'Atria: (Long pause). Scared.
Clinician: What was going through your mind?

D'Atria: (Long pause, and she began to cry). I thought, if I mess this up, she ain't never going to love me.

Clinician: Do you think you messed it up?

D'Atria: I didn't do nothing wrong, but I didn't comb it all the way. I was too scared.

Clinician: This is the first time I've seen you cry. It is very scary to think that your child may not love you.

D'Atria: (Nods her head).

Clinician: Remember when we talked about Miss Nellie; you would have loved her even if she never combed your hair so pretty, right?

D'Atria: Yeah, 'cause she loved me.

Clinician: And do you love Jakayla?

D'Atria: Yeah (cries more).

Clinician: I think some of what made you tense is how Jakayla didn't seem very comfortable with this, what do you think?

D'Atria: Yeah, I thought she was going to run away at first, but she stayed there.

Clinician: We have been taking baby-steps all along to help Jakayla feel comfortable, because that's what she needs, right? To me, it looked like you were working so hard to understand what she wanted and needed, and I think you did that beautifully because you were able to see that she wasn't completely comfortable. So, I know you think that you were too scared to comb her hair completely, but it seemed to me that you actually noticed she wasn't totally comfortable, and you understood that forcing her to do more than she could handle would be stressful for her. So, it seems to me like you just did everything that we've been practicing together. What do you think?

D'Atria: (Long pause) She still wanted to play with me after.

Clinician: And why do you think that was?

D'Atria: I guess she was ok with what I did.

Clinician: Yeah, that's how it looked to me, too. Would she have been ok if you had failed?

D'Atria: (Small smile) No, she's good at lettin' me know when I mess up.

For the next few weeks, we continued to use the video reviews to observe Jakayla's cues, discuss them and appropriate, sensitive responses, and plan for the next HCI. D'Atria's affect improved significantly, and she became more relaxed. This seemed to help Jakayla to be more relaxed, and the HCIs gradually increased in length. D'Atria still focused on the outcome of the hair in the beginning, but she slowly began to focus more on interacting with Jakayla over time; she responded well to this Clinician "speaking" for Jakayla to redirect her when she became too focused on the hair. She initially struggled quite a bit with recognizing Jakayla's cues, and she still often struggled to regulate her own responses when Jakayla pulled away from her. There were a few interactions that this clinician facilitated ending with statements like, "This is really hurting my head mommy, I think we need a break today." These instances became much fewer over time, and D'Atria soon began to speak for Jakayla, also, with statements like, "Ouch, that hurt," and "You don't want to do anymore today." D'Atria, remarkably, was always able to end the HCIs quickly, although she still shared frustration in her individual sessions about these times.

After approximately 6 full HCIs, Jakayla began to talk to her mom a bit more while having her hair combed. When they played together during the last few months, Jakayla's talk centered around the play, particularly in telling her mother how she wanted her to play. The content of these conversations was much different.

As they continued with the HCIs, Jakayla and D'Atria began to laugh together about things they did in past sessions, and D'Atria would often tell Jakayla about people she remembered, or they would talk about things they wanted to do. Jakayla began to physically relax her back against D'Atria's stomach and chest area, and sometimes D'Atria would absentmindedly stop combing and just snuggle with Jakayla; she occasionally tickled her, still, but Jakayla now seemed to enjoy it, and D'Atria continued to follow her cues about when to stop. D'Atria's and Jakayla's eye contact through the mirror increased significantly, and Jakayla often turned her head around to look up at her mother's face. D'Atria's overt reflection on Jakayla's cues decreased, but her responses to them became more natural and automatic.

In an individual session at this point, D'Atria told me that I could "skip the buttering up, let's just look at what I need to fix." D'Atria often made self-deprecating comments about not finishing high school, and she often stated that she could "never do anything right to make Jakayla happy." We reframed "I can't do this" as "These are things I'm not doing yet." D'Atria's self-confidence had improved so greatly from these HCIs that she began to look forward to mastering new skills. At the end of that same session, D'Atria made these remarks:

D'Atria: You know, I know I gots lots more to do before I get my baby back, but it's like I'm gonna get a new baby back.

Clinician: Yeah? What about her seems like a new baby?

D'Atria: Everything! She likes me now; she has fun with me. She feels happy when she is with me. (Note: D'Atria's talk at this point focused much more often on Jakayla's experiences, rather than her own at this point, demonstrating that her capacity for reflective functioning had improved.)

Clinician: Yeah, she definitely seems more relaxed and likes to spend time with you. What do you think caused that change?

D'Atria: (Long pause). I did.

Clinician: How so?

D'Atria: I started listening to her. I didn't know she had so much to say before, you know? I just thought she was a baby, and I was the mama, and she'd just love me. And when she didn't love me or listen to me, I got mad, and then I guess I scared her. But she ain't scared of me no more.

Clinician: No, she seems to enjoy being with you. And how do you feel the hair combing is going? Is it like you imagined?

D'Atria: I ain't no Miss Nellie, but I'm getting close.

Case 2: K'atrice

K'atrice was a 6-year-old Black girl who had been in foster care since she was 18 months old. Her history was described in detail in a previous publication (Lewis & Norwood, 2019), but, briefly, she witnessed significant domestic violence, which resulted in severe brain damage to her unborn sister, who died a year after she was born. K'atrice continued to have many more adverse experiences in the foster care system, and, as she was shuffled from foster home to foster home, her emotional and behavioral dysregulation worsened significantly. Each of these foster homes was with Black foster mothers. At the time of referral, K'atrice was in her 6th placement (and her 8th placement, as she was removed and then replaced in the same home); this placement, however, was with a White foster mother, Susan, and a diverse family. K'atrice finally began to receive appropriate behavioral health services and, more importantly, sensitive and nurturing care from her foster mother. This was a preadoptive placement, but there were significant concerns regarding K'atrice's behavior that may have jeopardized the adoption.

When K'atrice first arrived at Susan's home, her hair was shoulder-length and chemically straightened. Susan complained that it was "breaking off" due to damage from the chemicals; she brought K'atrice to a salon that specialized in Black hair, and she was reportedly told to "cut it all off and let it go natural so she can start over." They cut K'atrice's hair until it was about an inch in length, and it was now curly. Susan sent pictures to the DCFS workers, CASA volunteer, and this clinician, writing, "We've gone natural!! We both love her new 'do,' it feels so much healthier!" Shortly after that email was sent, DCFS called this clinician and stated that Susan had violated their policy on significantly changing a child's appearance without permission, and they were now going to immediately move K'atrice to a new home as a result.

At this point, K'atrice had been with Susan for several months, and we were just starting to see improvements in her behavior. I called DCFS and asked them to reconsider their decision, and they agreed to postpone the move until we could have a meeting. During this meeting, it was clear that their intense reaction to Susan's actions was not about their policy (which I had never seen enforced before), but, rather, their deep concern about the effect such a drastic haircut may have on K'atrice. The DCFS worker and supervisor had known and worked with K'atrice for many years, and her worker said, "K'atrice was so proud of her hair, it was her crown. How could Susan have done this? How can we trust that Susan will do what is good for K'atrice if she didn't even think about what this would do to her?" After a long meeting, during which they shared all their concerns, it was clear that they not only cared about K'atrice as a child, but they felt very protective of her as Black child (both the worker and the supervisor were Black). They agreed to allow K'atrice to stay with Susan only on the condition that Susan received "sensitivity training about Black girls' hair." They had no such services to offer, of course, so I, a White clinician, consulted with Dr. Lewis and met individually with Susan several times to discuss.

At this point in treatment, K'atrice was voicing many self-deprecating comments about her skin color, rejecting black dolls in play, and often wishing aloud that she could be White. We had recently begun working in a variety of ways to keep K'atrice connected to her race and culture (see Lewis & Norwood, 2019 for summary of activities), but this incident with the hair-cutting was an opportunity to strengthen the benefits of those activities. Susan had often met individually with this clinician to discuss K'atrice's behaviors and to brainstorm new responses. She was generally open to trying new interventions, she was consistent with attempts, and she was always motivated to do "anything needed" to help K'atrice to heal from her traumatic experiences. She struggled, however, with the disciplinary actions that DCFS initiated because of the hair cut:

> Susan: I just don't get it. I talked to everyone I know, I brought her to the salon, they all said the same thing. 'You have to cut it off to get it healthy again!' How can they think that this is harmful? How can they think that I would do anything to hurt her? After all I've done for her, and all I've done for my other kids I've adopted? I'm a good mother!
>
> Clinician: So, their reaction made it seem like they thought you were being a bad mother?
>
> Susan: What else could it mean? They practically accused me of child abuse!
>
> Clinician: They did have a very strong reaction. Honestly, at first, it shocked me that, after all the different homes and maltreatment K'atrice has experienced, they would consider moving her again when she is just now starting to improve. I initially thought that was incredibly insensitive of them. But then I had the chance to listen to them, and I actually understood that they were being very sensitive to her feelings and experiences, but they were paying attention to her experiences as a Black child in a White home, and a fairly White community. It was clear that they were worried that a White mother can't help K'atrice to love her skin and hair, and I think they felt this haircut on a personal level.
>
> Susan: Ok, so they're going to send her back to another Black foster home? They couldn't find one that worked, remember? Half of them literally abused her. How can they think me cutting her hair is worse than that? Plus, K'atrice even told you, she *likes* her new 'do. She was so happy to not have her hair break off anymore!

K'atrice had, in fact, told this clinician that she liked her new hairstyle. However, she was so invested in staying in Susan's home that she likely would not have expressed any dissatisfaction to Susan or this clinician. Her comment about her hair also seemed to parrot what Susan had been saying: "I like my short hair, it's healthy, and now I can grow it long again."

In addition to therapy to address K'atrice's dysregulation, Susan and I were working together to help K'atrice to feel more accepting of her skin color. Susan had been making great efforts to be "color blind" to all the kids in her home, who were of diverse races and had varying physical abilities. She often made well-intentioned statements like, "We are all the same," "I don't see any differences in any of us," and "Everyone is beautiful." We hypothesized that K'atrice may be rejecting her skin color, because she was trying so hard to be accepted by Susan, so we began to work on *acknowledging, accepting, and loving* differences, rather than acting like they did not exist. With the hair cutting incident, I wondered if adding HCI to the interventions may strengthen Susan's ability to talk about and accept the differences, which may lead to K'atrice beginning to value them.

Susan began to have individual time with K'atrice every evening as she combed her hair. They talked about a variety of things during these moments, and, over time, K'atrice became more accepting of her skin color. She progressed from using overtly rejecting statements ("When I go to heaven, I'll be White") to rehearsed platitudes such as, "We all have different skin, and we are all beautiful," to eventually choosing to play with Black dolls without any hesitation, as if it were now perfectly natural. Months later, Susan and I were reflecting on the progress that K'atrice had made, and Susan said,

> It's crazy. We've done so many different things, and I can see where everything helped with different issues. But you know, after we talked about the haircut and how it might have affected her, I noticed that I was always touching the other kids' hair, but I never touched

> hers. I think that was partly because it was so damaged, but I also have just felt, you know, clueless about what to do with her hair. I guess I felt incompetent. Looking back, I wonder if she knew that? I think by us having this time every day, it gave her some special time that she really needed that I didn't always get to give her, because there's always so much to do with all the kids. But making this time for her I think made her feel special. And I think she now thinks she has special hair because she gets this special time! I brush the other kids' hair, but I can just brush theirs until it looks brushed, and we rock and roll within just a few minutes, so it's not the same as us sitting there and talking like I get to do with K'atrice. And now I catch myself stroking her hair just as much as the others. I've always been affectionate with all the kids, but it seems like this is, um, I don't know how to name it, but it's just different. It's nice. And I think she just feels like she's more my kid now, you know?

Case 3: Keisha and Derrion

Keisha and her 4-year-old son, Derrion, were referred to treatment due to Derrion's aggressive behaviors. Derrion was in foster care for the second time after Keisha abandoned him and his sister at a hospital. She did this twice within the last year, thinking that the state's *Safe Haven* law allowed for children to be dropped off for a while until she felt like she could take care of them again. After the second time, though, DCFS kept the children in foster care to provide more services to the family to prevent Keisha from feeling so overwhelmed again.

DCFS staff noted that Keisha "seems to be afraid of Derrion. He yells at her, hits her, and throws things at her. She seems helpless to control him." Assessments revealed that Keisha had a long history of being in violent relationships, and her perceptions of Derrion reflected this. When asked about his personality, Keisha said, "He's just like his dad. I thought his dad was going to kill me, and it took me a long time to leave him. That's the first time I dropped the kids off at the hospital. But now I think Derrion might kill me when he gets older. And he's getting bigger and bigger." During the interaction assessments, Derrion had a consistently negative affect with his mother. As he struggled with the tasks, he rejected all attempts his mother made to help him, and he often pushed her hands away, yelled at her to "stop!" and threw toys at her. Keisha startled easily, and she nervously laughed and tried to act like the aggression was not happening. These dynamics continued as the dyadic therapy sessions began, and they were generally so stressful for everyone involved that even a social work intern cried after one of the sessions.

Keisha was a naturally sensitive mother even before intervention. She was able to understand his feelings and needs, but she was overwhelmed with the aggression. She participated in a Circle of Security group (Cooper et al., 2005), and she quickly emerged as a leader in that she could recognize what she was doing well and what she was not doing well yet, and she was very vocal about her children's experiences. She soon began to express insight as to why Derrion would act so aggressively, demonstrating that she was able to see him as a young child, rather than the dangerous men she knew. During one session of the group, Keisha said,

> You know, he needs me to be in charge and to take care of him, but I haven't done that. I abandoned him twice! I thought that he would be better off with someone else because I can't do this, so now he can't trust me. And now I feel like he don't need me because he knows he got someone else to take care of him. I want him to know that I'm not going to do that again, but he don't even want to give me a chance, and I don't blame him. Life has been really, hard for me, and when it was the hardest, I left him. I couldn't take care of him when it was so hard, and now he is being so hard. I gotta start showing him that I can do hard now.

Keisha began to reflect more often on Derrion's experiences during these groups and when in dyadic sessions. As a result, Derrion began to attend more to his mother, and his aggression and negative affect decreased slightly. Keisha's interactions, however, were still very "skittish," and she recoiled from him whenever he turned toward her, much in the same way that Jakayla did with her mother. Derrion usually stopped attempting to interact with her after these moments, and his aggression would typically increase immediately after. Being a young child and seeing such fear reflected in one's own mother's eyes during these attempts to engage must have been extremely distressing to Derrion and explained his subsequent behavioral dysregulation. This was something that I wanted to address as quickly as possible, as each fearful interaction seemed to chip away at their relationship and, I could only imagine, Derrion's sense of self.

In considering the major issues (fear of physical safety with proximity and "taking charge"), I proposed that we add HCIs during the therapeutic visitations. This would be a natural task that she would have been doing with him every day, it would create a normal situation that may require a parent to sensitively "take charge" to complete the task, and it would allow for physical proximity that would benefit each of them as they continue to try to recreate their relationship. Prior to trying this in session, Keisha and I discussed what it may be like to do this, and she replied, "I think he's going to take the brush from me and hit me with it!" We developed a plan on how to proceed nonetheless, and Keisha used a combination of skills that she had developed during her treatment to successfully have him sit near her so that she could brush his hair. They were still seated far apart during this first session, and Keisha had to stretch awkwardly to reach his hair. Derrion sat for approximately 30 seconds before he scooted across the room to start playing with a toy. Keisha looked at this clinician and exhaled loudly; she looked as though she had just survived an extremely stressful situation.

Each week, we started the dyadic sessions with these HCIs. There were several times when Derrion refused to sit for the combing; we balanced following his lead and giving Keisha opportunities to take charge throughout the sessions, and, as Derrion became better able to tolerate hearing the few commands Keisha gave him, and Keisha became more skillful at following through with her commands, Keisha began to insist that Derrion first sit with her for a few minutes at the beginning of each session to comb his hair.

While completion of the hair combing took less than a minute, Keisha began to feel more comfortable during these sessions, and they naturally began to last longer. Derrion began to sit closer and closer to her, and their conversations and joking with one another seemed to become easier for each of them. During one session, approximately three months after starting the HCIs, Derrion moved to Keisha's lap, where he remained for quite some time after the HCI had ended. As we later reviewed the video of that session after Derrion had left, I asked Keisha what that was like for her:

> At first, I was just like, 'Oh crap, what do I do now?' I didn't want to do anything to make him want to leave, I was excited, and I was scared. So, I just played it cool, and I think it all worked out.

As we continued to watch the video, I pointed out how Keisha stopped brushing his hair but continued to touch him; she was rubbing his arms, and, at one point, she embraced him for a moment. I asked her what that was like and she paused and started to cry, before saying, "I just never realized how small he is. He's just a little kid, he's my baby. And he needed me, he's always needed me."

Discussion

The degree of emotional attunement between the caregiver and child that occurs within the attachment relationship is the foundation for the child's internal working model, which then influences the young child's ability to self-regulate behaviorally and emotionally, develop trusting relationships with others, and develop a sense of self-worth. Complex trauma negatively impacts the child's ability to accomplish these developmental tasks, since the caregiver, who should be a "safe haven" for the child, is the very source of the distress. When dyads who have been affected by complex trauma are referred for treatment, the interactive behaviors of both the child and caregiver, along with their representations of one another and the attachment relationship, should all be considered as possible targets for intervention. There are numerous interventions that address one or more of these targets to varying degrees. This chapter has summarized three unique situations in which HCIs were effective at addressing these different elements of attachment relationships to improve the emotional attunement, reflective functioning, and coregulating of interactive behaviors between these dyads.

The cultural significance of hair combing for Black families has been discussed in earlier chapters of this book. It is this unique aspect of HCIs that made this intervention such an effective addition to standard infant mental health interventions for the 3 dyads described above. Like many Black women, D'Atria had very fond memories of having her hair combed by a loving, sensitive caregiver. We were having limited success with improving D'Atria's capacity for reflective functioning and decreasing her harsh caregiving behaviors until we specifically summoned this *angel* into her interactions with Jakayla. She was so motivated to share this nurturing experience with her own daughter that she became more receptive to intervention. We were able to use this simple, everyday task as a medium through which D'Atria was able to practice reading Jakayla's cues, mentalizing Jakayla's experiences when interacting with her, and responding more sensitively to Jakayla's needs. This experience gave D'Atria the hope that she could be a "Miss Nellie" to her own daughter, and we were able to begin a new self-perpetuating cycle of sensitivity and responsivity.

K'atrice was already in a sensitive, nurturing caregiving relationship with her adoptive mother, Susan, but the effects of her trauma were still evident in her emotional dysregulation, particularly in relation to her rejection of her own skin color. Susan loved K'atrice as her own child, but K'atrice had immense anxiety about their racial differences. Susan, with good intentions, tried to reassure K'atrice that those differences were not important, which may have led K'atrice to believe that, because of the way she looked, she was not important. As an extension of her skin, we were able to use hair combing to assist Susan and K'atrice with connecting with one another through this process that is so important to K'atrice's race and culture, thereby helping both K'atrice and Susan to accept and celebrate their racial differences. One can hope that this intervention will also help K'atrice as she engages in the same, daily hair combing one day with her own children.

While most HCI literature focuses on women and their daughters, I also illustrated how HCIs can be used with males, as well. Infants are primed to interact with their caregivers from birth, and the importance of physical touch, along with eye contact and face-to-face and vocal interactions, has also been well documented to impact infants' ability to regulate their emotions (Fonagy et al., 2002; Sroufe, 1997; Stern, 1998), affect their attachment relationships (Beebe & Lachmann, 2002; Bowlby, 1979; Tronick, 2003), and influence the development and functioning of the brain (Gunnar & Barr, 1998). Infant massage, for example, has long been used as an effective intervention with dyads in improving interactions and reducing crying (Field et al., 1996), among other outcomes, and is a traditional practice in many cultures and countries (Field et al., 1996). HCIs can offer similar opportunities for the caregiver and child to connect with one another physically, with the added benefit that it can be done with a child of any age. Derrion and Keisha were struggling, significantly, in their interactions with one another. Keisha was unable to feel safe when Derrion was near her, and Derrion's physical aggression was exacerbated by his mother's continued fear of him. HCIs in a supportive environment were an effective medium in which Keisha was able to become more comfortable with touching Derrion, and the physical interactions allowed her to finally *see* him as a small, vulnerable child, rather than as a threat. They also allowed her to appropriately take charge of his behavior when needed. These changes in Keisha, in turn, allowed Derrion to see his mother as someone who enjoyed him, rather than fearing him, and as someone who could manage his behaviors, which must have relieved his anxiety about being the monster he previously saw reflected in her eyes as she tried to interact with him.

All three of these mothers made assumptions about their children's mental states and acted accordingly on those assumptions, with D'Atria's and Keisha's assumptions being significantly distorted, which resulted in significant dysfunction in their interactions. Their HCIs were brief moments that encouraged them to wonder (Fonagy et al., 2002; Shai & Belsky, 2011) about their children's experiences (and their own influence on their children's experiences), giving them an opportunity to adjust their assumptions and their resulting interactions in a supportive environment. Although many interventions can effectively target the mental states and interactive behaviors of infant–caregiver dyads, thereby improving the sensitivity and responsivity of caregivers, HCIs can offer some of these same benefits but through a medium that also supports cultural traditions of Black communities, acceptance of racialized physical features (Lewis, 2013), and improvement in racial identity and self-concept (Lewis, 1999). Although the need for sensitive and responsive caregiving is universal, it is important for clinicians to recognize that the *angels* we should elicit to positively impact these dyads are transmitted from generation to generation in different ways, and HCIs may be an effective way to do that for many Black dyads.

Reflective Questions

1. What thoughts and feelings were aroused, personally and professionally, when reading these powerful vignettes about D'Atria and Jakayla, K'atrice and Susan, and Keisha and Derrion?
2. After reading this chapter, can you reflect on your own experiences or emotional responses regarding hair combing, hair styling, hair texture, or skin color?
3. How can self-awareness increase your professional capacity to engage, respond with empathy, and work effectively with a family whose culture, race, or ethnicity is different from yours?
4. In what ways might you use HCI to observe, understand, and create a relationship-centered intervention where you explore with parents their "angel in their nursery?"

References

Ainsworth, M. D., Blehar, M. C., Waters, E., & Wall, S. (1978). Patterns of attachment: Assessed in the strange situation and at home. *Infant Mental Health Journal, 1*(1). https://doi.org/10.1002/1097-0355(198021)1:1<68::AID-IMHJ2280010110>3.0.CO;2-3

Beyer, M. (2008). Visit coaching: Building on family strengths to meet children's needs. *Juvenile and Family Court Journal, 59*(1), 47–60. https://doi.org/10.1111/j.1755-6988.2007.00004.x

Beebe, B., & Lachmann, F. (2002). Organizing Principles of Interaction from Infant Research and the Lifespan Prediction of Attachment: Application to Adult Treatment. *Journal of Infant, Child, and Adolescent Psychotherapy, 2*(4), 61–89. https://doi.org/10.1080/15289168.2002.10486420

Bowlby, J. (1979). The making & breaking of affectional bonds. London: Tavistock Publications.

Bretherton, I., Ridgeway, D., & Cassidy, J. (1990). Assessing internal working models of the attachment relationship: An attachment story completion task for 3-year-olds. In M. T. Greenberg, D. Cicchetti, & E. M. Cummings (Eds.), *The John D. and Catherine T. MacArthur Foundation series on mental health and development. Attachment in the preschool years: Theory, research, and intervention* (pp. 273–308). University of Chicago Press.

Camoirano, A. (2017). Mentalizing makes parenting work: A review about parental reflective functioning and clinical interventions to improve it. *Frontiers in Psychology, 8*(14), 1–12. https://doi.org/10.3389/fpsyg.2017.00014

Crowell, J. A., & Feldman, S. S. (1988). Mothers' internal models of relationships and children's behavioral and developmental status: A study of mother-child interaction. *Child Development, 59*(5), 1273–1285. https://doi.org/10.1111/j.1467-8624.1988.tb01496.x

Cooper, G., Hoffman, K., Powell, B., & Marvin, R. (2005). The circle of security intervention: Differential diagnosis and differential treatment. In L. J. Berlin, Y. Ziv, L. M. Amaya-Jackson, & M. T. Greenberg (Eds.), *Enhancing early attachments: Theory, research, intervention, and policy* (pp. 127–151). Guilford Press.

Cyr, C., Euser, E. M., Bakermans-Kranenburg, M. J., & Van IJzendoorn, M. H. (2010). Attachment security and disorganization in maltreating and high-risk families: A series of meta-analyses. *Development and Psychopathology, 22*(1), 87–108. https://doi.org/10.1017/s0954579409990289

Fearon, R. P., Bakermans-Kranenburg, M. J., van Ijzendoorn, M. H., Lapsley, A. M., & Roisman, G. I. (2010). The significance of insecure attachment and disorganization in the development of children's externalizing behavior: A meta-analytic study. *Child Development, 81*(2), 435–456. https://doi.org/10.1111/j.1467-8624.2009.01405.x

Field, T., Grizzle, N., Scafidi, F., Abrams, S., & Richardson, S. (1996). Massage therapy for infants of depressed mothers. *Infant Behav. Dev. 19,* 107–112.

Fonagy, P., Gergely, G., Jurist, E. L., & Target, M. (2002). *Affect regulation, mentalization, and the development of the self.* Other Press.

Ford, J., & Courtois, C. A. (2009). Defining and understanding complex trauma and complex trauma stress disorders. In C. A. Courtois & J. Ford (Eds.), *Treating complex traumatic stress disorders: An evidence-based guide* (pp. 13–30). Guilford Press.

Fraiberg, S., Adelson, E., & Shapiro, V. (1975). Ghosts in the nursery: A psychoanalytic approach to the problems of impaired infant-mother relationship. *Journal of the American Academy of Child Psychiatry, 14*(3), 387–421. https://doi.org/10.1016/S0002-7138(09)61442-4

Gunnar, M. R., & Barr, R. G. (1998). Stress, early brain development. *Behavior, Infants & Young Children, 11*(1), 1–14.

Larrieu, J. A., Middleton, M. A., Kelley, A. C., & Zeanah, C. H., Jr. (2019). Assessing the relational context of infants and young children. In C. H. Zeanah Jr. (Ed.), *Handbook of infant mental health* (4th ed., pp. 279–296). The Guilford Press.

Lecompte, V., & Moss, E. (2014). Disorganized and controlling patterns of attachment, role reversal, and caregiving helplessness: Links to adolescents' externalizing problems. *The American Journal of Orthopsychiatry, 84*(5), 581–589. https://doi.org/10.1037/ort0000017

Lewis, M. L. (2013). Black mother-daughter interactions & hair combing rituals. In H. Jackson-Lowman (Ed.), *Afrikan American Women: Living at the crossroads of race, gender, class, and culture* (pp. 345–368). Cognella Press.

Lewis, M. L. (1999). The hair-combing task: A new paradigm for research on African-American mother-child interaction. *The American Journal of Orthopsychiatry, 69*, 504–514.

Lewis, M. L., & Norwood, R. G. (2019). "When I go to heaven, I'll be White": The ethics of transracial adoption within the context of childhood trauma and racial identity development. *Zero to Three Journal, 40*(1), 12–21.

Lieberman A. F., Padrón E., Van Horn P., & Harris, W. W. (2005). Angels in the nursery: The intergenerational transmission of benevolent parental influences. *Infant Ment Health Journal, 26*(6), 504–520. https://doi.org/10.1002/imhj.20071. PMID: 28682485.

Lieberman, A. F., Ghosh Ippen, C., & Van Horn, P. (2015). Don't hit my mommy: A manual for Child-Parent Psychotherapy with young children exposed to violence and other trauma (2nd ed.). Zero to Three.

Main, M., & Hesse, E. (1990). Parents' unresolved traumatic experiences are related to infant disorganized attachment status: Is frightened and/or frightening parental behavior the linking mechanism? In M. T. Greenberg, D. Cicchetti, & E. M. Cummings (Eds.), *The John D. and*

Catherine T. MacArthur Foundation series on mental health and development. Attachment in the preschool years: Theory, research, and intervention (pp. 161–182). University of Chicago Press.
Main, M., & Cassidy, J. (1988). Categories of response to reunion with the parent at age 6: Predicted from infant attachment classifications and stable over a 1-month period. *Developmental Psychology, 24*(3), 415–426. https://doi.org/10.1037/0012-1649.24.3.415
Main, M., & Solomon, J. (1986). Discovery of a new, insecure-disorganized/disoriented attachment pattern. In M. Yogman & T. B. Brazelton (Eds.), *Affective development in infancy* (pp. 95–124). Ablex Publishing.
Schuengel, C., Bakermans-Kranenburg, M. J., & Van IJzendoorn, M. H. (1999). Frightening maternal behavior linking unresolved loss and disorganized infant attachment. *Journal of Consulting and Clinical Psychology, 67*(1), 54–63. https://doi.org/10.1037//0022-006x.67.1.54
Stern-Bruschweiler, N., & Stern, D. N. (1989). A model for conceptualizing the role of the mother's representational world in various mother-infant therapies. *Infant Mental Health Journal, 10*(3), 142–156. https://doi.org/10.1002/1097-0355(198923)10:3<142::AID-IMHJ2280100303>3.0.CO;2-M
Stern, D. N. (1998). The Interpersonal World of the Infant: A View from Psychoanalysis and Developmental Psychology. London: Karnac Books.
Shai, D., & Belsky, J. (2011). Parental embodied mentalizing: Let's be explicit about what we mean by implicit. Child Development Perspectives. Wiley Online Library.
Sroufe, A. (1997). Emotional Development: The Organization of Emotional Life in the Early Years.Cambridge: Cambridge University Press.
Tronick, E. Z. (2003). Things still to be done on the still-face effect. *Infancy, 4*(4), 475–482. https://doi.org/10.1207/S15327078IN0404_02
Zeanah, C. H., Benoit, D., Hirshberg, L., Barton, M. L., & Regan, C. (1994). Mother's representations of their infants are concordant with infant attachment classifications. *Developmental Issues in Psychiatry and Psychology, 1*, 9–18.

Chapter 8
The Tilted Room of Colorism

Danielle K. Wright

Collective Shaming

I was a very curious child and during adolescence, I typically exercised my curiosity by being a good listener (during adult conversations) and asking a lot of questions. I can remember a specific conversation I had during adolescence, with one of my mom's dearest friends, Genevieve.[1] Genevieve was reflecting on her first marriage to her college sweetheart. We talked about how they met, how they fell in love, and we somehow landed on the topic of how her parents felt about him. Genevieve shared that her father did not like him and was not supportive of the marriage. I was baffled by this, as I knew Genevieve's first husband, Dr. Landry, and he seemed like a nice man and was a very well-respected dentist in our community. Genevieve went on to share that her father did not want her to marry Dr. Landry, because he thought Dr. Landry was unattractive. I thought this was odd, so I asked, "Well why did he think that?" Her response startled me…she said, "My dad thought he was unattractive, because he is dark skinned, and my dad did not want me to marry a dark-skinned man."

I will never forget how I felt at that moment. It was the first time I had ever heard of a parent disapproving of their child's significant other because of their complexion. I immediately wondered if one day I might encounter a significant other's parents not liking me, because I am dark skinned. Such a thought never crossed my mind prior to this conversation with Genevieve. While the immediate impact of that

[1]All names and other personal identifiers in clinical stories/vignettes in the chapter have been changed to protect privacy and confidentiality.

D. K. Wright (✉)
Navigate NOLA, New Orleans, LA, USA
e-mail: dr.deewright@gmail.com

M. L. Lewis, D. J. Weatherston (eds.), *Therapeutic Cultural Routines to Build Family Relationships*, https://doi.org/10.1007/978-3-030-83726-6_8

conversation was fleeting, I did not realize the kind of seed planted around being perceived as unworthy because of my complexion.

A couple of years later, I was a senior in high school, and I began dating a boy that I really grew to like. A mutual friend found out that we were dating and he told me that the boy's parents would never accept me, because I was too dark. At that moment, I recalled the conversation I had with Genevieve years earlier, and decided that it didn't make sense to continue dating him. I immediately pulled away from the dating relationship and accepted, without even experiencing rejection, that I was too dark.

As people of color, we have experienced the collective trauma associated with aligning ourselves to meet Eurocentric standards of beauty, and reporting that by doing so, we are standing upright. We impose these standards upon others, among our shared race, in the form of colorism, by using proximity to Eurocentric standards of beauty as the barometer for physical attractiveness, privilege, and access. The collective shaming of physical features such as darker hued skin, tightly coiled hair, wide noses, and full lips, gives rise to implications that are so pervasive and enduring that they continue to be perpetuated through intergenerational transmission. This collective shaming is what causes African Americans to align themselves to a tilted room and report themselves as sitting upright.

The Tilted Room Theory

A postcivil war cognitive psychology study employed several situations to investigate the roles of visual and bodily standards in perception of the upright, in an attempt to explore field dependence (Witkin et al., 1975). In one such study, study participants were placed in a tilted chair, situated in a tilted room, and then asked to align themselves vertically (Witkin et al., 1975). In some cases, an individual who tilted as much as 35 degrees, to align themselves with the room, reported being perfectly straight. In other cases, regardless of the position of the surrounding (tilted) room, other individuals adjusted their body to stand upright, despite the tilted room. Borrowing from scholar, political scientist, and professor, Melissa Harris Perry's application of this theory utilized as a lens to explore concepts related to the lived experiences of African Americans, we can use this tilted room theory to explore the concept of colorism and its implications for African Americans (Harris-Perry, 2011). If we apply this theory to colorism, the perceived upright, in this case, represents Eurocentric beauty standards

Self-Awareness as a Tool to Manage Emotions Surrounding Colorism

Given the complex nature of colorism's historical legacy of collective trauma among people of color, it is essential for therapists of color to practice self-awareness to manage their own emotions associated with their individual experiences with colorism. The absence of practicing self-awareness, while doing this work, exacerbates vulnerability to transference and countertransference across the continuum of the therapeutic relationship. Transference is when the patient/client transfers their thoughts or feelings on to the therapist (Hughes & Kerr, 2000). Countertransference is when the therapist transfers their thoughts or feelings on to the patient/client (Hughes & Kerr, 2000).

For example, I was working with a Black grandmother named Mable. Mable was articulating her frustration surrounding her granddaughter Bethany's mom Lisa, not properly grooming Bethany. When I asked Mable to give details, she went on to explain that Lisa does not perm (chemically straighten) or use heat to straighten Bethany's hair, and that she leaves Bethany's hair in an afro. Mable saw this as negligent, and a sign that Lisa did not care. As Mable continued to discuss the issue, she repeatedly made references to me about Bethany not having wash-n-go textured hair, suggesting that if Bethany had a different texture of hair, it would be okay for her to wear it in its natural state. Mable also made several references to me being a black woman and understanding that in order to be perceived as presentable, Bethany's hair needed to be straightened. In this case, Mable was looking to me to validate the ways in which she normalized appropriate hair presentation. Mable broad-stroked me into a category, and decided that because I, too, was a black woman, I subscribed to the same standards of beauty that she did. Mable was also expecting that I would deem Lisa's decision to leave Bethany's hair in its natural state as negligent. When I did not validate Mable's perception of the way that Lisa cared for Bethany's hair as negligent, Mable became frustrated with me.

At that moment, I was certainly bothered by the idea that a mother allowing her child to wear her hair in its natural state was somehow perceived by the grandmother as negligent parenting. However, I was self-aware enough to not impose my anger toward the underlying issue of colorism, to be projected on to an individual. In this case, Mable was a trigger for my larger frustration with colorism. If I would have become angry with Mable, that would have been an example of countertransference.

Practicing self-awareness allows us to expand our capacity to understand how experiences, such as colorism, have impacted us, how they show up in our interactions, and how we can better self-manage the difficult emotions that are cued up when we encounter these experiences.

As a woman of color, I spent most of my childhood dismissing experiences of colorism as ignorant. I convinced myself that my dismissal of colorism was an act of protest. It was my form of sitting upright in a tilted room and refusing to adjust myself to align with the tilted room. I held the opinion that the act of giving colorism any energy at all, further perpetuated within group prejudice, racism, and discrimination. My strategy to maintain my perspective was avoidance. The aforementioned avoidance functions similarly to the guise of color-blindness. In the same ways that the ideology of color blindness upholds racism, in that such a perspective allows individuals in our society to avoid confronting the issue of racism, my avoidance was allowing me to not confront within group prejudice and discrimination on the basis of complexion, hair texture, and facial features. I turned away from those who made hurtful comments about skin color and hair texture, pretending that these things were not happening all around me. I refused to confront the complex interplay of colorism and the impact that it was having on my emotional well-being. This represented years of missed opportunities I had to elevate my voice around my own experience and to create space for others to do the same. As an adult, this avoidance came back to haunt me in my work with children of color and their caretakers. I began to observe harmful experiences of colorism, transmitted intergenerationally from parent to child. Each time I was witness to colorism in my clinical work with families, it felt like gasoline illuminating the little fires all around me. I could no longer ignore those fires as I recognized that standing upright in a tilted room was just as emotionally harmful as adjusting oneself to fit in the tilted room. It became clear that the tilted room was what required the adjustment, not the individual(s) sitting in the room.

Case Study #1

A couple of years ago, I provided clinical support to an organization whose staff worked with African-American girls whose fathers had been incarcerated. I facilitated a series of therapeutic group sessions centered in expanding their capacity to heal themselves through shared identity, shared experiences, and collective power. I divided each group cohort by age; the youngest participants in one cohort ranged from 5 to 7 years old.

Conventional Wisdom gained from over a decade of clinical practice with children experiencing the adverse childhood event of parental incarceration informed my expectations of common emotional and meta-emotional themes among the target population. I envisioned themes such as distrust, betrayal, feeling misunderstood, shame, powerlessness, fear, isolation, loneliness, disconnection, numbness, sadness, disappointment, and hopelessness.

These emotions and meta-emotions place children, with an incarcerated parent, at an increased likelihood to isolate and suffer in silence, subsequently stripping away the opportunity to activate supports that may serve as a buffer to the negative outcomes associated with this adverse childhood experience. As expected, all these themes were present. However, one theme emerged that completely took me by surprise: colorism.

Tully, a 7-year-old program participant, began to talk about experiences of what she referred to as "racism." When prompted to explain the experience by giving examples, Tully stated that sometimes family members and kids at school referred to her as black and nappy headed and made fun of her darker hued skin. Other girls began to share similar experiences. They talked about these experiences in a very normalized way, accepting that if your hair is tightly coiled and your skin is of a dark hue, you are certain to be ridiculed for such characteristics.

As I listened to the girls, in the group, describe these experiences, I felt so many things. I began to worry about how I could give an appropriate clinical response. I wondered if there was a best practice for addressing colorism. In addition to the uncertainty of how to respond, I was also trying to manage intense and negative emotions from my own experiences with colorism that rose up in response to what the girls had shared.

I had been told that my brown skin made me less attractive. My skin color had been used as the barometer for "too dark." I had been ridiculed about my hair texture. I had also observed other individuals having similar experiences. Even in recent years, as an adult, I had a family member say, "During the time that I was growing up, you would not have had access to the privileges that you have enjoyed due to your darker complexion." His statement haunted me for many weeks. It made me feel like I was of less value and less attractive because of my complexion. This painful experience was yet another reminder that we cannot ignore these little fires, because they never go away. They live within us as we navigate throughout life. Although I was an adult when a male family member called out what he saw as a flaw in my darker complexion, it triggered the hurt feelings of a little girl. It was that exact kind of pain that allowed me to connect with the other little black girls sharing similar experiences in the group.

And so, I took a deep breath and began with emotional vocabulary. I first introduced the concept of colorism to the participants, so that moving forward they could identify the appropriate word to articulate their experience. Somehow, giving it a name, felt like the appropriate first step. In doing so, I began to feel a shift in the energy of the room. *Colorism is a collective trauma that all people of color have experienced on some level.* When the girls recognized that the adults in the room shared in some of the same experiences they were currently having, they began to feel understood. Acknowledging that I, too, had been hurt by experiences of colorism and continue to be impacted by its harmful effects as an adult was important to disclose as a facilitator.

The decision to disclose as a facilitator was informed by the tenants of Shawn Ginwright's Healing-Centered Engagement (HCE), a practice that expands how we think about responses to trauma and offers a more holistic, strength-based approach to fostering well-being. HCE advances a collective view of healing, and re-centers culture as a central feature in well-being. As such, I leaned into the capacity to heal through shared identity and shared experiences (Ginwright, 2018). HCE coupled with trauma informed practices presents the opportunity to fill the gaps that exist in trauma informed practices alone. Healing-Centered Engagement advances the importance of community and a sense of belongingness as an essential component to healing (Ginwright, 2018). The approach also recognizes the collective experience of healing and that it is cultivated by shared identity across race, gender, and sexual orientation (Ginwright, 2018). The integration of culturally grounded rituals, through activities rooted in indigenous culture and the sharing of experiences, creates an environment in which black girls can experience healing through interconnectedness (Ginwright, 2018). The choice to disclose as a facilitator was used to facilitate interconnectedness across experiences around colorism and presented a unique educational opportunity to discuss the harmful effects of colorism. It also presented an opportunity to celebrate within group differences across hair texture and skin hue. The girls began to compliment one another's braided and tightly coiled hairstyles and the diverse spectrum of brown hues that were represented in the room. We used this opportunity to push back against the normalization of derogatory comments about dark hued skin, tightly coiled hair, wide noses, and full lips.

Hair Combing Time

Hair combing time, for some African-American mother/daughter dyads, has historically been characterized by stress (Lewis, 2015). In the southern geographic region of the United States, where Jim Crow laws shaped politics of respectability, many African Americans conformed to politics of respectability through physical appearance. The ideological perspective that regarded one's ability to take control of their appearance as a protective factor that could prevent categorizations of negative stereotypes of African Americans was prevalent. Extending beyond this perception of protection from categorizations of negative stereotypes of African Americans, it was also thought to protect us from the inability to acquire a job, to protect us from not being regarded as "respectable," and to protect our sense of safety and security. It gave rise to the distinction between who was physically presenting themselves as "worthy" of respect and who was presenting themselves as unworthy of respect. While this country's legacy of racial terror continues to disprove the theory that presenting yourself as worthy of respect will serve as a protective factor, the underlying idea that worthiness of respect subscribes to a particular standard of appearance prevails. As such, throughout history, African-American women have utilized hair combing time as their opportunity to present their daughters to the world as "worthy" of respect, by achieving a hairstyle that meets the standards of "worthiness." Hair combing time is not simply about personal hygiene, it is about achieving a respectable look. It is through the process of achieving this look that many women of color transfer their own painful experiences of colorism on to their children and cultivate standards of beauty that their children pass down to their own children.

Talk, Touch, and Listen Hair Combing Interaction presents a unique opportunity to dismantle the intergenerational transmission of colorism, by creating new pathways to promote positive self-worth, as it relates to complexion and hair texture. Parents can utilize hair combing time to express positive sentiments about hair texture, during the hair styling process. I have personally observed this intervention transform the self-image of black girls.

Case Study # 2: Aiesha

Years ago, I worked with a mom, Aiesha, who shared that one of her deepest fears for her daughter, Dakota, was that Dakota would feel less attractive, because she did not have long hair. Aiesha stated that as a child, she never had long hair, and that she felt less attractive because of it. Aiesha began to use hair combing time as an opportunity to allow Dakota to tap into her creative expression and assert autonomy over her hairstyles. Dakota would excitedly pick out hairstyles and bows. During the styling process, Aiesha would complement Dakota's hair and express how much she enjoyed this special time spent between the two of them. Once the styling was completed, Aiesha would say, "Wow, you look beautiful." This became a part of their routine, and one day, Dakota beat Aiesha to the compliment and said, "Wow, I look beautiful."

Also during this time, Aiesha made the conscious decision to transition her own hair into natural styles (no heat or chemical straightening), so that she could normalize tightly coiled hair texture in the household. This proved to be beneficial, as Aiesha reported that when she decided to straighten Dakota's hair for the first time, Dakota cried at the sight of the finished product and stated that she wanted her curly hair back. To this end, Aiesha no longer straightens Dakota's hair. She alternates between natural hairstyles (allowing her curls/coils to be free) and braided hairstyles.

The HCI intervention created space for Aiesha to practice self-awareness and reflect on her own personal experiences with colorism and how they impacted her sense of self-worth. In doing so, Aiesha was able to better manage her negative emotions triggered by hair, preventing her from transferring those negative emotions on to Dakota, during hair combing time.

As practitioners of color, creating space for healing through the Hair Combing Interaction intervention, we must also do the deep work of self-awareness, to recognize our own triggers and negative emotions connected to colorism, so that we are less likely to engage in countertransference around the issue of colorism. To create spaces of healing for others, we must do the important work of creating space for our own healing.

Conclusion

The politics of skin tone and hair texture are deeply embedded into the lived experiences of African Americans. These experiences extend beyond the parent child dyad. African-American children encounter these experiences across the various systems with which they interface, such as schools, churches, extra-curricular activities, and social gatherings. These various systems represent the tilted room of colorism. If we are not acknowledging and working to dismantle this tilted room, we are allowing it to perpetuate within group inequities, and subsequently supporting a tilted structure. Addressing the tilted room will require a multi-systems level approach that begins with building connection and positive feelings of self-worth through the parent–child attachment relationship, coupled with community-based training across various systems and directly informing policy level change.

For example, the Crown Act (Creating a Respectful and Open World for Natural Hair) is the first legislation of its kind, prohibiting race-based hair discrimination in schools and workplace (H.R. 5309, 2021). In short, the Crown Act prohibits the denial of employment and educational opportunities because of hair texture or protective hairstyles associated with race. It was passed by the US House of Representatives in 2020. This multi-systems collaboration mobilized community members around the issue of race-based hair discrimination across the following entities: the CROWN Coalition, Dove, National Urban League, Color of Change, and Western Center on Law & Poverty. Working in tandem, across these various levels, is essential to creating real and lasting change.

As we continue to navigate inequities shaped by privilege and access, associated with Eurocentric beauty standards, it will be important to explore opportunities to shape policies that support dismantling colorism. This will be of particular importance in spaces where derogatory statements regarding skin color and hair texture have been normalized. Talk, Touch, and Listen provides a framework for elevating the psychological impact of such derogatory language. The HCI intervention tool is uniquely positioned to address colorism on the parent–child level (intrapersonal and interpersonal level), and has the potential to extend to the community and policy level.

Reflective Questions

1. In the opening paragraph of this chapter, the author shares a story that ends with *My dad thought he was unattractive, because he is dark skinned, and my dad did not want me to marry a dark-skinned man.* As you reflect on this, what stories, thoughts, or feelings – personal or professional – come to mind as they contribute to your own journey to self-awareness?
2. The author invites us to reflect on this: *Hair combing time is not simply about personal hygiene, it is about achieving a respectable look.* By what standard is "respectable" measured against and how does this lead to race--based discrimination?
3. How do you understand the meaning of "the tilted room of colorism" and why is it a powerful phrase, important to your work with children and families of color?
4. How can you bring the construct of colorism to your trainings or teachings or interventions with children and families of color?

References

Ginwright, S. (2018). *The future of healing: Shifting form trauma informed care to healing centered engagement.* Retrieved from https://medium.com/@ginwright/the-future-of-healing-shifting-from-trauma-informed-care-to-healing-centered-engagement-634f557ce69cGoogle Scholar

GovTrack.us. (2021). *H.R. 5309—116th congress: CROWN Act of 2020.* Retrieved from https://www.govtrack.us/congress/bills/116/hr5309

Harris-Perry, M. V. (2011). *Sister citizen: Shame, stereotypes, and Black women in America.* Yale University Press.

Hughes, P., & Kerr, I. (2000). Transference and countertransference in communication between doctor and patient. *Advances in Psychiatric Treatment, 6*(1), 57–64. https://doi.org/10.1192/apt.6.1.57

Lewis, M. L. (2015). Getting the parts straight: The psychology of hair combing interaction between African American mothers and daughters. In K. T. Craddock (Ed.), *Black Motherhoods(s): Contours, contexts, and considerations* (pp. 204–220). Demeter Press.

Witkin, H. A., Moore, C. A., Goodenough, D. R., & Cox, P. W. (1975). Field-dependent and field-independent cognitive styles and their educational implications. *ETS Research Bulletin Series, 1975*(2), 1–64.

Chapter 9
Infant Mental Health Practice and Reflective Supervision: Who We Are Matters

Karol A. Wilson

Introduction

The examination of race and its impact on relationships is a crucial part of working within the Infant and Early Childhood Mental Health (IECMH) service community. It can be challenging to address those parts of ourselves that feel uncertain, painful, or embarrassing as they relate to effective work with very young children and families. It is especially important to feel comfortable sharing our clinical vulnerabilities with another through supervision. To be truly open and honest about one's work and one's response to the work, a supervisee needs to feel assured that the supervisor can honor unique personal experiences without judgment and invite reflection thoughtfully and with sensitivity. Discussions regarding differences, culture, ethnicity, and race, essential to IECMH practice, require special courage and commitment. Some of the language that has been viewed in IECMH work as being attuned may feel dismissive in conversations regarding race and culture. It wasn't until I became a supervisor that I realized that saying, "I can't imagine what this is like for you," can create boundaries between a supervisor and supervisee that shut down honest conversations about cultural experiences, difference, or race. Intended to be supportive and empathetic, the message received may be that our differences are so great that I can't identify with how you might feel. The supervisor and supervisee may wonder how each could possibly understand how the other feels about race or cultural traditions or family values when neither one has had experiences that would have allowed our paths to cross.

As a Black woman, I thought that issues of race, ethnicity, and culture should be private and not necessarily talked about in the workplace. Failure to have coversations about our social identities creates missed opportunities to examine relationships

K. A. Wilson (✉)
Starfish Family Services, Dearborn, MI, USA
e-mail: wilsonkarol726@gmail.com

M. L. Lewis, D. J. Weatherston (eds.), *Therapeutic Cultural Routines to Build Family Relationships*, https://doi.org/10.1007/978-3-030-83726-6_9

whith families being served, colleagues and within RS. Equally important, misunderstandings about race can result in a disruption in the supervisory relationship, and, without an opportunity for repair, leaves the supervisee with regret for having tried to share her story. This parallels how families can feel when they share stories of vulnerability, including trauma, abuse, or neglect, and are not heard or understood. Like families, I felt at times rejected by my supervisor's silence or failure to respond to stories or feelings shared. Wondering if they were too difficult to handle, I tucked the stories away without any further discussion. I later learned, unless tackled, the supervisee will carry this feeling of rejection into future RS relationships and conversations that include race. My hope as a supervisor is to invite reflection and to be brave enough not to sweep these moments under the rug and talk about them. I suggest the following when issues of race, ethnicity, or difference arise in RS:

1. "I don't know what this is like for you, but I do know what it is like to feel judged or misunderstood."
2. "I know what it's like to have assumptions made about me. How can I support you?"
3. "I really want to understand. That sounds hard. I'm sorry that you have been feeling that way."

Unique cultural practices within the Black community have at times been embraced, imitated, misunderstood, and criticized. Hair and hair combing rituals have sparked conversation, admiration, curiosity, and, on occasion, an invasion of personal space. Because rituals and traditions reflect who and how we are, it is imperative to remember their importance. Personal memories, family rituals, and practices can trigger many thoughts and feelings. As well, there is a risk of feeling misunderstood when these moments are explored.

The following story is a personal one, describing an interaction I had with a mother and baby referred to me for IECMH services. I didn't share this experience with any of my previous supervisors. It wasn't until I entered into a relationship with a young white supervisor who was willing to be authentic vulnerable and genuinely interested in who I am, that I began to offer deeper reflections. The relationship we developed proved to be sturdy enough to engage in a conversation about diversity and family rituals. Sharing this story was not easy. I still worried about how my supervisor might perceive my reflections even though that had not been part of our experience together. As a Black woman, I know that Black hair and its history can result in emotionally charged conversations.

My Wonderings

I asked myself, "*Would my White supervisor understand what I had struggled with during that interaction even though it was years ago? Would she recognize it as being important to me? How much grace should I give her if she doesn't understand?*" These questions are important to think about in any RS relationship. As well, "*How much of an investment am I willing to make to deepen the RS experience?*" It would take courage.

The Story of Anita, Kathy, and Me

I am a Black social worker with many years of experience as an Infant Mental Health therapist. At the time this story took place, I was working in an Infant Mental Health (IMH) Home Visiting Program. Anita,[1] a 5-month-old White child and her young mother, Kathy, were referred to me for services. Kathy had been experiencing postpartum depression symptoms that had progressed over time and were making the care of her baby difficult. Kathy described feeling anxious about the increasing demands of having a baby who seemed to need so much. Even though Kathy felt she was developing a routine with her baby, she found herself feeling angry with her baby for wanting to be held, played with, and comforted. She said that she felt that she was responsive to her needs, but did not have the feelings of joy she always imagined having. She said, "I keep waiting for a connection with her that hasn't happened." As I listened to her story, I marveled at her reflective capacity to put into words some of her feelings about mothering and being a mother. After that, her baby, as if having understood her, reached up and touched her face with a chubby hand and a toothless smile. What appeared to be instinctive was Kathy's response, which was to take her baby's hand and gently kiss it.

Witnessing this gesture was comforting to me and gave me hope, but also made me wonder what had been making it hard for Kathy to fully enjoy the relationship that was developing between her and her baby, Anita. As I continued to sit with Kathy and Anita, the baby looked at me as if I had really caught her attention. To me, it felt as if she was taking in my face, my features, my skin, my hair, so unlike her mother's, and she reached out and grabbed one of my dreadlocks. Her grip was strong and determined. She looked very pleased with her accomplishment. I smiled at Anita and was going to pat her hand and note her curiosity, but before I could say anything, her mother grabbed Anita and told her, "You don't do that! I'm sure she doesn't like people touching her hair."

Assumptions: Disruptions and Repair

Mom looked visibly upset and I was taken aback, not understanding the intensity of the exchange. I assured mom that her touching my hair was ok, but her statement about not wanting people touching my hair struck me. I wondered why what I saw

[1] All names and other personal identifiers in the chapter have been changed to protect privacy and confidentiality.

as an innocent interaction caused her so much discomfort. *I wondered, what about me had made her uncomfortable.* Anita, startled by mom's response, began to cry and mom looked annoyed. My own internal working model was telling me there was something odd about my appearance and that even though mom appeared to be very courteous and welcoming initially, she may have been uncomfortable with me as a Black woman. I could feel my body grow tense. I began to feel defensive as I remembered times when I felt misjudged or discriminated against because of how I looked. *I wondered if my feeling was one of anger with myself for forgetting that everyone isn't comfortable with Black people.* I had felt comfortable with her and had assumed that what she had shared meant she was comfortable with me. *At the time, I was flooded with memories of times when I felt rejected.* I also thought about how I felt when I came into her home and sat down to talk with her. The vulnerability she expressed felt genuine. *Thinking now, how could I have been wrong about her when my initial experience felt so genuine?* Holding my initial feelings toward her in mind, I took a deep breath and said, "I noticed your reaction when Anita touched my hair and I'm wondering if you would tell me what you were feeling in that moment."

I braced myself feeling that mom would become defensive and end our visit. I was surprised when tears formed in Kathy's eyes as she said, "I had heard that African Americans don't like for White people to touch their hair, and I didn't want you to be angry and not come back." I was touched by her sensitivity to our differences and by her bravery to bring up race as I assumed this wasn't a topic easily entered into but is so much a part of who we are. Also, I was struck by seeing and understanding how much she needed and wanted support for her and her daughter.

Seeking Understanding

I told her "I thought Anita was just being curious." I said, "My appearance is very different from yours and Anita's, maybe she's trying to make sense of this new person in her space." *I found myself feeling less defensive but still unsettled as I felt there was more to the story, and I wasn't quite sure how to proceed. I was working hard to regulate my own emotions and feelings.* Before I began, I took a deep breath and asked if there was anything else that was bothering her. Kathy paused and said, "I remember being a little girl and I used to love to play in my mom's hair because it was long and curly. My mom would always push me away or tell me to go play. She wasn't affectionate at all."

I said, "You wanted to be close to your mom and it was really hard for her to give you what you needed." "Yes," Kathy said. "I thought her hair was so pretty and I was sad that mine wasn't as curly as hers. When I found out I was having a little girl, I was so excited. I imagined combing her hair and being so happy." As she spoke, she glanced at her daughter's hair that looked like a crown of tiny ringlets. I said, "Anita's hair is so curly. What's it like for you to comb her hair? Kathy replied, "I love her little curls and I thought I would love brushing her hair. I pictured adding tiny ribbons and bows and I would show her how she looked in the mirror. I just don't have the feelings I thought I would have. Sometimes I feel sad when I'm brushing her hair and sometimes I feel angry!" I listened carefully as Kathy spoke. I held in mind how it might feel to want to create positive experiences with your daughter, but unresolved feelings of loss and regret inhibit the opportunities for mutual enjoyment. We continued to talk. Kathy shared more information with me while her baby moved back and forth between us. When her baby tentatively touched my hair again, Kathy smiled. Kathy longed to have her mother's affection. Her feelings of longing were unresolved and had intruded into her present relationship with her daughter.

My Awakening

The awakening of my own feelings of rejection and discrimination emerged from my conversation with Kathy and impacted the new relationship I was building with Kathy and her baby. The above interaction sparked memories of having my hair combed by my mother and grandmother. I remember the smell of the pressing comb and holding my ear hoping to not get burned. I remember going to the beauty shop at 5pm and sitting in the chair surrounded by the ladies in various stages of hair grooming feeling so grown up and pampered. At home, my grandmother would hum as her fingers worked through my hair and I would lean into her legs as she massaged, braided, and brushed saying that she was making my hair strong. My mother would straighten my edges with the hot-pressing comb for special events and between visits to the beauty shop. I had to hold my ear to protect my skin from the heat of the comb. They were always so careful to avoid burning me but on the rare occasions when they did, I tried very hard not to cry, because it seemed to hurt them more than me. My hair was very thick; I perspired easily. I hated getting my hair pressed and longed for a permanent so that my hair would be straight with Shirley Temple curls.

I didn't like the pressing comb, but I loved the touch of my grandmother and mother's hands. I felt safe with these women and I knew how much I was loved. They would tell me how much they loved my pretty brown skin and thick hair. I didn't realize until much later that they were preparing me for a world where my dark skin and hair of wool would not be seen as beautiful in everyone's eyes. When I was discriminated against, I remembered the messages I received as a child. I would need to give these same messages of love and acceptance to my son and daughter as a protective shield of armor when they were faced with social injustice and systemic racism. It wasn't until I was married with children that I felt brave enough to wear my hair naturally. Each strand of hair holds stories of pain, shame, comfort, and joy. Although different in many ways, Kathy, Anita, and I connected in our desire to feel seen, heard, valued, and accepted. I hoped that in time I could support Kathy in freeing herself from the "ghost" that had invaded her relationship and create opportunities for fully delighting in her child.

As society has alternately been accepting and rejection of Black hair, so has my recognition of the importance of engaging in conversations to gain understanding to support diversity and honor culture. It takes a lot of effort and can be exhausting, but these conversations are too important to ignore.

Being Brave Can Be Difficult

My initial ambivalence about sharing this experience with my first RS supervisor made me a little uncertain about how to put into words with my new supervisor what I felt about the experience with Kathy and her baby and all that it awakened for me personally? What would she think about my early experiences and how they have impacted my work? Did it even make sense to share an experience that happened years ago? I was again reminded of some of the insensitive and intrusive questions I have been asked about my hair. Questions that made me feel as if I were on display. For example, "*Why does your hair feel like wool? Why do you burn it with that comb? Why do black women have so many hair styles? Sometimes their hair is long, sometimes it's short. What's up with that? Can I touch it?*" Would she understand the discomfort I feel and at times continue to feel? Would she defend or dismiss my feelings by saying that was just the sign of the times or would she be able to embrace how I might feel being thought of as "odd"? What I did feel with this supervisor was her deep compassion and desire to understand, which made each conversation easier. Over time my supervisor shared ways in which she felt like she had not always fit in and how inaccurate assumptions had been made about her. We were able to enter a space of generosity that has continued throughout our relationship.

Sharing in Vulnerability

What sparked my desire to share the above interaction I had with Kathy and Anita with my reflective supervisor was a case that had been presented to me by my current supervisee regarding a child's hair. My supervisee needed to talk about how this Black mom whose child was in foster care felt when she noticed during a visit that her child's hair was dry and breaking. This mother cried because despite the reasons for removal, this mother had always taken pride in her child's hair and appearance. I talked about how I offered support to my supervisee regarding the child's hair and how she talked about her own hair combing ritual. She shared that she would have been angry, too, if her child's hair had been damaged. My supervisee cried because the mother's pain had felt palpable. When I shared this story, my supervisor noted my compassion for my supervisee. We discussed how the supervisee had offered the same level of compassion and empathy to the mom. My supervisor then asked with interest about cases I might have had regarding hair combing. It was that simple question that reminded me of my experience with Kathy and Anita.

Feeling Heard

It felt as if I had been waiting to share the interaction. I wanted to be understood and hoped our carefully created rhythm would support what I wanted to convey. I began by talking about my observations regarding Kathy's postpartum depression symptoms and how she became more responsive to Anita's cues and developmental milestones. I talked about the pillars of Infant Mental Health I used and my affection for Kathy and Anita. I struggled to express what had been aroused in me regarding race and ethnicity. My supervisor sat patiently, quietly, present in our protected space, and invited me to think about my own history, early attachment relationships, and thoughts about diversity. Again, I reminded myself of the comfortable space we had created, and her genuine desire to know me and my work as a social work clinician and supervisor. Remembering this felt experience fueled me to share thoughts about my childhood, my parents, and the rituals I embraced. When I shared the interaction with Kathy and Anita, we wondered together about what might have been triggering for me. We talked about how memories of the past can sabotage our present, requiring attention and understanding.

Sharing Perspectives

As we continued to explore the interaction, my supervisor asked permission to offer her own initial reactions to what I shared. She said that she would not have thought about the mom feeling uncomfortable with her baby touching my hair or my race. She would have assumed that the mother was trying to prevent her baby from invading my space. I thought about how race and culture are so much a part of the lens in which I view the world. Sometimes it feels exhausting to be in settings where I am the only Black woman. I shared that my words and thoughts are always filtered to determine how I might be received and perceived. We were able to think together about our individual experiences as related to privilege and what it has meant to my relationships with families and in supervision. We also acknowledged how comforting it felt to have important conversations, because it has served to inform our work as supervisors. I thought about how I may have avoided conversations regarding race and missed opportunities to support families in more meaningful ways. We discussed the importance of not making assumptions and being brave enough to ask for clarity when there is a disruption and what I would need during our time together that would feel supportive. This space of emotional safety is not fixed but needs to be re-examined either internally or together when feelings of uncertainty and insecurity arise. It is the responsibility of both the supervisor and supervisee to make sure that safety remains consistent within the relationship (Noroña et al., 2012).

Concluding Thoughts

Predictability, reflection, and reciprocity are an essential part of reflective supervision (Wilson et al., 2018). Supervisor and supervisee cocreate a space for reflection, curiosity, and safety. We considered questions (see Reflective Questions) as we worked together.

Reflective Questions

1. How do my cultural and racial beliefs impact how and who I am in this RS space?
2. What cultural beliefs, biases, and misperceptions do I hold that may contribute to relationship disruptions in my work with families, with other professionals, or with people I supervisee?
3. What are my expectations and what do I hope to gain through an RS relationship?
4. How will I honor differences between us in this RS relationship?

References

Noroña, C. R., Heffron, M. C., Grunstein, S., & Nalo, A. (2012). Broadening the scope: Next steps in reflective supervision training. *Zero to Three, 33*(2), 29–33.

Wilson, K., Barron, C., Wheeler, R., & Estele-Avelini Jedrzejek, P. (2018). The importance of examining diversity in reflective supervision when working with young children and their families. *Reflective Practice, 19*(5), 653–665.

Chapter 10
A Case Study in Cross-Racial Practice and Supervision: Reflections in Black and White

Stefanie Hill

A Personal and Professional Journey

To be reflective and self-aware, two fundamentals important to the practice of Infant Mental Health have required me to take a long and difficult personal and professional journey. For one thing, I have struggled with uncertainty about my abilities. Then, as a Black woman, I have wondered if I would be accepted by other practitioners, primarily White professionals, in the infant mental health field. I took the fundamentals and the journey seriously. Many stories about families and relationships came to mind while writing this chapter, but one story was particularly life altering. A clinical story about a biracial baby and her family challenged the essence of who I was and forced me to take a deeper look within to find a part of me that I had long buried.

I learned to trust my reflective supervisor, a White male, with what I observed in my clinical work and the stories I heard, meeting for an hour every other week. We shared stories about families whose needs for guidance, emotional support, and infant–parent psychotherapy were extensive. It was within this reflective supervision relationship that I grew brave enough to explore my work, my own vulnerabilities, and my strengths. Up until this time, a pivotal point in my career, I had not thought that the color of my skin could influence my practice. I believed that if you were educated and skilled, clients would respect you. This is where the story begins.

First, a little about myself. A Black Woman, I have provided clinical services to infants, children, and families for over 30 years. I have worked for 23 of those years as an Infant Mental Health home visitor (Fraiberg, 1980; Weatherston & Ribaudo, 2020) and have provided reflective supervision (Heller & Gilkerson, 2009; Wilson et al., 2018) to mental health professionals for 15 years. Privileged to work with a

S. Hill (✉)
Starfish Family Services, Livonia, MI, USA
e-mail: stefhill1923@gmail.com

M. L. Lewis, D. J. Weatherston (eds.), *Therapeutic Cultural Routines to Build Family Relationships*, https://doi.org/10.1007/978-3-030-83726-6_10

great variety of families, my work has taken me in and out of many homes. Some have made lasting marks, personally and professionally, causing me often to think and wonder about them. The case story that follows comes from one of those families. I am honored to share the story of Traci,[1] a young White mother who accepted services from me on behalf of her 9-month-old biracial baby, Shay; Shay's father, Robert, a Black young man; Charlie, Traci's White step-grandfather; and Bill, my White male supervisor. My hope for sharing the story with you is to share my road to greater self-awareness through reflective supervision.

Black Therapist/White Mother/Biracial Baby

Traci is the 25-year-old White mother of Shay, a 9-month-old, biracial baby girl. Born at 40 weeks' gestation, Shay appears to be a healthy baby. She has thick, dark hair and a light brown skin tone. She is responsive and enjoys interacting with her mother when her mother can pay attention to her. The two live alone in a low-income, subsidized, racially diverse housing unit in a large, urban mid-western city. Traci is of large stature with fair skin and thick, curly, red hair. Shay's father, Robert, is a 26-year-old Black man. He met Traci when he was visiting relatives in a neighboring unit. Early in their relationship, Traci became pregnant. Robert does not live with Traci, but he visits, spends the night, and leaves without notice or explanation. He does not provide economically for Shay or Traci. When he does come around, it is to see if Traci has any money and to eat whatever is in the fridge. The area where Traci and Shay live consists of many young White girls who have relationships and children with young Black men.

Beginnings

Shay and Traci were referred to Infant Mental Health Home Visiting (IMH-HV) services by a pediatric nurse who saw Traci and Shay at the well-child pediatric clinic when Shay was 6 months old. At that time, Traci was minimally responsive to Shay, she presented with a mild cognitive delay, and did not appear to have any natural support to help her in caring for Shay. She reported that she had delivered Shay alone. No one came to the hospital to be with her during delivery or following the baby's birth. While in the hospital, she had difficulty figuring out what Shay needed and let her cry in the bassinet, terrified of picking her up or holding her. Upon discharge, she had called a public car service to get home.

[1]All names and other personal identifiers in the chapter have been changed to protect privacy and confidentiality.

I was the IMH-HV specialist who received the referral from the clinic nurse to work with Traci and her baby. At the time of this writing, I had been working with Traci and Shay for 3 months, meeting with them in their home every week for 2 h. The first few sessions consisted of paperwork and listening to the unraveling of their story. I kept in mind the words of my supervisor, William Schafer, "*You don't build rapport by being nice, but by getting the story.*"

The next few months were spent talking and sharing stories about Traci's own childhood and how much she wanted life to be different for Shay. Traci spoke frankly about not wanting to be pregnant but felt that her boyfriend would leave her if she did not agree to have a baby. Many of her girlfriends who live in the same housing unit had children with Black men and she wanted to be a part of something, to belong. Shay appeared clean, healthy, and relatively well cared for by her mother. It was their relationship that seemed problematic. Traci held Shay in her arms for most of the home visiting sessions, but rarely talked to her or looked down at her face. I spoke with Traci about her hopes and desires for her and her baby. We also discussed her need to increase her natural supports. She shared that she has a few friends in her housing complex, but they also have needs, so they are unable to help. Traci shared that she needed larger clothes for Shay, because she was growing quickly. Traci was very proud of Shay's size and weight. She was a pudgy little one with a beautiful round face. She was in the ninetieth percentile for weight and height. I was able to find a community resource near her home where we were able to secure clothes for Shay for the next 3–6 months. Toward the end of the first 3 months of our work together, I felt we were beginning the journey of building an alliance.

Reflective Supervision Across Race

Dr. William (Bill) Schafer,[2] a White male consultant, and I, a Black clinician, met years ago when I was beginning my work with families and young children in an Infant Mental Health home visiting program. I had no idea about the extent to which the impact of our work together would have on the rest of my career. While providing services to Traci and Shay, I was working for a Community Mental Health agency and Bill was the consultant who provided reflective group supervision (RSG) every 2 weeks to the IMH Home Visitor Team. Following each group supervision, he met with me, the IMH Team supervisor, for individual reflective supervision. What follows is a description of my supervision with Bill following an intensive home visit with Traci and Shay. I had been working with Traci and Shay for about 3 months.

[2] I am honored to include my experiences with Dr. William Schafer who died in 2019.

Reflective Supervision Same Day as the Home Visit

I began my supervision hour that day as I typically start each of our sessions, by relating what I observed, and the stories shared. At the time, I had been supervised by Bill for over a year. I felt it necessary to describe the family's physical appearance, because I wanted Bill to understand how race plays a major role in this family.

I admitted to Bill that I felt angry with Robert. "He is a Black man living with and taking advantage of a White girl with low cognitive ability and even lower self-esteem!" In supervision we explored my anger, attempting to get to the root of my feelings. Bill asked me, "*So who are you really mad at?*" I answered, "*What do you really mean?*" Bill was implying that Robert was bringing up some feeling for me and I needed to try and identify the trigger. My emotional response at first was to be offended, because he insinuated that my feelings toward Robert were not real and that I was allowing a personal feeling to get the way of helping my client. I recalled Bill's words, "*Reflection is being able to feel the feeling and then being able to describe it.*" It was apparent to him, but not to me, that Robert's behavior toward Traci was like someone in my personal life who was exhibiting the same arrogant behavior. I felt a little awkward, because I was talking to Bill, an older White man, about my anger and disappointment toward a client of my own race. It felt like betrayal.

I said, "Sometimes being a Black is hard because you can literally feel the weight of all Black people on your shoulders." I kept talking and Bill listened. He knew that I had four children around the same age as Traci and Robert. He wondered if my feelings stemmed from feelings toward my own children. I said, reluctantly, "Probably." I had shared with Bill in an earlier supervision that one of my sons was having problems working and felt that others should take care of him. Bill asked questions that led me to explore my feelings regarding my own son and how that could be contributing to my feelings about Robert. I responded, "*I feel embarrassed that my son is demonstrating some of the behaviors of a client.*" I struggled with sharing what I felt for my son and for these young Black men. I was angry because both Robert and my son fit the societal profile of young, lazy, Black boys who thought the world owed them. If I shared this with Bill would this reinforce beliefs that he had about Black boys and men? I was afraid that I might be selling out by sharing my feelings about these boys with a White man. I had trusted Bill up this point; he had never given me reason not to. The space between us felt safe. I shared my feelings with him about being a sellout. We continued to talk about my feelings toward Robert and how they stemmed from my feelings about my son. I could see the parallel between the two and it made me sad. "How could I have raised a child like that and why did he turn out that way?" I grew increasingly comfortable talking about these things in subsequent supervisions. I talked, and Bill listened.

Prior to reflective supervision, I had not made the correlation between Robert and my own son. "I didn't even realize that I had angry feelings toward my son!" Reflective supervision helped me become aware of my own feelings and how those feelings could affect my relationship with Traci and her family. I felt that if Bill had not helped me make the correlation, I might have punished Robert for the things I saw in him that reminded me of my son. Through reflective supervision, I was able to acknowledge feelings of shame and embarrassment toward one of my own children, a Black man, and how these feelings were parallel to those I had toward the Black father of Traci's young child.

Black/White/Black: Another Powerful Home Visit

During another visit, I felt frustrated because Traci had not followed through on some of the very basics of care for Shay. I tried not to show it. Although there had begun to be genuine, nurturing exchanges between Shay and her mother, Traci was either neglecting or could not understand the importance of establishing a routine for on time feeding, bathing, changing diapers, and combing Shay's hair. I worried about this. When I arrived that day and walked through the door, I could smell that Shay had soiled her diaper. Traci was holding Shay who enjoyed being nestled in her mother's arms. When I found a place to sit on the couch, I noticed that Shay had several bottles on the table. They all had different levels of formula and none of them looked fresh nor did they have lids. Shay's hair was considerably thick and looked dry and matted. As the visit went on Shay remained in her mother's arms and Traci gazed at her, but I was not able to fully enjoy the exchange because of the strong pungent smell. I wondered why Traci did not smell Shay's diaper. I struggled trying to find the right words to ask Traci about Shay's diaper. I did not want to sound like I was reprimanding her, so I gently began to ask questions about Shay's feeding and elimination schedule. After listening patiently to Traci's responses, I quietly suggested that Traci check Shay's diaper. She responded quickly by changing Shay's diaper. The rest of the visit went well, and I was able to help Traci set another schedule to guide and support her in Shay's care.

Black/White Reflective Supervision Following the Home Visit

I arrived at my reflective supervision session in a relatively good mood. I began talking to Bill about Traci and Shay. He congratulated me for sticking with the case and trying to work through some of my own feelings about the family and caregiving at the same time. By now I felt comfortable sharing with Bill what I observed on my home visits, what I experienced, and the more personal thoughts and feelings that I was aware of. I felt we had established a strong, trusting working relationship despite our racial and cultural differences. I was able to talk with him about almost anything. Today, I talked about Shay's hair, describing it as "dry and matted." Bill was not familiar with the importance of hair in the Black community. After explaining some basics to him about how to care for Black hair, he seemed to understand.

He felt comfortable enough to ask detailed questions and was especially interested in dreadlocks and how they were created.

Bill and I laughed throughout the supervisory conversation, which made it easy to talk about hard things. I brought up White people caring for Black children and my frustration with how their skin is often ashy and dry. I had strong feelings regarding the care of Black children's hair when they were placed with a White family. I expressed my frustration saying, "Many White people do not understand how to care for a Black child's hair!" Together we brainstormed a way to help Traci care for Shay's hair. I admitted that the "Black mama bear" was coming out. I just wanted to go in with all my hair products and comb Shay's hair myself, but I knew that would not help the situation in the long term. Instead, I would have to initially explore with Shay what she knew about Black hair care, just as I was exploring with Bill. This whole subject was so unfamiliar to Bill that he was only able to listen supportively. Bill asked a few questions, inviting more information from me to help him understand the importance of hair in the black community. This conversation went far beyond the issue of Shay's hair into the historical context of Black hair combing, bringing us into a closer trusting relationship through our reflective supervision.

A Third IMH Home Visit

During the next visit, Robert was in attendance. I had never met him. I saw a strong resemblance between Robert and Shay. I also noticed that Robert never spoke to or acknowledged Shay or Traci when he entered the home but went into the kitchen first thing to get something to eat. When Traci introduced us, Robert said, "Hello." I invited him to join us, and he reluctantly agreed. Robert was over 6 ft tall, large in stature, with a very dark complexion, and black dreadlocks that came below his shoulders. When asked, Robert was very forthright with his feelings about fatherhood. It was as if he felt he had something to prove. He reported that he was happy to become a father and he supported Traci's decision to have the baby.

I noticed how much easier it was to talk to Traci when Robert was around. The three of us talked openly about Shay and what she had brought to their lives. Robert talked about his mother and how happy she was about the baby. He reported that he did not know his father. It was then that I found out that Traci's family disliked him and baby Shay, because they were Black. Traci had never mentioned this during previous sessions. Robert joked and went on to say, "Shay's hair is thick like mine and because Traci's hair is also very thick and curly, Shay did not even have a chance to have 'good hair'." I felt comfortable with the conversation, because I had worked for a long time with mixed-race couples. I was very secure in my own identity and felt confident in my own racial and culture awareness. The conversation was rich and gave me much more insight into the lives of Traci and her ability to care for Shay, as well as Robert's place in this family. I felt that our relationship was growing stronger.

No supervision after this session

A Black Home Visitor in a White Neighborhood: The Fourth Home Visit

For this visit, Traci asked me to meet her with Shay at her mother's house. I wondered why she wanted me to meet her there and what else I might come to understand. I agreed to meet them at her mother's home in a more rural part of town, in a poorly kept trailer park. I felt apprehensive getting out of my car. Although I had worked many years in different neighborhoods, I felt particularly anxious because of the conversations I had had with Robert and Traci last week. Handling prejudice and racism is part of the job when you are meeting with clients in diverse communities, but for me, this felt different. I looked around and felt alone, vulnerable in this neighborhood where I had never been before.

Traci met me at the door and offered me a seat. Shay was on the floor playing with toys. Shay looked better, her clothes were clean, but her hair was the same, dry, and matted. As the session commenced, I wondered who else was in the house. Traci shared that her mother and her step-grandfather were in the other room. In the middle of the session, Traci's step-grandfather, Charlie, came out of the other room. He was a tall and very thin White man. His hair was pulled back in a long ponytail and the top of his head was bald. He was unshaven and had his shirt unbuttoned. I was surprised, because he looked younger than expected. He entered the room and did not acknowledge Traci, Shay, or me. I became increasingly uncomfortable and decided to break the tension by saying hello. He nodded his head and sat in the chair where the session was taking place. The conversation continued, but with caution. It was apparent that Traci was becoming uncomfortable. I wondered why Traci had not just cancelled or changed the day of the appointment. Curious, I wondered to myself what she wanted me to understand about her family and her relationship with them. When Traci blurted out, "I didn't know how hard it was going to be raising a child!" Charlie responded, "I told you not to have that 'N...' baby, you didn't need a baby! You cannot even take care of yourself." It happened so quickly and was so unexpected that it took me a minute to realize what he had said. Charlie must have realized this and followed up, "No offense to you, ma'am." I was so overwhelmed that I could not respond. I began to feel anxious and warm. I knew I had to leave the house but waited about 15 min before gathering my things to leave. I tried hard not to let my feelings show. I got in the car, left the trailer park, pulled into a nearby restaurant parking lot, and cried, for myself, and for Shay. I remembered Bill's words to me during one of our supervisions, "*Your goal is not about the people in the relationship, it is about the relationship.*"

Reflective Supervision Immediately Following the Home Visit

I pulled myself together and went straight to the office where I waited for 2 h until it was time for my reflective supervision with Bill. I was simply undone. I had a difficult time telling him that I had been in the presence of a man who referenced someone as "N….". Bill said thoughtfully, "*Words leave actual scars on a person's body,*" and then he was speechless.

I felt for Bill, because he looked so sad and ashamed. We had talked about many things in our time together, but not White guilt. I felt as though all the air had been sucked out of the room. I felt guilty for bringing this kind of overt racism to Bill, a White male, simply because even though we had a good relationship, this was more than we had ever tackled together. My feelings were all over the place. I needed to talk to him about feeling ambushed, disrespected, dishonored, and afraid. I found myself wondering how many times he had heard that term within his own family or with his friends. He grew up in the 1940 and 1950s when overt racism was more common. This was not a typical session.

Bill admitted that this was the first time that he really understood the pure ugliness of racism and its effects on Black people. He reported that he was so ashamed and felt so bad. I was careful that our session did not turn into me helping Bill to feel better. We continued to talk about the incident. I shared that I struggled with Shay being called a "N…" and asked, "What will that mean for her for the rest of her life?" I also thought about Robert's remarks about Shay never having a chance to have "good hair." I know just from being Black myself that Black people can be ashamed of their own hair texture, and they feel that White hair is "better."

I wondered aloud what messages Shay would receive about her hair from the Black side of her family. Bill and I continued to discuss the visit in Traci's mother's house and what that session must have meant to Traci. "If the step-grandfather felt so comfortable that he used that racist term in front of me, what must he be saying to Traci about her child? What messages is she receiving from the rest of her family about her child?"

This brought up so much for me. I realized then that it was not only my race, but my age and personal experiences that made working with this family so difficult. I also realized that for the first time in my social work career, I was afraid.

It took me a while to sort this out. I wondered what it must have been like for Traci living in a family that rejected her as soon as they found out she was pregnant with a Black child? Traci had reported that prior to her pregnancy, she spent every day with her family even though she had moved out of the house. Her family would shop, cook, eat, and hang out everyday either at her grandparents' home or at her house. When they found out that she was pregnant by a Black man, they begged her to have an abortion and when she refused, they stopped calling her and any interactions she had with them led to violent arguments. She told me that her family was racist, but she thought that they would eventually accept her back into the house and her baby into the family. Now, they no longer came to her house to visit and when she went to their house, they barely talked to her. I remembered Bill's words, "*When you are in a family that does not want you, then you are just lingering, and you are not safe.*" It was then that I realized my fears sitting with her family mirrored Traci's fears, leaving her feeling unsafe with family members who were racist, had rejected her baby, and withdrawn their support.

I felt guilty because I had focused so much on my own feelings following the home visit, not realizing that Traci must have felt afraid, too, in addition to feeling unwanted and unloved by her family. At least I could leave and seek support. This was the life that Traci and Shay live every day and will continue to live for the rest of their lives. Bill asked me why I felt guilty for having those feelings. I answered, "I am supposed to put my client's feelings first." Bill asked, "Where is that written? Your feelings are important, too." I smiled. This was a moment in time where I felt so understood and supported. "Reflection takes two. I need your awareness of me to become more self-aware."

Reflecting on an Important Relationship

Writing this case story has evoked many strong feelings. My 30-year adventure with my Reflective Supervisor, William (Bill) Schafer, came to a physical end, but not a psychological end, a few years ago when he died. Through our reflective supervision hours, he helped me to find out where I fit personally and professionally in the world of Infant Mental Health. In supervision, I had found it difficult to put on the mask that I often wore around my IMH colleagues. Bill saw through my façade, seeing and accepting the authentic me. As time went on, we met biweekly, and our relationship became reciprocal as he became comfortable in reaching out to me to make sure he was being racially and culturally respectful in different situations. The irony of it is that there were times when he was far off the mark in his thinking about Black people. Please don't get me wrong; there were missteps on my part, too. Without knowing it, this older White gentleman and I created a trusting bond that transcends time. Early in our supervisor–supervisee relationship, we bravely began to have honest conversations about racism, what it looked like for him, and what it looked like for me as a person of color. I think he appreciated my frankness and honesty as I did his. Years of working in foster care taught me to not shy away from hard conversations. I must put in this short story that will hopefully help in understanding the relationship that Bill and I built.

My mom died and I was out for several months. Bill provided reflective supervision to my team every 2 weeks, continuing to support them while I was away. When I returned, I knew it would be difficult. We were to meet for supervision, and I knew I would see Bill. I entered the conference room, but he was not there. I searched for him, going in and out of offices and other rooms. I remembered to check the playroom and that is where I found him. He was sitting calmly in a chair, alone, and had pulled up another chair next to him. He looked at me and said quietly, "Stefanie, I was waiting for you."

At that moment, the relationship shifted for me. It became personal and professional. Through the years, we had talked about our lives, but this was different. We talked about death, and I listened to his philosophy of life after death. We sat there for a long time. I realized that he had become my safe base, the person I turned to in difficult times with my work and now, with my life.

Bill's passing has led me on yet another journey to deeper self-reflection and awareness. I have had to "figure it out on my own" so to speak, but I talk with him often, and can hear his voice, his laughter. He continues to push me along. Bill was older, and his experience with racism was very different from mine. We managed to begin bridging the gap by having hard conversations in a safe and trusting reflective supervisory environment. His presence on this earth helped me to realize that race is just a thing we use to group ourselves into different categories. Our time together gave me faith that if this older White man and this younger Black woman could forge a bond that transcended race and prejudice, there is hope for us all.

Reflective Questions

1. Think deeply about these words: *Words leave actual scars on a person's body.* Have you ever experienced a hurtful racial slur or microaggression that left a deep wound? How might the experience affect you, personally and professionally? What leads to healing the hurt carried or restoring one's sense of self and well-being?
2. Have you ever engaged in supervision with a person of another culture, ethnicity, or race? What were some of the barriers experienced? What made it work?
3. What surprised you about this personal and professional case story? What are you still curious about?
4. In reflecting on the story about this reflective supervisory relationship, what story might you tell about someone with whom you have worked across race, Black-White?

References

Fraiberg, S. (1980). *Clinical studies in infant mental health: The first year of life*. Basic Books.

Heller, S. S., & Gilkerson, L. (Eds.). (2009). *A practical guide to reflective supervision*. Zero to Three.

Weatherston, D., & Ribaudo, J. (2020). The Michigan infant mental health home visiting model. *Infant Mental Health Journal, 41*(2), 166–177.

Wilson, K., Barron, C., Wheeler, R., & Estele-Avelini Jedrzejek, P. (2018). The importance of examining diversity in reflective supervision when working with young children and their families. *Reflective Practice, 19*(5), 653–665.

Part III
Reflections on Community-Based Interventions

Chapter 11
If Her Hair Isn't Right, then I'm Not a Good Mother: Reflections on the San Diego Caregiver-Child Connections Community Counseling Project

Nola M. Butler Byrd, Ojore Lateef Bushfan, Ava L. Gill, Kathleen Baca Leanos, and Michelle J. Rowe-Odom

Lies about the bodies of People of African descent and other People of Color have been highly effective in perpetuating the myth of White superiority. Black hair does matter, which is why I (Butler Byrd), as a community counselor educator, was attracted to the Early Connections Project© Hair Combing Interactions (HCIs) model presented by Dr. Marva Lewis (1993, 1999, 2001) at the Association of Black Psychologists Convention during the summer of 2012.

In order to develop culturally responsive community counselors, the program I direct, the Community-Based Block (CBB) Multicultural Counseling and Social Justice Education Program, stresses the importance of counselors developing and deliberately practicing relational knowledge and skills, including self-awareness, awareness of one's impact on others through feedback informed approaches and commitments to democracy, social justice, interpersonal and professional health, and well-being. Because of my own interpersonal and professional growth and development, I am very aware of my hair and my relationships with my caregivers. That was not always the case. My hair was a source of pride, pleasure, and pain. Growing up in a small, Black community, surrounded by a large privileged white community in rural Cincinnati during the Civil Rights and Black Power Movements, I remember my Granny asking me if my head hurt, because I didn't comb my hair that day. I remember the agony of my mother combing out and pressing my severely tangled hair after the ecstasy of shampooing it and massaging my scalp. I remember the creative craziness of making curlers out of twisted pieces of brown paper bags and the discomfort of wearing them to bed, where they snapped and crackled and disrupted my sleep all night so that I could have socially appropriate curls the next day. I remember my consternation and humiliation when people touched my hair without my consent, treating me like I was a zoo animal or freak. I remember the

N. M. Butler Byrd (✉) · O. L. Bushfan · A. L. Gill · K. B. Leanos · M. J. Rowe-Odom
San Diego State University, San Diego, CA, USA
e-mail: nbutler@mail.sdsu.edu

M. L. Lewis, D. J. Weatherston (eds.), *Therapeutic Cultural Routines to Build Family Relationships*, https://doi.org/10.1007/978-3-030-83726-6_11

pride of my giant, Angela Davis–inspired afro during the 1970s, with my fisted afro pick or a cake cutter sticking out of my bushy locks. I remember trying to make sense out of the double-messages that were directed toward my innocent, beautiful body.

Today, despite the pride I feel in wearing my Sisterlocks© for almost 30 years, I sometimes still feel shame about allowing my hair to grow as long as it has, mostly because of the disparaging looks and remarks directed toward me by White people and occasionally internally oppressed People of Color. The everyday hair combing interactions I had with my mother, grandmother, aunts, and sisters were an extremely meaningful way that I became aware of myself and our rewarding and painful relationships with each other.

When Dr. Lewis shared the *Touch, Talk, and Listen while Combing Hair!* model as a way for parents and primary caregivers to enhance their connections with their children, my soul leapt with excitement, and I began looking for a way to develop a project where Community-Based Block (CBB) Program graduate students could serve one of our disenfranchised communities.

The CBB program has been dedicated to serving the diverse needs of underserved students and communities for over 48 years. CBB is a pioneer in the training of culturally responsive counselors or change agents who specialize in working with communities. The program is called "community based," because it has always been held off campus, in the heart of two of San Diego's multiethnic, low-income neighborhoods and because it creates a learning community in which a team of faculty and a carefully selected, diverse group of students "partner" in the learning process to structure their affective, experiential learning experience. It is a "block" program, because all classes are required of all students, who stay together as a group (or "block") for the entire program. At the time of the San Diego (SDC3) project, the program was in transition from a one-year, Master of Arts (MA) in Education program, preparing students to become unlicensed counselors, to a two-year Master of Science (MS) in Counseling-LPCC program that fulfills the academic requirements for licensure in the State of California.

The CBB program helps students develop counseling skills, including relationship and community building; process and therapeutic intervention; the academic skills of critical thinking, systematic inquiry, program evaluation; effective written and oral communication; and the personal growth experiences and professional dispositions necessary to enable graduates to use their skills for the benefit of clients. The CBB program also helps students adapt counseling skills to the needs of different populations in order to prepare them to be competent multicultural counselors. The students are able to gain a unique experience of becoming counselors through live supervision at the Center for Community Counseling in City Heights, one of the most diverse communities in San Diego. The responsibility students assume for their own learning and community building and decision-making helps them develop the proficiencies they will need to become effective change agents in schools, colleges, and/or social service agencies and community-based organizations (Butler Byrd, 2010, 2009a, b; Butler Byrd et al., 2006, 2008).

The SDC3 Project

At the August 2012 CBB program retreat in the mountains of Southern California where incoming graduate student, Ava Gill shared her family's antique hot comb and its legacy in her family as her cultural artifact, and Kat Baca shared stories about her relationship with a school for homeless children and youth in downtown San Diego, we decided that we would develop an HCI service project to enhance relationships between caregivers and children at that school. After we were introduced to the Early Connection's HCI model, we decided to examine its efficacy and used the HeartMath emWave (n.d.) biomedical device to examine heart rate variability (HRV) and physiological coherence during hair combing interactions. HRV and coherence are indicators of stress and well-being that can also be used to help people learn how to manage their emotions and reduce stress. The San Diego Caregiver-Child Connections (SDC3) Project was developed to provided an opportunity for CBB graduate students to experience culturally responsive, community-based research, while serving a real community need – improving attachment relationships between homeless caregivers and their children. The Project helped caregivers become self-aware and connect with other caregivers in a culturally centered, six-week educational support group. The group also helped them enhance their existing parenting and caregiving skills using everyday hair combing interactions to strengthen their relationships with their children. Caregivers also learned emotional management techniques for stress reduction, and participated in a research study that assessed the effectiveness of the support group.

Southern California has become one of the most diverse, multiethnic/multilingual areas in the United States. This development occurred rather rapidly. In large part because of white supremacy, schools, colleges, business, industry, and government have been slow to develop inclusive engagement and service strategies that are responsive to the worldviews, strengths and needs of multiethnic and other diverse people. Adults and children in underserved communities are especially vulnerable, creating an urgent need for more competent cross-cultural counselors and culturally responsive services that support parents and alloparents (individuals who provide care for children other than parents) in healing from their own negative experiences and traumas developing resilience, stronger support systems and relationships with children. Alloparenting.

This chapter shares the experiences of four graduate students who participated in the SDC3 project. They discuss their backgrounds and experiences in developing and implementing the SDC3 Project, their observations about participants' experiences, and where these experiences lead them interpersonally and professionals.

Our Background, Experiences, and Reflections

As graduate students of color, we were very interested in HCI because of our own histories and hair combing interactions, so we agreed to collaborate with the Dr. Butler Byrd on the development and implementation of the support groups at a school for children affected by homelessness where one member of our team, Kathleen Baca Leanos, has worked as a program director for over 3 years.

Ava L. Gill

My interest in this project lies with my passion for helping others and wanting to know more about the effects of the mother–daughter relationship through the hair combing process with this population of participants. I also hoped to learn more about my own relationship with my mom and big momma and the attachment and/or detachment that took place, recalling my own hair combing experiences as a child. I also knew that the participants would learn from us and the possibility that I would learn from them, enriching my life as well.

Growing up as a little girl, hair played an important role in my self-worth. I spent many of my early years engaged in the process of hair combing interactions with my mother and big momma, especially my big momma. These hair combing times were alternately exciting, frustrating, enriching, and often cumbersome and overwhelming! The days leading up to getting my hair pressed, I would go through a plethora of feelings: sad, happy, confused, etc. I remember lying in a vertical position on the kitchen counter while my mother would wash my hair and then sit me in a chair and try and detangle my hair, mindful that the detangling process was very painful! She would have to take sections of my hair and try to comb through it. I don't really remember the conversations that we had in the process of pressing my hair. I think we would often listen to music or the TV would be on while this process was taking place. Even though it was very uncomfortable, it was nice to be with my mom, because she worked a lot.

When I would go to my big momma's house, the pressing experience would be much different. My mom would wash my hair the night before and drop me off at big momma's the next day and she would head to work. My big momma was serious about the hair pressing process. She would often say, "*You go hold a good head for big momma today*?" She wanted to make sure I wasn't going to move my head, while she was trying to press my hair. It was always, "*Hold your ear, bend your head so I can get those naps and that kitchen*" (the kitchen and naps are the tightly coiled hair on the nape of the neck.) This is the spot where I would often get burned with the pressing comb, because the hair was so small. Big momma would go on to say things like, "*Watch how pretty big momma's baby is going to look after I finish pressing your hair.*" Ultimately, those hair-combing sessions started to make me feel insecure with even thinking about wearing my hair naturally. And getting my hair wet after those long 2–3 h pressing sessions… that would never be a part of any conversation. I just knew better not to get it wet! As I look back at my adolescence, I realize that these negative "hair" self-images were embedded into my mind at an early age and took me through early years of my adulthood. I remember, throughout high school, I wore a hairstyle called the Jheri Curl (pretty much everyone in school was wearing this style), which consisted of applying liquid Jheri curl supplies to one's hair and inserting perm rods in the hair to make it curly. And as soon as that fad wore off, it was time to get a perm (straightening of the hair with chemicals to get it "Bone" straight). Again, being taught at an early age, the standard of beauty for a woman's (girl's) hair was to have it straight as can be, to be accepted in society even though when the beautician applied chemicals to my hair, it would sometimes be painful, especially if the chemicals were left on too long. I remember my beautician asking me, after applying the chemicals to my hair and letting me sit with it on my hair, "Is it burning yet?" I would often say "no" when I really wanted to say "yes," because I thought the longer, I keep it on the straighter it would be. Unfortunately, by keeping the perm on longer than It should, the perm would burn my scalp and I would sometimes get scabs in my hair. If I had told the truth to the beautician and said, "Yes! It's burning!" she would have immediately taken me under the water to wash out the chemicals. If only I had had the tools to know how to speak up!

While in graduate school, we were asked to share an item that represented our cultural identity. I automatically thought of and shared our family Pressing Comb that has been in our family for over 70-plus years. The family pressing comb was used for so long, the metal teeth of the comb started to bend. Shortly after my presentation at the graduate retreat, I was asked by Dr. Nola Butler Byrd, my practicum supervisor, to join the San Diego Caregiver-Child Connections Project. Unbeknownst to me, what I was about to embark on was going to be innovative and life changing to say the least. Work that would consist of hair combing interactions (HCIs) between female caregivers and their daughters, combined with the concept of "talk, touch and listen," was groundbreaking for me and I couldn't wait to learn more about and be a part of. I was really excited to learn about the HeartMath emWave® (n.d.) and how it would function with the participants in the interviews.

Before meeting with the participants, I felt overwhelmed with excitement and also anxious. I knew that the team and I had a lot of work ahead of us. I never dreamt that sharing my cultural item, the pressing comb, at our graduate retreat would lead to this awesome opportunity to work with this population of women and children. I also knew that going into this project would probably bring back some old memories that I had, while getting my hair straightened, while growing up. I was ready for the challenge. I remember before the actual project began, the team and I would have several GoToMeetings with Dr. Marva Lewis who is the pioneer of our project. Although I was learning a lot through these much needed meetings, I started to feel a little overwhelmed with the amount of paperwork and surveys that the participants had to complete. I was also wondering if they would feel overwhelmed as well, or if they would understand it, or if I would be able to explain it to them correctly. The process taught me that collecting large amounts of data, often in the form of surveys, is very much needed. When the interviews and workshop sessions were finally on the calendar and ready to be implemented with the participants, I started to feel more confident that the work we were doing as a team would 1 day turn out to really help develop true connections between a mother and daughter. Getting the "green" light from the IRB to move forward was a great feeling!

I would recommend that this type of work continues in some capacity, because it really promotes attachment relationships, teamwork, leadership, and humility. It was an awesome teaching tool for how, what, and why collecting data is important and needed. And for those who have a passion for helping the underrepresented populations, this type of work will hopefully be just what they've been looking for. I am also aware that this type of data collecting can sometimes change outcomes for the better. As well as being able to witness the pre- and post- of these incredible and resilient women with their daughters and having a safe space for them to process their feelings, as well as being able to process their personal challenges of their day-to-day lives, was very gratifying.

After graduating and obtaining my Master's Degree in Educational Counseling, I landed two Adjunct Counseling positions at two of the local community colleges, as an EOPS Counselor (Extended Programs and Services) and an EOPS / NextUP (Program for foster youth) Counselor Foster Youth Services. I also work with Project Restart students: men and women who have been incarcerated and are now going back to school. I feel that my graduate internship really helped prepare me for my current counseling positions. As a Counselor-in-training, my internship consisted of working with young students who were in foster care and students whose parents were incarcerated.

As a current Educational Counselor and a Foster Youth Liaison, it is my sincere duty and obligation to be as present with my current students as I was with the women in this study, internship and graduate school, clinic clients. Participating in the hair combing interaction experience has solidified my interest and calling in the helping profession. This experience came with many rewards and challenges. Having to wait a long period of time to start the actual project, having a hard time trying to retrieve the data from the 'emWaves. Rewards, being a first-time presenter at the 45th Association of Black Psychologist International Convention to discuss our findings, and being a first-time published writer in the Journal of Women & Therapy, was challenging and awesome. Most amazing of all was seeing the participants' relationships flourish with their daughters as they grew in understanding of themselves. One participant didn't want this project to end. She stated, "I'm not ready for this to end. I've learned so much about myself and about how to have a better connection with my daughter, I want more." For me, this quote is why I love being a Counselor and why the work that we were undertaking was so important. Moreover, it has confirmed the vital influence of touch, talk, and listen between female caregivers and their children during the hair combing process. This experience has definitely helped me with my current position, and I am thankful that I was able to be a part of such a rewarding and groundbreaking project. I feel very humbled to have been able to work with this population of women and children affected by homelessness. I really appreciated the guidance of Dr. Butler Byrd. She would give us the tools to do what was needed to make things happen but would allow us to go out and make our way. She trusted the team to go out and make it happen. Being under her direction allowed me to feel like the team and I could handle whatever was put in front of us. And if a problem were to arise (and they did), she was right there to get us through to the next step of the process. It was also an honor to work with the rest of the team as well, Kathleen Baca, Michelle Rowe-Odom, and Ojore Bushfan. Having team members you trust and feel supported by to bounce ideas, frustrations, highs, and lows was much needed and so appreciated. This project has allowed me to see the collection of data in a positive lens. This process has also helped me to open my eyes about how I currently feel about my own hair and the hair combing process today. I've concluded that I like wearing different hairstyles, depending on my mood. I love wearing my natural curly hair; different types of wings: long, short, straight, and curly. I also enjoy wearing braids and ponytails. This process has also allowed me to come to the realization that my mother and big Momma had their own set of tools and now I have my own tools as well! Tools that allow a lot of ongoing self-love and self-reflection, along with the help of this eye-opening project. I may carry a little residue from my past hair combing interactions, but I no longer allow my hair to define who I am. I humbly desire to learn more and do more data collection in the future.

Kathleen Baca Leanos

As a bicultural, bilingual, and cis-gendered woman in the United States, the physical aspects of my identity and gender expression have been a personal and public conversation. Over our lifetime, the body, with all its internal and external components, has become site of oppression and resistance. Individuals create stories about themselves, and others based on the socially constructed and accepted "truths" we learn from the moment we are born. Hair, the most prominent hair on our bodies, has been a complicated issue within communities of color, particularly within the black community. My personal hair journey and interest in community-based research is what cemented my connection to the project. During one of my first days in the Community Based Block Program, we were asked to bring a cultural artifact to share with the group. I remember my colleague; Ava Gill brought her familial hot comb to our retreat and shared the intergenerational memories that have been embedded into the comb. Ava's story triggered my own memories of my hair journey and the confusion and discomfort that surrounded those memories and my sense of self. I grew up in a Central American/Latinx/American family that did not know how to care for my thick, curly hair. As my hair continued to change throughout my childhood, my family made comments that made me feel othered. As a child of immigrants, I struggled to understand how my physical identity, more specifically my hair, was accepted or denied based on how well I assimilated to white beauty standards. I've always had a contentious relationship with my hair, which has slowly shifted toward acceptance as I better understand how my body is a site for my own resistance. Finding other individuals within the program who share similar struggles brought us together. Ava, Michelle, and I felt connected through our own hair stories and our passion to give back to the communities we call our own.

My experience at the Monarch School Project is what led me to pursue my master's degree through the Community-Based Block Program. The school has a unique organizational structure; the school is managed by their nonprofit (the Monarch School Project) and San Diego County of Education's Juvenile Court and Community Schools District. The Monarch School has been in existence since 1998 when a small group of individuals came together to address the increasing educational gaps faced by youth impacted by homelessness. The Monarch School aimed to address these educational disparities by recognizing the need to provide students and their families with ongoing support services and items such as toiletries, meals, etc., to help with the daily challenges they faced. The Monarch School continues to be an innovative organization focused on adapting to the needs of the students and their families. The Monarch School has grown and shifted their focus since their inception, but it has continued to address the dynamic demands of children and families who experience homelessness in San Diego County. The Monarch School has worked with numerous agencies and academic institutions to provide their community with unique opportunities to strengthen and address the emotional, mental, and physical impacts of homelessness.

As a program director, I was given the opportunity to create meaningful programming for youth and families impacted by homelessness. Although the school was able to successfully provide numerous resources and support to the students and their families, parents needed more intensive and innovative supportive services. Children who experience homelessness are subjected to ongoing stress that impacts their relationships with their parents, teachers, and other children. As mental health practitioners, we understand the importance of child–caregiver attachment and the impact it can have on a child's development and throughout their lifetime. Once my colleagues and I were exposed to the innovative work by Dr. Marva Lewis on hair combing interactions, Dr. Nola Butler Byrd formed the San Diego Caregiver–Child Connections Project with the aim of providing a unique, therapeutic resource to this underserved community. Combing someone's hair is a physically intimate interaction between two individuals; we saw this as an opportunity for our caregivers to use this interaction as a method for rebuilding and strengthening their connection with their child. Through my professional connection to the Monarch School, our team was able to receive support by the school and district to conduct this research with parents and their children. The process was challenging due to the unprecedented nature of the therapeutic work we were proposing.

Once we began to implement our research design, we were confronted with issues unique to the population we intended to serve. The Monarch School Project's student population tends to be more transient than traditional schools due to the issue of homelessness. Our initial participant group was targeted toward mothers and daughter dyads of color. We intentionally focused our recruitment of women of color, specifically African American and Latinx, due to the historical significance that hair and hair combing have in these communities. With the support of Monarch staff members, we utilized snowball sampling to recruit mother/daughter dyads with the intention of quickly building trust with the community. Once we solidified our first group, we began the data collection process, which incorporated written questionnaires and video interviews. Our pre- and post-surveys included the Brief Symptom Inventory (BSI), Adult PARQ, Adult Reading Survey, Childhood Experiences of Racial Acceptance-Rejection (CERAR), and Compassion Survey (for oneself and others). During the pre- and postinterview interactions, which were filmed, we utilized the emWave©. The emWave "collects pulse data through a pulse sensor and translates the information from your heart rhythms into graphics" (HeartMath, n.d.). We did not anticipate the technical difficulties we would face by videotaping our interviews or using the emWaves during group sessions. At times, we were not capturing data due to technical difficulties, which complicated our data collection efforts.

Due to the transient nature of our population, our group attendance was inconsistent. We were unable to have consistent communication with our participants due to the caregiver's inability to access technology. In each group session, we presented different topics on the importance of how they talked, touched, and listened with their children. Our training with Dr. Marva Lewis regarding The Early Connections Project and Talk, Touch, and Listen played a pivotal role in helping us create the structure and content of the group meetings. We provided a space for participants to discuss their own childhood experiences, including the elements that they wished to carry on to their children and those they wanted to change. These conversations provided an opportunity to discuss how parenting and caregiver/child interactions are intergenerationally passed on. Time was allotted during each session for caregivers and their children to experience a hair combing interaction. During these hair combing interactions, caregivers were encouraged to practice new skills and behaviors learned during the group discussion. All of these elements, the pre- and post-measures, videotaped interactions, and emWave data, were reviewed and analyzed once the eight-week group concluded.

Our participants expressed gratitude for the space provided for them by us and their fellow participants. Each participant had the opportunity to share parts of their story and were given the opportunity to reflect on how they want to continue that story with the children. Participants were able to express how they implemented the skills they learned within the group at home with their children. Overall, the experience appeared to have a positive impact in the caregiver's attachment relationship with their child.

Prior to initiating this project, my research experience was limited to qualitative research. Guided by Dr. Butler Byrd, our group embarked on creating a mixed methods research design with the goal of providing a meaningful treatment opportunity to the families, as well as a culturally relevant and distinct treatment modality for mental health providers. As graduate students, this project provided us with the opportunity to challenge ourselves and cocreate a project from its inception. From the Institutional Review Board (IRB) process to the data analysis and writing, each team member challenged themselves to learn new skills and practices. As graduate students, we are not often given the opportunity to participate in community-based participatory projects. Across all disciplines, access to resources and time to conduct new or unexplored research topics is not an opportunity many graduate students have access to. The support of Dr. Butler Byrd and the Monarch School project made it possible for us to pursue and execute this project. The experience we gained from this project augmented our therapeutic and research skills that goes beyond the classroom setting. Throughout the process, we had to adapt as changes occurred, navigate our roles as mental health practitioners and researchers, and think critically through the challenges we and the families faced. As researchers, we better understood how to manage data and technological difficulties that occurred during the process.

Since the completion of the project, I have obtained my Master's in Social Welfare and have become a Licensed Clinical Social Worker in Los Angeles and Ventura County in California. I have worked with families as a Children's Social Worker (Child Protection Services) with Los Angeles County Department of Children and Family Services and now as a Crisis Team Clinician with Ventura County Behavioral Health. This project inspired me to pursue my clinical licensure; I wanted to continue to expand my knowledge around parent and child connections. I continue to bring the lessons I learned from this project into the work I do with families daily. This project solidified my passion of working with families who are the most underserved in our communities, as well as help me share my experience with parents who want to strengthen their attachment with their child. My experience working with my colleagues on this project helped solidify the importance of building a diverse team. I have my own experiences, knowledge, and history, but continued to gain knowledge and skills to be a better clinician and researcher. Individually, we brought our own talents to the team and together, we were able to brainstorm issues and creatively address any challenges that arose during the process. This experience strengthened my desire to pursue community-based research projects and the importance of elevating the voices of our communities.

Michelle J. Rowe-Odom

Coming into the Work

At the time that I began the study, I had a 15-month-old daughter. I was introduced to Attachment Theory during my pregnancy. Even while pregnant, I felt deep commitment to connect with my daughter, especially through *talk* at that time. I will never forget how immediately after she was born the doctors placed her on my chest and explained to me that this skin-to-skin contact was vital to my daughter's well-being during her first moments in this world. From that moment, I've had an increased awareness of the importance of touch to my daughter's survival in this world. Working with this research team and the women participants in the San Diego Caregiver-Child Connections Project shifted my perspective as a counselor in training, especially regarding my counseling theory, which at the time was person centered. As a parent, I was learning to trust and feel confident that I had the skills to nurture the basic needs of my daughter, through a strength-based approach, while at the same time, knowing that this project would indeed call me to reflect on my upbringing, my hair story, the narrative that was developed, and how if or how I would want to change it moving forward. My original goal of research was to study educational outcomes and disparities between schools north and south of Interstate 8 in San Diego, California, and then it turned into black girls and academic achievement, which was a small tenet of our research before hair combing became the focus. But ultimately, I am glad it took this route. I think we did a fabulous job at bringing Marva's research to life in our own way. Her research is her heart/brainchild and is able to transform to give life to those who take it on in their own way.

Where I Came From

Rewind...I grew up in a community in Western Canada called Calgary. It is one of the five largest cities in Calgary, which occupies indigenous land of the Treaty 7 Blackfoot tribe. It has also become the home to many new arrivals from South America, Africa, the Middle East, Caribbean, and countless other countries. I, along with my cousins, and virtually every friend I had growing up were first-generation Canadians. Family was a big thing, and most of us had a large chunk of our families present, while others were back in countries of origin. Growing up we spent a lot of time with my grandma, and my cousins, my aunties would take turns every weekend babysitting all of us cousins, which was at least 10 of us on a given weekend. I would often go to play, but sometimes, I would also prepare to get my hair braided, and later in age, sometimes have my hair relaxed. This was always an ordeal. I had to have my hair taken out before I arrived. Sometimes, if my mom did not have time to help me take my hair out before I arrived, my auntie would be so upset that now we had another 4 h added to our already 8 h of hair combing, because now, we had to take out, detangle, wash, dry, and grease my hair. HCIs usually consisted of sitting for hours, being told to stay still, or listening to my auntie talk or complain about something or someone, but mostly watching TV shows, or watching my cousins and siblings run in and out of the apartment or house playing and having fun. It was also painful. To just sit there for 8 h and have your scalp tugged at and pulled, and just to endure. And if I cried or complained I was tender-headed, which was a bad thing, mainly because (what I understand now, was probably my aunty's guilt and annoyance that she was causing you pain, or that I made her look bad, or that I wasn't grateful enough and simply enjoying this labor of love; or duty). I just remember waiting until it was all over so that I could feel or be told I looked pretty. I mostly remember my dad telling me I looked pretty, but only after my hair was done, not braided, when it was relaxed. I also remember the times when I would take out my hair and then my aunt had to cancel or reschedule, and the fear I had about going to school with my hair naturally. I remember how my mom would relax my hair, because I would cry about not wanting to go to school or soccer practice with my "hair out." The times I had to, I would wear my hoodie on the bus and pull my hair back so tight to make a ponytail and could not focus in school, scared that the rubber band in my hair would snap and my hair would be out! Damn. What would it have been like if I was told that I was beautiful and didn't need extensions what my family called braid extensions, or that my hair was beautiful the way it was, and that there were other styles I could try to embrace my natural hair. What if I told stories about positive black women while getting my hair combed that reflected the inner beauty? What if? What if? This is what this research brought up for me. This is what I wanted to explore for myself, for my community, and for my daughter so that she would be proud of who she is, and that I would use 4380 opportunities for touch, talk, and listening while combing hair. What a concept! What a gift to know that I, every day, can build a stronger connection with my child while combing hair.

We also learned about proximity and closeness during the hair combing interaction. I was excited to do this in a deliberate way. The next time I did my daughter's hair. I kept her close in my lap, rubbed her scalp, and tried my best to make it an enjoyable experience for her. This research is a movement filled with moments of awareness and re-embrace and a call to do things differently. It is also a call to honor those who did this labor of love with the tools, knowledge, and love that they knew to be the best they could do. Whatever was passed down, whether positive or negative, is mine to fix, hold, or examine. I know the research we created with the mothers/caregivers in the HCI group is also a gift of reflection, awareness, and autonomy to do it "my way."

My Hair Story

In the beginning of the research, we would meet weekly with Dr. Marva Lewis and other colleagues around the United States who were interested in, or already conducting groups inspired by Dr. Lewis's research. One of the activities that we were introduced to, which we would later use as a tool for the women in the support group, was "My Hair Story." This activity asks you to "Draw a picture of your hair when you were younger and write one word that describes the feeling associated with that image." There were no other guidelines. It was endearing to see and hear about everyone's hair story. Some of us drew the face, the body, accessories, and others, like myself, drew the hair by itself. My image was a sorry attempt at drawing a head full of long black braids (or extensions, as we would call it growing up). The word I chose was "safe." We were asked to talk about our Hair Story and why we chose that word. I shared that growing up I usually had my hair in single braids with the added hair. This felt safe for several reasons; mainly because I played sports a lot as a child, so no matter how sweaty or kinky my hair was, it was woven tight into those braids, to me this was a safeguard. The other part about safety was that "I could wear my hair like the white girls." These were the words I said growing up. Growing up, this felt safe, especially because in sports, I was usually the only black girl, or in school one of the few without hair that didn't hang. But saying this out loud, in the group, felt painful. I was reminded of how much pain I carried. But at the same time, I was encouraged with my process in my current hair story, since I had just begun my natural hair journey, before entering the Community-Based Block program.

Building Rapport and Trust with the Caregivers

Because my colleagues will be discussing the main points of the research project itself, I will keep this section brief, and focus on other areas. Witnessing these mothers grow, learn, and be vulnerable was an unforgettable experience. One activity we conducted with the caregivers was to review their preinterview HCI video, and to learn to give and receive feedback. The caregivers were given feedback scales to help guide their feedback. We also showed a video beforehand that Marva shared with us, which was a compilation of hair combing interactions between caregivers and children, which showed a wide range of markers to look for: proximity (space between caregiver and child), or positive/negative verbal and nonverbal communication. At this point, the only participants were the same consistent caregivers, and while there was general discomfort with having to watch segments of their video with others, and discomfort in both giving and receiving feedback, the women committed to the activity. One of the prompts was to ask the mothers about any goals they wanted to set. This was the most memorable moment for me, where one mother shared that she wanted to talk more with her daughter after watching a silent HCI between her and her daughter, because her daughter was on the cell phone (used as a tool to distract her from the pain). It was beautiful to hear this mother return a week later and share her goal and how it brought her and her daughters closer, not just during the hair combing interactions, but in other family routines. It felt good as a researcher to know that the goals and outcomes, in this case, were entirely self-determined by this mother, and nurtured by the community we built. The short-term effects of positive and loving touch, verbal interaction, and effective listening were a testament not only to the theory itself, but to the power we have as human beings to rebuild painful generational narratives.

The Writing

The aftermath of writing and putting the project into words was a laborious, memorable, and healing process for me. This was another aspect of research that I was entering unfamiliarly as we were now seeking the goal of being published. A further analysis of the quantitative and qualitative data that we compiled during the study uncovered many of the joy and challenges in research as we uncovered information shared by the participants that, if we had reviewed during the project, or had more time, we would have explored more during the group sessions. For example, one measure, the CERAR (Childhood Experiences of Racial Acceptance and Rejection), gathered qualitative responses about parent/child relationships that helped to unpack the brief disclosures that participants shared in the sessions. We also uncovered unexpected shifts in the participants' levels of depression and anxiety from the Brief Symptom Inventory (BSI): a measure the participants were asked to complete at the start of each group meeting. We found that most of the participants' scores indicated an increase in depression overall. As researchers, we had to lean on the anecdotal, qualitative, and program outcomes to help us better understand this. We made the hypothesis that the activities and information shared in the support group about stress, mental health, and well-being increased the participants' awareness of their own mental health and childhood trauma, and deepened how they reported their levels as the weeks progressed. I could relate to this, as being in an emotion-focused counseling program naturally helped me to acknowledge and to take my mental health seriously.

Like much of my experience in higher education, I was introduced to terms that defined my lived experiences, bringing meaning, understanding, and proof of my existence. In this sense, alloparenting reminded me of my upbringing, and being raised by my mother, aunties, and my maternal grandmother. Understanding alloparenting helped to affirm our use of the word caregiver in the title of our project and in how we described the mothers and fathers that participated in the SDC3 support group and research. Alloparenting really helped to share the historical cultural influences from Africa, where the proverb "it takes a village" is realized in alloparenting. Moreover, in regards to attachment, alloparenting plays a role in the messages and narratives one develops as a child spends time under the care of different adults, and sometimes sibling care. If I ever continue this work further, I would like to incorporate alloparenting into the curriculum, to further unpack intergenerational trauma, strengths, and stories.

Recommendations for Community-Based Research

Understanding of the historical and traumatic conditions of the community and its members. Understanding what HCIs will look like for these communities. HCI can be used as a cross-cultural degree for understanding. It weaves us together, whether one has a hair story or not, the absence of a hair story is a story to be told. Also, this project involved children: a project that works with children and their parents/caregivers will always include an intergenerational component that will offer rich information and stories. Qualitative data is essential to capture the stories and lived experiences. Take lots of notes after each session, meeting, reflecting and journal your thoughts daily, or when they come up. Quantitative data is helpful for demographics and to track participant progress based on what question you are trying to answer. The BSI was a helpful and brief tool used each session that helped the participants to track their mood at the start and end of each session.

Ojore Lateef Bushfan

Coming on Board

At the time the SDC3 group was formed, I navigated the world as a male of African descent with a head full of locs, a growing interest in attachment theory, working part-time in the CBB program as a field site coordinator, and deciding on whether to apply to a social work or marriage and family therapy program. Prior to the start of the project, my hair was locked for 2 years. I was very much connected to my crown and had fully embraced my natural hair. I wore my hair in locs to move away from the gaze of "good hair." Growing up, I was often told that I had nice hair, because it was soft and naturally curly. Wearing my hair naturally was an important expression of my cultural identity. What I miss most about wearing locs was getting my locs tightened. I looked forward to seeing my Loc-tician and having my hair cared for while sitting comfortably in a chair catching up on each other's lives and sharing heartfelt laughs. While my locs and connection with my Loc-tician grew, so did my desire to understand more about attachment.

I developed a greater understanding of attachment theory during my interpersonal work with a body-centered therapist. As a result of my work in therapy, I gained insight into my attachment wounds and how they've impacted my relationships and ability to have close connections. I bought numerous books and read various articles on attachment theory to further explore my attachment styles, and what I needed to heal in order to develop and sustain closeness with others. My attraction to this developmental model became the bridge that brought me to find out about an opportunity to engage in a unique community-based project.

As a Field Site Supervisor in the Community-Based Block Program, my role was to connect incoming students with a field site or ensure their current field site was able to provide an opportunity for students to utilize their developing multicultural and social justice-oriented counseling skills, learn about their agency/site, and receive supervision. When I heard about the project, I felt an immediate curiosity that further developed into an interest in this community-based approach to strengthening attachment through hair care interactions; it was in alignment with where my interests were at the time. I was drawn to the idea that an everyday process (hair care) was an opportunity to establish and strengthen the connection between child and caregiver. The HCI became a space in which a community of parents/caregivers and their children were able to rediscover new ways of using a moment in time to bond with their child/children. While aiding the project, I became inspired by all the time and effort that went into bringing it to life and the participation of the group members. I began thinking about ways that I could do meaningful work with communities, families, and individuals that are often marginalized or forgotten.

While doing my interpersonal work, I decided to return to school to pursue a master's degree that led to clinical licensure. I was on the fence; I couldn't decide between applying to a social work or marriage and family therapy program. I talked with colleagues in both fields and got their input. During a personal therapy session,

I found my answer; I decided to become a Marriage and Family Therapist, since the bulk of my work in therapy focused on the family dynamics within my family of origin. In my application to the Marriage and Family Therapy Program, I expressed my desire to become a school-based therapist; my goal was to provide effective mental health services to middle-school or high-school students while being a change agent. I completed the majority of my clinical hours at a high school that provided various mental health services to students with an IEP and label of Emotional Disturbance and/or an additional qualifying diagnosis. My work at this site was heavily impacted by the study and the social justice/change agent approach to my work I developed as a student in the CBB program.

Attachment theory became an even more important part of my approach to building a therapeutic alliance with the students I worked with. I intentionally discussed the concept of attachment and explored the different attachment style(s) in hopes the students would develop insight as to how their attachment injuries impact their ability to connect with others. Most importantly, I was intentional about creating a space where students could take the risk to develop a secure attachment with myself, in hopes of creating secure bonds with others. I was able to experience the impact of cocreating a secure attachment and the dance of avoidance by students that were not interested in developing rapport. During my years as a school-based therapist, I experienced that dance of connection with many students I worked with; some of the dances were in sync and others were offbeat. Each dance of connection made me aware of my own attachment styles and what I needed to work on so that I could continue to be a secure base. In becoming a consistent person in a student's life also meant using my role/power as a therapist to challenge the status quo and do what I could to be about equity for all the students on campus.

Graduating from the CBB program has equipped me with an ability to notice when people in power positions are using their power in ways that perpetuate injustice and cause harm to others. In my role as an Associate Marriage and Family Therapist, I learned to use my voice to name and call out misuses of power and voice the need for structural change. Most importantly, I grew to use my voice to bring awareness to biased actions that were often directed to African-American and Latinx students (mostly female). Whenever I noticed or got wind that something shady happened, I woke up the social justice warrior and made a plan to address the inequity. I would often have to breathe and ground myself, because it appalled me that adults would direct such biases and racist actions toward students. And I would remember something said in a Wednesday circle in CBB. It was a reminder that when standing for social justice, you will be triggered and become angry; what will you do with that energy? How will you use it to propel you into action? I was reminded how I would sit with my anger before going to battle against the school system and its participants. I wanted to create change without losing my job, sometimes that was hard to negotiate. However, I found ways to make those negotiations numerous times. Challenging teachers' assumptions about students dealing with the effects of childhood trauma, challenging administrators' decisions to swiftly send home or suspend students of color and fighting decisions to remove students from campus. I realized that being a secure base has many different looks. Students knew that Mr. B (what the students called me) had their back. They were not afraid to let staff know that they had someone on site who would go to bat for them. The Community-Based Block Program laid a foundation of advocacy and social justice that I continue to stand on; it keeps me grounded and connected to the reason I became a school-based therapist.

I am very proud to share that I became a licensed marriage and family therapist on August 19, 2019. I continue to provide clinical services in postsecondary education settings. Currently, I am a full-time Clinical Therapist at San Diego State University. I have also become a certified practitioner of sound healing and am looking to further my knowledge and practice of this approach while integrating into my clinical work.

I still find myself talking about the research project anytime someone brings up attachment or discussions about black girls' hair. When I talk about the project, listeners find it interesting and want to know more about attachment through hair care interactions. They also seem to take a moment to reflect on their own hair care experience as a child growing up.

Trying It Out

We met via GoToMeeting to become more familiar with the initial work done by Dr. Marva Lewis at Tulane University and began a series of trainings to be able to implement the Talk, Touch, and Listen project in San Diego. Dr. Lewis shared a series of articles that explored race, hair, and attachment. The training walked the team through the curriculum for the project. During the training, the team participated in an activity called Hair Story. It was during this activity and discussion that I realized that I had a hair story and had been a witness to my sister's hair story as well. I recalled how as a child, my mother would wash my hair in the sink. I would have to get a washcloth and hunch over the sink; it wasn't the most comfortable position, but it was a moment I felt connected to my mother. After my mother would wash my hair, she would grease my scalp and part my hair (which I always struggled with her about because I hated having a part). As I got older, my mother stopped washing my hair and greasing my scalp. The message I received was that I was old enough to take care of my own hair, so I started washing my own hair and greasing my own scalp. Recalling and talking about my hair story made me miss the times my mother cared for my hair. There was something so connecting about my over the sink-washcloth-hair washing experience that made me miss those times with my mother.

Once the team finished the curriculum training, we developed a protocol to record the haircare interactions. One of the researchers knew a parent who was open to allowing the team to record her haircare interaction with her daughter. We discussed what equipment we would need to record the interaction; I checked out the video equipment and tripod from San Diego State University. The team met at the pilot project participant's house to record the haircare interaction. Once inside the resident, the team greeted the participant and thanked her for allowing us to record her doing her child's hair. Once we figured out where the interaction would take place, I set up the camera and a team member helped the participant get the emWave setup. Once the hair care interaction began, I observed the close proximity of mother and child, the way she combed the child's hair, and the conversation they had during the interaction. As I observed the interaction, I felt moved by the research we were planning to do; I felt privileged to witness this tender moment.

Equipment Guy

Recording the hair care interactions required the team to have access to video-recording equipment and tripods. The video cameras and tripods we used were essential to capturing the hair care interactions for group members to see their interaction and receive feedback from the group regarding the way they talked, touched, and listened. Capturing these moments required each team member to learn how to set up the camera and tripod; it was important to learn how to use the equipment, because we did not want to invite a caregiver and child to do a hair care interaction and spend half of the time fiddling with the camcorder. Also, we wanted to make sure we recorded the interaction successfully the first time; there was no director yelling "cut" and asking a parent and child to start over could have a negative impact on the participants. I felt it made the team look professional. Yes, there were some hiccups here and there, but taking the time to figure out how to record, capture audio, and save the recordings was paramount to the success of the overall project and participants being able to see themselves during their hair care interaction. While dealing with the recording equipment was necessary, it was also very challenging at times.

Borrowing the video equipment and tripod from the Multimedia Department at San Diego State University (SDSU) has its own set of challenges I had to navigate. One of the biggest challenges was being able to check out the equipment and returning the equipment on time. The equipment housed in the Multimedia Department was shared by campus faculty, so at times when I needed to check out a few camcorders, extra batteries, extension cords, and tripods, there was no equipment available to check out. Other times, after checking out the equipment, I would forget that it needed to be returned within a two-week period; the team was busy recording hair care interactions for their group, and I would miss the date to return the equipment.

Checking out the equipment was a challenge; at times, the team did not have it when it was needed, which would push back recording a hair care interaction. Constantly having to return the equipment every 2 weeks was a hassle. Loading up my vehicle and lugging the equipment across campus was not easy. It would have been easier if we had our own equipment; we would have had a certain kind of freedom/ability to record hair care interactions within our own time frame versus the two-week window the Multimedia Department gave us. Without access to the camcorders and accessories, extension cords, and tripods, the project would have struggled to find the equipment needed to capture the talk, touch, and listen moments the project was looking to strengthen, and caregivers and their daughters wouldn't have had an opportunity to see how they were currently using their moments to connect and received feedback on ways to have deeper connections.

Throughout the research project, I developed rapport with Nate,[1] an African-American male who worked in the Multimedia Department. The first time I went to the Multimedia Department to ask about checking out video equipment, Nate asked me several questions about my reason for using the equipment. I explained to him that I was part of a research group doing a study involving hair care interactions between caregivers and their daughters. He became intrigued by my description of the study, talking to me for almost an hour about how interesting he found the study and looking at hair care as a way to build closer connections between child and caregiver. We even spent some time talking about our own hair stories and realizing as men of African descent, we have hair stories too. I felt a sense of connection and shared experience with Nate. Our connection and conversations would develop throughout the duration of the study. It was helpful to have rapport with Nate, because I had to interact with him checking out and returning the equipment. He helped make the process smooth; when he was not in the department, I had to deal with someone else who often made it difficult to get what I needed.

Nate cut me a lot of slack. There were times when the equipment needed to be returned and I was a day or two late returning it. He would email me, then call me with a friendly reminder. When I arrived to turn in the equipment, he would ask me about the project. He would ask me if I still needed the equipment; if no other faculty put in a request, he would let me check it back out. Developing a connection with Nate allowed the team to have access to equipment that made it possible to record the hair care interactions. Nate and I spent many hours throughout this time talking about it being black boys and navigating our hair, and checking in with each other weekly made our connection meaningful. As the team thought about working on adding male caregivers to the project, he agreed that it would be a good addition to the research. I shared some ideas I had about recruiting fathers who have daughters; we would talk about the importance of fathers building close bonds with their daughters. He was one of the project's biggest fans. I made sure to often express my gratitude to Nate for being flexible with the rules and allowing the team to hold on to the equipment just a little while longer.

Working with Fathers

As a team, we discussed creating a group that included hair care interactions with fathers/male caregivers and their daughters as a part of a research project. We wanted to give male caregivers a space to strengthen their bond with their daughters as they carried out their normal hair routine. We discussed starting off with a few hair care interactions with male caregivers, so I took the lead on finding fathers/

[1] All names and other personal identifiers in the cases throughout the chapter are changed to protect privacy and confidentiality.

male caregivers who had a daughter, who would allow me to record their hair care interaction. I thought about the fathers I knew who had daughters and a couple of people came to mind. I reached out to a close friend to get her brother's contact information. She expressed that she was sure he would be open to it, since he does his daughter's hair often. I made the call and explained the nature of the research. He thought the research was interesting; he asked his daughter if she would be open to it, she agreed to participate in the project as well. I was extremely excited to have a willing participant. An African-American male in his 30s, from San Diego, who worked full-time and has a 10-year-old daughter. I contacted the team and shared the good news. We discussed the consent forms and measures I would need and the equipment. I took the documents and equipment home with me and practiced going through the consent forms and talking about the measures and setting up the tripod and camcorder. I also made sure I had an extension cord, fully charged battery, and a blank recording tape.

On the day of the recording, I arrived at the house and greeted the father and daughter and thanked them for being willing to allow me to witness their bonding time. After I greeted the participants, I went over the consent forms and informed the father and daughter that they could withdraw from the project at any time. After the consent forms were filled out and the study was further explained to the participants, the father filled out the needed measures. Once all the paperwork was completed, the recording equipment was set up adjacent to the space set up for the daughter's hair to be done.

I observed the hair care interaction from a distance to minimize any influence my presence would have on the interaction; thus, I sat like a fly on the wall witnessing the hair care interaction between a father and his daughter. The television was on during the interaction and the daughter was thumbing through her phone in between glances at the television. Father and daughter discussed what type of hairstyle was going to take place during the interaction. Once agreed upon, the father began. To his left was a table filled with hair products, combs, brushes, hair ties, and a water bottle. Like a detailed scientist, the father took his time to perfectly part her hair and then grabbing handfuls of hair and combing it (after applying sprays of water). I noticed the daughter making grimacing faces as her hair was being combed, but she did not express aloud that the combing hurt. Throughout the hair care interaction, father and daughter talked here and there; she was engaged with her cell phone and the television. The father took the utmost pride in doing his daughter's hair; when he finished, he had a look of pride and his daughter appeared to have appreciated the experience and hairstyle.

Afterward, I got the chance to sit down with the father and talk with him about the experience and how he started doing his daughter's hair. He shared that his mother told him that she is not always going to be around to do his daughter's hair, so he needed to learn how to comb and style her hair. He learned to style her hair by watching videos on YouTube; there was a lot of trial and error, but he has picked up a few skills along the way. He expressed that he enjoys doing his daughter's hair and that it is their time together. He enjoys their time together, even though she is on her phone or watching television, the little interactions they have during the hair care interaction are nice. He also made it a point to talk about his relationship with his daughter; for him, his relationship with his daughter is the first relationship she will have with a male, so it is important for him to set the standard for how she should be treated. With the success of capturing this hair care interaction and listening to this father's journey to caring for his daughter's hair, I became excited at the possibility of extending this project with other fathers/male caregivers.

In an effort to continue to capture hair care interactions between fathers/male caregivers and their daughters, I reached out to several fathers I knew but could not get anyone to commit to a date and time. Many fathers were interested in the project and thought it was nice that such a project existed, but they could not find time in their busy schedules or canceled before the day of the taping. In a further attempt, the research group attempted to include fathers/male guardians at the school site but were unable to because the child participant declined to participate in the hair care interaction and recording. I was bummed that the interaction would not be recorded, and the father/caregiver and daughter would not be participating in the study; however, the daughter participant had the right to decline their participation. In the future, it is my hope that the project will be able to include fathers/male caregivers and their daughters. There have been several pictures that have gone viral via social media showing fathers/male caregivers doing their daughter's hair, so hair care interactions are happening in households throughout the country.

I Can Do Research!

Through this process, I have realized that I can do research that I enjoy, has meaning to me, and makes an impact in peoples' lives. Prior to being a part of the SDC3 project, my interaction with research was for a research methods course in grad school. In this course, I learned how to set up a research project, collect and code data, and write about the findings. I wasn't connected to the project and my interest in doing the research assignment was very low. In contrast, the SDC3 project was totally opposite; I was really engaged and motivated to be a part of a project that aimed to increase connections between caregiver and child. I used to think that I couldn't be a researcher; however, what I found out is that I really connected with a project that spoke to my interest and had the potential to positively impact the lives of participants. I sincerely appreciated the opportunity to join this research team and project. Throughout this project's start to finish, I have grown as a person, researcher, and writer. May this research live on far more than a moment but become a movement.

Summary

Through the stories of four graduate students who participated in the SDC3 project, this chapter shared the power of community-based counseling, teaching, research, and service in the development of graduate counseling students. The project provided an opportunity for these students to experience community-based research that was culturally responsive and addressed a real community need – improved attachment relationships between homeless caregivers and their children. The project helped caregivers become more self-aware and connected with other caregivers in a culturally centered support group, where they enhanced their existing parenting and caregiving skills using everyday hair combing interactions. Caregivers also learned how to increase self-knowledge and emotional management for stress reduction.

Reflective Questions

1. The author shares this reflection: *As I look back as in adolescence, these negative "hair" self-images were embedded into my mind at an early age and took me through early years of my adulthood.* What memories, stories, or images about hair and hair care were awakened for you as you read this chapter and did these experiences, positive or negative, contribute to your self-image, then and now?
2. Can you reflect on your own hair combing story as a child, as a White person or Person of Color, as it contributed to your own development and beliefs about culture, ethnicity, race, equality, or inclusion?
3. Can you integrate the observation of Hair Combing Interaction (HCI) and the exploration of experiences, thoughts, and feelings about hair care and colorism into your research and practice with families, staff, undergraduates or graduates, or teaching and research faculty?
4. How can you "wake up the social justice warrior" and be heard when you notice racial disparity or injustice that is harmful to a family or peer?

References

Butler Byrd, N. (2009a). Historical identity development patterns and contemporary multicultural identity in first, second and third generation counseling students. *Penn GSE Perspectives on Urban Education, 6*(1), 21-31. Retrieved September 27, 2009, from http://www.urbanedjournal.org/Vol.%206%20Immigration%20Issues%20in%20Urban%20Schools/20-31%2D%2DByrd.pdf

Butler Byrd, N. (2009b). Preparing culturally responsive practitioners for social advocacy and systemic change using dialogic and democratic decision-making processes in multicultural context. *Social Advocacy and Systems Change, 1*(2) Retrieved September 27, 2009, from http://www.cortland.edu/ids/sasc/vol1_issue2/Butler Byrd%20Final.pdf

Butler Byrd, N. (2010). An African American supervisor's reflections on multicultural supervision. *Training and Education in Professional Psychology, 4*(1), 11–15. https://doi.org/10.1037/a0018351

Butler Byrd, N., Nieto, J., & Senour, M. N. (2006). Working successfully with diverse students and communities: The Community Based Block counselor preparation program. *Urban Education, 41*(4), 376–401. https://doi.org/10.1177/0042085906289706

Butler Byrd, N., Nieto, J., & Senour, M. N. (2008). Community-based multicultural counselor preparation as a site of praxis and social justice. *Journal of Praxis in Multicultural Education, 3*(1), 17–38. https://doi.org/10.9741/2161-2978.1010

HeartMath (n.d.) HeartMath tool.

HeartMath emWave2 (n.d.) HeartMath emWave2.

Lewis, M. L. (1993). *The Childhood Experiences of Racial Acceptance and Rejection (CERAR).* Unpublished dissertation. University of Colorado, Boulder.

Lewis, M. L. (1999). Hair combing interactions: A new paradigm for research with African American mothers. *The American Journal of Orthopsychiatry, 9*(4), 504–514. https://doi.org/10.1037/h0080398

Lewis, M. L., Turnage, B., Taylor, S. T., Francois, S., (2001). *The psychological residuals of Childhood Experiences of Racial Acceptance and Rejection: Theory and research.* Poster symposium: The development, reliability, and validity of the Childhood Experiences of Racial Acceptance and Rejection questionnaire (CERAR), Society for Research in Child Development, in Minneapolis, MI, USA.

Chapter 12
Reflections on the *Talk, Touch, and Listen* Facilitator Learning Community: Braiding the Personal, the Professional, and Liberation

Natasha Byars and Aditi Subramaniam

Introduction

"I am on a journey to accept my own hair – or at least not hating it as much as I did my whole life. I am more empowered to be intentional in my conversations about race, especially with my own children," reported a member in the Talk, Touch, & Listen Facilitator Learning Community. In 2018–2019, we, the authors, planned and subsequently facilitated Talk, Touch, and Listen While Combing Hair (TT&L) events in Boston, Massachusetts. The first was a half-day TT&L Train-the-Trainer workshop followed by a TT&L Parent Cafe, both facilitated by the curriculum's author, Dr. Marva Lewis. These one-time events were met with enthusiastic reception and a call for more TT&L offerings within the professional community. After several months of planning, we adapted the TT&L curriculum to launch a six-session Talk, Touch, and Listen Facilitator Learning Community, which carried on the rich professional and personal development that had been sparked at the half-day workshop. This chapter aims to describe and explore the deeply meaningful and complex experience of the learning community and the growth it supported among its members, as well as highlight some important considerations for the early childhood field.

The Talk, Touch, and Listen curricula, developed by Dr. Marva Lewis, is part of the scholarship of a Place for Natural Connections (PNC). The PNC works to promote caregiver–child relationships through the daily task of hair combing, which has the potential to support and strengthen emotional connections between

N. Byars (✉)
Southwest Human Development, Phoenix, AZ, USA
e-mail: Natasha.Byars@gmail.com

A. Subramaniam
Massachusetts Society for the Prevention of Cruelty to Children (MSPCC), Boston, MA, USA

M. L. Lewis, D. J. Weatherston (eds.), *Therapeutic Cultural Routines to Build Family Relationships*, https://doi.org/10.1007/978-3-030-83726-6_12

caregiver–child dyads, with community, and with culture. In addition to hair combing as a support for caregiver–child relationships, the TT&L curricula also focus on colorism and texturism – the valuing of lighter skin over darker skin and of straighter, smoother hair textures over curly or kinky textures, respectively – and how these insidious messages are passed intergenerationally, with roots in the historical trauma of slavery (Lewis et al., 2013). As a suite of manualized programs, including a parent cafe, and 4- or 8-week parent group, TT&L supports caregivers – in community with their peers – to challenge negative intergenerational and societal messages and build new, healing, affirming narratives for their families. More than a decade of research has validated hair-combing rituals and routines as a context to assess and support relationships between the child and caregiver (Lewis, 1999; Wilson et al., 2018). Though research initially focused on African-American caregivers, TT&L curricula has since been used with families across racial and ethnic identities.

In the words of legendary saxophonist Charlie Parker, “If you don’t live it, it won’t come out of your horn (Shapiro & Hentoff, 1955).” In the planning for the TT&L facilitator learning community, we (authors, N.B. & A.S.) willingly engaged with our whole selves, continuously returning to and reflecting upon our own multiple identities and intersectionality. The curriculum and learning community process held something for us that was deeply personal, in addition to its significant professional contribution. The author, Aditi Subramaniam, holds close to her identities of being a straight, cis-gendered, darker skinned South Asian woman from India, along with the layers of being an infant and early childhood mental health clinician, a dance movement psychotherapist, a dancer, a first-generation immigrant, and a parent raising a daughter bicultural with her husband in the United States. Navigating feelings of pain, confusion, and hurt as a child amidst the realities of being darker brown in a lighter brown–skinned community in India was always met by her family with empathy along with nurturing her to develop a sense of pride. She comes from a family (from both mother and father’s side) with thick black hair. In the retelling of her birth story, the family speaks of how it was only through seeing her thick head of hair that she was recognized by relatives. Hair interactions at home were a ritual! She fondly remembers rituals of oiling, massaging, and caring for hair as a family affair by her mother, passed generationally on to her. Along with it were also family practices of home remedies to nurture hair and very long weekend hours spent doing it. She belongs to a very large and closely knit family where relationships are seen as central. She values what the family values, e.g. commitment to the arts, cultural practices, and faith. Equally important, determination and hard work play a role in locating herself, personally and professionally. As a parent now, the intentionality to integrate positive and culturally proud practices with her daughter are a humbling, dynamic, and necessary journey of parenthood.

The author, Natasha Byars, identifies as a straight, cis-gendered, biracial Black and Hispanic woman. She comes from a mother with stick-straight hair, whose first language was Spanish and who proudly identifies as Texan and Mexican, retaining this connection to heritage even through generations of family living in Texas’s Rio

Grande Valley. Rooted in connection to family and culture, perseverance, faith, and justice-oriented compassion were some of the rich gifts handed down in this family. Still, there were also echoes of colorism in the stories of ancestors; *still*, there have been intentional, intergenerational efforts to combat these echoes. She comes from a Black father with generations of history in Alabama – a history, which included both legacies of slavery and legacies of family determination, love, and resilience. This family was instrumental in her positive formation of identity as a Black woman and her personal connection to the Great Migration, the Civil Rights Movement, and the richness of soul food and Black culture. A beloved family story from her childhood is her paternal aunt's concern at her lack of hair as a toddler, exclaiming to the author's mom, "Sylvia! When is she going to grow hair?!? I've never seen a Black child without hair!" She has fond memories from early childhood of male caregivers on both sides of her family who allowed her to "do" their hair – sitting on the top of the couch to grease her father's scalp, styling her uncle's hair with innumerable barrettes. At various time points, she has had hot combs, braids, chemical relaxers, flat irons, and ribbons, beads, barrettes, and "bolitas" – a Spanish term for bobble ponytail holders – applied to her hair; she eventually transitioned back to her natural curls in 2003. She had a family who celebrated her curly, kinky spirals and dark skin, though still had to navigate societal and internalized messaging of what constituted beauty.

The development and process of the TT&L learning community was personal, professional, and liberatory. Our journey together as cofacilitators highlighted for us the centrality of creating space together for the diverse aspects of identity, including but not limited to race, ethnicity, class, age, gender, and nationality. Such a multifaceted understanding of identity is elevated in the Diversity-Informed Tenets (St. John et al., 2012). Our similar experiences that spanned continents and generations led us to reflect on the impacts of colonialism, expanding on our understanding of racism. Our journey also highlighted the decolonizing nature of this work – our intentional, transformative effort to recognize, investigate, and courageously free ourselves from socialized, internalized, and oppressive messaging and valuations that have their roots in racism and colonialism. We see this liberatory work as necessarily starting within ourselves and then overflowing to our families, communities, and our world.

This chapter concludes with an invitation to center the important voices of the *people of the global majority* (Lim, 2020) in our shared field of early childhood, its research, and practice. There is important work yet to be done as a field in better understanding belonging, legacies of racism and colonialism inherent within our work, and embracing nondominant perspectives. It is our position that without this, what we understand as truths will never fully be universal.

We offer the following multifaceted experiences and theoretical foundations as a reflection, a source for learning – learning that is as deeply our own as we hope is that of the reader – and a call to the early childhood field. We also invite you – our reader and fellow human, in the fullness of your multiple identities – to join us in this important work of liberation.

A Spark Is Ignited: The Talk, Touch, and Listen Train-the-Trainer Workshop

In November of 2018, the Boston Public Health Commission (BPHC) organized a week of events with Dr. Marva Lewis, the author of the Talk, Touch, and Listen curricula, through their Massachusetts Multi-City Young Children's Mental Health System of Care grant, a SAMHSA-funded project focused on children from birth to age 6 years. Focused on strengthening early childhood mental health collaborations throughout the state, from the beginning of planning, BPHC decided that the events would carry on this vision of bringing partners together. The Boston Family Engagement Network (BFEN) joined as a cosponsor for a half-day Talk, Touch, and Listen Train-the-Trainer workshop, followed by a Parent Cafe, both facilitated by Dr. Lewis. BFEN is part of a state-funded network across Massachusetts, providing locally based child development and parenting services and resources. BFEN also trains and employs parent partners who work as leaders in family engagement, using their lived expertise as they connect within their communities. The authors of this chapter, Byars and Subramaniam, were managers of the BPHC System of Care and BFEN programs, respectively.

Open to the breadth of early childhood sectors, professionals came from across the state to attend the half-day Talk, Touch, and Listen (TT&L) Train-the-Trainer workshop with Dr. Lewis, including mental health, community health center, education, public health, child welfare, and family engagement professionals. A diverse group in many ways, attendees engaged deeply with the training content, sharing in one another's hopes, stories, childhood experiences, tears, and growth. The space created during the workshop was one of vulnerability and connection. Dr. Lewis led the group through the curriculum, engaging them as both learners and participants with their own stories. After the workshop was completed, attendees lingered, talking about the experience, some staying to also attend the afternoon's scheduled TT&L Parent Cafe.

The feedback, both written and verbal, in the moment and afterward, centered around gratitude for the experience and desiring more. Repeatedly, attendees asked if there would be a follow-up; the TT&L workshop had been impactful and they wanted to dive deeper into the content, reflect on their own identities and experiences, and work through some of the weighty topics that were covered. The recurring theme was that before facilitating the TT&L curriculum for others, attendees felt they first needed to have more understanding of their own connection to the content, that they had their own important self-work that they needed to do. As cosponsors who had also deeply resonated with TT&L, we, the authors, also felt what they were wanting and after much thought, discussion, and planning, decided to organize a six-session facilitator learning community. The goal for the learning community was to provide a multiweek reflective exploration of the Talk, Touch, and Listen curriculum, providing participants with an opportunity to engage in dual roles – attending for their own personal growth as well as professionals who planned to incorporate the TT&L curriculum into their future work.

Dr. Marva Lewis is a sociocultural developmental psychologist and is an associate professor in New Orleans, Louisiana, at Tulane University School of Social Work, with a clinical appointment in the Department of Child Psychiatry. Dr. Lewis is a ZERO TO THREE Academy Fellow (1994) and is the founder and director of the Place for Natural Connections, which promotes community-based interventions focused on hair-combing interactions as an effective, culturally resonant, and naturalistic means to support caregiver–child relationships. Dr. Lewis is the author of the Talk, Touch, and Listen curricula. In 2011, ZERO TO THREE commissioned her to design and conduct trainings on the historical trauma of slavery and child welfare system disparities for the Safe Baby Court Teams. She is a member of and consults for the national advisory board of the Quality Improvement Center for Research-Based Infant-Toddler Court Teams.

Planning the Talk, Touch, and Listen Facilitator Learning Community

Broad interest had already been established from the original, half-day Train-the-Trainer workshop feedback forms and we (authors, N.B. and A.S.) followed up with creating a survey to determine dates, level of commitment, an accessible location, transportation needs, food, and timing. The survey led to planning for a learning community of seven participants, most of whom identified as people of color, meeting over six biweekly sessions.

Group Design

The TT&L facilitator manual served as a compass for us to reflectively plan the biweekly sessions. Our focus was on planning with the community, as copartners in this growth work, and not for them. Topics over the six sessions included reflection on family values, understanding the unique personality of each child, responsive communication, and active listening, understanding emotions and stress, colorism and texturism, searching for strengths in hair-combing interactions and among peers, and a final session of celebration and connection.

Per the manual, each session includes:

1. Announcements/Mindful check-ins
2. Opening Ritual (including review of psychological safety rules)

3. Minilecture
4. Experiential Activities
5. Thinking Points and Preview of Next Session
6. Closing Ritual: *Pass the Comb*

As we (authors, N.B. and A.S.) were focused on creating a learning community that involved members to reflect on both their professional and personal identities, we intentionally worked to balance fidelity to the Talk, Touch, & Listen curriculum with tailoring it to meet the group's composition and needs. For example, in planning for the session, which covered searching for strengths in hair-combing interactions, we planned for a discussion on reframing potential challenges when working as facilitators to identify strengths in the families we serve. We were also very aware of the truly diverse and global nature of our city and sought out videos that spoke to experiences of texturism and colorism across races, ethnicities, and nationalities, intentionally confronting colonialism, and including the experiences of fathers with caring for the hair of their children. Some items in the curriculum were skipped and others, such as some of the assessment tools, were assigned as homework for reflection.

Necessity of Building Trust as Cofacilitators

Working collaboratively to wonder, brainstorm, and codesign with each other as cofacilitators was a gift. We (authors, N.B. & A.S.) were able to weave our personal and professional experiences and learnings into the planning. In reflecting back on our process of coming together to do this, something that stood out was the ease, comfort, and ability to question – supported by our already strong working relationship – which served us well as cofacilitators. Our relationship was a key ingredient in being able to sit with our own vulnerabilities, holding each other in the planning process, and eventually in cofacilitating the group. This was weighty, evocative ground. We each were engaging in our own continuous liberation, with the benefit of a strong working partnership within which vulnerability and sharing could flourish.

Diversity-Informed Tenets

The Diversity-Informed Tenets are a set of ten aspirational principles that serve as a guide to strengthen the commitment of professionals, organizations, and systems to embed diversity, inclusion, and equitable practices into their work. We saw a crucial connection between a set of Tenets that elevates nondominant ways of knowing and the TT&L curriculum, which utilizes everyday dyadic interactions as modes of healing and relationship. From the beginning of our process, we embraced the organizing principle of the first Diversity-Informed Tenet, "*Self awareness leads to better services for families*" (St. John et al., 2012, p. 16), sharing and learning from each other's experiences and journeys while adapting the curriculum for the learning community. We deliberately reflected on and wove the Tenets into our planning and implementation.

Experience of the Talk, Touch, and Listen Facilitator Learning Community

Our Talk, Touch, and Listen facilitator learning community was multigenerational and multiethnic, participants carrying within them a variety of stories and orientations to the topics of hair, texturism, and colorism. They were Latinx, Asian, Black, and White and all identified as women. Some were grandmothers who spoke from their own experiences as children, then in mothering and grandmothering roles; others were still actively parenting their own children. They came from family engagement, mental health, and early childhood programs. All had been introduced to TT&L previously, most through the original TT&L Train-the-Trainer Workshop. They were seeking to incorporate what they had learned more fully into their work, but wanted the experience of navigating the topics on a personal level in advance of bringing it into their professional roles.

A Necessary and Brave Space

In setting the psychological space together, cocreation of a *brave space* was crucial. A brave space, a conceptualization described by Arao and Clemens (2013), invites a collectivist approach to honoring full engagement from all participants, with social justice at its core. It calls upon facilitators and group members to pay deep attention to and notice how power, privilege, and oppression can operate within a group, often unacknowledged. This conceptualization also calls upon facilitators and groups to understand the varying vulnerabilities and inherent risks that different identities carry with them into a space. Too often a sense of safety and comfort comes at the expense of nondominant identities, calling upon group members and facilitators to work together, to pause, to make explicit, to repair, and to change.

In our learning community, we expanded on the TT&L curriculum's creation of psychological rules of safety to weave in the concept of brave space. We took the time to cocreate this necessary brave space as crucial not only in the first session, but throughout the six sessions. It served as a ritual to come together in relationship with oneself and one another in the group. Together, we as a group reviewed and reflected on the brave space agreements and what it would mean to pause, to name, to take responsibility, and to repair when moments of *oops* and *ouch* were elevated in the group process. Spending ample time on this in the context of relationship building was of paramount importance to having the space be a *collective space* versus a directed space.

We heard stories of experiences fraught with tears and ultimately needing a family friend to do a child's hair, of bringing new memories and hair pride to a grandson, and of feeling new to this deep, entangled experience of texturism and colorism. Some learning community members came from multiethnic families and spoke to the variations in texture and color among relatives, siblings, or their own children. For others, parenting stirred up within them their own histories and meaning making when it came to hair texture. Among us, there were views of hair combing as a joyous time for connection, of ritual, full of energy to proclaim beauty, relationship, and worth, and others spoke of the ongoing difficulty and feeling of being lost. Even as facilitators, we ranged from comparing the "chore" of doing hair to cleaning a toilet to having multistep, family rituals in which caring for hair carried a deep sense of connection and culture. Though experiences were varied, what was shared was a deep resonance with the richness of what can happen, what can be communicated, what can be passed along when a caregiver engages in hair combing with a child. An example that elucidates this was the *Neck-Up Drawing* activity from the TT&L curriculum, which engages participants in drawing a picture of themselves from the neck up as a child – and their hair – and then to reflect on their experiences. This activity led to the collective holding of stories, history, memories, and the deep feelings of both pain and hope.

A multimodal pathway. We also wanted to create a multimodal pathway for members to reflect upon both the content and process of the group. As early childhood practitioners, grounding in relationships brought a natural and predictable way of comfort. To support the group's self-reflection, both personal and professional, we created and incorporated an activity called "A-ha moments" to invite all participants, and ourselves, to wonder and reflect on times outside of our group space when elements of the TT&L resonated. Whether from professional interactions with families or personal experiences, "A-ha moments" provided us a way to reflect on our continuing journeys beyond the sessions.

While engaging in the transformative process of the learning community, members also connected with one another for resources and ideas. For the most part, the learning community was not shy or reticent to share, and conversations of shared challenges or suggestions being made were a common feature each week. Two members had either Black sons or grandsons who were more frequently part of their conversation, and discussion over shorter styles and the required care and responsibility, as well as tools that made a significant difference, such as specific brushes, were brought forth to the group. Some would ask about hair care products and receive a variety of recommendations.

At the close of each session, and in keeping with the Talk, Touch, and Listen curriculum, we would pass a comb around and state a hope for a child close to us, or for ourselves, regarding identity or experiences around hair and color. While each member of the learning community was in a professional role in which they might utilize the Talk, Touch, and Listen curriculum with families with whom they worked, biweekly the impetus for the group was re-lived: we were people for whom these issues were a part of our daily lives and we wanted to work them out authentically for ourselves, our families, and those we served.

Holding

Through the six sessions of the learning community, we cocreated a way of holding one another in our vulnerable and authentic experiences. Each and every member brought wisdom and deep courage with their own stories, as parents, grandparents, aunts, or reflecting on their experiences as children. Holding another in mind was experienced at multiple levels in the group. This occurred when a member of the group was not present and the rest of the group "held," invited, and wondered about the absent member's ways of knowing, being, and doing from stories shared previously together. When the group member returned the next time, the group intentionally found ways to bring to the forefront what was missed and how we thought of them and their stories. The unfolding of the learning community process with both content and authentic participation of each group member made the experience very rich. The learning community also offered the opportunity to wonder about the possible parallel experiences of families with whom we work. These included *how might each group member as a facilitator in their community draw upon their own experience here to cocreate a space for TT&L groups with families and their children? How might our own identities and experiences create space and tenderness in noticing and holding families and their children's experiences through TT&L?* Just as we as facilitators intentionally brought both our personal and professional selves into our roles, we deliberately reflected with learning community participants on doing the same in their future work with TT&L.

Reflections and an Invitation to Center Nondominant Perspectives

In preparation for this chapter, we (authors, N.B. & A.S.) resurveyed the seven learning community participants to see how the experience has influenced their work and way of being in the year plus since the learning community's conclusion. Participants reported utilizing the curriculum within family-based work to offer opportunities for connection and empathy building, intentionally bringing in messages to children and families to combat colorism, and the relational and antiracist power in engaging families around the everyday task of hair combing. One participant specifically named holding empathic space for the challenging experience hair combing can have for both the child and the caregiver, reminiscent of several of the group's conversations during the learning community when participants spoke of the difficult experiences on both sides of the comb.

Throughout the weeks together in the facilitator learning community, the lived experiences and emotions of being bodies who have navigated the world's messages were never beyond reach and did not leave us. We had invited our multifaceted selves to the table, allowing emotion, pain, and resilience to be right there with us. Each of us had journeyed a lifetime with the ever-present legacies of colonization on perceptions of beauty and worth, many of us continuing the ongoing liberatory work of resisting and disentangling ourselves from such corrupt messages. We had also been introduced to a curriculum that had engaged us in a new way, connecting us deeply and thoroughly from both the personal and professional. From the first Train-the-Trainer workshop to the follow-up facilitator learning community, the participants were diverse in a multitude of aspects, but still resonated with the Talk, Touch, and Listen research and curriculum. In the survey, one participant wrote, "it made me think deeply about my own experience with my hair, my race and all the scars I had and wasn't aware of."

The response to the TT&L curriculum reminded us of the incredible call of the Diversity-Informed Tenet #4 – "Recognize and Respect Nondominant Bodies of Knowledge: Diversity-informed practice recognizes nondominant ways of knowing, bodies of knowledge, sources of strength, and routes to healing within all families and communities" (St. John et al., 2012). TT&L took something simple, something every day, something accessible that spoke to people's experiences as children, as adults, and as caregivers. It evoked something deep within participants as they reflected on their identities and the impact the legacies of colorism and texturism had had on them, reflecting on how such a curriculum could also bring a new path to healing for the families with whom they worked. This was not a dense theory with which they had to grapple and translate to make sense of it in the real world; it was brilliant and immediate and resonant and made sense not only to lived experience, but also to our *lived expertise*. Identities and experiences were seen, and it was through this clear seeing that core principles of early childhood mental health and family well-being found sure footing for professionals across a broad spectrum of disciplines. This was and is a rare gift within the field.

However, such professional development and intervention need not be so rare. We authors hold that early childhood disciplines, including infant and early childhood mental health, would benefit from interventions and theories that were for communities, created by diverse people who were more representative of the intended benefactors. Perhaps, in some part, TT&L resonate so deeply and broadly, because it was coming from a nondominant perspective, and was a little less "WEIRD," an acronym Heinrich, Heine, and Norenzayan coined in a 2010 article. According to their review, while the vast majority of studies across multiple disciplines come from Western, Educated, Industrialized, Rich, Democratic (WEIRD) societies and from European-descended subjects, these typical research subjects represent one of the least generalizable segments of the world's population. Put more simply, out of the billions of people in the world, basing our knowledge, theories, and interventions on largely White, Western populations has limited utility across other groups, yet far too often this is exactly what is done. "Researchers often implicitly assume that either there is little variation across human populations, or that these 'standard subjects' are as representative of the species as any other population... The findings suggest that members of WEIRD societies, including young children, are among the least representative populations one could find for generalizing about humans." (Heinrich et al., 2010, p. 1)

Belonging. Additionally, we have experienced and have heard from colleagues who are people of color and immigrants, also known by the emerging term *people of the global majority* (Lim, 2020), needing to "translate" material into a context or application that can fit better for us and our experiences. Included in this, early childhood mental health theories and applications often hold their own preponderance of WEIRD-ness, and we authors have found ourselves, and our colleagues, needing to deliberately sort through seminal offerings of the field and try to recognize the elements of universality, regardless of the culture-ized packaging.

In her book, *I'm Still Here: Black Dignity in a World Made for Whiteness,* author Austin Channing Brown wrote of similar experiences in reflection of having her first Black teacher:

> The gift of Professor McMath's presence went beyond the fact that she looked like me, though that was special all by itself. The true gift was that I didn't have to create my own sense of belonging in her class. In every previous classroom, I had been responsible for decoding teachers' references to white middle-class experiences... having gotten used to white teachers' assumption of universality, we (Black students) would all nod our heads and move on. Who had time to teach the teacher?
>
> But Professor McMath was different. One day, while illustrating a point regarding business planning, she decided to use the example of opening a beauty shop. Our conversation moved along as usual until Professor McMath made an analogy to "getting a relaxer." My head snapped up in recognition, but all the white students looked toward the lectern completely baffled. I was the only one who understood the reference...
>
> I relished the sense of belonging I felt in her classroom. Suddenly I wasn't content to feel like I was attending a college made for someone else. I paid tuition like every white student (2018, pp. 50–51).

Colonialism and Liberation

The international nature of our learning community – members who knowingly hailed from or who had origins from five different continents – also brought to the forefront the concept of colonialism, or colonization. Across our diverse backgrounds, we identified similar impacts on conceptualizations of beauty in our communities, including colorism and texturism, even in societies and nations primarily composed of black and brown people. The *Encyclopedia of Race, Ethnicity, and Society* describes colonialism as a "system of domination and value based on the belief that the subjugated people are inferior to the colonizers. The development of the European colonial project since the 16th century coincided with the development of the concept of racism and ethnocentrism... *even though most colonial countries have been liberated, the legacy of colonialism continues to affect them* [emphasis added]" (Schaefer, 2008, p. 317). The concept of colonialism allowed us to better connect experiences across our different cultures, as well as connect to those who came before us and others who were not represented in the group.

In deep ways, it was this knowing within ourselves that legacies of colonialism and racism had their ongoing effects, which led to the formation of the group. We felt the need, or at least the desire, to do more of our own work in understanding the insidiousness of colorism and texturism, and their effects on conceptualizations of self, value, and identity, before we deeply engaged families in this work. In other words, we wanted to practice our own piece of decolonization, intentionally working to remove from within us colonization's effects on our ways of thinking, ways of being, and ways of connecting. In the anthology, *For Indigenous Minds Only: A Decolonization Handbook* (2012), Waziyatawin and Michael Yellow Bird wrote, "decolonizing actions must begin in the mind, and that creative, consistent, decolonized thinking shapes and empowers the brain, which in turn provides a major prime for positive change… When we regain a belief in the wisdom and beauty of our traditional ways of being and reject the colonial lies that have inundated us, we will release the pent-up dreams of liberation and again realize the need for resistance to colonization" (p. 2). In its own way, our TT&L group held a piece of this ongoing liberation work for us.

Conclusion

The journey of the Talk, Touch, and Listen Facilitator Learning Community began as deeply personal and grew, in the collective, into something larger than us and our roles: a call to reflection and action for our field. We see an immense need within our field to center more interventions and theoretical frameworks that are diverse and representative by design, not relegated to the obligatory cross-cultural practice seminar or a time-limited focus on equity and inclusion, but front, center, and *deep*. If it only were to strengthen caregiver–child relationships, Talk, Touch, and Listen would be much needed in our field. If it only were to increase empathy from caregiver to child, Talk, Touch, and Listen would deserve to be commonplace across our practice. However, TT&L offers our field much more than a way to connect and strengthen caregiver–child relationships; it offers a piece of deep, liberation work. We authors believe that children, families, researchers, practitioners – and we, too – still have much to learn in the braiding of liberation, healing, and early childhood and family practice. After having experienced the power of this different approach to healing, on multiple levels, and understanding relationships that Talk, Touch, and Listen provided, we want more of it. We hope you join us – your personal and professional selves are welcomed.

Reflective Questions

1. How might you bring the Talk, Touch, and Listen curriculum to your community, embracing culture, ethnicity, and race as crucial concepts to explore through reflective group work?
2. What did you find yourself reflecting on as you were invited to think about the Talk, Touch, and Listen curriculum and the Parent Cafe, braiding the personal with the professional, and considering hair combing as a pathway to healing difficult memories, thoughts, and feelings about hair texture, colorism, and parent–child relationships?
3. Aware of the importance of the term "belonging," how might you bring this concept into your work with families, as well as your own understanding of where and how you "belong?"
4. What does liberation mean to you and why is it so important for social work professionals and others to engage in exploring its meaning and embedding it in practice with children and families?

References

Arao, B., & Clemens, K. (2013). From safe spaces to brave spaces: A new way to frame dialogue around diversity and social justice. In L. Landreman (Ed.), *The art of effective facilitation: Reflections from social justice educators* (pp. 135–150). Stylus Publishing.

Brown, A. C. (2018). *I'm still here: Black dignity in a world made for whiteness*. Crown Publishing Group.

Heinrich, J., Heine, S. J., & Norenzayan, A. (2010). The weirdest people in the world? *Behavioral and Brain Science, 33*(2-3), 61–135. https://doi.org/10.1017/S0140525X0999152X

Lewis, M. L. (1999). Hair combing interactions: A new paradigm for research with African American mothers. *American Journal of Orthopsychiatry, 69*, 504–514. https://doi.org/10.1037/h0080398

Lewis, M. L., Noroña, C. R., McConnico, N., & Thomas, K. (2013). Colorism, a legacy of historical trauma in parent-child relationships: Clinical, research, and personal perspectives. *Zero to Three Journal, 34*(2), 11–23.

Lim, D. (2020). *I'm embracing the term 'people of the global majority'*. Medium. https://regenerative.medium.com/im-embracing-the-term-people-of-the-global-majority-abd1c1251241

Shapiro, N., & Hentoff, N. (1955). *Hear me talkin' to ya: the story of jazz as told by the men who made it*. Rinehart.

Schaefer, R. T. (Ed.). (2008). *Encyclopedia of race, ethnicity, and society*. Sage Publications. https://doi.org/10.4135/9781412963879

St. John, M. S., Thomas, K., & Noroña, C. R. (2012). Infant mental health professional development: Together in the struggle for social justice. *Zero to Three Journal, 33*(2), 13–22.

Waziyatawin, & Yellow Bird, M. (Eds.). (2012). *For Indigenous minds only: A decolonization handbook*. School for Advanced Research Press.

Wilson, I., Mbilishaka, A., & Lewis, M. (2018). "White folks ain't got hair like us": African American mother–daughter hair stories and racial socialization. *Women, Gender, and Families of Color, 6*(2), 226–248. https://doi.org/10.5406/womgenfamcol.6.2.0226

Chapter 13
PsychoHairapy Through Beauticians and Barbershops: The Healing Relational Triad of Black Hair Care Professionals, Mothers, and Daughters

Afiya M. Mbilishaka

Introduction

Caring for highly textured hair is a complex process. To be skillful in caring for the textures of Black hair often requires a level of expertise in product choice, creativity, and dexterity (Neil & Mbilishaka, 2019). However, Black mothers are often tasked with the hair care of one or more children without formal training or education to do so (Wilson et al., 2018; Mbilishaka et al., 2020c). Many mothers intentionally choose to delegate the task of hair care to a professional. Here, the hair care professional is involved in the process of hair styling, creating a triad in the mother–child relationship.

Hair care professionals are ideal lay health advisors who offer microcounseling to individuals and families as they provide hair care within their settings (Mbilishaka, 2018a, b). Further, the practice of PsychoHairapy includes mental health professionals training hair care professionals in psychotherapy skills, for example, active listening, imparting helpful information, assessing for harm, and referring to mental health professionals in the community (Mbilishaka, 2018a). Mothers bringing their daughters to the hair salon can be understood as a Black cultural routine to build family relationships, especially if the stylist is trained in PsychoHairapy.

Further attention is required to identify the value of hair care professionals entering the relational triad and offering emotional support to mother and child. This chapter will (1) unpack the complex history of hair care, (2) describe the unique relationship between hair care professionals and communities' members, and (3) suggest techniques for collaboration between hair care professionals and mothers.

A. M. Mbilishaka (✉)
University of the District of Columbia, Washington, DC, USA
e-mail: afiya.mbilishaka@gmail.com

M. L. Lewis, D. J. Weatherston (eds.), *Therapeutic Cultural Routines to Build Family Relationships*, https://doi.org/10.1007/978-3-030-83726-6_13

Getting to the Root of Hair Care

The history of Black hair tells an intriguing story that takes root in ancient African societies. Beginning with the archeological digs of the excavated pyramids of Egypt, our ancient Kemetic ancestors clearly documented their hairstyles and hair care regimens through pictorial designs and through hieroglyphs (Mbilishaka, 2018a, b, c). Dynastic families wore intricately braided styles and their hair could only be cared for by the spiritually initiated as hair was decidedly sacred. The priest and priestesses of thousands of years ago documented the procedures of cleansing and moisturizing hair with milk and honey (Walker, 2011). Because the hair care process was viewed as highly spiritual, these initiated hair care providers applied plant-based medicines through castor oil and almond oil to cure various illnesses (Walker, 2011). Here, we can see that being a hair care professional was not embedded into a mother's daily activity but was a sacred ritual to be orchestrated by someone with specific spiritual skills. These ancient professional hairstylists could spend hours to weeks creating hairstyles (Mbilishaka, 2018a).

The Yoruba ethnic group of Nigeria has well documented the hair care profession through spiritually guided rituals. From birth, babies ritualistically have their hair shaved as an offering to the spiritual world for health (Sherrow, 2006). In traditional Yoruba societies, all girls are taught the art of hair braiding (Byrd & Tharps, 2014). And yet, only those who are best are tasked with braiding hair for their whole community. From this cultural lens, the head is viewed as a spiritual center of the body. Hairstylists are responsible for feeding and cleansing rituals of the physical and spiritual head. Therefore, their status is one of the top ranked professions and highly regulated with ritual and taboo. For example, no one should ever bargain with a hairstylist about money, because it is believed that she holds your destiny (Mbilishaka, 2018a).

Rituals across the lifespan involve the hair care professional. Like the Yoruba tradition, within the first few days of the birth of a baby in Kenya, a mother presents her child to get the first haircut (Sherrow, 2006). This haircut serves to be a spiritual offering for the safe birth of the child during a community baby naming ceremony. For the Masai of Kenya, the mother joins her child in getting his/her hair shaved as part of this first haircut ritual to strengthen the mother–child bond (Beckwith & Fisher, 1999). During rites of passage for the Shai of Ghana, girls must get their hair adorned with various talismans and elements in nature that includes medicine that prepares them for womanhood (Beckwith & Fisher, 1999). For adolescent males in the Maasai ethnic group of Kenya, they begin a warrior initiation through getting their hair braided and twisted to form locs as part of their uniform (Beckwith & Fisher, 1999). Further, the boy's mother is the only person in the warrior's life that is allowed to cut his hair. Stylists also played an important role in the wedding ritual as well. For the Tuareg of Mali and Niger, the hair care professionals must rub the hair of the bride with special medicines to bless the marriage (Beckwith & Fisher, 1999). Additionally, several death and grief rituals require families to either not comb or shave their hair in response to a family death (Byrd & Tharps, 2014). Hair facilitated these rituals and hair was deeply embedded into the daily way of cultural life.

Conversely, hair care translated into an instrument of maltreatment when European slave captors and masters stole Africans from their homes. To initiate the process of servitude, Europeans would publicly shave the hair of their new "cargo" (Byrd & Tharps, 2014). This process was a tool to disconnect African people from the great beauty of their hair and their cultural rituals (Morrow, 1990). Yet, even on the boats to the Americas, there is a record of African people grooming themselves and their hair in the belly of the ships (Sherrow, 2006). On plantations, enslaved Africans were not permitted to groom their hair consistently, due to the laborious routines of daily life and because of the aesthetic threats perceived by plantation mistresses. White women would humiliate Black women through mutilating their hair or not permitting them time to groom themselves as conscious and unconscious attempts to regulate the appearances of these beautiful Black women (Mbilishaka, 2018a). Many mistresses knew that Black women were used for sexual labor by plantation masters and felt in competition with the victims of their husbands. Enslaved Africans, if permitted to do so, would use the tools identified for animals to groom their hair (Byrd & Tharps, 2014). Their hair was also deemed as "fur" or "wool" as a method of dehumanization. Scalp diseases and hair loss were the norm in plantation life, due to high levels of stress and malnutrition.

A caste system was organized around hair texture during chattel slavery (Morrow, 1990). Those enslaved Africans with tightly coiled or curly hair were often forced into tasks of manual labor in the fields, while those with straighter hair textures were privileged to cooking and cleaning indoors (Morrow, 1990). A Eurocentric ideal was enforced through an operant conditioning process of social rewards, causing many enslaved Africans to damage their hair and scalp to conform with the unrealistic and unhealthy standard (Morrow, 1990). For example, enslaved African women would heat irons in a fire, lay their hair on a flat board, and apply the blazing instrument to their hair as a means to alter their hair texture to meet the aesthetic requirements of servitude (Mbilishaka, 2021). Often, mothers traumatized their daughters through this styling methodology. With hopes of increasing the level of acceptance of their child in the Americas, Black mothers styled their daughters hair in a fashion that satisfied the needs of the outside world (Lewis, 1999). Black mothers would not only engage in the process of squeezing their children's noses to try to make them narrow like Europeans, bathe their children in citrus to lighten the skin, but they would also pull and stretch their hair as an attempt to remove all possible kinks (Morrow, 1990). These beauty rituals between mother and child were survival tactics in a system of extreme racial oppression. This process of attempting to change the texture of a child's hair was laborious and anxiety provoking for mothers. These approaches to mother–child grooming still exist today, because of intergenerational racial trauma (Lewis, 1999; DeGruy, 2005; Wilson et al., 2018). Today, many Black mothers include the hair salon in the practice of styling the hair of their children.

Finding Relationships in Black Salons

The period of Reconstruction in the United States offered Black women with income and money to invest in their physical appearance (Gill, 2010). Consequently, the emergence of the Black beauty salon space provided an opportunity for building community in large urban centers and rural towns for Black women. Black women who were now generating incomes could rely on hair care professionals, also known as "beauty culturalists" to create highly coiffed hairstyles to represent their access to financial resources (Byrd & Tharps, 2014). Rarely during enslavement, did Black women have the time or economic weight to spend money on hair care. Black women flocked to get their hair shampooed, conditioned, moisturized, and straightened in the salon setting, not only for the styling outcome, but for the fostering of social bonds with other Black women (Gill, 2010). Clearly, social support would entice women to spend hours in the salon chatting about personal life and exchanging news about the political state of Black women in the country at the time (Mbilishaka, 2018a, b, c). Often, Black political leaders would even come to organize social justice campaigns in the salon setting, because the salon was clearly a site of in-depth discussion and supportive counsel (Mbilishaka, 2018b).

Black hair stylists offer space in their salons for meeting the complex needs for Black communities (Gill, 2010; Solomon et al., 2004; Mbilishaka, 2018b). The Black hair salon is set up in a way to facilitate group conversation, with chairs set up in a circle rather than aisles or between partitions like in White salons (Solomon et al., 2004). These floor plans create an openness for all in the space to be seen and allow for "cross talk" between the hair care professionals and clients in the space. Here, the hair professional not only talks to their client, but is involved in conversation with multiple customers and professionals at once. Black hair care spaces also offer room for meeting nutritional needs, through selling food themselves or having vendors that visit the site to sell food. Offering food makes Black women stay in hair care spaces longer, and social scientists have observed that this may be necessary as Black women tend to spend more time – like over 4 h – getting their hair done and will therefore work up an appetite during the styling process (Solomon et al., 2004). This experience of eating together aligns with the cultural value system of people across the African Diaspora, bonding through meals and having thoughtful conversation (Terry, 2014). Additionally, significant media (music, magazines, movies, television) is consumed during the Black salon experience (Solomon et al., 2004). Each sense can be stimulated through the Black hair salon experience in this way.

One of the variables that brings uniqueness to the Black salon experience includes noncustomer visits, and this is mixed with the oral tradition. Solomon and colleagues (2004) observed that stylists have visitors attend the salon, but also customers bring visitors with them while getting their hair done. These visitors include friends or relatives. Often, community members will even enter the salon space and have no intention of getting their hair groomed. Black women will gather in the salon to give and get life updates from their community members. Solomon et al.

(2004) observed several Black stylists engage in layered storytelling with their customers, visitors, and colleagues.

Although understudied, hairstylists serve a vital role in helping mothers to displace the labor of mothers in the task of hair combing (see Ashley & Brown, 2015). Here, mothers are still involved in the process of financially addressing the hair care needs of their children, but do not need to manually exert the energy required to properly care for the hair of their daughter. Hair care professionals take systematic approaches to creating hairstyles in the salon (or even for home visits) that can last for weeks. This creates freedom for the mother to address other personal needs, either staying to chat with the community members present or read, or it offers childcare in being able to run errands, while the child is occupied and safe in the salon chair.

PsychoHairapy Collaboration Between Mothers and Hairstylists

The intervention model of *Talk, Touch, and Listen While Combing Hair,* developed by Dr. Marva Lewis, has significantly impacted family dynamics through supporting mothers in the hair care process. Here, mothers are the key stakeholders to have deep conversations and gentle touch. Through community approaches, groups of mothers can learn how to be sensitive, on a physical and emotional level, to care for their children. However, many mothers still struggle with the skillset and frankly say, "I don't know how to comb her hair." *Talk, Touch, and Listen* can be extended to these mothers who are distressed by taking on the task of hair combing.

PsychoHairapy should be extended to include the healing triad among hair care professional, mother, and daughter to provide support and guidance without interrupting the family attachment. PsychoHairapy is defined as using hair as an entry point into mental health services (Mangum & Woods, 2011; Mbilishaka, 2018a). This includes mental health professionals training hair care professionals in basic counseling techniques and then hair care professionals offering supportive services to their communities (Mbilishaka, 2018b). Often, Black women have more contact with a hair care professional than their own physician (Browne, 2006), and often never seek services from a mental health professional (Mbilishaka, 2018a). Therefore, by hair care professionals providing emotional support services and respectful referrals, this public health approach to mental health care is accessible and culturally informed. Hair care professionals are often tasked with the emotional labor of styling the hair, and it may be an ideal time to have conversations that include advice giving, as well as active listening.

A major emotional stressor of Black mothers can include the hair care process with their daughters (Lewis, 1999; Wilson et al., 2018; Mbilishaka et al., 2020a, b, c). First, the hair care process can take several hours between Black mother and child. This process takes a long time because of the process of washing and detangling coiled hair, which can get knotted and the scalp can become tender in response to the excessive parting and pulling. Combing Black hair therefore requires ambidextrous movement, creativity, and patience. These are all difficult skills, and they require an ability to carry them out simultaneously. Second, mothers often have to reflect on their aesthetic value system and phenotype during the hair-combing interaction (Lewis, 1999). As a parent now, women navigate their hair-combing experiences of acceptance or rejection related to hair texture, length, and style. While some Black women had very positive experiences of getting their hair done, others had traumatic grooming, which may make them want to avoid the hair care process for their child (Wilson et al., 2018; Mbilishaka et al., 2020a, b, c). Further, many Black women have to negotiate the shame of improper hair care growing up and the bullying that occurred in school due to the way their mother chose to style – or not style – their hair (Mbilishaka & Apugo, 2020).

In a world of constant maternal stress, hair care professionals can provide support. Hair-combing interactions between Black mothers and hair care professionals offer mothers an opportunity for close physical contact and caring touch. From the shampoo to the combing and brushing, and even the application of special oils and creams, mothers often find reprieve in getting their hair done. This nurturing touch through the hair care process can form a tight attachment between Black mothers and hair care professionals (see Mbilishaka, 2018a). Hair-combing interaction offers emotional intimacy between Black mother and hairstylist too (see Mbilishaka, 2018c). Mental health professionals should be extremely mindful that Black mothers need this type of support and have heightened awareness that the care received to a Black mother can extend to her daughter (see Wilson et al., 2018).

There have been existing therapeutic interventions that include pairing professional hair care services with emotional support, where the mother is not responsible for grooming her child's hair. Ashley and Brown (2015, p. 1) argued, "hair care can provide a context and vehicle for attachment, nurturing, and positive self-worth." They note that this hair care process does not need to include the mother in the position of hair styling. Specifically, the concept of "Attachment tHAIRapy" connects a licensed psychotherapist with a licensed hairstylist to offer behavioral support services to African-American foster youth. Caregivers were invited to verbally participate in the therapy. These sessions were an "an opportunity to reframe hair issues as they connect to psychological and emotional health" (Ashley & Brown, 2015, p. 7). Several themes emerged in observations and focus groups related to this intervention, such as feelings about being in the foster care system, negotiating significant relationships, thoughts on therapy, emotions related to hair, and negotiations of racial identity development. The physical act of getting their hair professionally styled improved the self-esteem of these Black youth (Ashley & Brown, 2015). Black girls and adolescents also shared the desire to learn to take care of their hair from a professional, as it was very frustrating to have their hair styled by a caregiver that did not have the skills to groom their hair or themselves being confused on how to care for their hair. Black girls often have the desire to change the texture, length, and style of their hair due to pressures from larger society, and they face even greater stress if they make attempts that cause harm to their own hair (Mbilishaka & Apugo, 2020).

Process in a Healing Space

Now, PsychoHairapy offers an opportunity to integrate *Talk, Touch, and Listen* with Attachment tHAIRapy. The hair care professional can now offer therapeutic services to both mother and child. Black mothers can bring their daughters with them to the salon environment to both get their hair done and get their daughters' hair done. This ritual allows for the mother to be cared for and destressed, while also delegating the task of hair combing to a professional. It is often only in family therapy that the family is seen as a unit, but now with PsychoHairapy, the mother–daughter dyad can be a unit to receive hair care services. The hair care professional has the opportunity to have private and public time with them both.

First, special attention should be paid to the hair washing portion of this hair intervention. For example, the hair washing process in a professional bowl can allow the mother to have an opportunity to have her hair washed in a cleansing ritual and offers private conversation time. During this time, the physical process of detangling the hair and cleaning the hair may be a chance for the stylist to physically provide comfort to the dyad individually. This part of the process can be used for information gathering and intention setting for the service.

Next, hair styling can occur where the mother and child can listen to each other, within developmental language skill sets. While having the hair cared for and transformed, there can be certain age-appropriate prompts that the hair care professional can ask in this group setting to share stories and experiences that appear to be important to the family dynamics. This could be a negotiation of rules at home, stress from work or school, and matters of other family members. Similar to a therapist, the hairstylist can foster relationship enhancement skills, like encouraging the dyad to make "I statements" and clarify any confusing parts of the conversation.

Finally, there can be moments of summary and resolution. This stage of the hair care process occurs at the end, where mother and daughter can say how they felt about getting their hair done together and intentions that they would like to set once they return home. This can be something as simple as committing to fix the bed each morning to deciding how to manage stress better as a family. Here, the stylist is an audience to the resolution and does not interrupt but affirms that goal and recommitment of family during the hair care process.

These are just the beginnings of how to affirm both mother and child in a healing space and with a healing member of the community, the hairstylist. We can notice that the hair care professional's relationship to the mother impacts the mother–daughter relationships. The triad serves to help the mother and the child feel good about themselves, both aesthetically from a beautiful style, but also through the experience of talking, touching, and listening. Future studies and research will be carried out on how to address hair and mental health within and between families.

Conclusion

The intent of this chapter was to guide readers into the interdependent nature of hair care within Black families. We know that hair-combing interaction extends to outside of the home. Black mothers engage in hair care within a complex ecology of hair care professionals in their local communities. Mother–child hair care often becomes a triadic relationship, where there is a delegation of hair-combing tasks. To further broaden the *Talk, Touch, and Listen* intervention, this chapter highlighted the incentive of Black mothers bringing their children to hair care spaces for support, to simultaneously receive support as they care for their child.

Reflective Questions

1. What do you find yourself reflecting about after reading the rich history of hair and hair care traditions within African cultures in Nigeria, Kenya, Ghana, and Mali?
2. What was your response to learning that "hair care translated into an instrument of maltreatment when European slave captors and masters stole Africans from their homes?"
3. Have you ever thought about "the nurturing touch through the hair care process" between a hair stylist and parent or child and its healing potential?
4. Hair care offers a time and private space for personal conversations, as well as a collective social experience in which women talk, eat, and gather. Reflect on your experience of having your hair cared for or styled by a family member or in a professional salon.

References

Ashley, W., & Brown, J. (2015). Attachment tHAIRapy: A culturally relevant treatment paradigm for African American foster youth. *Journal of Black American Studies, 46*(6), 587–604. https://doi.org/10.1177/0021934715590406

Beckwith, C., & Fisher, A. (1999). *African ceremonies*. Harry Abrams.

Browne, R. C. (2006). Most black women have a regular source of hair care—But not medical care. Journal of the American Medical Association, 98(10), 1652–1653.

Byrd, A., & Tharps, L. (2014). *Hair story: Untangling the roots of Black hair in America*. St. Martin's Press.

DeGruy, J. (2005). Post traumatic slave syndrome: America's legacy of enduring injury and healing. Milwaukie, Oregon: Uptone Press.

Gill, T. (2010). Beauty Shop Politics: African American Women's Activism in the Beauty Industry. Champaign, IL: University of Illinois Press.

Lewis, M. L. (1999). The hair-combing task: A new paradigm for research on African-American mother–child interaction. *The American Journal of Orthopsychiatry, 69*, 504–514.

Mangum, A. M., & Woods, A. M. (2011, July). *'Psychohairapy': Integrating psychology, public health, and beauty shop talk*. Presented at the 43rd Annual Association of Black Psychologists Convention, Crystal City, VA.

Mbilishaka, A. M. (2018a). PsychoHairapy: Using hair as an entry point into Black women's spiritual and mental health. *Meridians: Feminism, Race & Transnationalism, 16*(2), 382–392. https://doi.org/10.2979/meridians.16.2.19

Mbilishaka, A. M. (2018b). Black lives (and stories) matter: Race narrative therapy in Black hair care spaces. *Community Psychology in Global Perspective, 4*(2), 22–33.

Mbilishaka, A. M. (2018c). Strands of intimacy: Black women's narratives of hair and intimate relationships with men. *Journal of Black Sexuality and Relationships, 5*(1), 43–61. https://doi.org/10.1353/bsr.2018.0014

Mbilishaka, A. M., & Apugo, D. (2020). Brushed aside: African American women's narratives of hair bias in school. *Race Ethnicity and Education, 23*(5), 634–653. https://doi.org/10.1080/13613324.2020.1718075

Mbilishaka, A. M., Clemons, K., Hudlin, M., Warner, C., & Jones, D. (2020a). Don't get it twisted: Untangling the psychology of hair discrimination within Black communities. *American Journal of Orthopsychiatry*. https://doi.org/10.1037/ort0000468

Mbilishaka, A., Mbande, A., Gulley, C., & Mbande, T. (2020b). Faded fresh tapers and line-ups: Centering barbershop hair stories in understanding gendered racial socialization for Black men. *Psychology of Men & Masculinities*. https://doi.org/10.1037/men0000317

Mbilishaka, A. M., Mitchell, D. S. B., & Conyers, C. (2020c). Grandma's hands: Memories of hair styling interaction with African American grandmothers. *Journal of Intergenerational Relationships, 18*(2), 139–155. https://doi.org/10.1080/15350770.2019.1658008

Mbilishaka, A. (2021). PsychoHairapy: Brushing up on the History and Psychology of Black Hair. Eye on Psi Chi. 25(3), 26–29.

Morrow, W. (1990). *400 years without a comb: The untold story*. Black Publishers.

Neil, L., & Mbilishaka, A. (2019). 'Hey curl friends!': Hair care and self-care messaging on YouTube by Black women natural hair vloggers. *Journal of Black Studies, 50*(2), 156–177. https://doi.org/10.1177/0021934718819411

Sherrow, V. (2006). *Encyclopedia of hair: A cultural history*. Greenwood Press.

Solomon, F., Linnan, L., Wailewski, Y., Le, A., Katz, M., & Yang, J. (2004). Observational study in ten beauty salons: results informing development of the North Carolina Beauty and Health Project. Health Education & Behavior, 31, 790– 809. doi:10.1177/1090198104264176

Terry, B. (2014). Afro-Vegan: Farm Fresh African, Caribbean, and Southern Flavors Remixed. Ten Speed Press.

Wilson, I., Mbilishaka, A., & Lewis, M. (2018). 'White folks ain't got hair like us': African American mother-daughter hair stories and racial socialization. *Women, Gender, and Families of Color, 6*(2), 226–248. https://doi.org/10.5406/womgenfamcol.6.2.0226

Walker, R. (2011). When we ruled. Halethorpe, Maryland: Black Classic Press.

Chapter 14
Reflections on Experiences in a Community-Based Parent Support Group: Parent Whisperers

Olivia Saito, Barbara Cheatham, and Marva L. Lewis

Purpose and Structure of the Community-Based Support Group

The Talk, Touch, and Listen While Combing Hair program is a community-based parent support group that offers a culturally appropriate curriculum built around the everyday task of hair combing to address issues around parent–child relationships. The curriculum is modeled after the World Cafe model designed for groups of community peers to discuss difficult topics that impact them all (Brown & Isaacs, 2005, 2010; Brown et al, 1999). Hair combing interaction involves specific behaviors involving verbal interaction (talk), touch, and reading and responding appropriately to cues given by the child (listen), which can be used to strengthen attachment between parents and children (Crawford & Lewis, 2012). This is particularly beneficial for low-income African-American mothers and children who are often disproportionately affected by mental health and sociocultural issues.

During the summer months of 2012, the *Talk, Touch, and Listen* (TTL) curriculum was piloted with a group of mothers at the New Orleans Women's Shelter as well as the New Orleans Healthy Start Program. Two different groups of mothers met weekly at these two locations to complete the 8-week curriculum. Three Tulane University public health graduate-level students participated as parent peer coaches

O. Saito (✉)
Los Angeles, CA, USA
e-mail: osaito88@gmail.com

B. Cheatham
Toledo, OH, USA

M. L. Lewis
School of Social Work, Tulane University, New Orleans, LA, USA

M. L. Lewis, D. J. Weatherston (eds.), *Therapeutic Cultural Routines to Build Family Relationships*, https://doi.org/10.1007/978-3-030-83726-6_14

or "parent whisperers" to provide individual support to the mothers during the sessions.

Through the TTL program, parents were supported through experiential learning techniques to increase unconditional acceptance of their children, knowledge of their child's unique temperament and personality, and enhance the parent's positive communication style. The topics presented in the curriculum build on the skills required for emotion regulation and the promotion of healthy attachment relationships between parents and their children. Parents were taught to recognize and increase the type of talk that enhances self-esteem in their children and communicates warmth and acceptance. The parents were also taught that there is a difference between positive and negative physical touch with children. Furthermore, a critical skill they learned is how to use active listening to hear all the ways that children communicate verbally and nonverbally. A sample of the topics for each section are presented in Table 14.1.

Another goal of the curriculum was to help the parent become aware of emotional legacies from the historical trauma of slavery surrounding hair and skin color. Parents were able to reflect on their own childhood experiences and emotions regarding their skin color and hair texture (Lewis & Swift, 2015). These self-reflective activities and practices allowed parents to be more engaged and aware of themselves, which resulted in being able to understand their children better.

The group was structured to include these components in every session: Review of Rules, Jokes, Announcements, Opening Ritual, "Go-Rounds," Minilecture, Thinking Points, Closing Ritual, and Fun and Humor (Lewis, 2008; Lewis, 2013).

Learning About My Role as a Parent Whisperer: My Reflections as an Asian-American Woman

For many years, lay, nonprofessional community members have provided support to professional healthcare providers in treatment and preventative health services for several health outcomes. Many of them are labeled as "peer" support workers or coaches and play an integral role in the success of many interventions. There are three characteristics that increase the effectiveness of peer coaches: (1) They share certain characteristics with the target group and they usually have similar experiences especially in regards to the targeted health outcome. (2) They receive training in the delivery of specific interventions, yet they lack professional status. (3) They function outside of their naturally occurring social networks, intentionally engaging and interacting with individuals who will benefit from their guidance and training. Many studies have shown that peer coaching or support is beneficial to helping patients cope and improve self-efficacy. Furthermore, it has been found that peer support is especially effective with disadvantaged populations that may have previous histories of mistrust with the healthcare system.

Table 14.1 Example of *Talk, Touch, and Listen Sessions*[a] with parent whisperers' duties

SESSION #1 –WHAT ARE MY Family VALUES?				
Supplies	MINILECTURE (by Cofacilitator)	Experiential exercises	GO-ROUNDS Community Share (CS) Dyad Share (DS)	CLOSING RITUAL: *Pass the Comb*
Name Cards Crayons & paper Newsprint to put on walls Handouts of 'My Values' sheets. White & Colored Index Cards Hat/Basket Large Comb or drawing a comb to put on the floor. Consumer Satisfaction Surveys. TIP Sheet	Announcements Welcome & overview of TT&L series. (Pass out Caregiver/Child TT&L Notebook) Introduce ***Parent Whispers*** & their role **Mini-lecture "*Do as I Do!*"** Our values shape our behaviors with our children. Preview of Session #2 – The Road To PATH & RICS; Tender-headedness strategies & Guest beautician Reflective Processing If participants need to talk more. (referral list) **Post Group Processing**	Ice Breaker- Childhood nicknames *Hopes & Fears Questions in the Hat*. HOPE "On the white index card write one thing you would like to learn about parenting your child and one thing you fear for your child." The *Neck-up Drawing*, "*Draw a picture of yourself from the neck up. Write one emotion word that summarizes your feelings about your hair.*"	**CS: Nickname Go-Round Each person in the circle responds. Say your childhood nickname, why you got it, and did you like it.** **CS: *Rules for Psychological Safety*.** **Write on Newsprint, Post on walls each week.** **CS: Generate a community list of "What I Value for all children" on Newsprint.** **DS – Individual Family Values; write your Top 3 Values from the community list. *What behaviors will I do to teach my child these values*?** **Share with the parent Whisperer. Share your response to the following statement: *Why I selected the Emotion word for my Neck-Up drawing*.**	Every person states the following and then passes the comb to the next participant. *What I wish for my child [name] _____ to know about our* ***family values*** *is that we value. …* Thinking Point: *How do my behaviors this week match my values?* Color the TT&L Notebook Cover Sheet. Bring back for next week to put in Notebook.

[a]From, *Talk, Touch and Listen While Combing Hair* © Parent Group Facilitator Manual, M. L. Lewis

During our eight-week *Talk, Touch, and Listen While Combing Hair* sessions, parent whisperers served as peer coaches who provided individual support to mothers in the group sessions. The main role of a parent whisperer was to be an active listener to the mother, to create and identify values and goals that were important for the mother, to encourage them and reframe their negative self-talk, and to provide acknowledgement that reaffirms their positive qualities. Parent whisperers supported mothers through understanding, accepting, encouraging, and empowering, helping parents discover a new way to interact with their own children that modeled the same type of supportive behavior.

Often during the one-on-one interactions, mothers seemed to be more comfortable in sharing their personal feelings and stories, something that was more difficult in group settings with anywhere from three to ten mothers. Creating these individual connections provided a safer environment for both the mother and parent whisperer where the two could get to know each other on a level separate from the group. Listening and giving positive feedback were two main supportive actions that the parent whisperer took when having one-on-one conversations with the mothers.

Flexibility: Attending to the Needs of Children During Group Sessions

Although the curriculum for each session was decided upon before the sessions, flexibility was key to holding a successful group. To carry out a successful program for mothers, the barriers had to be identified and reduced. One of the potential barriers to a parent participation was the presence of their children. As a result of children wanting attention from their mothers during the session, the mother's attention was often divided between what was going on in the session and the needs of their child. As a parent group focused on enhancing attachment between mother and child, it seemed ironic to remove the children in these types of situations. However, at times when children were present, providing some sort of childcare was often the most effective solution to having the mother's undivided attention and engagement. In many instances, parent whisperers were asked to support the mothers by watching their children in a separate room. In this way, mothers felt comfortable knowing that their children were simply a few doors away, leaving them to fully focus on the sessions and getting the most out of them.

As a parent whisperer, there were many times when my mindset had to quickly shift from parent whisperer to caretaker. Often, I would enter a session thinking I was going to be able to interact with the mothers, yet I was asked to take care of the children in the play area. Although I enjoyed being with the children, it was often disappointing to think that I was missing out on the conversation that was happening between the mothers in the session. However, as I continued to take on this role, my relationship with the children enabled me to get closer to the mothers as well. Through my relationship building with their child, a trust was formed between the mother and me. This kind of flexibility in the end was beneficial to my role as a parent whisperer and it enabled me to create a deeper connection with the mothers.

"But I Don't Have Children!"' My Thoughts on Sharing as a Full Participant in an Experiential Group Model for Parents

In the *Talk, Touch, and Listen* (TTL) sessions, parent whisperers also engaged in discussions as participants of the group, offering thoughts, stories, and experiences with the mothers. Research shows that peer coaches or navigators are more effective when they have had similar life experiences to the target group. Simoni et al. (2011) state, "Matching the marginalized or stigmatized status of a target group (i.e., impoverished, sexual minority) is often an important aspect of parent peers." In our group, many of the women were low-income, young, African-American mothers between the ages of 25 and 35 years. As an Asian American, Master of Public Health candidate with no children, I felt ill-equipped to relate to the mothers or support the mothers in the TTL sessions. However, after attending several sessions, I found that the experience of motherhood and growing up as a child is similar across cultures. Questions that were asked of the mothers could be modified and fit to participants with no children. By addressing the questions from the perspective of the child, participants who had no children could offer a child's point of view and often allowed mother's to reflect on their childhood as well as their child's perspective on many issues.

In order to break down cultural perceptions and barriers, it was necessary to have individual interactions. It was through the individual interactions as well as the sharing of stories and experiences that enabled everyone to see each other as a fellow woman versus an "other." Human beings often share similar emotional experiences and stories, by sharing these with each other, the sense of "other" can be diminished and a common ground can be established.

However, that is not to say that mothers were completely comfortable. Some mothers expressed feeling uncomfortable being "supported" by young students who did not have any children of their own and therefore had no good advice to offer and might not be able relate to what they were going through as a mother. While a cordial relationship could be created, it may have been to the benefit of the participants to feel like they could connect with their parent whisperers on a greater level. Mothers may have benefited more from parent whisperers who were women who went through the experience of childbirth and have experienced the joys and struggles of child rearing. Furthermore, mothers expressed that it was hard to open during an eight-week session to parent whisperers who they knew they would not speak to after the sessions were over. It may be beneficial to extend the relationship of mothers with parent whisperers beyond the TTL sessions to ensure that genuine relationships are created between the mothers and parent whisperers.

In conclusion, the most important role of the parent whisperer was to develop relationships of trust with the parent caregiver, who could then model that same type of relationship with their own child. In the society we live in today, these interactions and conversations between parent and child are more crucial than ever.

Reflective Questions

1. Is the role of a "parent whisperer" one that you can imagine taking on in your interactions and relationships with infants, children, and families who are referred to your practice?
2. What makes a "parent whisperer" successful in engaging and supporting another?
3. What can you, a professional, learn from peer coaches who were instructed to model skills from Talk, Touch, and Listen While Combing Hair, especially, active listening, acceptance, and empowerment through positive support, when working with parents, and do you think you can embrace these strategies in your practice?
4. What did you find yourself wondering about as you read the reflections of a parent whisperer?

References

Brown, J., & Isaacs, D. (2005). Conversation as a core process: Co-creating business and social value. *Reflections: The Sol Journal, 6*(4-5), 23–28.

Brown, J., & Isaacs, D. (2010). *World Cafe design principles*. http://www.theworldcafe.com/principles.html

Brown, J., Isaacs, D., Margulies, N., & Warhaftig, G. (1999). *The World Cafe: Catalyzing large-scale collective learning. Leverage: News and Ideas for the Organizational Learner* (Pegasus Communications), 33, 1–2. http://www.theworldcafe.com/wp-content/uploads/2015/07/catalyzinglearning.pdf

Crawford, D. & Lewis, M. L. (2012, July 12). *Strengthening family relationships through routines of combing hair & family stories*. A Webinar for the March of Dimes Family Support Specialists.

Lewis, M. L. (2008). Talk, Touch & Listen While Combing Hair. Facilitator's Manual, Unpublished manuscript, Tulane University, New Orleans, Louisiana, USA.

Lewis, M. L. (2013). *The historical roots of African-American mother-daughter relationships and the psychology of hair combing rituals*. In H. Jackson-Lowman (Ed.), *Afrikan American women: Living at the crossroads of race, gender, class, and culture*. Cognella Press/University Readers.

Lewis, M. L., & Swift, A. L. (2015). What my momma gave me while combing my kinks: A culturally informed program to strengthen relationships between mothers and daughters and community connections. In A. D. Yarber, D. Davis-Maye, & T. Perry (Eds.), *What my momma gave me: conceptualizations of womanhood* (pp. 54–72).

Simoni, J. M., Franks, J. C., Lehavot, K., & Yard, S. S. (2011). Peer interventions to promote health: Conceptual considerations. *American Journal of Orthopsychiatry, 81*(3), 351–359. https://doi.org/10.1111/j.1939-0025.2011.01103.x

Chapter 15
Culture, Creativity, and Helping: Using the Afrocentric Perspective in Community Healing

Samuel L. Bradley Jr. and Marva L. Lewis

Introduction to a Puppet Show

In the summer of 2013, a team of social work students, under the guidance of their professor, Marva Lewis, constructed Miranda's Puppet Show, a community-based psychoeducational intervention used to teach parents and children about emotions and getting their hair combed. In this chapter, we will discuss Afrocentric theory, using creative arts in community-based interventions, and practical strategies for social workers and other professionals seeking to make use of their own culturally rigorous techniques.

Miranda's Puppet Show is a world not unlike our own, one in which a community of helpers shows up to support parents in their day-to-day quest to provide a rich and meaningful upbringing for their infants and young children. Miranda is a child like most children. She is precocious and smart, inquisitive, and trusting. As our team engaged in the sketching of *Miranda's Puppet Show,* we all called to mind images of childhood shows that reflect the best ideals of community, tenderheartedness, and loving engagement, with a village of citizens all working toward a common goal.

Perhaps, one of my favorite themes in *Miranda's Puppet Show* is carried out through all three acts of the show, the parent–child relationship or attachment. It features Miranda running away from her mother to protest having her hair combed. The central tenet of attachment in Bowlby and Ainsworth's Attachment Theory (Tracy & Ainsworth, 1981) suggests that Miranda uses her mother as her secure base, her anchor as she runs away, testing her own reality in the larger world, and

S. L. Bradley Jr. (✉)
School of Social Work, Boston College, Boston, MA, USA
e-mail: Samuel.Bradley@bc.edu

M. L. Lewis
School of Social Work, Tulane University, New Orleans, LA, USA

M. L. Lewis, D. J. Weatherston (eds.), *Therapeutic Cultural Routines to Build Family Relationships*, https://doi.org/10.1007/978-3-030-83726-6_15

keeping her mother in mind all the while. Miranda protests as she runs away, and yet, rather than ignoring her mother, she brings her up to every adult she comes in contact with on her adventure. This is much like young children who run away from their caregivers as a means of reality testing and playfulness, and then return to the safety of the parent–child relationship.

When I discovered the method, *Talk, Touch, and Listen While Combing Hair!* (TT&L), developed by Marva Lewis (Lewis & Butler Byrd, 2016) to support healthy parent–child interaction, and based on my deep love of the arts, I was drawn to become a member of her team. I couldn't wait to get home after our initial brainstorming meeting to watch several episodes of the Punch and Judy Show on YouTube. I had long admired that style of comedy. I remembered staying up late to watch old TV shows and movies with my parents. Memories of *I Love Lucy* and other *Nick at Nite* grainy black & white TV shows flooded my dreams. It felt like a treat to study the ways in which puppetry had brought lessons for understanding and great joy to so many children and adults. Following a study of as many episodes as I could get my hands on, I worked with the team of graduate students as we set out on a mission to craft a show that would be fun for students and easy for amateur performers to read and understand. We stayed up all night with a skeletal framework created by Dr. Lewis, writing dialogue and interaction for *Miranda's Puppet Show*.

Attachment and Talk, Touch and Listen While Combing Hair

Attachment Theory helps us see that young children learn about the world of relationships from sensitive caregiving and responsive interactions with parents, caregivers, and other community members. Appropriate and contingent responses between a primary caregiver and young child result in a strong attachment relationship, providing emotional and psychological safety, encouraging the child to explore the world of people and things with curiosity and enthusiasm (Ainsworth, et al., 1978).

Central to TT&L is the idea that hair combing, something that parents do when caring for their children, allows parents time to pay attention and express a host of concepts including love, support, affection, sympathy, encouragement, excitement, and empowerment, just to name a few. These interactions lead to a strong and healthy attachment relationship that sets the foundation for positive relationships with other people throughout the lifespan (Sroufe et al., 2005).

The Conceptual Framework: An Afrocentric Lens for Creative Social Work Practice

The Afrocentric perspective, largely developed in historically Black colleges and universities, and contributed to by many modern-day researchers such as Jerome Schiele, Tricia Bent-Goodley, Colita Nichols Fairfax, Iris Carlton-LaNey, focuses on using African philosophies, history, and culture as a starting place for understanding the world (Bent-Goodley et al., 2017). The Social Work field needs to integrate Afrocentric theories into its educational and training curricula while seeking new opportunities to put it into practice.

The benefit of *Talk, Touch, and Listen* is its alignment with core social work values and ethics such as our obligation toward social justice, person-in-environment perspective, and strengths-based approach when working with clients. As social workers, we have a responsibility to seek justice in all that we do in pursuit of social change. Social work practice requires us to consider the history, culture, and needs of the peoples of Africa and the diaspora, which includes those from the African continent, the Caribbean, Latin America, and African Americans. In considering specific culture and needs within the culture, professional social workers are advised to use an Afrocentric perspective to apply culturally rigorous approaches to practice.

Our collective professional obligation is further exemplified in the person-in-environment perspective, an approach that has long been a tenet to good, evidence-based practice. The Afrocentric perspective invites practitioners to pay attention to both strengths and needs of children and families who are historically and socially different from other cultural groups. Many times, the conflation of cultural competency is rooted in knowing the broad strokes of history that affected a large so-called minority community. The person-in-environment perspective asks us to approach this problem of marginalized and minoritized peoples differently. When applied, the person-in-environment approach helps us to carefully inspect and respect people, their physical surroundings, and their social and historical surroundings.

Finally, the infusion of an Afrocentric approach, alongside our professional ethics for social justice and social change, combined with the person-in-environment approach, allows us to approach our clients from a strengths perspective. Knowing one's history, culture, and philosophies helps both practitioners and clients to ground themselves in identities that are unique and powerful. For instance, the storytelling tradition of the African-American community creates a powerful opportunity to tap into creative endeavors like puppet shows, spiritual gatherings, and simple cookouts to bring a new message about healing from the trauma of historical oppression and slavery. Leveraging these gifts is powerful and also skill based. Storytellers within communities have a powerful ability to tap into the shared experiences that the dominant group is often oblivious to. By using the *Talk, Touch, and Listen* model as a point of reference, we hope to create an accessible tool for social workers that reflects an Afrocentric way of thinking.

Afrocentric Social Work Practice

Talk, Touch, and Listen While Combing Hair! flows from research that focuses on the importance of the mother and child's attachment relationship to the developing child's healthy social, emotional, and cognitive development (Wilson et al., 2018). The attachment relationship, optimally defined as secure and trusting, develops out of many sensitive and responsive interactions between parent and child. The *Talk, Touch, and Listen* experience honors and reflects this theoretical frame, with a unique focus on the hair combing experience within the African-American community.

Important to understand, Afrocentric social work demonstrates that an intervention focused on supporting Black women and children is possible. This important approach should be integrated into practice, rather than something that is additional to treatment and intervention. In a world where anti-Black racism creates psychological impacts on all peoples of the African diaspora, the professional social worker should pursue with haste and vigor methodologies like *Talk, Touch, and Listen* that build psychological resilience.

Creating the Puppet Show: "Have You Ever Seen the Punch and Judy Show"?

Translating abstract statistics from research findings into pragmatic tools to support children and families is a challenging task. Much of evidence-based practice builds on techniques and theories established as appropriate with different populations. Translating a cultural practice of hair combing into a clinical intervention was daunting. A brief image seen while scrolling through the pages of a website on an unrelated topic was the catalyst for the development of Miranda's Puppet Show. What I saw was a still photo of the wildly popular Punch and Judy puppet show, a staple of street entertainment in Britain in the 1600s. What attracted my eye was how it was centered in the heart of the community, surrounded by throngs of laughing children and adults.

Briefly, the plots were short, depicting lively interactions between two puppets with exaggerated features. The central male puppet, Punch, and his wife, Judy, often engaged in shouting matches, arguments, or fights, with Punch using manipulative techniques or even hitting his wife over the head. You may wonder what this depiction of family violence has to do with promoting loving parent–child interaction while combing hair? How could a puppet show about an old white couple with the husband regularly beating his wife in jolly old England inform social work practice with Black children and families?

Prior to seeing the images of the Punch and Judy Show, I (Lewis) had read through the latest draft of a children's book created by a dear friend, Dollwyn Pierre from New Orleans, Louisiana. Familiar with the focus of my research on the importance of the hair combing task as an opportunity to bond with young children, Dollwyn created Miranda's Green Hair© (Pierre, 2004). The book normalizes the hair combing task and helps children connect emotionally to their daily hair combing experiences. The story is about a little girl who doesn't want to get her hair combed. She runs away from home, has some frightening experiences in the forest, and gets help from the animals and trees in the forest to find her way home.

The "aha" moment was how a lively, boisterous puppet show in the tradition of *Punch and Judy* could serve as a vehicle to reach communities of parents and children together on the emotionally charged topic of hair combing. The photo of the old English puppets wildly chasing each other around the stage evoked images of wild-haired two-year-olds chased by a frustrated parent with comb-in-hand trying to get the child to sit still to get their hair combed. The theme of violent interactions between two family members could be translated into the depiction of intense emotions that children feel in response to getting their hair combed. With a large dose of humor, the puppets could act out the emotions felt by both the child and the parent. Thus, Miranda's Puppet Show was born.

After developing an outline focused on the expression and recognition of emotions, a puppet show could serve as a community-based vehicle to help parents and young children to recognize the emotions of a young girl of color who doesn't want to get her hair combed. What emerged from this creative process was the idea of adding *Miranda's Puppet Show* as a companion to the *Talk, Touch, and Listen While Combing Hair! Parent Café*. Both could support learning to listen, creating opportunities to interact positively with one another, and entering into everyday conversations that are respectful.

What Is The Parent Café?

The *Talk, Touch, and Listen* Parent Café was originally designed to address the legacies of historical trauma for African-American descendants of enslaved African survivors of chattel slavery in the United States. For example, Colorism, valuing light skin over dark skin, is an unrecognized legacy of centuries of group oppression. The strong emotions associated with these experiences are not often discussed within families. These emotions may become part of intergenerational patterns of acceptance or rejection of children due to the parent's internalized stereotypes about racial features. The TT&L *Parent Café* provides a safe neutral space for parent peers to unpack their memories of childhood experiences of colorism, hair combing, and other racial traumas of acceptance or rejection by loved family members or unthinking neighbors and friends.

During the Parent Café, children sit in a setting that is separate from their parents or other caregivers, and follow a curriculum of interactive, artistic activities such drawing, painting, or learning how to recognize and understand the meaning of different emotions. They also spend time preparing items for the puppet show that follows the cafe.

Based on the World Wide Cafe model (The World Café Community Foundation Creative Commons, 2015), TT&L Parent Cafés are a series of "drop-in" groups that are offered to parents and families as a regular part of the community agency's early childhood services. The Cafés provide an informal place for parents to connect over a meal. Agency staff trained in the cafe model lead a gently facilitated tabletop discussion about tough topics of colorism and the meaning of terms like "good" hair.

Miranda's Puppet Show parallels the topics of acceptance, rejection, and conflict resolution that parents discuss in the monthly Parent Cafés and that are covered in the 8-week parent support group *Talk, Touch, and Listen While Combing Hair!* offered at the sponsoring community agency.

This is a two-generation approach to raise emotional awareness and create social support for parents. Through the voice of Miranda learning to express her emotions, we aim to interrupt historical or intergenerational family patterns, shining a light of hope so that children can be accepted for who they are. Primary goals are to encourage unconditional acceptance of children and to recognize the hurt caused by racialized Colorism. The Parent Café and *Miranda's Puppet Show* are relevant to people of color from marginalized, oppressed racial, ethnic, cultural, and minority groups around the world.

This entertaining activity engages parents in the ritual and routine of hair combing and storytelling as a daily opportunity to talk, touch, and listen to their child while combing hair. After participating in these gently facilitated conversations with other parents at a *Parent Café,* caregivers and children come together to enjoy an interactive and fun puppet show.

The Development of *Miranda's Puppet Show*

Miranda's Puppet Show was adapted from the original story, *Miranda's Green Hair*© by Dollwyn Pierre of New Orleans, Louisiana, and produced in 2013 by Samuel Bradley, Kaley Gerstley, Ian Farrell, Abbey Cettel, and Kendal Jackson, MSW graduate students at the Tulane University School of Social Work. The puppet show centers on a lively little girl of color with green hair. Her mother wants to comb her hair, and she has strong feelings about getting her hair combed. The central theme of the show is that Miranda does not know how to express her emotions and resolve the conflict she feels. Her mother wants to comb her hair and she has strong feelings about getting her hair combed. Her best friend, JoJo the Clown, leads her through a hilarious journey through the neighborhood, where she encounters a nosey neighbor and friendly postman or police officer.

The Structure of the Puppet Show

The interaction takes place on the front porch of a single-story house in the neighborhood of an urban city, similar to New Orleans, Louisiana. There are three scenes that tell the story of Miranda's efforts to avoid getting her hair combed. Throughout the show, the audience urges Miranda to express her emotions using rhythmic chants accompanied by musical instruments such as drums or rainmakers. The encouraging chants tell Miranda to show her feelings and seek help from other adults or the helping community. The seven basic emotions include *joy, surprise, anger, fear, sadness, disgust, and interest* (Izard, 1992) and are incorporated throughout the dialog of Miranda's Puppet Show. Each emotion is painted on a hand-held sign that the puppet Miranda holds up in front of her face as the audience loudly chants for her to express her emotion. Another puppet, JoJo, the Clown, reads the signs that Miranda holds and instructs the audience of children and parents to shout out the emotions as loudly as they can. Separate musical instruments are played to emphasize each specific emotion.

Our goal is to jointly build the parents' and children's emotional vocabulary. With this nonthreatening intervention, parents observe other children's responses to the emotions that their child might experience during hair combing. Seeing other children's responses to the task of combing hair may normalize their own child's reaction to what could be a painful or pleasurable experience.

By following the lighthearted antics of a little girl puppet that may look like their own child or remind them of themselves as children, parents and children learn to recognize and label seven universal emotions and normalize the expression of basic emotions in all children. Parents also can practice active listening skills in a nonthreatening environment with other peers. As parent caregivers comb hair, it will be important for them to listen carefully to their own child's verbal and nonverbal ways of expressing emotions. They can take the skills learned at the puppet show and in the Parent Café, back to their homes and everyday routines of combing their child's hair.

Finally, the two-generation goal of all these activities is to strengthen the parent–child bond, the parent's sense of self-efficacy, increase the recognition of basic emotions and emotional literacy, and ability to recognize and resolve conflict.

Build Community Among Parent Peers

Parents come together through food, fun, and being heard. The scenes presented in the puppet show are designed to demonstrate the positive roles of a variety of community members for social support. The characters of the nosey neighbor and the helpful policeman or postman are easily recognized by both young children and their parents.

Parenting children with the stresses of today's world provides many challenges. Participating in traditional parenting groups often has the very defined goals of addressing behavioral challenges in children, learning new child management techniques, or simply complying with the order of a juvenile court to attend "parent training." The final goal of this puppet show is to give parents an opportunity to relax, laugh, and learn with both their children and other parents in a safe, nonthreatening environment. To have *fun!*

Igniting Social Workers' Imagination Through Art and Creativity

Readers may wonder to themselves what some key takeaways are regarding building a puppet show and igniting social work practitioners' imagination. First, the process does not need to be expensive. The puppet stage built in the New Orleans production cost just under $100 using PVC piping, bed linen, and tape. The puppets themselves were constructed using puppet arts and crafts cut-outs easily searchable on the internet. However, some of our other colleagues have purchased puppet theatres, stages, and puppets online for ease of convenience.

We borrowed sound makers (small drums and rainmakers) from musically inclined colleagues, but practitioners can also build their own sound makers or involve children in making them in an arts and crafts activity. To create the sound of a pair of maracas, you can fill a plastic cup with beads or peas and then tape a second cup to it right at the rims of both cups. When shaken, the cups with the beads/peas inside will give the distinct cha-cha sound of the maracas. This is an inexpensive and easy activity. Building puppet shows, singing songs with clients, and working on productions together are wonderful ways to build rapport and create opportunities for discussion with children and adults, supporting both the parents' and children's development.

Combing the Arts and Afrocentric Social Work Practice: Personal Reflections

Music, dancing, drawing, and storytelling are central components of the human condition. Across numerous cultures, beliefs, and values, people share the common trait of attempting to offer parts of themselves, their cultures, and their ideas through artistry. Art isn't limited; it can include puppetry, martial arts, graphic design, cooking, and a host of other activities that are designed to bridge the human experience with a shared and communal storytelling experience.

Not everyone talks, not everyone speaks the same language, and when we are talking, we might not know what we are saying or what we need to say. To circumvent this difficulty in connecting, we need the same tools our ancestors have relied on for thousands of years: art.

Why am I talking so much about art? I want to encourage social work practitioners to feel free to use the arts in their own practice. Whether you consider yourself to be creative or not, there is no better way to get started than to try it. Asking clients to draw, write, or sing about their experiences is an excellent option for helping them to express their lived experiences.

I encourage you to consider using your own cultural experiences to teach lessons, create space, and encourage creativity with your clients. They will be thankful for your thoughtfulness in this space.

The beauty of Miranda's Puppet Show is its simplicity. It allows us, the puppeteers, and showrunners, to take a playful approach to engaging children who may be at one of the most painful points of their young lives. In our case, we took the puppet show to the New Orleans Women's Shelter (NOWS), where many of the women were in the middle of transitioning away from living conditions made dangerous due to intimate partner violence.

While our team of performers and social workers in training worked with the children during playtime activities, the Parent Café's would take place. This was an opportunity for parents to share their concerns, questions, and engage in knowledge development around best practices for parenting. At the same time, at a moment in time in which our clients were most in danger of foregone and distant attachment, we were able to model healthy exploration of the world through Miranda's Puppet Show.

When I discuss creativity with other professionals, they say that they don't feel qualified to try new approaches to service or create new ways to reach children and families. While I advocate for the use of evidence-based practices in social work and other health allied fields, it is also important that practitioners with real lived experiences are given latitude to create and problem solve in the field. What follows are basic guidelines to creative thinking for social workers or other helping professionals:

Guidelines for Creative Thinking for Helping Professionals

STEP #1: To kick off a creative process, gather a group of trusted colleagues who represent diverse cultures, varied experiences, and different academic disciplines.

STEP #2 Explore the problem that you are trying to work on. Is it a community--based intervention at a women's shelter? An attempt to reach a particular community that is hard to interact with? Exploring the problem, the client, the community, and the environment is just as important as the solution and the creative process. Set a timer for 10 minutes, giving yourself an opportunity to define the problem, acknowledge the constraints of the problem, and focus on developing your critical thinking and creativity skills. Jot your ideas on post-it notes. Reflect for 10 min and place your sticky notes on a wall where everyone can see it. Refrain from discussing the sticky notes until the 10 min are up.

STEP #3: Explore the problem through more research. Libraries, online knowledge communities (often found on social media), and research scholars may be able to provide insight into the tough social problems that social workers and others face in the field. These important resources should help in discussing the group's ideas around the problem. Try reframing the problem several times.

STEP #4: Brainstorm the solution to the problem with your team. Suspend judgment; be playful and imaginative. Listen to each other. Reach agreement to try something out.

STEP #5 Create a test product or prototype. Test out your idea without investing too much time.

STEP #6 Take time to rehearse the finished product. Practice until you feel confident.

Conclusion

Miranda's Puppet Show demonstrates an attempt to set the framework for a world that isn't always friendly, warm, and endearing by creating a world that is a little less traumatic than the one that surrounds us. As a social worker or helping professional, you can foster creativity and healing with your clients. Building on the everyday cultural practices provides a template for creativity, healing, and identity building. Be curious, explore, and take action!

Reflective Questions

1. How can you bring an Afrocentric approach to your practice with Black children and families, using Talk, Touch, and Listen as a creative centerpiece for novel strategies to encourage positive parent–child interaction leading to a healthy attachment relationship?
2. What thoughts came alive for you as you thought about the pleasure that children and families enjoyed and what they learned watching *Miranda's Puppet Show?*
3. Reflecting on the art of storytelling that is at the center of Bradley's creative puppet show, what other stories about culture, ethnicity, race, or belonging could you tell that might capture the minds and hearts of children and parents and lead to healing?
4. How can you "think outside the box," and bring the creative arts, including music, dancing, drawing, and storytelling, into your social work or early childhood practice?

References

Ainsworth, M. D., Blehar, M. C., Waters, E., & Wall, S. (1978). Patterns of attachment: A psychological study of the strange situation. *Infant Mental Health Journal, 1*(1), 68–70. https://doi.org/10.1002/1097-0355(198021)1:1<68::AID-IMHJ2280010110>3.0.CO;2-3

Bent-Goodley, T., Nichols Fairfax, C., & Carlton-LaNey, I. (2017). The significance of African-centered social work for social work practice. *Journal of Human Behavior in the Social Environment, 27*(1-2), 1–6. https://doi.org/10.1080/10911359.2016.1273682

Izard, C. E. (1992). Basic emotions, relations among emotions, and emotion-cognition relations. *Psychological Review, 99*(3), 561–565. https://doi.org/10.1037/0033-295x.99.3.56

Lewis, M. L., & Butler Byrd, N. (2016). *Translating research to practice: A community-based parent curriculum, talk, touch & listen while combing hair*. Biennial meeting of the Society for Research in Child Development, Seattle, WA, USA.

Pierre, D. (2004). Miranda's Green Hair. Unpublished manuscipt. New Orleans, LA, USA.

Sroufe, A., Egeland, B., Carlson, E., & Collins, W. (2005). *The development of the person: The Minnesota study of risk and adaptation from birth to adulthood*. Guilford Press.

The World Café Community Foundation Creative Commons (2015). https://www.theworld-cafe.com.

Tracy, R. L., & Ainsworth, M. D. (1981). Maternal affectionate behavior and infant-mother attachment patterns. *Child Development, 52*(4), 1341–1343.

Wilson, I.-P., Mbilishaka, A., & Lewis, M. L. (2018). White folks ain't got hair like us: African American mother-daughter hair stories and racial socialization. *Women, Gender, and Families of Color, 6*(2), 226–248. https://doi.org/10.5406/womgenfamcol.6.2.0226

Part IV
Tools for Observation, Assessment, and Intervention

Chapter 16
Tools to Disrupt the Legacies of Colorism: Perceptions, Emotions, and Stories of Childhood Racial Features

Marva L. Lewis and Virginia White

Do you remember getting your hair combed as a child? What emotions did you feel as you got your hair combed? Was it an ordeal or a painful time to be endured? Or was it time that you felt loved and cared for by a special person?

Culturally sensitive infant and early childhood practitioners have few systematic tools to assess the impact that psychological residuals of historical trauma have in developing parent–child and family relationships (Lewis et al., 2013). Within African-American communities, the topic of hair and skin color has long been a focus for popular media and interdisciplinary studies (Byrd & Tharps, 2001; Prince, 2009). Researchers in diverse regions of the world, such as India and South Africa (Erasmus, 2000), Brazil, (Hordge-Freeman, 2015) and Puerto Rico (Neal-Barnett et al., 1996), report the impact of hair and skin color on Black women's self-concept and children's development. These emotionally toxic intergenerational legacies may permeate the everyday interactions of Black caregivers with their young children.

The historical trauma associated with racialized African features, specifically light or dark skin tone and kinky-curly hair type remains a modern-day standard to judge the beauty of African-American women and girls. A colorist-historical trauma framework views colorism as a function of historical trauma impacting the psychological and physical well-being of African Americans (Meyers, 1999; Ortega-Williams, Crutchfield, & Hall, 2019). The racial environment may be one of the most profoundly influential factors in the feelings that children of color have about themselves and their relationships with their caregivers. The structured tools, the *Neck-up drawing*© (Lewis & Joseph, 2017), and the CERAR story are introduced in this chapter. The *Neck-up drawing*©, a projective measure, will help adults and primary caregivers share their memories and tell stories based on freestyle drawings of

M. L. Lewis (✉) · V. White
School of Social Work, Tulane University, New Orleans, LA, USA
e-mail: mlewis@tulane.edu

M. L. Lewis, D. J. Weatherston (eds.), *Therapeutic Cultural Routines to Build Family Relationships*, https://doi.org/10.1007/978-3-030-83726-6_16

their racialized self as a child from the neck up. Several case examples are presented in the chapter to illustrate the childhood memories and emotions associated with hair texture and skin color to adults using the *Neck-up drawing*©.

Broaching the Topic of Race

At the first meeting with a client or family, seasoned practitioners may become stymied with the question, "*How do I ask about race?*" Race may be a difficult topic to broach when meeting a client of color (Day-Vines et al., 2007). The routine of combing hair presents a nonthreatening entry point to begin these conversations. Joining with a parent or caregiver for mutual observations of videotaped hair combing interaction presents opportunities for both parental insight eg., reflective functioning and mentalizing), and therapist assessment and intervention.

In 2019, the fastest growing populations in the United States will be identified as "multicultural" based on diverse social identity groups including gender, race, ethnicity, sexual orientation, and social class (Vespa, Medina, and Armstrong, 2020). In this chapter, we present a clinical protocol using drawings and narrative techniques to assess the impact of negative childhood messages of colorism, the parent's internalized stereotypes about skin color and hair type, on the quality of their behaviors, attitudes, during hair combing interaction (HCI) and developing attachment relationship. These stereotypes may become triggered during hair combing times.

The concept of broaching race is described by Day-Vines et al. (2007), to prepare counseling students to work with clients on issues of race, ethnicity, and culture during the counseling process. They state, "*Broaching refers to the counselor's ability to consider the relationship of racial and cultural factors to the client's presenting problem, especially because these issues might otherwise remain unexamined during the counseling process.*" (p. 401).

A therapist's broaching behaviors are characterized as an attitude of openness coupled with a commitment to continually explore issues of diversity with the client. It is the therapist's role to initiate race-related dialogues, or this topic may remain taboo in a racially stratified society where race is not sufficiently discussed (See Wilson, Chap. 9).

Day-Vines et al. (2007) present a continuum of broaching styles that they argue parallel the counselor's stage of racial identity formation (Helms, 1990). We adapted this broaching continuum to help understand challenges that might arise in the therapist-client discussion of the racially charged topics of race and hair combing interaction (HCI). The stages of racial identity formation may explain both the therapist's and client's levels of internalized stereotypes.

The Neck-up assessment protocol allows the therapist to explore racial trauma associated with the client's internal working model of their early attachment relationships. Observed parenting behaviors, attitudes, and beliefs can then be understood within the larger racial context and history of oppression (Meyers, 1999).

These racialized trauma memories can trigger a mental alarm in clients who do not have the ego strength to address unresolved attachment issues. Their psychic defenses may lead to perceptions of the therapist's questions as challenges and criticism to their idealized image of their mothers.

Understanding the Practitioner's Childhood Experiences of Colorism

Countertransference refers to the therapist's unresolved intrapsychic or personal conflicts, which may have occurred in early childhood (Crawford & Lewis, 2017). We address these issues through the reflective practice questions at the end of this chapter. Culture-based countertransference includes the therapist's culturally held assumptions, stereotypes, norms, beliefs, and values; attitudes related to race, ethnicity, and gender; political, religious, and moral worldviews; the influence of family of origin beliefs and intergenerational messages (Lewis & Ghosh-Ippen, 2004).

A lack of awareness of culture-based reactions may significantly impact the practitioner's ability to provide authentic and respectful service to all individuals (Crawford & Lewis, 2017). For a different-race or same-race clinical practitioner, bringing up the emotionally charged topics of race, skin tone, hair, and a client's mother are fraught with potential landmines. Three interpersonal dynamics must be considered by the therapist/practitioner during an HCI assessment: how ready is the client to assessing the sensitivity of the topic of the client's internal working model with their primary attachment figure; assessing the client's level of internalized oppression; and the practitioner's skill in broaching issues of race. Careful consideration of these three areas will support the practitioner's understanding of the role of racial trauma in Hair Combing Interaction (HCI) assessments.

A Client's Internal Working Model

The structure of a client's internal working model (Bowlby, 1969) developed over the course of many interactions with their primary attachment figure helps tell the story of race-based trauma, and guides the use of the HCI tools for assessment and intervention. When a parent is asked to recall early caregiving experiences, many thoughts and feelings come to mind about the quality of care and the resulting attachment relationship with parents and other primary caregivers. The quality of care given may have been nurturing or not, leading to a working model for relationships described as loving and secure or abandoning, avoidant, and insecure. Memories around hair combing are particularly evocative. For example, after completing the Neck-up drawing, one parent shared the emotion word, *nothing*, when asked to describe feelings about getting their hair combed. The parent explained, "*I have no memories of my birth mother completing this routine task.*" She went on to relate that her hair had often been uncombed or "neglected" by her substance-abusing mother. She then burst into tears after sharing these memories. It offered a moment for empathy and greater understanding about all she had lost. A tool to enhance parental reflective functioning is provided at the end of this chapter.

Internalized Oppression

A second emotionally charged area may emerge when assessing the client's level of internalized oppression. As we discussed in the ethnobiography of the parent or primary caregiver, they may be at a different stage of awareness of their racial identity as a person of color (See Lewis & Weatherston, Chap. 4). When unrecognized negative stereotypes of a racial group become internalized and are seen as "normal" within a network of family members, these messages may be passed down through the generations (Parmer et al., 2004). For generations the practice of teasing and joking about a child's "nappy hair" or "ashy dark" skin is expressed with laughter and normalized at family events. Thus, a parent who spontaneously blurts out the same message to their child, "*You got some bad, nappy hair to comb!*" may minimize or justify the continued practice of these messages in the presence of the therapist. The therapist, after listening carefully, may ask the parent who might have said that to them, and then wonder how those words felt long ago. The parent may deny that these messages have a negative, emotional impact on their relationship with their child or their child's self-image. The psychic defenses in place when it comes to critiquing anyone's mother may have layers of protection from outsiders seeking to break in (Crawford & Lewis, 2017). Intentionally listening, responding with empathy, and addressing these messages are critical for the therapist when conducting a racially informed assessment or intervention using parent or primary caregiver–child hair combing interactions.

Disrupting Intergenerational Nappy-Haired Legacies of the Historical Trauma of Slavery

The Neck-up drawing© helps the practitioner to answer the question: *What was this parent's childhood self-image of their racialized features*? The answer gives the practitioner an emotional window into understanding a parent's feelings about their hair and their racial features including skin color, nose, lip size or in the case of lighter-skinned or white/Caucasian adults, their red hair and facial freckles. Drawings completed by adult caregivers of color from a variety of backgrounds and different family backgrounds will be used throughout the chapter to illustrate these points.

Telling the CERAR Story

The second part of the *Neck-up drawing*© protocol uses the storytelling technique of the Thematic Apperception Test (TAT) (Westen, 1991). Using the parent's drawing of racialized features of their childhood self as a stimulus, the practitioner asks the parent to tell a story to explain the two emotion words they selected to describe feelings about their hair, as well as feelings about getting their hair combed. These stories may provide clues to the counselor or therapist about underlying dynamics of the person's interpersonal relationships and racial self-attitudes. Beginning the session with this protocol may complement trauma treatment for individuals reporting traumatic HCI memories. The *Neck-up drawing*© may be used as a single administration for assessment or as a series of drawings over several sessions. The repeated use of a drawing protocol provides the practitioner or therapist with a themed-based structure to support the client in processing childhood memories of racial trauma associated with their hair type or skin tone. The practitioner or therapist, in turn, will need to have a place to reflect on what is shared and their own memories awakened in the assessment and intervention process (See Part II, Reflective Supervision and Practice).

In a formal assessment by a clinical researcher, this drawing may be used with standardized measures of ethnic identity, internalized stereotypes, or coping with racial discrimination. Caution should be used with the *Neck-up drawing*© as a formal projective assessment tool. For example, the degree of shading used by a client in some clinical contexts may be an indicator of depressed mood (Cox, 1993). But, in the context of drawing a picture of your racialized self, it may be an accurate depiction of their skin tone.

The *Neck-up drawing*© provides a practitioner with the opportunity to explore further questions about memories of positive, negative, or ambivalent messages about race from diverse members of a child's network of relationships. The following pictures and stories describe the impact of early messages of racial acceptance or rejection on the adult's depiction of their racialized self-image from the "neck up."

The Neck-up Drawing Protocol: The Internal Model of the Adult's Perception of their Racial Self-image

Projective tests assume that the way a test taker perceives and responds to an ambiguous scene reveals inner needs, feelings, conflicts, and desires (Cox, 1993; Hass-Cohen et al., 2018). An adult recalling childhood experiences of chronic trauma of stigmatized racial features may include unconscious emotions associated with their features. For parents, the racial features of their newborn infant or young child can become a trauma trigger. With this projective test, the therapist may be able to explore with the parents or caregiver their emotions and feelings in response to their infant or child's racial features and the possible origins of their response in their childhood experiences of racial acceptance or rejection based on these same racial features.

Memorialized Representations

We ask adults to recall their childhood image of their racialized features at about age 5 years of age. In the analysis of children's drawings, Cox (1993) uses the term "memorial representation" to describe the adult's production of the drawing having abstracted the distinguishing and invariant features of an object. These are then stored as an internal model or a memorial representation. We suggest that you think of the racial features depicted in the drawings as memorialized representations.

To explore childhood experiences with hair texture and skin color, we undertook a case study approach using a projective measure, the *Neck-up drawing*©, and the informal scores from the *Recognition of the Impact of Colorism on Children Scale* (RICS) (Lewis & Comer, 2015) completed by the participants. The case studies allowed an in-depth view of the impact of skin tone and hair texture on children. Case studies were conducted with seven participants who were selected based on demographics. The semistructured interviews typically lasted 10–20 min and were recorded. Four participants were female, three were male and ages ranged from 26 to 59 years old. In the beginning of each interview, participants were given a consent form describing details of the study. The order of the protocol used with each participant was for them to complete a brief form of their background demographics, draw a picture from the neck up when they were a young child, identify their hair type and skin color from forced-choice descriptions, and complete the Recognition of the Impact of Colorism on Children Scale (RICS).

What will be presented next are the pictures and brief summary of the stories participants developed based on the emotional reactions to their drawings (Figs. 16.1, 16.2, 16.3, 16.4, 16.5, 16.6, and 16.7). All names of participants are fictional[1], and each signed a consent form for their stories and pictures to be shared. There will be no clinical interpretations of these drawings. What will be discussed are the stories that the participants shared about their choice of emotions to describe their hair and experience getting their hair combed.

Case Study #1 Jane – Positive Emotion – "Patience," Negative Emotion – "Insecure"

Jane's Story

Jane is a 27-year-old African-American female from Washington, D.C. She was fully engaged throughout the survey and openly discussed childhood experiences in relation to her paternal twin sister, Jill. The *Neck-up drawing*© specifically requested the participants to draw a picture of themselves from the neck up when they were

[1] All names and other personal identifiers in the cases in this chapter have been changed to protect privacy and confidentiality.

Fig. 16.1 Jane: A dark-skin twin's Neck-up drawing of her light-skin twin sister

young children. Jane's interpretation of the exercise shed light on the dynamics of the relationship with her twin sister. Jane drew a full body picture of herself and twin sister as children. She identified herself as tall and her twin sister, Jill, as "much shorter." Written below Jill's depiction in parenthesis was the word, "twin." Interestingly, Jane drew herself bigger and used "twin" instead of sister or twin sister to identify Jill. Jane frequently paused while completing The Neck-Up exercise. She would stare at the drawing and even place her hand to her mouth as if she was in deep thought about what to add next.

Jane stated she felt insecure about her hair as a child, and was patient when getting her hair combed. Jane's explanation of her feelings was somewhat unfocused as she stared off to the background. She stated,

> "I was insecure about my hair because I didn't realize how magical it was or could be because I didn't have…" Jane then looked back at the screen and continued, "My mom didn't know how to do hair…um and it was a lot. I have a lot of hair."

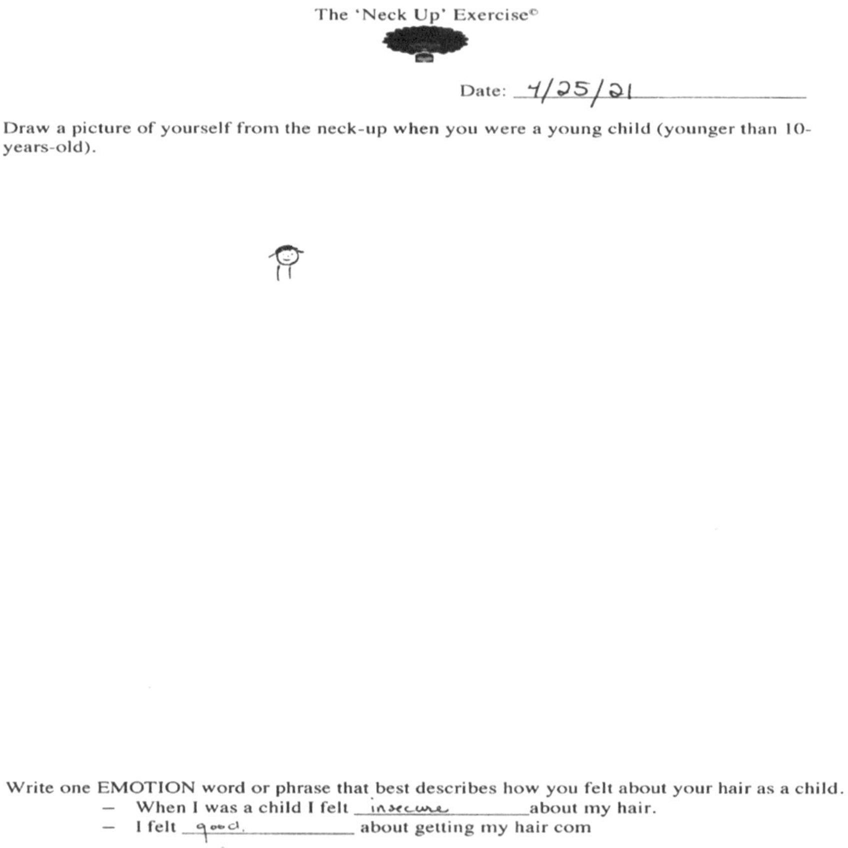
The 'Neck Up' Exercise©

Date: 4/25/21

Draw a picture of yourself from the neck-up when you were a young child (younger than 10-years-old).

Write one EMOTION word or phrase that best describes how you felt about your hair as a child.
– When I was a child I felt insecure about my hair.
– I felt good. about getting my hair com

Fig. 16.2 Anne's Neck-up drawing of positive and negative emotions

She returned her focus to the background and described how her hair looked as a child. It's important to note how Jane's focus returned back to the screen when explaining that her mother didn't know how to comb her hair as a child. She stated, "My mom didn't know how to handle it." Jane said her mother would put their hair in plaits and tell them to, "go on about their business."

Jane folded her arms and explained she had patience when getting her hair combed because it would look "halfway decent." She exhaled deeply while briefly rocking back and forth before answering the next question. Jane often stared to the background when responding to questions. She would look back at the screen toward the end of her statement. This consistent ritual of body language suggested the intimate childhood experiences she shared.

Jane described various hairstyles her cousins would put in her hair. She stated they would put, "cornrows in it, putting beads on the end of barrettes, pigtails with barrettes." Jane's face looked tense as she nodded her head and shared how she had her first hair relaxer before the age of 10 years. She rocked side to side and explained

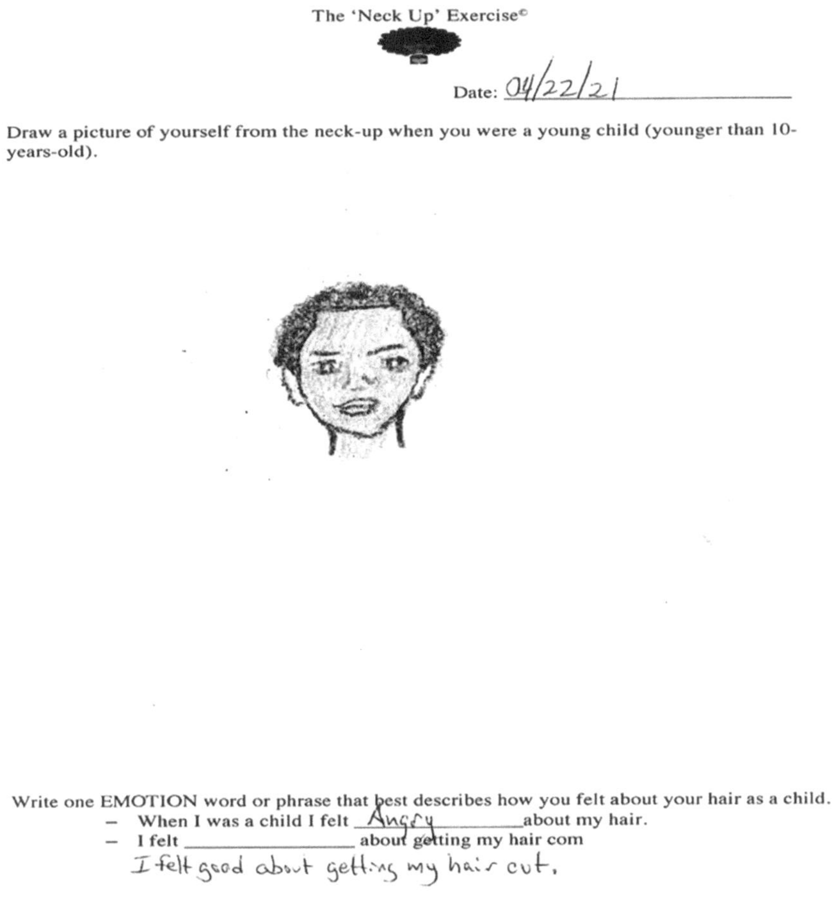

The 'Neck Up' Exercise©

Date: 04/22/21

Draw a picture of yourself from the neck-up when you were a young child (younger than 10-years-old).

Write one EMOTION word or phrase that best describes how you felt about your hair as a child.

- When I was a child I felt Angry about my hair.
- I felt ________ about getting my hair com

I felt good about getting my hair cut.

Fig. 16.3 A Black Male's Neck-up drawing: "I felt good, I felt angry"

why she wanted a relaxer as a child. Jane exclaimed, "My twin and I wanted to resemble Tia and Tamera." Tia and Tamera Mowry are identical twin actresses who had a popular television show named, "Sister, Sister."

Jane described her sister's hair as, "not as thick and long as mine." She stretched her hair to show its length and explained it wasn't like this as a child because, "relaxers pulled out my hair." Jane continued to describe physical characteristics of herself and twin sister. She said, "I am 5' 10, brown skin with lean build." She shared that her sister was, "about 5'4, light skinned and she's a bit more curvy than I am." While pointing to herself, Jane stated, "My mom looks like this and my father is much shorter and light skinned." She stated that her sister was referred to as, "the daughter of the milkman" when they were children. Jane explained this was, "just a joke from around the way, if your mom is sleeping with the milkman, the man who delivers milk while the father is away at work, because she was lighter than I was." She shared they both had the same hair texture but "within the past 10 years, mine

The 'Neck Up' Exercise©

Date: 4-24-21

Draw a picture of yourself from the neck-up when you were a young child (younger than 10-years-old).

Write one EMOTION word or phrase that best describes how you felt about your hair as a child.

- When I was a child I felt lovely about my hair.
- I felt good about getting my hair com

Fig. 16.4 Jon's Neck-up drawing and positive emotions about hair combing interaction

just went a different direction." Jane explained that her sister likes to get her hair flattened and cut. She also shared that she was compared to her twin sister's physical attributes as a child. Jane further explained, "For example, when it came to dating, men, young boys would befriend me and hope that I put in a good word for them with my twin." She said that they would associate her darker skin complexion with "difficult." Jane stated that she used to get called, "Black Jesus" as a child. While using air quotes, she said her sister was referred to as the "golden child". They were never treated differently at home. Jane said they were always seen as twins in the home; however, outside of the home, people would "start to separate us."

The 'Neck Up' Exercise©

Date: 4-24-21

Draw a picture of yourself from the neck-up when you were a young child (younger than 10-years-old).

Write one EMOTION word or phrase that best describes how you felt about your hair as a child.

- When I was a child I felt bad about my hair.
- I felt horrible about getting my hair com

Fig. 16.5 Sara's neck-up drawing: 'I felt horrible'

Jane shared the differences caused issues within herself. She stated, "Just growing up during that time, where you're trying to figure out who you are and certain things are growing in certain areas and other things are not and you think…oh wow, now we're comparing." Jane explained that she wished she would have learned how to appreciate her hair as a child. She said she regrets she didn't have those things but tries to implement them with her nieces and nephews.

Jane stated that if she could give advice to her 10-year-old self, she would say, "Don't compare yourself to what you see on TV and learn who you are or want to be at a very young age, so that way you can kind of fight off forces that tell you who you are."

The 'Neck Up' Exercise©

Date: 4/24/21

Draw a picture of yourself from the neck-up when you were a young child (younger than 10-years-old).

Write one EMOTION word or phrase that best describes how you felt about your hair as a child.

- When I was a child I felt Good about my hair.
- I felt i liked it about getting my hair com

Fig. 16.6 Lee: Black male Neck-up drawing, "I felt good"

Case Study #2 Anne – Positive Emotion – "Good", Negative Emotion – "Insecure"

Anne's Story

Anne is a 49-year-old mother of three from Kansas. She quickly completed the Neck-up exercise, taking a very small portion of the paper to illustrate herself as a child. Anne hesitated before writing the emotion words describing her hair as a child. She felt "insecure" about her hair as a child, but felt "good" about getting her 4a/4c hair combed (for more information on different types of hair: https://www.

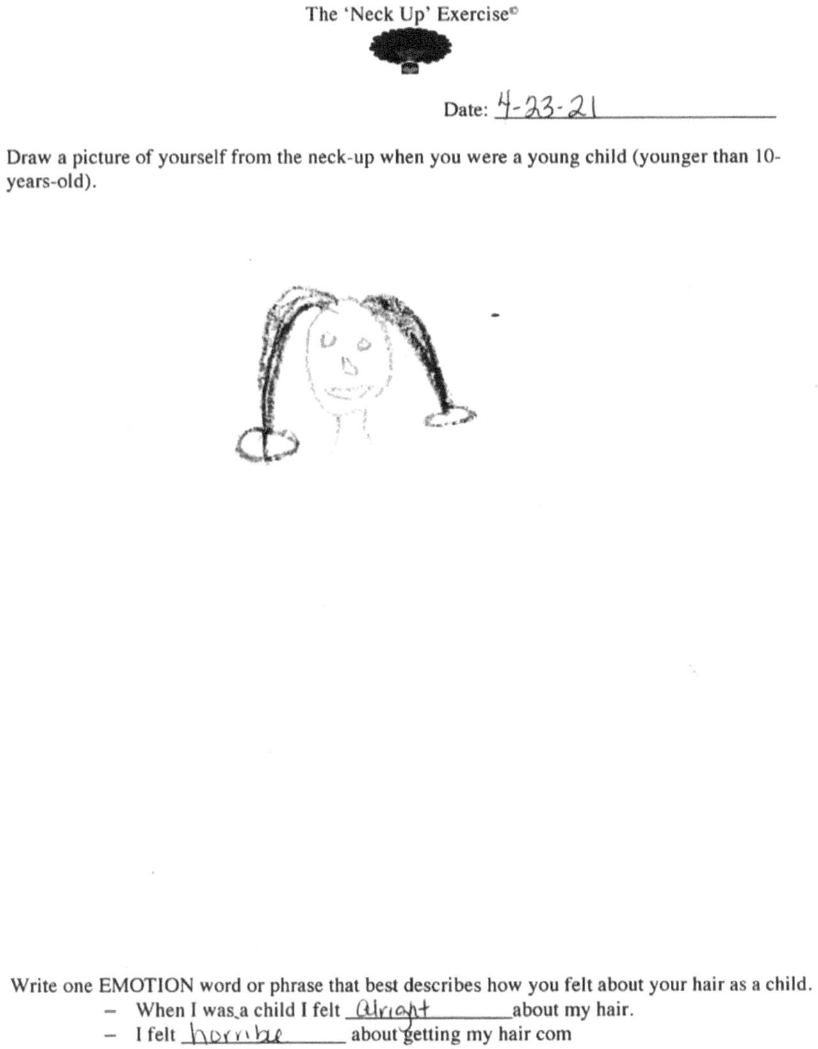
The 'Neck Up' Exercise©

Date: 4-23-21

Draw a picture of yourself from the neck-up when you were a young child (younger than 10-years-old).

Write one EMOTION word or phrase that best describes how you felt about your hair as a child.

- When I was a child I felt alright about my hair.
- I felt horrible about getting my hair com

Fig. 16.7 Pam's Neck-up drawing: I felt "alright"

medicinenet.com/what_are_the_four_types_of_hair/article.htm). Anne spoke with transparency when reflecting on childhood experiences with her hair. Following a brief pause, Anne exhaled deeply and stated, "I would think, as a child, I didn't value, you know African-American hair, kinky coily hair." She noted that as she grew up, she began to learn, "that our hair is actually very beautiful."

Anne passionately shared that she was motivated to "embrace" and "master" her hair through seeing representation of natural hairstyles. She stated, "I was the Queen of wigs and weaves, but now I really value my own natural hair." Anne shared society played a role in not valuing her natural hair as a child. She said,

> As a child, when you go to school, you see Caucasian girls, they have long, silky, pretty hair flowing and then as African American children, we had kinky coily hair that didn't move, that you know we wore braids, pigtails, braided-up, but it wasn't…you know, it was a difference. And I think later on, I kind of learned that black hair could be beautiful too.

I think it's important to note how Anne described the qualities of Caucasian hair in present tense.

Anne described her skin tone as medium. She was not teased about skin tone or hair type as a child. Anne agreed that light skin is prettier than dark skin. She also feels Black men prefer light-skinned women with straight hair and light-skinned people have more opportunities than dark-skinned people.

Case Study #3 Jaylen – Positive Emotion – "Good," Negative Emotion – "Angry"

Jaylen's story

Jaylen is a 30-year-old African-American father from Louisiana. Changes were observed in his voice and tone throughout the interview. Specific questions and topics elicited various feelings and emotions .

After completing the Neck-up execise, Jaylen calmly shared he felt angry about his hair as a child. We continued to explore his description of anger in relation to his hair as a child. Jaylen stated, "Because I always was," he briefly paused and continued, "I guess under the impression I had bad hair." His voice changed to informative and matter of fact as he explained, "In society, it was a norm that Black people had bad hair."

Jaylen described the opposite reaction to getting his haircut. While laughing, he exclaimed, "I loved getting my hair cut because my hair wasn't nappy then." Continuing to smile, Jaylen reaffirmed his prior statement. He said, "So, yeah, uh, I used to like to get my hair cut". Jaylen laughed and agreed that there are people in his family who value light skin and straight hair in children. He shared that it was always the assumption light skin is prettier than dark skin when he was a child. Jaylen stated, "That's what society tells you, now that I'm older, I mean I love my skin complexion." His voice began to shake as he laughed and continued, "But when I was younger, I used to pray that I…I used to wish that I was light skinned, so I know what that's about."

Toward the end of his interview, Jaylen shared that at this point in his life, he doesn't care to know more about why people value one skin color and hair type over the other. He concluded, "At this point, it is what it is."

Case Study #4 Jon – Positive Emotion – "Lovely," "Good"

Jon's Story

Jon is a 26-year-old African-American male from Missouri. He does not have children. Jon's demeanor during the interview was reserved and quiet. During "The Neck-up exercise," he briefly hesitated with a sigh before quickly completing the drawing and identifying an emotion word. Jon felt lovely about his 4c hair as a child, and shared he felt good about getting his hair combed.

It is important to note that I (V. White) interviewed Jon with a female participant, who was more vocal during the survey. Jon remained quiet as the other participant asked questions concerning the survey. He murmured a brief chuckle when she asked what number on the Hair Type scale represented "nappy" or "thick" hair.

Jon described his skin tone as dark and strongly agreed that things people say about skin color or hair type have an impact on children. As a child, people made fun of his skin color or hair type. Jon expressed he has forgiven those who hurt his feelings as a child. He agreed that dark-skinned people are treated differently than light-skinned people, but Jon does not feel light skin is prettier than dark skin.

Case Study #5 Sara – Negative Emotions – "Bad", "Horrible"

Sara's Story

Sara is a 53-year-old African-American female with children. She resides in Missouri. Unlike the other participants interviewed with her, Sara was outspokenly vocal about childhood experiences with her hair and skin tone. She described her hair type as 4b and dark skin tone. When asked to identify an emotion word or phrase that best describes how she felt about her hair as a child, Sara responded, "bad" and "horrible" with no hesitation. As she approached the following section on hair type, Sara calmly presented a question. She asked, "What does this indicate, 'what is your hair type like, would it be referred to as nappy?' She shared that her hair was often referred to as coarse and thick when she was a child. Sara noted she felt her hair was "nappy" as a child, because it was hard to comb through. Her tone became low and somber. Sara's voice sounded shaky as she continued to reflect on her hair combing experiences as a child. When getting her hair combed, Sara stated, "They would have to oil it, put that grease in it, and I used to hate it when they did that."

Similar to other participants, Sara agreed that dark-skinned people are treated differently compared to light-skinned people. She shared, as a child, people made fun of her skin color or hair type. Sara described her skin tone as dark and shared she has forgiven people who hurt her feelings as a child about skin tone or hair type. Overall, she expressed satisfaction with her skin tone and hair type.

Case Study #6 Lee – Positive Emotion – "Good"

Lee's Story

Lee, a 54-year-old African-American male from Arkansas, was interviewed with Pam, a 50-year-old African-American female from Missouri. Both participants are parents; however, their childhood experience with their hair contrasted in interesting ways. During the Neck-up exercise, Lee playfully laughed at Pam's attempt to draw hair barrettes. He glanced at her drawing and remarked, "Really?" as to question the accuracy of the image. Pam laughed and gleefully added, "That's all I got." Lee's playful demeanor continued throughout the survey. He shared that he felt good about his hair as a child and liked getting his hair combed. Lee identified his hair texture as 4c and dark skin tone.

When asked to rate the statement, "the blacker the berry, the sweeter the juice," Lee chuckled and stated, "Oh, y'all getting personal" with a grin. He similarly agreed that things people say about skin color or hair type can hurt a child's feelings. Lee also was teased about skin tone and hair type as a child. He does not think light skin is prettier than dark skin, but he agreed that Black men prefer light-skinned women with straight hair. Lee feels light-skinned people have more opportunities than dark-skinned people. He is satisfied with his skin tone now but has not forgiven family or community members who hurt his feelings about skin color or hair type as a child.

Case Study #7 Pam – Positive Emotion – "Alright," Negative Emotion – "Horrible"

Pam's Story

Pam is the 50-year-old African-American female mentioned in a previous interview. She put great emphasis on the Neck-up exercise. While drawing, she laughed and stated, "I am not a good drawer. It is not gonna be pretty." Then she pointed at the hair on her drawing and exclaimed, "These are supposed to be ponytails."

Pam stated she felt "alright" about her hair as a child, but she felt "horrible" about getting her hair combed. She identified a mixture of 2b and 3b as her natural hair texture and categorized her skin tone as medium. Pam shared she didn't like getting her hair straightened as a child. She passionately described getting her hair straightened as a "brutal" experience. She agreed that some things people say about skin color can hurt a child's feelings. She also was teased about her skin color or hair type as a child. Pam believes Black men prefer light-skinned women with straight hair; however, she does not personally think light skin is prettier than dark skin. Pam is satisfied with her skin tone and has forgiven family or community members who hurt her feelings as a child.

Summary of the Neck-up Stories

The drawings and interviews exposed a range of experiences of trauma and positive memories (Hass-Cohen et al., 2018). These memories included their personal internalized racial stereotypes as they reflected on their childhood experiences of acceptance or rejection based on their skin tone and hair type. While listening to the rich and colorful stories of each respondent, I (V. White) often felt an intangible cutural string that connected our childhood experiences of colorism and hair texture. I observed participants gain insight throughout the interview as their experiences were finally recognized. Listening to each case acknowledged and confirmed the long term impact and importance of recognizing Childhood Experiences of Racial Acceptance and Rejection CERAR (Lewis & Comer, 2015).

All participants expressed some degree of emotions about their childhood experiences with their hair type and/or skin color. We discussed responses using the following themes: 1) impact on children, 2) skin color satisfaction, and 3) hierarchy of light or dark skin color and hair type.

A Caution for Reflective Conversations

It is difficult to engage clients in working on psychic material that has long been repressed (See chapters on Reflective supervision). There is a risk factor that the client will not return to therapy if they experience the topic as too difficult for them to cope with at that time in their therapeutic journey. When introducing the concept of race there may be a similar response from the client who may not yet be at the point of trusting that a different race therapist is genuine in bringing up the topic. Similarly, if the topic of race in relation to their presenting clinical problem and their interactions with their child during the hair combing task is brought up too soon with a same race therapist, the response may be, "Why do they only want to talk about race?" Reflective supervision should be entered into with great care and respect for the thoughts and feelings of each other.

Accessing Memories of Mama: 'Yo Mama! – Playin' the Dozens'. The formation of an attachment partnership is created by a cacophony of emotional memories that build up during HCI (Green, 1990). These memories are ultimately about memories of the caregiver's primary attachment figure whether that person be the mother, grandma, dad, or foster mother. Talking about a person's mother and their childhood relationship may be fraught with potential (landmines) that can derail a client/therapist relationship. The added layer of race increases the potential lethality of introducing the topic of memories of mother and race.

In African-American communities, a long-standing practice among young adolescent males is what is known as "verbal dueling" (Wald, 2014). This practice, also called "playing the dozens," is designed to allow a man, the descendant of oppressed and marginalized men, to prove to an observing audience of male peers, just how tough he is. The central focus of the "Dozens" are derogatory remarks about the other man's mothers. The criteria for the depth of the remark are its humor and comedic value. For example, "Man, yo' mama so fat, when you called the ambulance to take her to the hospital, they had to send a semi-truck!" The amount of laughter from the admiring peers signals approval of the "cut." The recipient of the joke must quickly and loudly respond with an even more intense and comedic attack on the mother of the attacker. This back-and-forth repartee is one of the few culturally appropriate ways for members of the Black community to criticize anyone's mother.

As a guide for therapists to use to broach the subject of race we present the key areas of assessment to be considered as you broach the topic of race with a client. This guide can also be used within a context of reflective supervision to support the therapist building their skill level in broaching the topic of race and ethnicity with clients showing varying degrees of awareness and resolution of their internal working model of their attachment figure, the client's and therapists' stage of racial identity, and concept of broaching race to set goals for strengthening their relationship with their child using hair combing interaction. Most importantly, by listening and addressing the racial context of parent–child relationships and the risks and vulnerabilities such as acceptance and rejection based on skin color and hair type, the therapists aid the client in interrupting longstanding intergenerational patterns that had its origin in the trauma of slavery (Branch, & Newcombe, 1986; Wilkerson, 2020). Similarly, when engaging in reflective supervision, the supervisor is wise to listen and support the therapists' experiences, stories and self-awareness about racial identity, acceptance, and rejection within a protected space.

Generations of families of color, living with the toxic stigma and stereotypes, invisibility, and oppression, may have family structural systems reflecting this racial wounding. Surviving and nurturing darker-skinned children in communities where fears of violence and little access to support services are a constant reality of daily life (Fromm, 2012; Wilkerson, 2020). Further, the unrecognized media-based psychological triggers, such as the repeated showing in social media and television images of darker skinned people, and acts of race-based, authority-perpetrated violence directed at darker-skinned people, may continue to traumatize families of color (Ashing et al., 2017). The unconscious reminder of the lethality and danger of dark skin color may revive old internalized stereotypes that "black is bad" and accompanying emotions of anxiety, shame, or rage (Cheek, 1984). The current social climate of highly publicized, race-based police shootings of Black people serve as continuous triggers for protective survival behaviors that may be expressed through harshly authoritarian parenting styles with children.

Trauma-informed interventions typically focus on individual and family level resources to address children's experiences of trauma and violence (Fromm, 2012). We suggest these resources include knowledge of race-based historical trauma responses and implications for infant and young child development (Wright, 1998). Unrecognized, these legacies impact the quality of working relationships as well as parent–child relationships. The culturally sensitive and racial-informed early childhood practitioner has the opportunity to provide guidance for families to recognize the emotional impact on young children of message colorism, or even simply joking about a child's skin color or hair type. Parents and families of multi-racial or bi-racial children will gain understanding of the significance of messages about racial features on children with this protocol (Miller & Miller, 1990). With these simple narrative tools of the Neck-up drawing© protocol, the CERAR interview, and the listening ear of the practitioner, parents have the experience of being validated. Their racial stories are heard by a "powerful other," their therapist, or helper. Using the Neck-up tool as an interactive activity in parent groups, parents experience becoming visible and validated through social support from parent peers hearing their story. The parent may then use these tools with their child in the form of storytelling with their child during hair combing time interrupting the intergenerational transmission of historical trauma responses. Most importantly, they reinforce positive memories for their child's routine time of having their hair combed.

Reflective Questions

1. The Hair Combing Interaction assessment protocol, Neck-Up Drawing, and the CERAR Interview are tools that invite inquiry and reflection about racial identity, ethnicity, and culture. How can you sensitively use these tools in your practice or teaching of undergraduates or graduate students working with families of color?
2. Who combed your hair as a young child? What thoughts or memories are awakened in you as you think about hair combing experiences, pleasurable or painful, and what does it help you to think more deeply?
3. How comfortable would you, as White person or a Person of Color, be in broaching the topic of culture, race, or ethnicity with a client family?
4. Take time to reflect on why it is so important in 2021 to bridge the gap in our understanding of each other, as White or a Person of Color, by talking courageously and sensitively about race, culture, ethnicity, and inclusion?

Tools for Reflective Parental Functioning

Yale Child Study Center provides tools for enhancing parental reflective functioning.

Minding the Baby: http://mtb.yale.edu/training/index.aspx

Clinical Model: https://medicine.yale.edu/childstudy/communitypartnerships/mtb/model/

References

Ashing, K. T., Lewis, M. L., & Walker, V. P. (2017). Thoughts and response to authority-perpetrated discriminatory, and race-based violence. *Journal of the American Medical Association, Pediatrics, 171*(6), 511–519. https://doi.org/10.1001/jamapediatrics2017.0137

Bowlby, J. (1969). *Attachment and loss: (Vol. 1). Attachment.* New York: Basic Books.

Branch, C. & Newcombe, N. (1986). Racial attitude development among young black children as a function of parental attitudes: A longitudinal and cross- sectional study. *Child Development, 57, 712–721.*

Byrd, A. D., & Tharps, L. L. (2001). *Untangling the roots of Black hair in America.* St. Martin's Press.

Cheek, D. K. (1984). *Assertive black . . . puzzled white. A Black perspective on assertive behavior.* Impact Publishers.

Cox, M. V. (1993). *Children's drawings of the human figure.* Lawrence Erlbaum Associates.

Crawford, D.E. & Lewis, M. L. (2017). *Talk, touch and listen: Hair combing interaction and caregiver-child relationships.* Training Manual for clinicians. Unpublished Manual, Tulane University.

Day-Vines, N. L., Wood, S. M., Grothaus, T., Craigen, L., Holman, A., Dotson-Blake, K., & Douglass, M. J. (2007). Broaching the subjects or race, ethnicity, and culture during the counseling process. *Journal of Counseling & Development, 85,* 401–409.

Erasmus, Z. (2000). Undoing the locks: the politics of black hairstyles in South Africa. In S. Nuttail & C. Michael (Eds.), *Senses of culture.* Oxford University Press.

Fromm, M. G. (Ed.). (2012). *Lost in transmission: Studies of trauma across generations.*London/ New York: Routledge.

Green, B. A. (1990). What has gone before: The legacy of racism and sexism in the lives of Black mothers and daughters. In S. Brown & M. P. Root (Eds.), *Diversity and complexity in feminist therapy* (pp. 207–230). Harrington Park Press.

Hass-Cohen, N., Bokoch, R., Findlay, J., & Witting, A. (2018). A four-drawing art therapy trauma and resiliency protocol study. *The Arts in Psychotherapy, 61,* 44–56. https://doi.org/10.1016/j.aip.2018.02.003

Helms, J. E. (Ed.). (1990). *Contributions in Afro-American and African studies, No. 129. Black and White racial identity: Theory, research, and practice.* Greenwood Press.

Hordge-Freeman, E. (2015). *The color of love: Racial features, stigma, and socialization in black Brazilian families.* University of Texas Press.

Lewis, M. L., & Ippen, C. G. (2004). Rainbows of tears, souls full of hope: Cultural issues related to young children and trauma. In J. D. Osofsky (Ed.), *Young children and trauma: What do we know and what do we need to know?* (pp. 11–46). Guilford Press.

Lewis, M. L. & Comer, E. W. (2015). The Process of Change in Attitudes About Colorism. Unpublished manuscript, New Orleans. Louisiana, USA.

Lewis, M. L., & Joseph, M. (2017). *Why don't you listen to me, dammit! Communicating across the provider-client divide.* Presented at the Beyond ACES: Building Community Resilience. Petersburg, Virginia, June 1 & 2.

Lewis, M. L., Noroña, C. R., McConnico, N., & Thomas, K. (2013). Colorism, a legacy of historical trauma in parent-child relationships: Clinical, research, & personal perspectives. *Zero to Three Journal, 34*(2), 11–23.

Miller, R. L. & Miller, B. (1990). Mothering the biracial child: Bridging the gaps between African-American and White parenting styles. *Women and Therapy, 10(1), 169–179.*

Meyers, S. A. (1999). Mothering in context: Ecological determinants of parent behavior. *Merrill-Palmer Quarterly, 45, 332–357.*

Neal-Barnett, A. López, I. & Owens, D. (1996, August). Neither Black Nor White. The Impact of Skin Color in the Puerto Rican Community. In A. Neal Barnett (Chair), Women of Color on Color: Healing wounds, and building legacies. Round table discussion conducted at 104th annual meeting of the American Psychological Association, Toronto, Canada.

Ortega-Williams, A., Crutchfield, J. J., Camille Hall, J. C. (2019). The colorist-historical trauma framework: Implications for culturally responsive practice with African Americans. *Journal of Social Work,* 0(0) 1–16. https://doi.org/10.1177/1468017319890083

Parmer, T., Arnold, M. S., Natt, T., & Janson, C. (2004). Physical attractiveness a process of internalized oppression and multigenerational transmission in African American families. *The Family Journal, 12*(3), 230–242. https://doi.org/10.1177/1066480704264931

Prince, A. (2009). The Politics of Black Women's Hair, London, ON: Insomniac Press.
Vespa, J., Medina, L., & Armstrong, D. A. (2020). *Demographic Turning Points for the United States: Population Projections for 2020 to 2060, Current Population Reports*, p25–1144, U.S. Census Bureau, Washington, DC.
Wald, E. (2014). *Talking 'bout your mama: The Dozens, snaps, and the deep roots of rap*. Oxford University Press.
Westen, D. (1991). Clinical Assessment of Object Relations Using the TAT. *Journal of Personality Assessment, 56(1), 56–74.*
Wilkerson, I. (2020). *Caste: The origins of our discontent*, New York: Random House
Wright, M. A. (1998). *I'm chocolate, you're vanilla: Raising healthy Black and biracial children in a race-conscious world.* San Francisco, CA: Jossey-Bass Publishers.

Chapter 17
Guidelines to Identify Child-Endangering Hair Styling Practices: Medical, Legal, and Psychosocial Perspectives

Marva L. Lewis, Mumbi Dunjwa, and Constance Cohen

Guidelines for Hair Care

Infant and early childhood educators, medical personnel, child welfare workers, and therapists are mandated reporters of child maltreatment. However, few guidelines are available to assess the safety of hair styling practices with infants and young children (Brissett-Chapman, 1997; Costa, 2003; Rudolph et al., 1973). The multi-billion-dollar hair care industry directly and aggressively markets chemical hair products as "kiddie perms" with no age-appropriate guidelines provided. Using a flat iron or chemical dye comes with warnings of their danger to adults. There are no clear and consistent professional cosmetology guidelines that exist regarding best practices for the use of heat and tightly braided, pulled-back styles. Historian Henry Louis Gates (1994) has spoken of the positive emotional memories associated with what can be a painful process of styling African texture hair. In this chapter, we focus specifically on the unique issues related to hair styling practices with African-American children and multiracial children - a growing population of children in the United States, with African textured, tightly curled and coily hair, and the associated psychological, legal, and medical risks. Parents of multi-racial or bi-racial children often ask for guidance in the care of culy/coily hair textures.

Conflict of Interest: Mumbi Dunjwa has business and financial interests in Naturaz Inc.

M. L. Lewis (✉)
School of Social Work, Tulane University, New Orleans, LA, USA
e-mail: mlewis@tulane.edu

M. Dunjwa
Natural Hair Care, Oaks, PA, USA

C. Cohen
Des Moines, IA, USA

M. L. Lewis, D. J. Weatherston (eds.), *Therapeutic Cultural Routines to Build Family Relationships*, https://doi.org/10.1007/978-3-030-83726-6_17

Community hair stylists are revered service providers and recognized as a more important caregiver than health providers (Browne, 2006; Cowen et al., 1979). As discussed in the earlier chapter by A. Mbilishaka (Chap. 13), there is a complex, sociocultural, and historical context of African-American hair. There is limited research on normative hair styling practices with African-American mothers (Rooks, 1996). The complicated history includes legacies of toxic, emotionally charged, negative stereotypes associated with natural African hair. Terms like "nappy," "kinky," "coarse," "unruly," and, simply, "bad" hair carry with them a variety of emotions including anger, frustration, and shame. Thus, some African-American mothers report feeling that the orderliness of their child's hair reflects their worth as a mother and a signal to the African-American community of the quality of care they provide their child (Lewis, 2015; Patton, 2006).

We briefly examine existing literature about best practices with different styling techniques. We then conclude with guidelines for members of the child welfare system including social workers, judges, and lawyers to use for legal decisions involving the safety of various hair styling practices with young children. We offer criteria and propose standards for use by child welfare team members related to child-endangering hair care routines.

Keisha[1] gets a 'perm'

In recent years, the issue of hair styling practices for young children in foster care has been brought to the attention of the juvenile court. The case of Keisha, a 3-year-old African-American child, was placed in a foster home for neglect. Her case illustrates the colliding cultural beliefs and practices of what constitutes healthy hair care by the mother, social worker, and foster care mother who were all African American. The 19-year-old mother, Jennifer, was granted weekend visitation with her daughter and took her home for overnight visits. On three different occasions, Jennifer put a permanent relaxer in Keisha's hair. According to the packaging, the relaxer was a chemical-based, caustic product "made specifically for children," but there were no product guidelines regarding the youngest appropriate age for use. On each occasion the foster mother, also African American, contacted the foster care social worker expressing concern that the child was too young to have a chemical relaxer. She felt the biological mother was excessive in repeated use of the chemical-based product. The social worker (also African American) called for a special hearing with the judge overseeing the case to render a decision about this issue. With no guidelines on the legality of the situation, the worker was only able to present the foster mother's concerns and the biological mother's belief that it was her right to style her child's hair as she saw fit. The judge treated the concern as an issue of safety and subsequently ordered the biological mother to cease putting chemicals relaxers in the 3-year-old child's hair.

[1]All names and other personal identifiers in the cases in the chapter have been changed to protect privacy and confidentiality.

The Unique Styling Needs of Natural, Curly/Coily Textured Hair

The structure and daily styling needs of natural African hair is distinctive, often misunderstood, and requires specialized styling products (Draelos, 1997; Jackson, 1998). There are unique skin and hair care issues and needs among women of color (Grimes, 2000; Loussouarn et al., 2005). Healthy styling practices, especially those involving the use of chemicals, with young children's hair require sophisticated knowledge and a set of professional guidelines. This information is not often readily available to everyday parents and caregivers. Combing the wide variety of textures of children's hair can pose a challenge for some African-American parents and foster parents caring for African-American children (Jacobs-Huey, 2007; McMichael, 2007).

In one of the earliest *Talk, Touch & Listen While Combing Hair community-based* parent groups of African-American mothers, they asked if a hair stylist could speak to the group about how to care for natural textured hair. There is a growing population of biracial children with African-texture hair, as well as an entire community of cross-racial adoptive and foster parents seeking guidance on how to care for young African-American children in their care (Aldridge & Gaber, 1994; Miller & Miller, 1990). Foster care social workers often report a common concern expressed by biological parents with children in foster care is the way their child's hair is cared for while the child is in someone else's care. The perception of some parents that a foster parent of a different race does not know how to adequately care for their child's hair only fuels their feelings that the child welfare system does not "understand" the needs of their child.

There are currently few readily available guidelines regarding healthy hair styling practices or medical, legal, or psychological standards to use when evaluating child-endangering hair styling practices (Caldwell, 1991). Recent review of the limited research for adult women highlights the racial disparities and increased risk of breast cancer among African-American women exposed to estrogen and endocrine-disrupting chemicals from use of over-the-counter hair products (James-Todd et al., 2016; Stiel et al., 2016). Little information is available to child protection social workers, members of the judicial system, or medical professionals regarding the unique issues related to hair styling practices with young children who have tight curly/coily hair (McMichael, 2007; Wolfram, 2003). Each of these professionals makes critical decisions regarding the physical and emotional safety of children and their well-being, as well as the assessment of the quality of care provided by the caregiver, including attention to their hair during the early years.

A Universal Worry

Although this chapter focuses on African-American hair styling practices and the unique texture of African-origin hair, the issues described affect children from various racial and ethnic backgrounds including African, biracial, Latina, Aboriginal, Asian, and more (Hordge-Freeman, 2015; Neal-Barnett, et al., 1996; McMichael, 2003). For example, there are Dominican-American salons nationwide that service people from different racial backgrounds. These salons are well known for thoroughly straightening hair so that it is sleek and shiny, primarily using blow dryers and sometimes by adding chemicals to shampoo (Dunjwa, personal communication, October 2016). Although adult women mainly patronize these and other salons, children are also brought in for professional services by caregivers who may want to "train" or loosen curls and coil patterns to make combing and styling the child's hair easier.

To ground our discussion, we provide a brief description of the distinct structure of curly/coily hair and then review the scant research from the medical community about the risks associated with each of the three major hair styling practices: natural styles, the use of chemical straighteners, and the use of metal hot combs and electric curling irons. We will also present research about the developmental physiology, permeability, and vulnerability of the skin to hormones and chemicals prematurely introduced to the porous, immature scalp of infants and young children. Finally, we make recommendations for guidelines and policies for the medical, social work, and judicial professions regarding child-endangering hairstyling practices. The broad questions discussed in this chapter include the following:

- At what age is it appropriate to put a chemical permanent hair relaxer on a young child's hair?
- When is continued use of certain hairstyles and products considered to be neglectful?
- What are the cultural and community standards for what constitutes abusive hair styling practices?
- What are the hair combing/styling practices by caregivers of young African-American children that require intervention from child protective services?

The Medical Risks Related to Common Hair Styling Practices

In a recent study of the 96 children admitted to two major children's hospitals for caustic ingestions, 34% of the admissions were attributed to chemical hair relaxers (Aronow et al., 2003). Of the patients admitted, the average age was 14 months, 51% were male, and all were African American (Aronow et al., 2003). While the discovery of intentional or unintentional second-degree burns on the neck, face, or back of a toddler in a hospital emergency room will likely be reported to a child protection agency and possibly the police (Kerner et al., 1988), parents, caregivers, and licensed beauticians (cosmetologists) regularly place Africa-American infants and young children at risk for these types of physical burns through their hair styling practices including the use of heated metal combs ('hot-combs').

As previously noted, there is little information regarding the unique needs of coily/kinky hair in terms of normative hair combing and styling practices and the histories tied to them. For example, braiding hair with intricately patterned cornrows and dreadlocks has been widely prevalent among African communities for centuries (Mastalia & Pagano, 1999).

Today, African-American mothers use these same braiding styles alongside heat or chemically straightened styles with their young daughters. From birth, African-American infants' hair (including infant boys) may be styled with gels, pomades, ribbons, and bows. Parents, teens, and licensed and unlicensed beauticians perform these hair techniques in their homes, back porches, and beauty shops. Combing or braiding hair – which may take anywhere from a few minutes to several hours – is viewed by many caregivers and members of the African-American community as a requirement for a well-groomed child and a reflection of responsible parenting (Lewis, 2015; Patton, 2006).

While these hairstyles have specific historical and cultural contexts, clearer definitions are needed for what crosses the line into child endangering styling practices. In the case of braids and other hairstyles such as pigtails and buns, these can pull the hair from the scalp and, when done too tightly, can cause lasting damage (McMichael, 2003, 2007). Other potentially damaging hair styling practices include the use of heated metal combs, blow dryers, and caustic chemicals such as sodium hydroxide and guanidine hydroxide (Giles, 1972; Joyner, 1988). These styles present a risk for physical harm or accidental injury to young children. The US Food and Drug Administration (FDA) lists chemical hair straighteners and hair dyes among the top consumer complaint areas. Guidelines for use with young children and the population as a whole need to be put in place to raise awareness and to proactively alleviate practices that can unintentionally put children in harm's way.

As addressed in earlier chapters of this book, many curly, coily-haired girls have not had positive hair styling experiences, for various reasons of racial acceptance and rejection based on texturism (Butler, 1990; Byrd and Tharps, 2001). They may develop a negative self-image because of damaging hair styling practices and related commentary that is innocently directed at them during hair styling sessions. Whether at home or in a salon, without the right knowledge and techniques, styling a child's tangled, coarse, dry, curly, or coily hair can be onerous. In salons around the country, you may find young girls crying while their hair gets combed and blow-dried. Without the right information, products, techniques, and tools, the hair styling process can be painful for both the hair comber and the one having their hair styled. Salon professionals may encounter a frustrated mother requesting that a chemical relaxer be applied to her 2-year-old daughter, because her hair is difficult to manage. This experience can be terrifying for the young child on many levels, and caustic chemicals may cause damage to the child's delicate hair and developing scalp (Seidel, 1994).

The Structure of Hair

Hair is composed of keratin, a protein that is also found in nails, and is made up of three components: the inner medulla, the cortex, and the outer (Loussouarn et al., 2005). A cross-section of the **medulla**, which is the innermost layer, is typically found in thick or coarse hair strands. It may not be present in thin, fine hair types. The **cortex** makes up 80–90% of the hair shaft and is the innermost layer if the medulla is absent. This is the layer that gives hair its pigmentation, strength, and elasticity, and it is made up of protein chains. The **cuticle** is the protective outermost layer that is made up of fatty acids and proteins. Under a high-powered microscope, it appears to be made up of five or more overlapping layers of cells arranged like roof shingles. The cuticle layers can decrease based on natural wear and tear or damage caused by hair styling practices. The follicle, which sits below the scalp, is critical because it is where the hair is "born"; if it is damaged, it can no longer play a role in populating the head with healthy hair.

The Distinct Nature of African-American Hair

The degree of curl in natural African-origin hair varies radically from straight with no curl pattern to very kinky hair with tight curls (Wolfram, 2003). As the level of curls increases, the simple twisted oval-rod shape of the hair shaft makes it vulnerable to fractures and other trauma. To combat damage, healthy styling practices require a sophisticated interaction between the geometrically complex shaft and a brush or comb. Due to the hair's curly nature, sebum (oil produced by the scalp) does not efficiently travel along the shaft, so moisturizing and applying external oils to this type of hair is crucial to prevent it from getting very dry and tangled and breaking easily (McMichael, 2007). Physician and dermatologist Draelos (1997) writes that because of this lack of sebum, individuals with kinky hair may only require shampooing once a week or less to achieve an optimal appearance. There are also specialized shampoo products designed to remove sebum from the hair shaft and replace it with a layer of oily conditioner that adds shine.

The Use of Chemical Relaxers

Sodium hydroxide (commonly known as "lye") is a chemical that can be found in household cleaning products such as Drano and, despite its common name, guanidine hydroxide (often advertised as a "no lye" relaxer) contains harsh chemicals as well (Gillum, 1996; Wise et al. 2012). When looking at the chemical composition of these products, both have pH levels ranging between 10 and 14. It is important here to note that the pH scale measures the acidity or alkalinity of a substance and runs from 0 to 14. On this scale, a measure of 7 is neutral and numbers above 7 indicate an increasing degree of alkalinity and corrosiveness, with 14 being the highest. The use of either type of chemical relaxers can result in hair breakage, scalp irritation, scalp burns and damage, and hair loss (McMichael, 2003, 2007). Because there are no specific labeling guidelines that provide legal or federal guidelines for the appropriate age range for use, parents and caregivers have reported using the products on children as young as 2 years old (Tiwary, 1997).

Alopecia and Hair Styling Practices

Alopecia is a condition where hair stops growing where it normally would, and it is characterized by areas where the hair has significantly thinned out or is balding. The most common form of alopecia is male pattern baldness, or androgenetic alopecia, although it has become common to find widespread alopecia among Black women due to hair styling practices. Alopecia in children of African descent can be caused by various factors including genetics, autoimmune disorders, improper diet, frequent heat treatments, traction (defined later), and the use of chemical products. In this article, we will mainly cover chemically induced and traction alopecia, as well as thinning and damage to skin and scalp caused by heat treatment. We believe that this type of alopecia and related problems can be avoided if caregivers and styling professionals are armed with the right information, techniques, tools, and products to help them make the best choices for their children and clientele.

Chemically Induced Alopecia and Its Effect on Children Chemically induced alopecia is a type of hair loss that is caused using hair relaxers. Many children may have their hair straightened, because it is easier to manage or because their caregiver likes the aesthetic. Chemical relaxers straighten hair by permeating the cortex, or cortical layer of the hair shaft, and breaking apart the protein bonds, effectively loosening the natural curl pattern. The broken bonds then rearrange themselves such that hair appears straighter. Once this process is performed, it is irreversible on the hair that was treated, and the hair is left extremely weak and susceptible to breaking and further damage, because the relaxer also causes the cuticle layers to lift and become more porous. This increased porosity means the hair absorbs and loses moisture very easily, something that can cause trauma to the hair, which, as outlined previously, is already prone to dryness and breakage.

During the application process, gloves are normally needed when handling relaxers to protect the skin from chemical burns. Once applied, the relaxer needs to be washed out quickly, because it starts chemically burning the scalp if left too long. When applied on young children's hair, the experience can be traumatic on a physical, psychological, and emotional level. This is because the chemical inevitably gets applied very close to or directly on the scalp to straighten as much of the hair strand as possible. Areas where the chemical touches the scalp can result in chemical burns and cause discomfort and pain. The fact that gloves are worn during this procedure should be an indication of how dangerous this practice can be, especially for very young children (Tiwary, 1997). Once the initial relaxer is applied, "touch-ups" are required every 6–8 weeks to address new hair growth, increasing the likelihood of damage to hair, scalp, and skin.

Traction Alopecia and Its Effect on Children Traction alopecia is caused by the constant tugging and pulling of hair caused by very tight braids/extensions, cornrows, twists, weaves, pigtails, and other pulled-back hairstyles (McMichael, 2007). Although these hairstyles can be low maintenance, the frequency with which they are done, and the degree of tightness applied to the hair, will determine the extent of hair loss over time.

The reality is that most women who get their hair braided often complain of tightness and pain due to tugging when braids are freshly done. Painkillers are often taken to alleviate pain associated with tight braids and this discomfort can persist for several days until the individual braids loosen as hair grows. Caregivers or salon professionals may unintentionally braid a child's hair too tight, and it is likely that children might experience similar discomfort but be unable to express their discomfort as well as an adult can. Because their scalp is so delicate, if tight braids or other pulled-back hairstyles are not remedied immediately, a child's scalp, follicles, and hair may face hair loss or thinning, sores, and more. It is therefore very important to handle a child's hair very gently when braiding it.

Guidelines to Evaluate Risk of Hair Styling Practices

While The Child Welfare League of America published one guidebook directed to caregivers for the care of hair and skin for children of African descent placed in the foster care system (Costa, 2003), these guidelines do not address the risks of various hair styling practices. Infants and young children with kinky or tightly curled African-origin hair in its natural state require considerable time and effort to manage the hair daily (Ferrell, 1999) and there are currently no evidence-based guidelines to evaluate the risk of potentially child-endangering hair styling practices with these children.

Three typical strategies used by African-American caregivers to manage young children's hair are "natural" styles where the hair is arranged in its original state with the aid of oils and moisturizers into plaits, multiple braids, cornrows, or twists; "permanent" styles where the hair is primarily straightened with chemicals and may then be styled with an electric blow dryer, hooded dryer, and curling iron; and "hot-combed" styles where wavy, curly, and coily hair is temporarily straightened with either an electric pressing comb or a metal hot comb that has been heated on a stove. Each of these strategies involves potential physical risks to children ranging from unintentional burns on the scalp and upper body to infections of the scalp and loss of hair. Based on a review of the scant medical literature cited throughout the chapter, we have summarized each of these common practices and their associated medical risks in Table 17.1.

Table 17.1 Categories of common styling (combing) practices for natural, chemical, and metal-combed styles with curly/coily hair and associated medical risks

Hairstyling practice	Medical risk(s)
NATURAL HAIR STYLES	
Tightly pulled hair (e.g., pigtails, twists with rubber bands)	1. Traction alopecia
	2. Scalp infection
	3. Pain in scalp
Cornrows, braids, or tight plaiting	1. Cornrow alopecia
	2. Scalp infection
	3. Traction alopecia
	4. Pain in scalp or tender-headed scalp
"Kinky Hair Syndrome"	Chronic uncombed, unwashed hair
Cornrow extensions	1. Traction alopecia
	2. Scald burns to the face, neck, and/or arms from hot water used to melt the ends of braids so that the braided hair stays in place
	3. Burns from cigarette lighters used to finish the ends of braids as outlined above
Vigorous combing of hair to prepare for styling (afro, pigtails, braiding, etc.)	1. Tender-headed scalp
	2. Pain in scalp
Natural bush or afros	Pediculosis (i.e., lice) – very rare
CHEMICAL 'PERMANENTS'	
Permanent hair relaxers and hair activation products	1. Chemically induced alopecia
	2. Scarring alopecia
	3. Thinning hair
	4. Burns to the face and/or scalp
	5. Hair breakage
	6. Hair loss
	7. Damage to hair follicles
	8. Pain in scalp and possible infection
	9. Chemical toxicity through scalp (specifically with infants)
Products containing hormones and placenta	Risk of breast cancer in adults and premature development of sex characteristics in prepubertal children
Keratin treatments	Exposure to formaldehyde, which is a known carcinogen
HEATED METAL COMB ('HOT-COMBED')	
Straightening by metal hot comb or electric curling iron	1. Hot comb alopecia
	2. Burns to the face, scalp, and/or neck
Blow drying with a blow dryer on high heat setting or tugging on scalp with blow-drying combs or brushes	1. Possible burns to the scalp and skin on neck, ears, face when heat setting is on high
	2. Tender-headed scalp
	3. Pain in scalp

Judicial and Legal Guidelines, Thoughts, and Suggestions

The issue of hair care for children involved in the child welfare system can be very complex (Caldwell, 1991; Lawrence-Webb, 1997). Judges, attorneys, social workers, therapists, medical professionals, and other individuals serving families are often undereducated about the physical and emotional ramifications of recommendations and decisions regarding healthy care of children's hair. The importance of these choices may be minimized, because it is not typically the type of safety or harm issues that are brought to the attention of juvenile courts. In the context of a case brought to court, it is often overlooked unless and until it rises to the level of further adjudicatory harm.

In the instances where severe blistering, burning, and other physical injuries meet the definition of abuse or neglect, and if there are no other presenting issues, the juvenile court would not become involved and child welfare intervention would generally involve community-based services. Voluntary services targeted at preventing further injuries might include parent coaching and education, supervised visitation, and medical treatment. If the caregiver provides insight into the dangers of harmful hairstyling practices and demonstrates the ability to change their methods, the voluntary case will be closed successfully.

However, if the harmful practices continue following initial intervention or if the severity of the physical harm merits legal intervention, a petition alleging that the child needs the court's protection will likely be filed. If the harm is extreme, there will generally be a request to remove the child to an out-of-home placement with kin or in foster care. In the event of visitations where a child is placed in foster care and is subjected to dangerous hair styling practices while in the care of the birth parent, restrictions may be placed on the visit.

State-Specific Considerations

Each state has its own legal criteria for the removal of a child, for the definition of child abuse, and the standards of proof to consider. For example, in Iowa, to approve an immediate ex parte (i.e., outside the presence of all affected persons) request to remove a child, the court must find substantial evidence that the child's immediate removal is necessary to avoid imminent danger to the child's life or health (IA Code § 232.95 (2017)). At the first hearing following the actual removal, after all parties have received proper notice, the court must find substantial evidence that the removal is necessary to avoid imminent risk to the child's life or health to approve the removal (IA Code § 232.95 (2017)). Removal hearings are held anywhere from 1 to 10 days, depending on individual state laws. At these hearings, each party is represented by legal counsel and evidence is presented by way of testimony and/or reports. The court must also make specific findings that continuation in the home would be contrary to the welfare of the child and that reasonable efforts have been made to eliminate the need for removal (IA Code § 232.95 (2017)).

A lower standard of proof applies at the removal and removal hearing because of the high bar of "imminent risk to the child's life or health" and because the investigation is often still in very early stages. A higher standard of proof generally applies at the jurisdictional or adjudication hearing where the court determines if the allegations of the petition are satisfied and if the court's aid is required. In Iowa, the standard is clear and convincing evidence, which is less than the criminal standard of beyond a reasonable doubt, but more than the standard typically applied to civil cases such as contract or personal injury cases (IA Code § 232.95 (2017)).

When it comes to the definition of child abuse and neglect, in Iowa, Iowa Code Section 232.2(6) defines a child in need of assistance as one whose parent, guardian, other custodian, or other member of the household has physically abused or neglected the child or is imminently likely to abuse or neglect the child; or a child whose parent, guardian, or custodian or other member of the household failed to exercise a reasonable degree of care in supervising the child resulting in the child suffering or imminently likely to suffer harmful effects due to poor supervision.

If the court adjudicates the child to need assistance but does not sustain a prior removal or remove the child, a lower standard will apply to a removal after adjudication: a preponderance of evidence that the child will be exposed to further adjudicatory harm and meet the definition of a child in need of assistance if they are not removed (re A.M.H. 516 N.W.2d at 867 (Iowa 1994)).

A Case Study

Suffice it to say, there are many moving parts to judicial proceedings. To clarify, consider the following scenario: pediatrician Dr. Reed, a mandatory reporter, has contacted the child welfare agency on three separate occasions after observing chemical burns on her 7-year-old patient's scalp. The child's school has also called the agency to report the child's burns and pain. After investigating the reports, the agency determined that the mother's sister, who babysits the child, was routinely chemically straightening the child's hair without permission from the mother.

Dr. Reed repeatedly informed the mother about the harm the chemical was doing and, while the mother seemed to understand the conversations, she did nothing to stop her sister from continuing the practice. The mother worked nights and had no other daycare alternative, and her sister was always quick to say that if she didn't like the way her child was being cared for, she could find daycare elsewhere. The sister historically straightened her own hair and that of her 12-year-old daughter and believed the mother was derelict in her duties by allowing her daughter to have "bad hair."

After unsuccessful efforts to work with the family informally and the continued straightening of the child's hair, the agency filed a petition in court alleging physical abuse and lack of supervision and sought an emergency removal. The judge granted the emergency removal and placed the child with their grandmother with directions not to allow any chemical hair treatments. At the removal hearing 5 days later, the mother informed the court that she had found another full-time daycare provider and she convinced the judge that there was no imminent risk to the child's life or health. The judge returned the child to the mother's care with restrictions placed on the aunt's unsupervised contact. At the adjudication hearing, the court dismissed allegations of physical abuse regarding the mother but sustained the petition on grounds of improper supervision. The mother retained custody and agreed to comply with the case plan.

Three months later, the teacher again noticed and reported scalp injuries. The agency requested immediate removal. The mother admitted that she became desperate for childcare for 2 weeks and had no one to help her other than her sister. The court did not grant the request for immediate removal but set the matter for a hearing. After hearing testimony, the court declined to remove the child, but modified the case plan to include daycare assistance and additional safeguards. The mother was able to demonstrate compliance and the case successfully closed 6 months later.

While this case is illustrative, the scenario itself is not uncommon. In juvenile courts, issues involving hair care are usually collateral to other issues. For example, the birth parents may be angered because the foster parent cut their child's hair without permission. In most cases, unless and until the court transfers guardianship, the parents retain guardianship even when they are not the custodians who provide day-to-day care such as food, clothing, and housing; decide what time a child goes to bed; or protects, trains, and disciplines the child (IA Code § 232.2 (2017)). Because guardians make important decisions that have a permanent effect on the life, development, and general welfare of the child, unless there is an emergency, if the court has not appointed another guardian, the birth parents should continue to make guardian-type decisions (IA Code § 232.2 (2017)). While the foster parent may believe, for example, that a haircut is in the best interest of a male child who is teased by his peers, the birth parents should have the larger voice in such decisions. Where there are legitimate reasons for contention, a judge should decide the matter.

To make the best possible decisions for children who cannot make their own decisions, it is imperative that the advocates and decision-makers understand the consequences of hair styling practices that impact a child's safety and well-being. Education by knowledgeable professionals across disciplines is the best way to improve outcomes. As outlined in previous sections, there are several medical conditions and injuries of the skin and scalp often seen in African-American children such as alopecia and tinea capitis (Brauner, 1983). Without adequate information, these medical conditions associated with hair styling practices and darker skin color may be misdiagnosed as child maltreatment (Brauner, 1983; Verschoore, 2012), potentially causing trauma and fractures to family structures and attachments.

Conclusions

The perception of natural curly/coily hair and healthy styling practices with children is at the center of our discussion. The paradox of the need for safety with use of chemicals on the scalps of children whose brains are still forming, and the care required for curly/coily hair is paramount. Many caregivers require simple education into healthy styling practices. We recognize that the continued marketing of the use of chemical products without sufficient guidelines for the infants and toddlers by the billion-dollar hair care industry adds another level of complexity to the decisions that caregivers will make regarding safety of hair styling practices. The medical, legal, and psychological decisions associated with popular hairstyles for children remain complicated.

The Need for Resources There is growing attention to the distinct nature of African-American hair styles that will add to the number of resources, research, and understanding of healthy hair styling practices for children. There is a growing movement of natural hair styles and embracing the beauty of natural, African textured hair. Currently, there are many natural alternatives presented by cosmetologists and hair styling proponents for African-origin hair. In addition, children's books, such as Spike Lee's *Happy to be Nappy*, are examples of the growing positive cultural shift to acceptance and celebration of natural curly/coily hair in children.

The Need for Research We have yet to determine if a primary caregiver or attachment figure social and ethnic characteristics are associated with their choice of hairstyles, harsh and punitive behavioral parenting styles during the hair task, or the frequency of use of specific hair styling practices. For example, are caregivers with low racial self-esteem or high internalized stereotypes more likely to introduce chemical straighteners to their child at an earlier age? Are girls with significant alopecia at age five also associated with significant disturbances in the parent–child attachment relationship? More research is needed to truly understand these connections.

Considering the intense emotions stimulated by any discussion of hair with African-American women, it is important to separate these emotions from decisions about the safety of practices with very young children (Harris et al., 2001). Further, the emotions elicited from perceptions and feelings of evaluation of being a "good enough" mother are also important to take into consideration (Fontes, 2005). Identifying community standards and cultural norms associated with healthy hair combing practices remains to be done in this current age of natural hair styles and the incorporation of artificial hair in styling practices (weaves). These community standards may then form the basis of establishing assessment techniques for child maltreatment and designing culturally valid parent training programs.

More research is needed to understand the presence of child-endangering hair styling practices as part of an array of neglectful or abusive caregiver behaviors, especially in dysfunctional environments where young children are unable to advocate for themselves. Clinical and medical research is needed to determine acceptable standards of practice of various hair styling practices with very young African-American children. Based on our review of the current medical and legal literature, knowledge of developmental needs of young children, and evidence from qualitative research with normative groups of African-American mothers and women about cultural standards of healthy hair (Lewis, 2015), we recommend the following guidelines:

- The use of tightly braided hairstyles should be limited during the first 5 years of life.
- No chemical styles should be used on young children under the age of 12.
- The use of heated metal hot-combs should only be used with children over the age of eight

With these broad guidelines, we make the following recommendations for parents, foster parents, social workers, lawyers, judges, and professionals regarding the need for safety of young children having their hair styled. By using these guidelines as a reference tool, caregivers and all relevant entities involved in caring for a child can recognize problems and mitigate them in a timely fashion to protect young children where hairstyling practices are involved.

Recommendations for Hair Styling Practices for Young Children with Curly/Coily Hair

1. Parents must be given clear information about the dangers and risks they are exposing their young children to with their choice and techniques of hair styling practices. A nationwide campaign using a public health approach to educate parents is required. Globally, parents are using chemical-based products in countries such as Nigeria, Kenya, South Africa, and Brazil with limited information available about potential risks and dangers to their children. In these countries, as in the United States, hair styling practices involving chemicals and heat have resulted in hair loss, especially in women. Many children are also subjected to similar hair- and scalp-damaging practices and, without the right information, many caregivers and professionals may not be able to make informed decisions regarding care for children's hair.
2. Legislation is needed to regulate the billion-dollar hair care industry that includes product manufacturers and retail outlets. They must be required to inform consumers of the potential dangers of their products through

clear labeling and truthful advertising. Furthermore, explicit guidelines should be made regarding the use of chemical products on children under the age of 12.

3. Pediatricians, emergency room personnel, nurse practitioners, and public health professionals should all receive uniform education and information about the potential risks associated with various hair styling practices used with young children, specifically those with curly/coily hair types. While this chapter focused mostly on children of African descent, some of these hairstyling practices extend to children of other races and these guidelines can serve as a foundation for all training and conversations, especially where hair-altering chemicals or hot implements are concerned.
4. The use of chemical relaxers by hair care professionals, including licensed cosmetologists and unlicensed practitioners, should be regulated, especially when it comes to young children.
5. Child welfare workers must be educated and informed about appropriate risk assessment considerations to use when working with families of African descent reported for child maltreatment.
6. Finally, this task of hair styling and hair combing can be used as a structured task during therapeutic visitation by social workers and other professionals working to reunite parents with children and strengthen their attachment relationships.

Questions Judges and Lawyers Should Ask

1. Parent, are there any hair care techniques or advice that you want to share with the current caretaker?
2. Does the child ever complain about pain or discomfort associated with hair care?
3. Are the processes or products you are using for hair care approved for children under the age of 12?
4. Is the child experiencing symptoms associated with any hair care products or processes (e.g., burning, itching, headaches)?
5. Are there any health risks associated with current styling products or processes?
6. Who makes decisions regarding the child's hair care?
7. Do you know of any allergies or negative reactions from specific hair care products or processes?
8. Who are the people who typically care for the child's hair?

Reflective Questions

1. Intense emotions are stimulated by any discussion of hair, hair combing, or hair styling among Black and Indigenous people of color. Reflect on your reactions to understanding that medical risks, burns, painful scarring, and discomfort are associated with many hair styling practices and unregulated processing products, and are especially toxic for infants and young children.
2. Was your hair ever temporarily straightened using chemicals and blow drying, was your scalp burned, or did you lose hair following a hair styling process as a young child or adolescent? As you reflect on this now, what memories about your hair and hair combing experiences have you carried with you into adulthood and how are they woven into your Hair Combing story now?
3. How can you bring information about hair care endangering processes and chemical risks to Black and Indigenous families of color in your practice whose Black and Brown children have hair that is kinky, curly, or tightly coiled and difficult to manage?
4. How can you educate judges, lawyers, and child protection workers in your community about the need for hair styling care guidelines to protect Black and Indigenous young children of color from health, medical, and psychological damage due to toxic and painful hair styling processes?

A Personal Note to Parents

We applaud parents and caregivers and the effort they put into caring for and raising their children. We, the authors, are mothers and spend a lot of time styling our children's hair. We recognize that some hair styling choices are made very innocently and with the best intentions in mind, but also know that these choices may endanger young children with consequences that range from the ingestion of corrosive chemicals to damaging a child's hair, skin, and scalp. While wearing our professional hats as a psychologist, chemist, and judge, we found no clear guidelines to help us with the hair styling choices we make as parents. This chapter is intended to provide caregivers of young children, and the professionals who assist them, with basic guidelines that can be used to evaluate the risks associated with common hair styling practices. We hope that this chapter will help parents and caregivers make healthy choices about hair styling practices that can affect the health of their children's hair and scalp. Above all, we hope that by illuminating the current lack of standards for the use of hair straightening chemicals, such as sodium hydroxide, we will highlight the inherent risks involved in their use. We hope these guidelines will help ensure the safety of infants, toddlers, and young children who are unable to advocate for themselves.

Glossary

1. Alopecia: A condition in which hair is lost from some or all areas of the body, usually from the scalp, causing noticeable bald spots. This condition can be temporary or permanent.
2. Braids: Lengths of hair made up of three or more interlaced strands. Braids can either be formed with natural hair or with hair extensions made from human or synthetic hair.
3. Chemically induced alopecia: Hair loss induced using harsh chemicals on the hair and scalp. Chemicals that may induce alopecia if not used correctly include sodium hydroxide, sodium thioglycolate, and guanidine hydroxide.
4. Coily hair: Natural hair texture that describes the size and tightness of a curl, which can range in size from a spring coil to the diameter of a pencil.
5. Combing: A grooming and styling technique where a comb is used to detangle or rearrange hair by passing it through the hair from the roots to the ends.
6. Cornrows: Style of hair grooming where the hair is braided very close to the scalp to produce a continuous, raised row. Cornrows can be formed in simple, straight lines or complicated geometric, curvilinear designs. Cornrow extensions made with synthetic or human hair can be applied for additional volume and length.
7. Hyperpigmentation: A condition where patches of skin become darker in color than the surrounding skin. This is caused when an excess of melanin, the brown pigment that produces the primary skin color, forms deposits in the skin.
8. Pediculosis: Infestation of lice.
9. Relaxed/processed hair: Hair that has undergone a chemical process to transform it from being curly or coily to straight or "relaxed." Curly kits and texturizers use chemicals such as sodium hydroxide, sodium thioglycolate, and guanidine hydroxide to loosen or make curls/coils larger.
10. Sodium hydroxide (NaOH)/Lye: A very strong alkaline, caustic, and corrosive chemical used to permanently straighten or "relax" curly/coily hair. Due to the damage it can cause to hair and skin such as alopecia and burns, it is recommended that a trained professional apply this hair treatment. In addition to hair products, this chemical is used by many industries as a base in drinking water, soaps, toothpaste, and household cleaners.
11. Tangles: Knots created by the shedding of hair, the natural growth pattern of curly hair, or by techniques that intertwine hair in a haphazard way (e.g., circular/zigzag motion of hands on the surface of hair when cleansing).
12. Tender-headed scalp: Scalp becomes hypersensitive and painful to touch often due to severe pulling on the hair.
13. Tinea capitis: Ringworm of the scalp.
14. Traction alopecia: Hair loss induced by frequent pulling or tugging forces on hair due to braids, weaves, or tight pulled-back hairstyles such as pigtails and buns. Traction alopecia mainly affects the hair around the temples or the entire hairline.

Resources and Information on Culture and Hair Care

These sites present information on hair care and cultural practices:

- Virginia Commonwealth University: Center for Culture and Experiences in Prevention, https://ccep.vcu.edu/about-us/
- S.H.I.E.L.D.: Research on culture, race & ethnicity and emotional well-being, https://www.shieldlabresearch.org/
- The CROWN Act: Working to eradicate race-based hair discrimination (Dove). This site has legal resources and cases of experiences of hair discrimination: https://www.thecrownact.com

References

Aldridge, J., & Gaber, I. (Eds.). (1994). *In the best interests of the child: Culture, identity, and trans-racial adoption*. Free Association Books.

Aronow, S. P., Aronow, H. D., Blanchard, T., Czinn, S., & Chelimsky, G. (2003). Hair relaxers: A benign caustic ingestion? *Journal of Pediatric Gastroenterology & Nutrition, 36*(1), 120–125.

Brauner, G. J. (1983). Cutaneous disease in black children. *American Journal of Disease and Children, 137*(5), 488–496.

Brissett-Chapman, S. (1997). Child protection risk assessment and African American children: Cultural ramifications for families and communities. *Child Welfare, 76*(1), 45–63.

Browne, R. (2006). Most black women have a regular source of hair care – But not medical care. *Journal of the National Medical Association, 98*(10), 1652–1653.

Butler, J. (1990). *Gender trouble*. Routledge.

Byrd, A., & Tharps, L. (2001). *Hair story: Untangling the roots of Black hair in America*. St. Martin's Press.

Caldwell, P. (1991). A hair piece: Perspectives on the intersections of race and gender. *Duke Law Journal, 2*(4), 365–396.

Costa, J. M. (2003). *Making cultural connections: Hair and skin care for children of African descent*. Child Welfare League of America Press.

Cowen, E. L., Gesten, E. L., Boike, M., Norton, P., & Wilson, A. B. (1979). Hairdressers as caregivers. A descriptive profile of interpersonal help-giving involvements. *American Journal of Community Psychology, 7*(6), 633–647.

Draelos, Z. D. (1997). Understanding African-American hair. *Dermatology Nursing, 9*(4), 227–231.

Ferrell, P. (1999). *Kids talk hair: An instruction book for grown-ups & kids*. Cornrows & Co.

Fontes, L. A. (2005). *Child abuse and culture: Working with diverse families*. New York,New York: Guilford Press.

Gates, H. L. (1994, April 18). In the kitchen; From a childhood view of a mother's home beauty parlor to adolescent dreams of a perfectly greased flat head, a history unfolds of the politics of the hair do. *The New Yorker*.

Giles, S. F. (1972). Hair: The nursing process and the black patient. *Nursing Forum, 11*(1), 78–88.

Gillum, R. F. (1996). Hyperpigmentation associated with selenium sulfide lotion. *Journal of the National Medical Association, 88*(9), 551.

Grimes, P. E. (2000). Skin and hair cosmetic issues in women of color. *Dermatologic aspects of cosmetics, 18*(4), 659–665.

Harris, J., & Johnson, P. (Eds.). (2001). *Tenderheaded: A comb-bending collection of hair stories*. Pocket Books.
Hordge-Freeman, E. (2015). The color of love: Racial features, stigma, and socialization in black Brazilian families. University of Texas Press.
Jackson, F. (1998). The ABC's of black hair and skin care. *ABNF Journal, 9*(5), 100–104.
Jacobs-Huey, L. (2007). *From the kitchen to the parlor: Language and becoming in African American women's hair care*. Oxford University Press.
James-Todd, T. M., Chiu, Y., & Zonta, A. R. (2016). Racial/ethnic disparities in environmental endocrine disrupting chemicals and women's reproductive health outcomes: Epidemiological examples across the life course. *Current Epidemiological Reports, 3*(2), 161–180. https://doi.org/10.1007/s40471-016-0073-9
Joyner, M. (1988). Hair care in the Black patient. *Journal of Pediatric Health Care, 2*(6), 281–287.
Kerner, E., Matheney, K., Boertman, J. A., & Sullivan, W. G. (1988). Facial and scalp burns from hair activator products. *The Journal of Burn Care & Rehabilitation, 9*(5), 524–525.
Lawrence-Webb, C. (1997). African American children in the modern child welfare system: A legacy of the Fleming rule. *Child Welfare, 76*(1), 9–30.
Lewis, M. L. (2015). Getting the parts straight: The psychology of hair combing interaction between African American mothers and daughters. In K. T. Craddock, (Ed.), *Black Motherhoods(s): Contours, contexts, and considerations*. pp 204–220, Bradford, ON: Demeter Press.
Loussouarn, G., Rawadi, C., et al. (2005). Diversity of hair growth profiles. *The International Society of Dermatology, 44*, 6–9.
Mastalia, F., & Pagano, A. (1999). *Dreads*. New York, NY: Artisan.
McMichael, A. (2003). Hair and scalp disorders in ethnic populations. *Dermatologic Clinics*, 629–644.
McMichael, A. (2007). Hair Breakage in Normal and Weathered Hair: Focus on the Black Patient. *Journal of Investigative Dermatology Symposium Proceedings, 12*, 6–9.
Miller, R. L., & Miller, B. (1990). Mothering the biracial child: Bridging the gaps between African American and White parenting styles. *Women and Therapy, 10*(1), 169–179.
Neal-Barnett, A. López, I. & Owens, D. (1996, August). Neither Black Nor White. The Impact of Skin Color in the Puerto Rican Community. In A. Neal Barnett (Chair), Women of Color on Color: Healing wounds, and building legacies. Round table discussion conducted at 104th annual meeting of the American Psychological Association, Toronto, Canada
Patton, T. O. (2006). Hey girl, am I more than my hair? African American women and their struggles with beauty, body image, and hair. *NWSA Journal, 18*(2), 24–51.
Rooks, N. M. (1996). *Hair raising: Beauty, culture, and African American women*. New Brunswick, NJ: Rutgers University Press.
Rudolph, R. I., Klein, A. W., & Dechard, J. W. (1973). Corn-row alopecia. *Archives of Dermatology, 108*(1), 1334.
Seidel, J. S. (1994). The danger of scald burns during hair braiding. *Annals of Emergency Medicine, 23*(6), 1388–1389.
Stiel, L., Adkins-Jackson, P. B., Clark, P., Mitchell, E., & Montgomery, S. (2016). A review of hair product use on breast cancer risk in African American women. *Cancer Medicine, 5*(3), 597–604. https://doi.org/10.1002/cam4.613
Tiwary, C. M. (1997). A survey of use of hormone/placenta-containing hair preparations by parents and/or children attending pediatric clinics. *Military Medicine, 162*(4), 252–256.
Verschoore, M. (2012). The physiology of the African hair and skin was not fully investigated until the last two decades when dedicated laboratories aimed to identify its specificities. *International Journal of Dermatology, 51*(1), iv–v. https://doi.org/10.1111/j.1365-4632.2012.05552.x
Wise, L. A., Palmer, J. R., Reich, D., Cozier, Y. C., & Rosenberg, L. (2012). Hair relaxer use and risk of uterine leiomyomata in African American women. *American Journal of Epidemiology, 175*(5), 432–440.
Wolfram, L. (2003). Human hair: A unique physicochemical composite. *Journal of the American Academy of Dermatology, 48*(6), 106–114.

Chapter 18
Conclusions

Marva L. Lewis and Deborah J. Weatherston

In this book, we have presented several tools based on hair combing interaction (HCI) and colorism for social workers and infant and early childhood educators to use to support Black and Indigenous children and families of color. From an attachment, relationship-based framework these conceptually connected tools may be used with parents or primary caregivers of children, and early childhood educators and teachers. Each of the developmental, culturally based, trauma-informed tools is illustrated throughout the book and designed to understand the influence of caregiver and child factors that may shape behaviors during HCI.

We began with the Ethnobiography *of the caregiver,* designed to provide a structure to systematically assess the individual and sociocultural factors that shape the social context of the neighborhood and the historical context of the caregiver. Two standardized tools to assess skin tone and hair texture are included for use by researchers or clinicians. The projective tool of the Neck-up Drawing provides a method to understand the caregiver's self-perception of their immutable racialized features. These drawings and the selection of emotions to describe their feelings about their perception of their racialized self provide areas for clinical exploration and opportunities for parental insight. In the Appendix, we provide several tools referenced throughout the book, the *Childhood Experiences of Racial Acceptance and Rejection* (CERAR), a semistructured interview, the Tender Headed Rating Scale to assess the degree of physical pain experienced by children during the hair combing time, and the survey, *The Recognition of the Impact of Colorism*© (RICS). This brief survey can be used by both therapists and researchers to assess a parent's understanding of how children emotionally experience negative messages of colorism.

M. L. Lewis (✉)
School of Social Work, Tulane University, New Orleans, LA, USA
e-mail: mlewis@tulane.edu

D. J. Weatherston
Alliance for the Advancement of Infant Mental Health, Southgate, MI, USA

M. L. Lewis, D. J. Weatherston (eds.), *Therapeutic Cultural Routines to Build Family Relationships*, https://doi.org/10.1007/978-3-030-83726-6_18

A Growing Recognition of the Beauty of Natural Hair

In the past decade, there has been an explosion of social media including books and movies, such as comedian Chris Rock's movie on *Good Hair*, and, more recently, Oprah Winfrey's showing of the movie, *Dark Girls*. This movie by actor Bill Dukes and released in 2013 documents the experiences of dark-skinned African-American women's emotional pain of racial rejection by members of their families and community. He has since released a movie on Light Girls to tell their stories of acceptance and rejection based on skin tone. Social workers and infant and early childhood practitioners may use this video to structure their conversations about race with parents.

A recent nationwide movement of a coalition of community organizations has worked for the passage of legislation titled the CROWN Act, which stands for Creating a Respectful and Open World for Natural Hair (2019). This law prohibits discrimination in the workplace based on an employee's hair texture and hairstyle.

We hope that the antidote to these unconscious memories of the race-based trauma of colorism can be the use of healthy cultural practices such as the routines and rituals of combing natural hair. Connection to culture – the traditions, values, and practices that reflect an ancient African philosophy of resilience, and collectivist community practices – benefits parent–child relationships (Miller & Goodnow, 1995). Through interventions based on the hair combing interactions, social workers, therapists, and other infant and early childhood practitioners can support and strengthen parent–infant socioemotional relationships. Joining with parents for observation and listening, lively talking, and storytelling, during this routine interaction, supports positive perceptions of a child's skin color and hair type, reinforcing parents' unconditional acceptance of their child. Through daily routines of loving and gentle physical touch during hair combing time, parents and other caregivers communicate acceptance of their child through the sensory experience of touch. Finally, paying close attention, then listening and responding carefully to the child's cues during the routine of combing hair, strengthens the attachment relationship. More simply stated, touch, talk, and listen. The positive interactions with young children during hair combing time begin to disrupt toxic legacies and stereotypes and reconnect families of color to a rich cultural heritage (Mbilishaka, Chap. 13).

Implications for Research

The scientific study of hair combing interactions between caregivers and young children as a developmental context for research is in an embryonic stage of development. The central research questions for basic and applied research centers on the question: Does hair combing interaction shape the quality of parent–child attachment? Other potential research questions that may be explored by interdisciplinary behavioral scientists – developmental psychologists, social workers, educators, and the medical field – cover critical developmental processes of early childhood. These questions include: How does this repetitive, predictable hair combing routine contribute to a child's emotion regulation, neurological, linguistic, and cognitive development? Does this repetitive behavior reduce stress in the parent or caregiver? What are the long-term implications of the positive practice of HCI for the child as a future caregiver for the quality of the relationships with their children?

There remains a need for continued evaluation research on the incorporation of the topics of colorism and childhood experiences of racial acceptance and rejection based on skin color and hair type into parent education curricula. Evidence-based, culturally grounded resources to support parents of color.

Implications for Practice

Hair combing time offers opportunities for parents or primary caregivers to connect emotionally with their infants and young children – talking, touching, and listening – and, most optimally, can lead to secure and stable relationships over time. These behaviors are fundamental to healthy growth and development in the early years (Ainsworth et al., 1978). The social work or behavioral health practitioner or early childhood educator who witnesses hair combing interactions between parents and young children are in a position to observe, assess, and comment on positive exchanges that affirm parental capacities to nurture and protect.

Furthermore, hair combing provides a portal for helping professionals to learn from parents about their own earlier hair combing experiences, understanding past interactions and relationships that were pleasurable, as well as those that were harsh and rejecting. Taken together, stories create a parent's *ethnobiography* and can include cultural, ethnic, and racial experiences that helped to form parental beliefs and attitudes about racial features, especially hair and skin tone, now communicated in interactions with their children. Inviting persons of color to reflect on their intergenerational experiences of racial trauma and discrimination in a therapeutic or caring environment, and to share their stories, can lead to the reduction of risk and enhancement of caregiving strengths, offering an effective strategy for healing. What a parent shares is invaluable in helping both the parent and professional appreciate parental strengths and vulnerabilities, leading to change in the developing parent–child relationship. Furthermore, stories invite the professional's empathic response to what is told, inviting personal and professional reflections within the context of a supervisory relationship, about hair combing and relationship experiences, leading to greater self-awareness and cultural understanding, using the lens of ethnicity, culture, race, and inclusion as a centerpiece.

Our hope is that these intentional tools and techniques invite Black and Indigenous persons of color to reflect on their intergenerational experiences of racial trauma and discrimination in an environment that leads to healing, growth, and change. We also hope that these tools, related to hair combing interaction and the exploration of colorism, will be adopted by professionals and complement traditional professional practice strategies such as observing, assessing, gentle questioning, listening, and responding with empathy for caregivers.

We have incorporated relationship-based, racially informed reflective practice throughout each chapter in this book. Engaging in Reflective Supervision nurtures professional growth and personal self-awareness, using the lens of ethnicity, culture, race, and inclusion as a centerpiece. In the reflective supervision process, applying the central principle of the Diversity Tenets "awareness of self" opens the door for understanding the experiences of others (Thomas et al., 2019; Van Horn, 2019). We hope you will become more aware of experiences that have shaped your own beliefs about diversity, ethnicity, culture, and race, reflect on them, and share them with others in a protected space. Such awareness contributes to effective service and quality social work practices. In the process of joining with parents to explore their childhood experiences of racial acceptance or rejection, social workers and helpers can also reflect on thoughts and feelings that come to mind about their childhood experiences of being treated differently based on a personal, immutable physical characteristic, such as facial freckles or red hair.

Finally, to understand the depth of this complex interaction of combing hair, we presented a colorist-historical trauma framework as a conceptual foundation for reflective supervision and applied practice. This Framework provides the basis for the psychosocial tools introduced in the book. Each chapter provides reflective questions tied to the social, cultural, and emotional content described regarding colorism and hair type. These questions invite the reader to think reflectively about the information shared and, at the same time, to consider personal thoughts and feelings about culture, ethnicity, and race that may have been evoked by the experiences and materials described.

In summary, *Talk, Touch, & Listen!* creates a new awareness among parents, White professionals, and Professionals of Color about the importance of hair combing routines and rituals to promote healthy growth and change. With a new recognition of the power of hair combing experiences and colorism, past and present, to affect young children, parents can then become empowered through community based interventions to disrupt the intergenerational cycle of rejection, racial trauma, and psychological harm. We hope this reflective practice framework will help parents and professionals use the hair combing time to assess or provide mutually rewarding, therapeutic support for caregivers and their young children.

References

Ainsworth, M. D., Blehar, M. C., Waters, E., & Wall, S. (1978). *Patterns of attachment: A psychological study of the strange situation*. Lawrence Erlbaum.

C.R.O.W.N. Research Study. (2019). *Conducted by JOY collective*. https://www.thecrownact.com/

Miller, P. J., & Goodnow, J. J. (1995). Cultural practices as contexts for development. In *New directions for child development* (Vol. 67, pp. 5–16). Jossey-Bass.

Thomas, K., Noroña, C. R., & St. John, M. S. (2019). Cross-sector allies together in the struggle for social justice: Diversity-informed tenets for work with infants, children, and families. *Zero to Three Journal, 33*(2), 23–28.

Van Horn, J. (2019). Exploring professional ethics through diversity-informed reflective supervision. *Zero to Three, 40*(1), 5–11.

Appendixes

Glossary of Hair Combing Interaction Terms

A Place for Natural Connections – Website: https://drmllewis.com/
Tulane University

Word	Definition
African American	The nomenclature of African American is used to refer to the broader culture and traditions of African origin people descended from slaves. In the United States, the term "Black" is a sociopolitical term used to identify the race of any person of African phenotype.
Allomothers	(Also referred to as alloparent care) It is parenting in which individuals other than the direct genetic parents act in a parental role, either for a short, or extended, period. This definition does not exclude alloparents who are genetically "related" to the offspring, such as siblings and aunts. An individual other than the biological mother of an offspring that performs the functions of a mother
AMDIS-1	African-American Mother–Daughter Interaction Study
Attachment Theory	Attachment Theory is an emotional bond with another person. John Bowlby, the first attachment theorist, believed that the earliest bonds formed by children with their caregivers have a tremendous impact that continues throughout life. Attachment can vary across cultures.
Bias	A preference or inclination that inhibits impartially. Social stereotypes about certain groups of people that individuals form outside their own consciousness. Patterns based on small bits of information. Often incompatible with our conscious values. Also called schemas, cognitive biases, stereotypes, default thinking.
BIPOC	Black, Indigenous, and People of Color.
Black People	People of African descent who may live in various places around the world. In the United States, these are the descendants of enslaved Africans.
CERAR	Childhood Experiences of Racial Acceptance and Rejection

M. L. Lewis, D. J. Weatherston (eds.), *Therapeutic Cultural Routines to Build Family Relationships*, https://doi.org/10.1007/978-3-030-83726-6

Word	Definition
Chattel Slavery	Chattel meant that once you were deemed a slave by law, you now become the property of your owner. You became his and his descendants' property for you and your children's lifetime. Your status as a slave was determined at your birth by the status of your mother, not your father. So, if the slave owner fathered children by a slave, these children became his property to do with what he pleased including selling them.
Colorism	The allocation of privilege and disadvantage according to the lightness or darkness of one's skin (Burke, 2008). In oppressed, minority groups, this practice is within a racial group phenomenon where lighter skin tones are valued over darker ones. These internalized beliefs reflect the values and standards of the dominant group or the oppressor. The practice of colorism is currently prevalent in multiple cultural and ethnic groups around the world.
Culture	A shared set of beliefs, values, material traits, social forms, and traditions that provide meaning to the everyday life to individuals within a group. Individuals are socialized into the standards of behavior for the group through language and everyday practices.
Disparity	The condition of being unequal, referring to the difference in outcomes and conditions that exist among specific groups as compared to other groups due to unequal treatment or services. Racial disparity occurs when the rate of disproportionality of one racial group, (e.g., African Americans) exceeds that of a comparison (e.g., White Americans).
Disproportionality	The overrepresentation of a particular race or cultural group in a program or system compared to their representation in the general population. In child welfare when factors of poverty, single-parent households, and risk level are taken into consideration, the rate of removal for African-American children remains higher, keeping them disproportionate in the system.
Ethnicity	A social group defined by cultural values, traditions, and beliefs that an individual chooses to identify.
Fair Skinned	In African-American communities, a term is used to refer to African American with lighter toned skin colors.
HCI	Hair Combing Interaction
Historical Trauma	"A cumulative emotional and psychological wounding over the lifespan and across generations, emanating from massive group experiences" (Brave Heart, 2003, p.7).
Historical Trauma Responses by Systems of Care	The transmission of historical trauma is not just an individual, group, or community experience, but is deeply embedded in our systems of care. Systems of care can be described as systems that work with families across the prevention, intervention, and treatment continuum. Child welfare, public education, healthcare, and other services may be described as systems of care.
Hot Comb	A metal comb developed by Madame C.J. Walker that could be heated and used to straighten naturally curly African hair.
Implicit Bias	The unconscious automatic prejudicial judgment triggered by some form of discernible difference such as skin tone, hair type, vocal accent, body size, or height.

Word	Definition
Implicit (Unconscious) Bias	The attitudes or stereotypes that affect our understanding, actions, and decisions in an unconscious manner. They are activated involuntarily without awareness or intentional control. Can either be positive or negative. Everyone is susceptible (Kirwan Institute, n.d.).
IECMH	Infant and Early Childhood Mental Health
Internalized Oppression	A population targeted for psychological terrorism through acts and threats of violence, racial hate crimes, and other forms of social oppression, racism, or sexism. These are internalized beliefs by the targeted group. They show responses of shame, denial, and disconnection that reflect societal values that derogate the group, erode individual sense of value, and undermine collection action for change.
Institutional Racism	An institution's policies and practices that result in discrimination based on social caste systems occurring in organizations or institutions that serve to preserve the social hierarchy of a dominant racial group.
IWM	Internal Working Model of Attachment Relationships
Loc-tician	A beautician or hair stylist who specializes in the care of natural "locs."
"Nappy" Hair	Very curly and coarse hair type (hair type 4). Originally, used to negatively stereotype African origin hair textures.
Oppression	The intentional subjection of one dominant group by another.
Plait	*Plait,* three or more lengths of hair, rope, or other material together, you twist them over and under each other to make one thick length. A *plait* is a length of hair that has been plaited.
PATH	Positive Attitudes Toward Hair
PsychoHairapy	The use of micro counseling and listening skills by beauticians and barbers.
Race	A sociopolitical category of social difference externally imposed designed to privilege one group and oppress another based on skin color or religious affiliation (Jews, Muslim). Race maintains a social hierarchy that categorizes groups of people according to skin colors: white, (Caucasian), yellow, (Asian) red, (Native Americans), brown, (Latinx, Hispanic), and black (African American).
Racism	"Racism is a system – consisting of structures, policies, practices, and norms – that assigns value and determines opportunity based on the way people look or the color of their skin. This results in conditions that unfairly advantage some and disadvantage others throughout society." (CDC, 2021).
Reflective Supervision and Consultation	The offer of a regularly scheduled meeting that invites thoughts and feelings about work and oneself within a supportive and trusting relationship with a supervisor or consultant.
RICS	Recognition of the Impact of Colorism on Children
Social Justice	Where the barriers are dismantled, and the courts' challenges and supports are in place for targeted, marginalized, and oppressed groups to achieve equity.
Stereotype	A generalization and oversimplification of an ethnic group or race's traits.

Word	Definition
Stereotype Threat	When an individual of a targeted social identity group internalizes the stereotypes used by the oppressor group and develops an expectation of failure or are incapable of performing well because of the social groups to which you belong.
Structural Racism	A system in which public policies, institutional, practices, cultural representations, and other norms work in various, often reinforcing ways, to perpetuate racial group inequity. It identifies dimensions of our history and culture that have allowed privileges associated with "Whiteness" and disadvantages associated with "color" to endure and adapt overtime (The Aspen Institute, n.d.).
Sundown Town	Communities that kept out African Americans (or sometimes Chinese Americans, Jewish Americans, etc.) by force, law, or custom. These communities are sometimes called "sundown towns," because some of them posted signs at their city limits reading, typically, "N . . ." Don't Let the Sun Go Down on You In ___ [name of town]."
Texturism	Discrimination of curly/coily hair types and natural textures.
White Privilege	This is a term for societal privileges that benefit people identified as White in Western countries beyond what is commonly experience by non-White people under the same social, political, educational, or economic circumstances.

Childhood Experiences of Racial Acceptance and Rejection (CERAR) Interview Questions & FAMILY COLORGRAM[1]

Marva L. Lewis

Date: ___________________________ Time Started: ____________

Time Ended: _______________

Permission to be part of Research Study:

Use your clinical discretion as to when to broach this topic with the client.

At the outset of the interview, ask client's Permission to be part of research. Have them sign an Informed consent form.

> ***"At the end of the interview, you will have the option of not participating in the research and we will simply use this interview in our ongoing work together. Do you understand that the research is voluntary and in no way interferes with our counseling work together? Yes, or No?"***

At the conclusion of the interview, please invite participants to allow de-identified transcription and anonymous family tree to be used as part of a research study.

Introduction

[1] Marva L. Lewis, (1993). Childhood Experiences of Racial Acceptance and Rejection Interview Guide. University of Colorado, Boulder, Colorado, USA.

The next set of questions are about young children and messages they hear about skin color and racial features. First tell me your Childhood home city, state, & country at age 5–6: ________________________________

I will be audiotaping this interview to transcribe it. In some communities, these physical features may be used to treat people differently. Sometimes people within the *same community* may discriminate against other people based on a physical characteristic like skin color or hair type or nose size or lip size. Sometimes people within the *same family* may say things to children about their physical features or make fun of their features using words like "good or bad hair" or "nappy" hair or "light skinned" or "dark skinned.'"

I would like to discuss with you your childhood experiences, when you were a young child about 5 or 6, related to messages you heard from people in your family and community about your physical features.

WARM-UP OPTIONS: To get you thinking back to that time in your life can you remember the name of your school you attended in first grade? Do you remember the name of any of your favorite teachers? How did you feel about her or him?

Or ask about nicknames. When you were about 5 or 6, did you have a nickname? Who called you that name? Did you like that name? Does your family still call you by that name?

OK, let's get started. I'm turning on the recorder now.

TURN ON AUDIO RECORDING.

Let's make a simple Family Tree to use for our discussion about today. We will use squares for males and circles for females. We will start with you and your birth parents. Then we will build the people who lived in your house when you were five to six and then add any other family members who were part of your childhood.

I. **HAIR TYPE or COLOR**

a. During your childhood, did everyone in your family have the same HAIR TYPE? Was it straight, or Wavy, Very curly, thin or thick? What did people in your family or community call that type of hair? What was the range of HAIR TYPE of people in your family? [AS CLIENT TALKS, HAVE HIM/HER DRAW IN STRAIGHT, WAVY, OR CURLY HAIR TYPES AROUND THE NAMES OF EACH PERSON ON THE FAMILY TREE.]
b. What were your experiences as a child growing up based on your HAIR TYPE?
c. Were you treated differently than other children in your FAMILY OR community based on your HAIR TYPE?
d. Did any of these experiences based on your hair TYPE lead to feelings of acceptance or rejection or other feelings as a child?

II. **SKIN COLOR**

Now we will discuss skin tone or skin colors in your family.

When you were growing up, was everyone in your family the same skin color? What were the range of colors of people in your family? IF THEY REFER TO EXTENDED FAMILY, BE SURE TO DRAW THEM INTO THE FAMILY TREE TO UNDERSTAND THEIR EMOTIONAL CONNECTION TO THE CLIENT.

a. Using the **language** of your family and community what were these skin colors?
b. Were you treated differently in your family than your brothers and sisters because of any of your features? What were your experiences as a child growing up based on your skin color?
c. What were your experiences in your family or community based on your skin color?
d. Did any of these experiences based on your skin color lead to you feeling accepted or rejected or other feelings you may have had as a child?

IF THESE AREAS HAVE NOT BEEN REFERENCED, ASK THE FOLLOWING:

a. How did you experience differences based on your racial features?
Racial Physical features, e.g., lip or butt size, freckles.

III. **BUFFERS. During your childhood, describe any persons, events, or experiences that helped you cope, or inspired you, or you felt safe and protected.**

a. Did you tell *anyone* about _____ [use their specific words to describe the one or two of the experiences they describe.]

Then what happened?
As a child, is that what you would have liked to see happen after [this experience]?

b. Did anyone help you manage the experience [use words they used to describe their experience.] What did the adults say when this happened?

IV. As you look back on these experiences, how do you think or feel about these experiences now as an adult?
V. Is there anything else about the way children are given messages about skin color, hair texture, or other physical features you would like to share?

Tender-Headed Rating Scale© (TRS)[2]

The following questions ask about how "tender headed" (painful sensitivity to physical touch to the scalp) were you and, your physical and emotional responses to your hair combing when your hair was combed as a child (younger than 5 years old).

1. Who was the primary person who combed your hair as a child?

__Mother __Father ___Someone else ______________________(Please specify your relationship, e.g., Aunt, Hairdresser, sibling)

2. How tender headed were you as a child?

___Not at all ___A little ___Somewhat ___Moderate ___Severe

[2] The Tender-Headed Rating Scale (2020). Marva L. Lewis, New Orleans, LA, USA.

3. How much pain did you experience in your scalp when your hair was combed?

Pain Score 0–10 Numerical Rating

0 1 2 3 4 5 6 7 8 9 10
No pain possible Moderate pain Worst pain

4. **How did you respond** when it was time to get your hair combed? (Check all that apply).

___Cried ___Screamed __Argued __I hid __ Tried to run away

Other behaviors ______________________________.

5. How **aware** was the person who combed your hair of how tender headed you were as a child?

___Not at all ___Slightly ___Moderately aware ___Very aware ___ Extremely aware

6. What did the person do to **get you to sit still** to get your hair combed? (Check all that apply)

____Gave me toys or snacks ___Waited for me to calm down ___Talked patiently to me ____Threatened me ___Took away my toys ___ Yelled at me ___ Made promises to me ___Punished me ___Ignored me

____Hit me with the comb or brush ___Hit me with a belt

___Gave up and didn't comb my hair

Other responses ____________________________________

7. Did that person **make any changes** in how they combed your hair, because you were tender headed?

___Never ___Rarely ___Sometimes ___Often ___Always

8. Were you ever seen by a medical doctor about your physical reaction to getting your hair combed?

__No __Yes

9. Were you ever prescribed any medical treatment for your reaction to the touch of your scalp? __No __Yes
10. Were you ever referred for counseling or psychiatric services for your tender-headed reaction?

___No ___Yes

Other comments:

The "Neck-Up" Exercise[3]©

Date: ____________________________

Draw a picture of yourself from the neck up when you were a young child (younger than 10 years old).

Write one EMOTION word or phrase that best describes how you felt about your hair as a child.

When I was a child, I felt ________________about my hair.

I felt ________________ about getting my hair combed.

[3] The Neck-Up exercise created by Marva L. Lewis and Maureen Joseph

Bibliography and Additional Resources

Adams, C. (2020, June 18). Not all black people are African American. Here's the difference. *CBS News*. https://www.cbsnews.com/news/not-all-black-people-are-african-american-what-is-the-difference/.

Agyemang, C., Bhopal, R., & Bruijnzeels, M. (2005, December 1). Negro, Black, Black African, African Caribbean, African American or what? Labelling African origin populations in the health arena in the 21st century. *Journal of Epidemiology & Community Health*. https://jech.bmj.com/content/59/12/1014

The Aspen Institute. (n.d.). https://www.aspeninstitute.org/

Brave Heart, M. Y. H. (2003). The historical trauma response among natives and its relationship with substance abuse: A Lakota illustration. *Journal of Psychoactive Drugs, 35*(1), 7–13.

Burke, M. (2008). Colorism. In W. Darity (Ed.), *International encyclopedia of the social sciences* (Vol. 2, pp. 17–18). Thomson Gale.

CDC. (2021). *Health Equity: Racism and Health*. https://www.cdc.gov/healthequity/racism-disparities/index.html

Children's Bureau. (n.d.). *Racial Disproportionality and Disparity in Child Welfare*. Child Welfare Information Gateway. https://www.childwelfare.gov/pubPDFs/racial_disproportionality.pdf.

Coen, R. (2020, December 2). *Sundown Towns*. https://www.blackpast.org/african-american-history/sundown-towns/.

Colorism. NCCJ. (n.d.). https://www.nccj.org/colorism-0.

Garcia, S. E. (2020, June 15). *Where did BIPOC come from? The New York Times*. https://www.nytimes.com/article/what-is-bipoc.html.

Implicit Bias Explained. Perception Institute. (2017, May 17). https://perception.org/research/implicit-bias/.

Infant and Early Childhood Mental Health. ZERO TO THREE. (n.d.). https://www.zerotothree.org/espanol/infant-and-early-childhood-mental-health.

Kirwan Institute. (n.d.). *Kirwan Institute for the study of race and ethnicity at The Ohio State University*. https://kirwaninstitute.osu.edu/

Li, A. P. (2021, March 26). What is the internal working model of attachment: Psychology. *Parenting For Brain*. https://www.parentingforbrain.com/internal-working-model/#:~:text=An%20internal%20working%20model%20of,in%20human%20behavior%20among%20people.

Mcleod, S. (1970, January 1). *Bowlby's attachment theory*. John Bowlby | Maternal Deprivation Theory | Simply Psychology. https://www.simplypsychology.org/bowlby.html#:~:text=Bo.

PSYCHOHAIRAPY. (n.d.). http://www.psychohairapy.org/.

Recognizing and Addressing Colorism in Schools. Learning for Justice. (n.d.). https://www.learningforjustice.org/magazine/recognizing-and-addressing-colorism-in-schools.

M. L. Lewis, D. J. Weatherston (eds.), *Therapeutic Cultural Routines to Build Family Relationships*, https://doi.org/10.1007/978-3-030-83726-6

Rutgers School of Arts and Sciences. (n.d.). *Stereotype threat*. https://philosophy.rutgers.edu/climate-v2/climate-issues-in-academic-philosophy/stereotype-threat.

Staats, C. (2014). *State of the Science: Implicit Bias Review* (2014). Kirwan Institute for the Study of Race & Ethnicity. W. K. Kellogg Foundation.

Sussex Publishers. (n.d.). Internalized oppression: We need to stop hating ourselves. *Psychology Today*. https://www.psychologytoday.com/us/blog/unseen-and-unheard/201509/internalized-oppression-we-need-stop-hating-ourselves.

Trauma. Administration for Children & Families. (n.d.). https://www.acf.hhs.gov/trauma-toolkit/trauma-concept.

The San Diego Foundation. (2020, September 24). *What is social justice?* The San Diego Foundation. https://www.sdfoundation.org/news-events/sdf-news/what-is-social-justice/.

University of North Carolina Chapel Hill. (n.d.). *What racism looks like*. https://fpg.unc.edu/sites/fpg.unc.edu/files/resource-files/What%20Racism%20Looks%20Like%2010.pdf.

Walker, N. C. (n.d.). *Is it time to reclaim the word "nappy"?* Allure. https://www.allure.com/story/is-nappy-hair-a-negative-term#:~:text=The%20term%20is%20one%20that,blogger%20and%20natural%20hair%20influencer.

What is Slavery?: The Abolition of Slavery Project. (n.d.). http://abolition.e2bn.org/slavery_40.html.

Index

M. L. Lewis, D. J. Weatherston (eds.), *Therapeutic Cultural Routines to Build Family Relationships*, https://doi.org/10.1007/978-3-030-83726-6